CW00525796

Transitions to Good Governan

Transitions to Good Governance

Creating Virtuous Circles of Anti-corruption

Edited by

Alina Mungiu-Pippidi

Chair of Democracy Studies, Hertie School of Governance, Germany

Michael Johnston

Charles A. Dana Professor of Political Science Emeritus, Colgate University, USA

 Edward Elgar
PUBLISHING

Cheltenham, UK • Northampton, MA, USA

© Alina Mungiu-Pippidi and Michael Johnston 2017

Cover photograph by Bruce Wilson. Photo: Bronze sculpture 'Circulation of Money' in Aachen, Germany.

All rights reserved. No part of this publication may be reproduced, stored in a retrieval system or transmitted in any form or by any means, electronic, mechanical or photocopying, recording, or otherwise without the prior permission of the publisher.

Published by
Edward Elgar Publishing Limited
The Lypiatts
15 Lansdown Road
Cheltenham
Glos GL50 2JA
UK

Edward Elgar Publishing, Inc.
William Pratt House
9 Dewey Court
Northampton
Massachusetts 01060
USA

A catalogue record for this book
is available from the British Library

Library of Congress Control Number: 2017939808

This book is available electronically in the **Elgar**online
Social and Political Science subject collection
DOI 10.4337/9781786439154

ISBN 978 1 78643 914 7 (cased)
ISBN 978 1 78643 916 1 (paperback)
ISBN 978 1 78643 915 4 (eBook)

Typeset by Servis Filmsetting Ltd, Stockport, Cheshire
Printed on FSC approved paper
Printed and bound in Great Britain by Marston Book Services Ltd, Oxfordshire

Contents

Contributors

Alessandro Bozzini is an international development practitioner in the field of governance, specializing in transparency, accountability, anti-corruption, parliamentary support and civil society strengthening. He has worked for various organizations, such as Transparency International and the United Nations Development Programme (UNDP).

Dr. Daniel Buquet Corleto holds a PhD in Political Science from the Latin American Faculty of Social Sciences (FLACSO-Mexico). He is a professor in the Faculty of Social Sciences of the University of the Republic of Uruguay. He has lectured as guest professor in several universities in Latin America and Spain, specializing in political parties and electoral systems in Latin America, and has published dozens of articles in books and magazines nationally and internationally.

Dr. Christian Göbel is Professor for Contemporary Chinese Studies at the University of Vienna. His current research is concerned with the political economy of innovation in authoritarian regimes. Dr. Göbel is author of *The Politics of Rural Reform in China* (Routledge, 2010) and *The Politics of Community Building in Urban China* (Routledge, 2011, with Thomas Heberer).

Michael Johnston is an Emeritus Professor at Colgate University, New York State. His publications include *Syndromes of Corruption: Wealth, Power, and Democracy* (Cambridge University Press, 2005); the edited volumes *Public Sector Corruption (SAGE, 2010)* and *Civil Society and Corruption: Mobilizing for Reform* (University Press of America, 2005); *Political Corruption: Concepts and Contexts* (Transaction Publishers, co-edited with Arnold J. Heidenheimer, 2002); *Political Corruption: A Handbook* (Cambridge University Press, co-edited with Arnold J. Heidenheimer and Victor LeVine, 1988); *Fraud, Waste, and Abuse in Government* (Institute for the Study of Human Resources, co-edited with Jerome B. McKinney, 1986); and *Political Corruption and Public Policy in America* (Brooks/Cole Pub., 1982). He has been a consultant to many international organizations and development agencies, including the World Bank, the OECD, the Asia Foundation, the New York State Commission on Governmental Integrity, USAID and the United Nations.

Dr. Valts Kalniņš was awarded his doctorate in political science from the University of Latvia. He has been a senior researcher at the Centre for Public Policy PROVIDUS, a Riga-based non-governmental think-tank, since 2003. He is also an assistant professor at the University of Latvia. He consults for the OECD and the European Commission (DG Home).

Dr. Lina Khatib is Head of the Middle East and North Africa (MENA) programme at Chatham House in London. Formerly she was the director of the Carnegie Middle East Center in Beirut and the co-founding head of the Program on Arab Reform and Democracy at Stanford University's Center on Democracy, Development, and the Rule of Law. Her research focuses on the international relations of the Middle East, Islamist groups and security, political transitions, and foreign policy, with special attention on the Syrian conflict. She has published seven books and has also written widely on public diplomacy, political communication, and political participation in the Middle East.

Dr. Alexander Kupatadze is an assistant professor at King's College London, studying organized crime and corruption issues in post-Soviet Eurasia. He is the author of numerous articles and book chapters on smuggling, policing, and criminality. He holds a PhD in International Relations from St Andrews University. In 2012–14 Dr. Kupatadze was Oxford-Princeton postdoctoral fellow in Global Governance. Apart from academic research he has been advising various government, commercial and non-government institutions on corruption, crime, and informal politics in post-Soviet countries.

Maira Martini holds a Master of Public Policy (MPP) degree from the Hertie School of Governance in Berlin, and is a senior researcher with the Transparency International (TI) secretariat in Berlin.

Dr. Alina Mungiu-Pippidi chairs the European Research Centre for Anti-Corruption and State-Building (ERCAS) at the Hertie School of Governance in Berlin. Her theory of corruption has been published in various journal articles, most notably *Nature*, and at greater length in *The Quest for Good Governance* (Cambridge University Press, 2015). Dr. Mungiu-Pippidi has designed several corruption assessment methodologies, for instance to evaluate integrity in public universities or parliaments. She has consulted more recently for the governments of Sweden and the Netherlands, the World Bank, the European Commission and the Council of Europe. She designed the EU FP7 ANTICORRP project, which examined corruption and the responses to corruption around the world, and was the principal investigator of Work Package 3, which was the origin of the present book.

Dr. Patricio Navia holds a PhD in political science from New York University. He is currently a Master Teacher of Global Studies in the Liberal Studies Program and an adjunct professor at the Center for Latin American and Caribbean Studies at the University of New York. He is also a professor in the School of Political Science, Universidad Diego Portales, Chile. He has been a visiting professor at several universities, including Princeton and the University of Chile. Dr. Navia has published on democratization, institutional design and electoral laws in Latin America in book chapters and scholarly articles.

Dr. Rafael Piñeiro holds a PhD from Pontificia Universidad Católica de Chile and is an assistant professor with Universidad Católica del Uruguay, Department of Social and Political Sciences. He is the author of several papers on Uruguay and Chile politics.

David Sebudubudu is a professor in the Department of Political and Administrative Studies (PAS) of the Faculty of Social Sciences, University of Botswana. His research interests are democracy and development in sub-Saharan Africa.

Evelyn Villarreal (MPhil Latin American Studies, University of Oxford) is Research Coordinator at Programa Estado de la Nación (PEN), Costa Rica and has taught courses on Central America politics and methodology at UCR and UNED. She is a founding member and vice president of Costa Rica Íntegra, the national chapter of Transparency International.

Dr. Bruce M. Wilson is Professor of Political Science at the University of Central Florida, Orlando; Associated Senior Researcher, Chr. Michelsen Institute; and Global Fellow, Centre on Law and Social Transformation, Bergen, Norway. His peer-reviewed research has appeared in *Comparative Political Studies*, *Journal of Latin American Studies* and *Comparative Politics*. His books are *Costa Rica: Politics, Economics, and Democracy* (Lynne Rienner, 1998) and, as co-author, *Courts and Political Power in Latin America and Africa* (Palgrave Macmillan, 2010).

Dr. Jong-sung You holds a PhD in public policy from Harvard University. He has taught at the University of California, San Diego and Australian National University (ANU). His research interests include comparative politics and political economy of inequality, corruption, social trust, freedom of expression and election campaign regulations, with regional focus on Korea and East Asia. His book entitled *Democracy, Inequality and Corruption: Korea, Taiwan and the Philippines Compared* was released by Cambridge University Press in 2014. Dr. You's articles on the causes of corruption and social trust were published in the *American Sociological*

Review and Political Psychology. Before pursuing an academic career, he worked for democratization and social justice in South Korea, being imprisoned for more than two years because of his active role in the anti-dictatorship student movement under the military regimes.

Bianca Vaz Mondo, Aare Kasemets, Denise Misleh, Roberto Martínez Barranco Kukutschka, Dr. Ramin Dadašov and Sindy Natalia Alvarado Pachon were associated with the project in the early phases as ERCAS associates, and contributed documentation and statistical work. Christian van Soest and Thomas Richter were in charge of the project on behalf of the German Institute for Global Studies (GIGA). Philip Keefer, Michael Johnston and Robert Klitgaard reviewed the individual contributions. Special thanks go to the editors of *Journal for Democracy*, Larry Diamond and Marc F. Plattner, for publishing an advance sample of the present book in their winter 2016 issue.

Abbreviations

GENERAL

CoC   Control of Corruption Indicator, Worldwide Governance
          Indicators
CPI   Corruption Perception Index, Transparency International
CSO   Civil Society Organization
EC   European Commission
EU   European Union
FDI   Foreign Direct Investment
FH   Freedom House
GCB   Global Corruption Barometer, Transparency International
GDP   Gross Domestic Product
GNI   Gross National Income
GRECO   Group of States against Corruption, Council of Europe
HDI   Human Development Index
ICRG   International Country Risk Guide
IMF   International Monetary Fund
IPI   Index of Public Integrity
MEP   Member of the European Parliament
MP   Member of Parliament
NATO   North Atlantic Treaty Organization
NGO   Non-Governmental Organization
OECD   Organisation for Economic Co-operation and Development
PPP   Purchasing Power Parity
SOE   State-Owned Enterprise
TI   Transparency International
UN   United Nations
UNCAC   United Nations Convention against Corruption
UNDP   United Nations Development Programme
WEF   World Economic Forum
WGI   World Bank Worldwide Governance Indicators

BOTSWANA

BCP	Botswana Congress Party
BDC	Botswana Development Corporation
BDP	Botswana Democratic Party
BEC	Botswana Examination Council
BMD	Botswana Movement for Democracy
BNF	Botswana National Front

ESTONIA

CPSU	Communist Party of the Soviet Union
ECP	Estonian Communist Party
ESSR	Estonian Soviet Socialist Republic
EU-FS	European Union-Former Socialist
USSR	Union of Soviet Socialist Republics

COSTA RICA

ANEJ	Judicial Employees National Association [Asociación Nacional de Empleados Judiciales]
CCSS	Costa Rican Social Security Agency [Caja Costarricense de Seguro]
CEPN	Center of Studies for National Problems [Centro de Estudio para los Problemas Nacionales]
CGR	Office of the Comptroller General of the Republic [Contraloría General de la República]
CICIG	International Commission against Impunity in Guatemala [Comisión Internacional contra la Impunidad en Guatemala]
CONARE	National Council Proctors of Public Universities [Consejo Nacional de Rectores]
DHR	Office of the Ombudsman [Defensoría de los Habitantes de la República]
FAPTA	Probity, Transparency, and Anti-corruption Prosecution Unit [Fiscalía Adjunta de Probidad, Transparencia y Anticorrupción]
FATF	Financial Action Task Force
ICE	Costa Rican Institute of Electricity [Instituto Costarricense de Electricidad]

ISI	Import Substitution Industrialization
LAFPP	Financial Management and Public Budget Law [Ley de Administración Financiera y Presupuestos Públicos]
MESICIC	Mechanism for Follow-up on the Implementation of the Inter-American Convention against Corruption [Mecanismo de Seguimiento de la Implementación de la Convención Interamericana contra la Corrupción]
MP	Prosecutor Office [Ministerio Público]
OIJ	Judicial Investigation Branch [Organismo de Investigación Judicial]
PAC	Citizen's Action Party [Partido Acción Ciudadana]
PASE	Access without Exclusion Party [Partido Accessibilidad Sin Exclusión]
PEP	Office of the Inspector of Public Ethics [Procuraduría de la Ética Pública]
PLN	National Liberation Party [Partido Liberación Nacional]
PSD	Social Democratic Party [Partido Social Demócrata]
PUN	National Unity Party [Partido Unidad Nacional]
PUSC	Social Christian Unity Party [Partido Unidad Social Cristiana]
SALA IV	Constitutional Chamber of the Supreme Court [Sala Constitucional, Corte Suprema de Justicia]
SNE	National Electricity Service [Servicio Nacional de Electricidad]
TCA	Administrative Dispute Tribunal [Tribunal Contencioso Administrativo]
TSE	Tribunal Supremo de Elecciones [Supreme Elections Tribunal]

1. Introduction: identifying and explaining governance virtuous circles

Alina Mungiu-Pippidi

1.1 WHAT IS INSTITUTIONALIZED CORRUPTION? OUR CONCEPTS

From the beginning of government, humans have struggled with the problem of fair distribution of joint resources, and with the difficulty of preventing those with greater power and access from cutting the lion's share off for themselves. Democratization and the exponential growth of the state, and therefore of common resources, have made this problem paramount; and presently there is no day when we do not witness serious challenges to executive leaders on corruption grounds: from the prime minister of Iceland stepping down over mere allegations, to the presidents of Brazil and South Korea who were impeached. The high integrity standards have expanded from a minority of developed countries by norm promotion and modernization, culminating in the United Nations Convention against Corruption (UNCAC) in 2003. The UNCAC establishes fairness, equality, transparency, accountability and public participation as the foundations of good governance. More and more citizens from a growing number of countries, who are probably unaware that the convention even exists, have presently come to demand that their governments deliver good governance. The unprecedented extension of elections after the Third Wave of democratization brought roughly half the world's countries into a situation where their people have sufficient freedom to demand equal treatment by the government, only to discover that public corruption is the chief obstacle. Achieving control of corruption thus becomes the indispensable final stage of a successful democratization process (Johnston 2014).

In the academic world as well, after many years of being marginal, corruption has resurfaced as a major issue. Following the post-Washington Consensus revelation that governance matters greatly in explaining development, the issue of institutional change, which a few decades ago was of interest only to students of Mancur Olson or Douglass North, has risen to the forefront not only for economists but also for the international donor community. Corruption, of course, is ubiquitous. Johnston (2005) showed how corruption takes the form of different syndromes across societies according to power distribution, natural resources and societal constraints: driven by elite cartels (as found in Botswana, Italy and Korea) or oligarchs and clans (as in Mexico, the Philippines and Russia, with rival groups competing for government favors in an institutionally weak state) or official moguls (as in China, Indonesia and Kenya, where political leaders used to despoil public resources with impunity). Even when institutions and legal systems are relatively strong, an undue business–politics connection might try to influence markets to get favorable treatment (as in Germany, Japan and the United States). We may not know much about why some societies managed to evolve to have better control over corruption and others not, but we do know quite well how the former differ presently compared to the latter. In a time-series model, Mungiu-Pippidi (2015a, ch. 4) showed that corrupt societies have not managed to balance the opportunities for corruption (such as natural resources, red tape, high power inequality and lack of transparency) with the constraints on elite behavior (through independence of the judiciary, freedom of the press and enlightened citizens).

But how to reach this equilibrium, or in other words how to engineer this development, remains far less consensual, if altogether known. As Claus Offe has argued, we still have insufficient knowledge of what could bring countries out of the vicious circle of corrupt institutions: "which motives, values, and political forces would actually push forward the reform project . . . what are the incentives to introduce incentives designed to control corruption or to redesign opportunity structures?" (2004, p. 91). In other words, what makes a governance order based on what Max Weber described as patrimonialism evolve to ethical universalism (equal and fair treatment for everyone) by design, rather than through a long historical evolution; and can such transformations be engineered by human agency? These are the main questions of this book.

The concept of the virtuous circle had been used for quite a while in development studies before the best-selling *Why Nations Fail* suggested that a virtuous circle is based on a passage from extractive to inclusive institutions (Acemoglu and Robinson 2012a); or, in other words, that it accomplishes in the initial stage exactly the kind of transformation of interest to us in this research. Explaining the difference in economic performance across countries by some governance virtuous circle is tempting, except that such governance virtuous circles need explaining themselves. In terms of neo-institutionalism theory, an equilibrium can only change when those who profit from the status quo (the so-called institutional winners) give away some of their advantage in favor of institutional losers. While historians are generally reluctant to put forward, or even admit, that such developments can be theorized, social scientists have been attempting in recent years to advance such explanations for the advent of rule of law in the West (North et al. 2009; Fukuyama 2011) or for democracy (Acemoglu and Robinson 2005). Other works have attempted to explain how control of corruption came about in modern Western countries: either due to enlightened despots who developed meritocratic recruitment and regular audits to increase state capacity—as for instance in Denmark (Mungiu-Pippidi 2015a, ch. 3)—or through a far longer path of intra-elite competition and growth of a mass of critical citizens in democracies like the United States (Wallis 2006). The reproduction of such historical mechanisms in contemporary settings cannot be taken for granted, however. Present-day societies enjoy better education, communication and mobility, on the one hand; and, on the other, traditional ties have been weakened or have vanished (with a few exceptions in a handful of Asian traditional monarchies). The challenge these days is increasingly not how to disrupt corrupt rulers as much as how to prevent new rulers from becoming corrupt in their turn. Current corrupt democracies outnumber corrupt autocracies by two to one if we combine the World Bank's Control of Corruption with Freedom House's count of electoral democracies; although, with a couple of exceptions (like Bhutan or Singapore), the least corrupt countries in the world are the oldest democracies (Table 1.1). This simply shows that democratization, despite its current challenges, has been a tremendous success, but the reduction of patrimonialism far less so.

Table 1.1   Distribution of countries across control of corruption and democracy categories

2015	CoC Lowest Tercile	CoC Mid Tercile	CoC Top Tercile	Total
Free	4	32	46	82
Partially Free	31	23	4	58
Not Free	32	13	4	49
Total	67	68	54	189

Notes: *N* countries = +171. Freedom categories as provided by Freedom House; terciles determined with CoC scores for 2015.

Sources: Freedom House's *Freedom in the World* and World Bank Worldwide Governance Indicators.

The main question guiding our research is precisely what explains the transition of a society from a governance norm where public resource distribution is systematically biased in favor of the power privileged to a society where the state is largely autonomous towards private interest and the allocation of public resources is based on ethical universalism (everyone treated equally and fairly) and the pursuit of social welfare (for the benefit of the majority) and if and how such a process can be engineered. In other words, we study the few governance 'virtuous circles' which have materialized after the Second World War. The collection of process-tracing cases in this volume follows the theory of development of governance espoused in books such as Johnston's *Corruption, Contention and Reform* (2014) and Mungiu-Pippidi's *A Quest for Good Governance* (2015a). The field research was carried out over a five-year project funded by the European Union (FP7 ANTICORRP).

"Any attempt to analyse the concept of corruption must contend with the fact that in English and other languages the word corruption has a history of vastly different meanings and connotations" (Heidenheimer and Johnston 2002, p. 3)—hence the importance of clarifying what we understand by corruption and its opposite, control of corruption, in the context of this book. Simply, but hopefully clearly, the widespread definition of corruption as 'deviation' from the norm of integrity applies to the individual level, while the discussion of governance orders is at a macro level. When corruption is the norm in a society, we need to understand it as a social practice or institution, not just as a sum of individual corrupt acts. We call a country 'corrupt' when we find a governance regime where corruption is institutionalized as a rule of the game; and we call the opposite 'control of corruption' when a society reaches the capacity to constrain corrupt behavior in order to enforce the norm of individual integrity in public service and politics, to prevent state capture by particular interests and thus to promote the public interest and social welfare. Control of corruption and rule of law overlap within a complex equilibrium that includes a government subject to the law; equality of citizens before the law; respect for individual rights; equal and fair distribution of public resources; and corresponding societal norms such as respect for rules and widespread observation of the ethical universalism norm. These optimal equilibria are grounded in a social order which is based on individualism and low power distance (Eisenstadt and Roniger 1984; Hofstede 1999; Husted 1999; Mungiu-Pippidi 2015a). In contrast, institutionalized corruption is based on particularism, a feature of collectivistic and status-based societies (Mungiu-Pippidi 2015a, chs. 1–2).

1.2 WHEN IS A COUNTRY SUCCESSFUL IN CONTROLLING CORRUPTION? THE DIAGNOSIS

To understand how a country develops control of corruption—in other words a governance context where corrupt acts are a mere individual deviation from an otherwise enshrined integrity norm—we have to understand its opposite: a governance context where corruption is the norm and a widespread social practice, so it cannot be defined as a 'deviation'. Patrimonialism, as espoused by Max Weber, is a feature of governance where the public–private border is not enforced, with the consequence of authority holders appropriating public office and its benefits for themselves and their cronies (Weber 1991, p. 298). Particularism—a concept developed by Talcott Parsons (1997, pp. 80–82) on the basis of Weber and further developed by Mungiu-Pippidi (2006)—is an exchange mode of collectivistic societies, encompassing a variety of interpersonal and personal–state transaction types such as clientelism, bribery, patronage, nepotism and other favoritisms, some of which imply at an individual level some degree of patrimonialism. Particularism is defined as the deviation from the ethical universalism norm of social allocation (as defined by law, rules and the modern principles of administrative impersonality, impartiality and equality, as well as by market relations) resulting in private benefit not warranted by merit.

Particularism defines not only the relations between a government and its subjects, but also between individuals in a society, and it explains why advancement in a given society is based on merit or, on the contrary, status or particular connections with influential people. If particularistic exchanges, which are carried out on the basis of status and connections versus impersonal factors (such as merit of product, price and rules), are the dominant mode in a society, markets cannot evolve from a state of imperfect competition. Similarly, particularism of transactions between state and citizens makes democracy a mere façade, as resources are systematically spoiled by authority holders and the state never manages to become autonomous from private interest, with bureaucrats and rulers colluding in the public resources spoliation game.

The existence of particularism limits access to public resources (some applicants are favored and some are discriminated against), resulting in unfair treatment. Particularism is a broader concept than corruption as it includes both criminalized forms of corruption (favor in exchange for undue profit) and what Kaufmann and Vicente (2011) labeled 'legal corruption'. In its extreme form (most government transactions are particularistic) a state can be entirely 'captured' by private interest. The current scholarship and policy literature on corruption uses a variety of overlapping and differently theorized concepts that mix the social and individual level, such as state capture, grand corruption, regulatory capture, government favoritism, administrative capture and petty corruption. They all describe a specific case of particularism—for instance, in clientelism parties trade favors for votes and in petty corruption tiny bureaucrats deliver public services only incentivized by bribes; but by and large all these remain particular categories of a general situation, the distribution of public resources on the basis of favoritism. If we picture governance as the set of formal rules and informal practices determining who gets what in terms of public resources, we can then imagine a continuum of public resource allocations with full particularism at one end and full ethical universalism at the other.

The outcome of particularism—a regular pattern of preferential distribution of public goods—is called 'limited access order' by North et al. (2009), 'extractive institutions' by Acemoglu and Robinson (2012a) and 'patrimonialism' by Fukuyama (2014). But essentially all these categories overlap, and all these authors acknowledge that particularism, rather than universalism, is closer to the state of nature (or the default social organization), and that the building of the opposite (a norm based on open and equal access or public integrity) is by no means guaranteed by some evolution, and has only been reached in a few cases so far. This did not deter the promoters of UNCAC, which clearly spells out the principle of ethical universalism: to date, it has been signed by over 160 countries, which have thus pledged to implement it.

Although the literature on corruption from the nineties labeled state capture as a phenomenon related to liberalizing economies after the fall of communism (Hellman et al. 2003), state capture can be a very stable governance context that can hardly be seen as 'transitional'. Moreover, political regimes and governance orders are not tightly linked. For example, in Poland, the largest and most successful of the new European Union (EU) member states, control of corruption—as measured by the International Country Risk Guide (ICRG) since 1984—was largely unchanged between 1989 and 1998, despite the country's dramatic improvement in political pluralism. In 1998, control of corruption actually began to decline slightly, and it remained at a lower level throughout the EU accession process and even after Poland attained membership in 2004. As governance orders reflect fundamental patterns of social organization and power distribution in a society they tend to be stable once they reach a certain equilibrium, and therefore hard to transform even by means of a political regime change (Mungiu-Pippidi 2015a).

How many exchanges are particularistic versus universalistic and which of the two norms is dominant in any society can be measured fairly precisely, as well as indicated by most public opinion survey respondents (Mungiu-Pippidi 2015b). A simple but effective proxy is the people's expectation, as indicated in public surveys, of the accessibility of a public resource in the absence of a personal connection or bribe. Once this is established, the nature of the particularistic exchanges—status, family ties, party ties, oligarchs, moguls or monetary advantage in the form of bribes—should be investigated next, as each society has a mix of its own. Establishing what is norm and what is exception seems an anthropological venture; but the high correlation between experts and public opinion surveys shows that awareness is generally high for everyone in corrupt countries, where journalists and ordinary people alike can fairly describe how 'it works' (Kaufmann et al. 2006).

Despite the development in recent years of fact-based measurements of particularism, grounded for instance on public procurement patterns, few states have sufficient open data to allow the use of such measures for big n cross-country and cross-time comparisons. We have to resort again to aggregate perception indicators, which have been severely criticized for the lack of validity, reliability and theoretical foundation they provide (Kaufman et al. 1999; Knack 2006). To place a country on the continuum we use three indicators:

1. the Control of Corruption (CoC) indicator of the Worldwide Governance Indicators (WGI) project, an aggregate measure in existence since 1996 and including most expert scores and public opinion surveys (scores are recoded from 1 to 10, with 10 the best performer);
2. the Corruption Risk indicator from the PRS Group's International Country Risk Guide (ICRG), an expert score (ranging from 1 to 6) in existence since the early 1980s; and
3. indicators of particularism from country diagnoses undertaken by our group of researchers.

Using the first indicator (which basically covers all corruption ratings for all countries since 1998), we can obtain a range from closed access with particularistic exchanges at one end to open access with universalistic exchanges at the other. This shows a compact group of ten countries with the best quality of governance in the world, with another 30 or so in the upper tercile; but the majority of countries score 5 or less. Simply put, the evidence seems to indicate that the world is more particularistic than universalistic. Very few developing countries are to be found in the

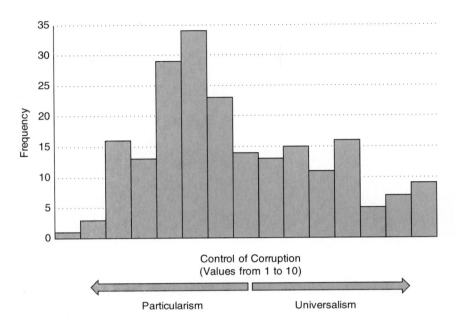

Note: WGI CoC frequency distribution, recoded 1–10 with Denmark 10. *N* = 209

Figure 1.1   Distribution of countries on the particularism–ethical universalism continuum, 2015

upper tercile; and, with the exception of Japan, the 'achieving' group is composed of early European modernizers and early Anglo-Saxon colonies such as Canada, the US, New Zealand and Australia (Figure 1.1). Exceptions to the rule come only in the form of small islands or city states.

The transition away from a regime based on particularistic governance and the evolution to governance based on universalism does not come easily. Both public opinion polls and expert surveys concur in the assessment that few countries have made it, and even fewer seem to have succeeded on this path in recent times, since we have data allowing comparisons across countries and time (North et al. 2009; Mungiu-Pippidi 2015a). Furthermore, the efforts of the anti-corruption community since the birth of international promotion of good governance have yet to produce a final undisputed success case, other than what self-promoters report in general as incremental evolution (Klitgaard 2014). Many anti-corruption policies and programs have been declared successful, but no country has yet achieved control of corruption due to international assistance and its standard prescriptions, though a few have succeeded on their own.

The definition of success also needs clarification. 'Success' can only mean a consolidated dominant norm of ethical universalism and public integrity. Exceptions, in the form of corrupt acts, will always remain; but as long as they are so numerous as to make the rule virtually indistinguishable, a country cannot be seen as an achiever. A successful transformation requires both the dominance of the norm of public integrity (the majority of acts and public officials are not corrupt) and its resilience against an eventual backslide, as happened in some Eastern European countries after EU accession. *Reducing corruption to the status of exception in a sustainable way thus defines a successful evolution.* Backsliding to lower quality of governance is frequently observed, since we have some indicators to trace it; but none is known from the situation when corruption has become an exception to the norm yet again (South Africa may be a strong candidate), which argues in favor of a 'tipping point' between governance orders (Wallis 1989). However, quite a few developing countries seem to be presently struggling on the borderline, where the old norm and the new norm confront one another; hence the anti-corruption headlines from such countries, where popular demand for integrity of leaders has increased substantially over the years.

The diagnosis of a governance context where particularism has become either exception or norm cannot rely only on aggregate perceptions, even if they are grounded in observations and experiences, but essentially needs fact-based indicators as well. This study surveyed six areas and observed a wealth of indicators to establish the nature of the governance order and its change across time. A summary is presented in Table 1.2, but each case study resorts also to additional indicators. The main research question guiding the choice of indicators is empirical: what are the most common practices and norms (expectation shaping behavior) in every area surveyed which encompass particularism and its outcomes for public policy? A more comprehensive discussion can be found in Mungiu-Pippidi (2015a, chs. 1–2).

Table 1.2   Diagnosis tool for assessing particularism as governance norm

Diagnosis questions	Indicators
Power distribution	
● Is influence distributed unevenly, resulting in constant preferential treatment of certain groups by the state?	● Real power held by the same individuals or networks regardless of the outcome of elections
● Is it only one group (network/estate) which enjoys privileges?	● Persistence of widespread popular perceptions of government corruption despite changes in government
● Is this consistent over time or does it change with elections or government succession?	● High political migration from opposition parties to the party in government in search of political rents
● Is there one particular group that constantly loses due to power inequality?	
● Does the 'loser' group have any voice?	
Autonomy of the state towards private interest	
● Is the state autonomous from, or captured by private interests?	● Degree of politicization (to what level personnel reshuffling occurs at government change)
● How politicized is the administration and the public sector in general?	● Presence of business politicians. To what extent rulers and politicians are also successful private entrepreneurs
● Is there a permanent bureaucracy which does not change with elections and how much influence does it have over policy formulation and implementation?	● Share of the market for businesses with political ties
● Is this bureaucracy well trained and paid to fulfil its functions?	● Main fortunes related to government favoritism (public contracts, monopolies, subsidies) rather than market
● Are policy formulation and public spending transparent, observable by and consulted with civil society and stakeholders?	
Public resource allocation	
● Is the main goal of the state to cater to everyone, or to special interests or groups?	● Government subnational transfers per government versus opposition areas

Table 1.2   (continued)

Diagnosis questions	Indicators
● Does the party/clan in government distribute mostly to itself (connected local governments or regions, favorite companies)?	● Pork barrel allocations by MPs
● How much of the total spending budget are rents? Does this change from one government to the next?	● Size of rentier public companies ● Wages in the public sector compared to private ● Existence of companies which are successful only due to political connections manifested in preferential public contracts, concessions or subsidies
Public private separation	
● To what extent is the norm that a public position or advantage is passed down in a family or used for family profit?	● Nepotism in the executive, legislative, judiciary
● Is it customary that rulers/officials use public funds (or administrative resources) to cover private expenses?	● Cases of use of administrative resources for private goals
● Is there any public scrutiny and disclosure of such expenses?	● Offices or actual jobs in the public sector passed on by holders or managers without any real competition
● Is there any moral outrage at such disclosures or is the practice accepted?	
Relation formal-informal institutions	
● Is the dominant norm closer to the formal or the informal institution?	● Multitude of unimplemented and unobserved rules and regulations
● Is the formal institution subverted/competed by the informal one?	● Discretionary application of law, but roughly according to status
● Is there an effort to enforce formal (legal) norms?	● Existence of well-known patterns of making the inefficient state sector deliver (connections, bribe to gatekeepers, brokers, etc)
● How long has the gap existed between formal and informal institutions?	

Table 1.2   (continued)

Diagnosis questions	Indicators
Accountability versus culture of impunity	
● Has anyone belonging to the chief status group (clan, party, or family) ever been deposed from an official position or sentenced by a court?	● Widespread perception in surveys that politicians are above the law, perception of political parties as top 'status groups' and political affiliation as indispensable for economic success
● Are reports of wrongdoing by such people ever followed up with public investigations?	● Open and outrageous displays of unjustifiable wealth by public officials
● Do people as a rule officially complain of unfair treatment from authorities?	● Cases of notorious rule or law breaking by status holders (not only corruption, but, for instance, traffic accidents) not followed, as a rule by prosecution of every kind
● Are there any whistleblowers?	
● Do regular reports on government activity exist at end year/mandate, including information on objectives which were not reached and measures taken to rectify them?	

1.3   HOW MANY SUCCESSFUL TRANSITIONS IN CONTEMPORARY TIMES? TRENDS AND CASE SELECTION

Although we do not have systematic comparative assessments of corruption to go further back than the 1980s, there are enough historical indicators of when countries have reached certain governance benchmarks. A wider historical compass would thus divide the achievers of good governance into generations. The first generation, which we call 'historical achievers', is comprised of 14 countries, including atypical polities such as Andorra or Liechtenstein. This generation includes:

- the Scandinavian countries, which were created as a result of diverse secessions but which have forged their own paths to good governance, despite their common origins;
- Britain, the classic historical performer, and the United States, its most prodigious colony;

- the Benelux countries, which have shared the same political space for many years, although modern and post-modern Belgium might have reached somewhat lesser standards of governance than the Netherlands;
- three historical German-speaking principalities (Austria, Prussia and Bavaria); and
- France and Switzerland (Mungiu-Pippidi 2015a).

Their achievement in governance has largely coincided with their modernity, leading to the belief reflected in UNCAC that the two can only go together, despite serious skepticism on this account voiced in the past (Nye 1967; Huntington 1968). This group of countries retains a considerable advance in their performance on governance, including control of corruption (Figure 1.2), government effectiveness and the rule of law.

The second generation of 'early' achievers reached modern governance between the two World Wars. These were generally new states that seceded from a first-generation achiever, mainly British Empire splinters mostly populated by European Christians (Ireland, Australia and New Zealand, whose evolutions continued after World War II) that continued to follow the tradition of British legal institutions, mixed with their own democratic developments. In some cases, like Ireland, the further independence was from this origin, the more control of corruption declined, according to recent accounts (Byrne 2012). Also included in this group is Iceland, a splinter of Denmark.

Finally, contemporary 'achievers' came close to the good governance benchmark after the Second World War, starting with two countries which evolved as Western protectorates following military occupation: Japan and West Germany, both on preexisting roots. More recent achievers included a new round of former British colonies, in particular Caribbean islands, a handful of Mediterranean and Eastern European countries, plus some continental exceptions. This suggests that, historically, only a few countries achieved the benchmark of 'control of corruption' independently. There appear to be only a few streams and a few exceptions from broader continental contexts. And since the World Bank began monitoring the WGI in 1996, it seems that very few countries have managed to evolve in controlling corruption, despite the development of an international legal anti-corruption framework and increased awareness of the systematic nature of corruption as a result of efforts by non-governmental organizations (NGOs) such as Transparency International. CoC, due to its aggregate nature, is not very sensitive to change; but we do find changes on the lower part of the scale. It is just transformation from the middle to the top tercile where we see insufficient change, despite a good number of

Note: Control of corruption recoded 1–10 best; the darker shades mean more control of corruption. *N* = 209.

Source: World Bank, WGI Control of Corruption (CoC).

Figure 1.2 National performance in average control of corruption, 2010–2015

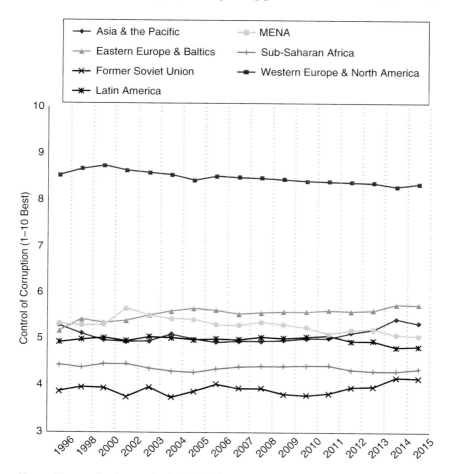

Note: The sample of countries for 1996 includes 190 countries, whereas the sample for 2015 includes 209 countries.

Source: WGI CoC (1996–2015), recoded 1–10 best.

Figure 1.3 Evolution of WGI Control of Corruption average by region, 1996–2015

countries being clustered on the borderline (Figure 1.3). But very few have made it to the group of top performers so far. Some of the countries that had evolved within the previous decades have in fact regressed since global anti-corruption efforts from around 2000.

We can therefore make two observations with high certainty. The first is that few successful transitions exist, and that they tend to unfold

over greater intervals of time than just 15 years. The second is that little
positive change has occurred in general for the past 20 years for which we
have some measurements (and not many more for the past 30, as ICRG's
measure lags even more than CoC). According to the WGI CoC indicator, there has been little statistically significant change in this period, and
Eastern Europe (which includes only the Baltic states from the former
Soviet Union that are now EU members,) is the only region which has
registered constant, albeit small, progress (see Figure 1.3). Surveys are
more difficult to compare across time; but, taking into account the number
of countries polled, they also fail to show significant positive evolution
(Mungiu-Pippidi 2015a, ch. 1). Positive changes were experienced in two
regions: post-communist Central Europe and South East Asia. The former
progressed constantly, more so in the decade of the fall of the Berlin wall
than afterwards; the latter first regressed after the global economic crisis,
but then redressed, ending with small progress. Governance average trends
across continents are matched by individual countries' trends, where also
very few have made it to the threshold defined as the upper tercile or a
rating of 6. With the exception of the EU, Oceania and North America,
which are mostly doing well with not so much internal variation, few countries manage to escape the continental context and posit themselves as
positive exceptions. These are, of course, the cases of interest.

Four criteria determine our selection of transition cases. First, a
country must either rank in the upper third of all countries on the World
Bank's Control of Corruption scale *or* be performing significantly better
than other countries in its neighborhood or the expectation set by its
human-development scores. This position has to be sustainable, in other
words to have resisted at least one change of government. Second, no
country can make the list unless it is on Freedom House's roster of
'electoral democracies'—autocracies cannot reasonably fulfill the ethical

Table 1.3   Significant change in control of corruption, 2000–2015

2000–2015	Free	Partially Free	Not Free	Total
Progressed	12	7	3	**22**
Regressed	11	7	7	**25**
Total	**23**	**14**	**10**	**47**

Notes: *N* countries = +171 (1996–2015). Freedom categories as provided by Freedom
House. Regression and progression determined taking into account the confidence intervals
provided by the WGI.

Source: WGI CoC (1996–2015), own calculation, recoded 1–10 best.

universalism criteria, even if they have few bribery cases, able bureaucrats and a business-friendly climate, simply because rulers who do not risk losing power enjoy de facto immunity. Third, a country must have compiled the bulk of its corruption-control achievements in the last thirty years, since our oldest corruption indicator dates from 1984. Finally, a country has to be unexceptional, in other words have a population larger than a medium-sized city and not be a small island or a fiscal paradise for other countries to find meaningful sources of inspiration in its transition. This is why we discarded all the Caribbean candidates, despite many of them progressing in charts in the last decade, as their tiny polities profited increasingly after the economic crisis from their tax haven status.

A more recent picture of change based on the CoC (15 years) returns only 12 free countries which progressed, compared to 7 partly free and 3 not free. The 12 free cases, which registered a positive evolution from Table 1.2, would have been perfect candidates for transition; however most of them did not evolve all the way up to the upper tercile (Estonia and Uruguay are the notable exceptions), so their progress does not satisfy the transition criteria (although Latvia and Croatia made great progress in charts). From the countries selected under the first criterion, actually, quite a few cases have recorded negative evolution. The economic crisis hurt some small economies, so new EU member countries like Poland, Slovenia or Cyprus regressed (the last, dramatically, with information of it being a fiscal paradise becoming quite salient). Poland, for instance, which is the largest borderline case from Eastern Europe, also has the highest proportion of non-competitive tenders in Europe (at over 40 percent), and in areas like education and research the percentage is even higher (Mungiu-Pippidi 2015a), so it cannot be seen as an accomplished transition. Romania, which has become the latest poster child due to its assertive anti-corruption agency jailing over 20 ministers, prime ministers and generals after 2011, is still on a par with the rest of the Balkans at around 5, and its corrupt magistrates and academics have already released many imprisoned corrupt officials on pardons for their 'academic' papers written in jail (outside jail, they were never academics). This further restricts our pool of countries.

Meanwhile, some authoritarian or semi-authoritarian countries (as well as Singapore, Qatar, the United Arab Emirates or Rwanda) have risen spectacularly to the upper tercile, well above East European cases, Israel or Mediterranean Europe (with the exception of Portugal). We therefore applied our diagnosis tool (Table 1.2) to all these countries in order to check if, beyond ratings, we are really dealing with successful transitions (Table 1.4). None were confirmed.

The situation of control of corruption (CoC, recoded 1–10, with 10

Table 1.4 Selected cases performance in indicators across time and region

Country	Region	Score change in CoC (1996–2015)	Control of CoC (0–100)	CoC 2015 score	Average CoC Score of the Region in 2015	CoC Difference from Regional Average	Index of Public Integrity (1–10)	Rank in Index of Public Integrity (1–105)
Georgia	Former Soviet Union	3.65	72	6.65	4.15	2.49	7.33	30
Rwanda	Sub-Saharan Africa	2.88	75	6.71	4.35	2.36	4.63	90
Estonia	Eastern Europe and Baltics	2.36	87	7.75	5.73	2.02	8.82	12
Qatar	Middle East and North Africa	1.93	81	7.27	5.07	2.20	6.31	48
Uruguay	Latin America	1.05	89	7.84	4.83	3.01		
Botswana	Sub-Saharan Africa	0.45	77	7.01	4.35	2.65	6.08	54
South Korea	Asia and the Pacific	0.40	70	6.38	5.34	1.04	8.12	16
Taiwan	Asia and the Pacific	0.37	77	6.94	5.34	1.60		
Costa Rica	Latin America	0.24	75	6.77	4.83	1.95	7.98	18
Chile	Latin America	-0.35	87	7.77	4.83	2.94	7.54	26

Note: All CoC scores are on a scale of 1–10 best.

Source: WGI CoC, Index of Public Integrity, www.integrity-index.org.

the best) by region with individual country average scores (2010–2015) can be examined in Appendix I. Botswana, Cape Verde and Rwanda top sub-Saharan Africa with best performance, with an average of 4.35 per continent and the former with scores over 7. Rwanda's evolution is the greatest over this interval, so it is worth studying to see if indeed an evolution towards ethical universalism is taking place there; its 2010–2015 average score is 6.61. For the Middle East and North Africa (MENA) the top performers are three traditional monarchies: Qatar (7.6), United Arab Emirates (7.5) and Bhutan (7.1).

Latin America has registered little recent progress (actually quite some involution), and two countries emerge as best performers, closely trailed by a third: Chile (8.1), Uruguay (7.8) and Costa Rica (6.6); but again their evolution spans more than 15 years. A wealth of Caribbean islands has recorded progress in recent years, but, due to their exceptional small size and situation as fiscal paradises (the Cayman Islands are among them), they are not included in our analysis. For Eastern Europe, Estonia (7.4) is the absolute performer, followed by Slovenia (6.9, but regressing not progressing) and Poland (6.4); however only Estonia's trend has been constantly upward. From the former Soviet Union, Georgia (6.0), has the world's largest positive trend. For Asia, Japan (8.4), an earlier achiever, remains high, with city states Singapore (9.3) and Hong Kong (8.6) the top achievers.

From more recent democracies, positive trends exist for Taiwan (6.8)— catching up with older achievers who backslid, like Israel (6.9)—and South Korea (6.3), with an overall positive trend. Oceania has always done remarkably well, and Western Europe shows more involution in recent years than positive evolution: Spain (6.9), Italy (5.4), Greece (5.1), Cyprus (7.4).

By and large, excluding fiscal paradises, sparsely populated islands and city states, we are left with a list of contemporary achievers who come close to (Georgia, Costa Rica, Rwanda, Slovenia, Poland) or satisfy (Estonia, Chile, Uruguay, Botswana, Qatar, Taiwan, South Korea) our 'success' criteria. A first, mostly cross-sectional analysis of these cases exists in Mungiu-Pippidi (2015a, ch. 5). In the present volume we return with detailed country cases in order to understand what made these countries progress and to what extent this can be reproduced elsewhere. In a first stage, we identify specific progress indicators for each country in order to verify whether their advance towards ethical universalism is based on more than perception. For instance, it seems unlikely that Rwanda is indeed doing better than EU member states Romania and Bulgaria (as the WGI CoC shows) or that Qatar is better governed than half of Europe. The next chapter will discuss in some detail the discarded countries, in other words the achievers in the World Bank's CoC ratings that were not fully confirmed under in-depth country analysis. For the remaining cases, country experts undertook process tracing of the change process, and this is the main core of the present book.

By and large, countries could achieve control of corruption in two ways. One is surreptitious, with an incremental change of institutions until open access, free competition and meritocracy become dominant. However, they were not always (or indeed, ever) a main collective goal, but have reached accomplishment rather as a side effect or a by-product, with a gradual buildup of ethical universalism following traditional particularism (patriarchalism, as Weber called it) rather than patrimonialism. Adam Graycar's (2015) account of Australia after the Second World War suggests that major steps in control of corruption came about as a by-product. According to him, this former colony of convicts developed a high integrity (and high performance) state by addressing issues of administrative capacity rather than corruption directly. The complex of institutions built (administrative ombudsmen, for instance) were meant primarily to increase public satisfaction with service delivery—and public integrity was delivered as a side effect. This account is largely consistent with the path that Max Weber described for Germany, where particularism was gradually reduced and eliminated due to the rise of bureaucracies as tools of domination and state performance in an intra-state competition, and not due to some deliberate anti-particularism campaign.

Johann Graf Lambsdorff (2008) discussed as a theoretical possibility a similar mechanism that he called the 'invisible foot', whereby competition and other market mechanisms deliver control of corruption as an unintended consequence. The opposite way is, of course, when rule of law and control of corruption are delivered as collective goods after collective agency and investment—for instance after sustained anti-corruption campaigns. In Britain in the nineteenth century, both royal privilege and electoral corruption were curtailed after many years of such campaigns undertaken by a minority. In France, the Dreyfus affair at the turn of the twentieth century made a decisive contribution to a shift in public opinion, and also in government, with a more universalistic view of rule of law taking hold following a campaign which had lasted for nearly two decades (Mungiu-Pippidi 2015a, ch. 3). The United States also had such campaigns, particularly after dramatic increases in particularism associated with some catastrophe, such as the assassination of President Garfield in 1881 by a disappointed supporter who expected to be appointed ambassador after the victory.

The difference between these alternative paths matters both for our definition and for accounts of transitions from particularism. We define transition as the distance between the last moment when the rule of the game was not yet ethical universalism and the moment when ethical universalism becomes the norm. In the case of Denmark, as reported by Jensen (in Mungiu-Pippidi 2011, pp. 64–70), this can be approximated as between the last moment the chiefs of staff were mostly aristocrats related to the Danish royal family and to each other (regardless of merit) and the moment aristocratic origin by itself (without merit) could no longer guarantee any such position. By 1824, very much by royal design (as wars were lost due to the incompetence of the aristocratic military class), no high public office could be occupied without a law degree from the University of Copenhagen or equivalent.

Transitions can vary in length and visibility from country to country, according to how much 'unintended consequence' versus 'agency-driven' the evolution had been. But it should always be possible to establish a moment zero and a tipping point after which the norm has shifted and people expect ethical universalism rather than particularism, so they no longer seek a connection to access a service, for instance, but just apply anonymously as any citizen. Process-tracing is carried on between these two points with the goal of producing an analytic narrative, exploring how and why the change came about. The process is undertaken with all hypotheses open and has two main advantages: it eliminates reverse causality and endogeneity problems, as it can follow the succession of events in time; and it does not seek a single variable explanation, the largest source of error in most corruption and institutional quality theory. As Talcott Parsons put it (1968, p. 229):

> actions do not take place separately each with a separate, discrete end in relation to the situation, but in long complicated 'chains' . . . [and] the total complex of means–end relationships is not to be thought of as similar to a large number of parallel threads, but as a complicated web (if not a tangle).

In other words, governance cannot be understood in terms of simplistic models based on one dependent variable; rather they are understood as a path model, where variables affect one another and the tangle of reciprocal influences determines a specific path by which change does or does not happen. As transitions only exist where change took place, our main strategy in this book is to study recent achievers by means of process-tracing. We also explore, in limited time series, the main hypotheses across all cases; but since our time series suffer from multiple limitations—the dependent variable is an expert score (ICRG, 1984 to the present), is not a sufficiently long time series and, any complex model would have major endogeneity problems as well as missing data—we combine qualitative and quantitative methods. Other methods have been tried for related research questions: case studies in North et al. (2013) or paired comparisons such as North versus South Korea by Acemoglu and Robinson (2012a). We did not choose this path as comparisons would again have had to use as a dependent variable control of corruption itself, rather than change across time in control of corruption. Also, a detailed account, both quantitative and qualitative, of the former dependent variable exists in our previous work, especially Mungiu-Pippidi (2015a, chs 3–4).

1.4 UNDERSTANDING THE EVOLUTION TO ETHICAL UNIVERSALISM: THE MODELS

At any given moment in time, control of corruption results from the equilibrium between opportunities (or resources) for corruption and the capacity of a society to constrain its most powerful members from extracting privileged rents. This mechanism cuts across state and society and is identifiable as a specific *policy context* (the inner-ring factors), as illustrated in Figure 1.4, which is however the product of a specific development history (the outer ring of the circle). Factors in the outer ring are 'structural': they

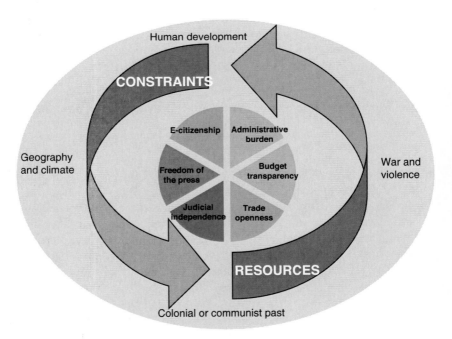

Figure 1.4   The contextual balance determining corruption control

come from a specific geography or history and cannot be changed; they create a legacy that constrains development paths. They influence corruption indirectly, through shaping the balance between more direct factors generating *opportunities for corruption* (power discretion, excess regulation and bureaucracy, competition restrictions, material resources such as foreign aid, natural resources and so on) and factors creating *constraints on the spoilers of public resources*, such as independence of the judiciary and collective action capacity of citizens (Mungiu-Pippidi 2015a). The interaction between these factors delivers an equilibrium that can be closer to control of corruption or to actually institutionalized corruption (Mungiu-Pippidi and Dadašov 2016).

Institutions are endogenous to contexts for the most part, which makes them hard to change. This is why we only consider from Figure 1.4 those factors from the outer ring that can change, and we discard the usually tested and significant factors such as 'former British colony' or 'island' or 'mineral resources'. We built this policy framework more recently into a new Index of Public Integrity (IPI), which measures public integrity national contexts through objective and actionable data. The time series model reported in Mungiu-Pippidi et al. (2014), Mungiu-Pippidi (2015a) and Mungiu-Pippidi and Dadašov (2016) are robust on both expert scores and survey data and have very high explanatory value (see Table 1.2). The IPI also correlates highly with fact-based indicators of corruption, such as non-competitive tenders in the European Union. Here we depart from this cross-sectional model and try to explain the evolution to the optimal equilibrium rather than its components.

In our previous work, we argued that the development of corruption control is not linear in time as political modernization increases constraints; but the growth of the state scope in modern times increases opportunities, which explains the Huntington paradox: why modernization outside Europe seems to have increased corruption instead of decreasing it (Huntington 1968; Mungiu-Pippidi 2015a, ch. 5). Furthermore, it may be precisely the failure of government rationalization (the persistence of particularism, the growth of patrimonialism) that generates what Fukuyama calls "modernization without development." As we do not agree with Fukuyama that "development is a *coherent* process that produces general as well as specific *evolution*—that is, the *convergence of institutions across culturally disparate societies over time*" (Fukuyama 2014, p. 38; italics added)—we suggest that perhaps top-down modernization (modernization by imitation) may only increase the distance between formal and informal institutions, with negative consequences for the rule of law, state capacity and legitimacy. Huntington, in *Political Order in Changing Societies*, had already intimated that this was a possible development. The existence and persistence of a large informal economy, a companion of corrupt societies, may be the best proxy for the incapacity of some societies to avoid a suboptimal equilibrium of high opportunities for corruption and low constraints (Mungiu-Pippidi 2015a, ch. 4). With low constraints and high resources offered by mineral resources or external aid, governments never arrive at social welfare as their main goal (and development as its byproduct), but remain focused on extraction of rents (with underdevelopment as a negative externality).

What then is the solution for change from this rationalization trap? In a very synthetic way we summarize the grand alternatives.

Path 1 consists in modernization of the state. It means making changes directly to the failed organism, which is the non-rational state that has not evolved to autonomy towards private interest, public–private separation and so on. In this narrative, the solution to the failure to create a substantive rather than just nominal modern government (by not managing to create, for instance, an autonomous bureaucracy and independent judiciary) is just more top-down modernization. By and large, this path means addressing the outcome, the state as an extractive machine, rather than the causes that made it so in the first place (for instance, the large profit that rulers derive from the status quo), and building capacity of administration and judiciary as well as some transparency. This has been the path pursued most often by the anti-corruption community, leading to an explosion of integrity legislation and para-legislation and much stress on anti-corruption agencies and actions against corrupt acts after they had already occurred. In some ways, this is what the king of Denmark did in the nineteenth century, and we know that with a strong enlightened principal, in the presence of traditional authority and without a contested supreme office, this path worked.

What we lack so far are democracies to have evolved on this path in recent times, and this is what we check in our process-tracing. After all, Pritchett and Woolcock (2004) have described an intellectual fallacy of development called "when the solution is the problem," which comes dangerously close to this mechanism. Furthermore, successful anti-corruption should not take for granted that a plausible principal who is committed to advancing reform either exists or is the head of the government or institution that needs to reform. Enlightened despots are rare, and cannot be engineered. In their absence, Susan Rose-Ackerman (1997) insightfully noted that while the World Bank is concerned that its projects are not sufficiently 'owned' by borrowing countries, ownership at the top is not desirable if patronage and corruption are rife or if projects help keep corrupt regimes in power.

Path 2 can be called modernization of society. As Frank Fukuyama remarked (2014, pp. 184–6), the attempts to replicate the Western modern state around the world were seldom grounded in a society similar to, for instance, the British one of the nineteenth century. It is to be expected that the more similar a society grows to Western Europe at the advent of its modernization—more educated, urban, secular, gender equal, achievement oriented rather than consumption oriented—the better control of corruption it would develop. After all, the colonies that succeeded (Oceania or Canada) had the most similar societies to their European metropolis. The tipping point is then a convergence point, where social structures, economic institutions and culture align sufficiently to the Western modernization template. Historically, Peter the Great and Alexander II in Russia (Mosse 1992; Cracraft 2009) and the Meiji Restoration (1868–1912) in Japan (Beasley 2000) tried to engineer such processes of creating a modernized nation, with uneven results. Surveys of modernization as a consequence of transfer and imitation exist, allowing assessment of how national goals were set and how deep the Western imitation ran (Nettl and Robertson 1968).

The mechanism by which a society modernizes successfully enough to also experience a transition to ethical universalism is not clear. In one variant, Glaeser et al. (2004), for instance, argue that accumulation of human capital causes both economic development and superior political institutions. On the particular case of corruption, Uslaner and Rothstein (2016) argue in a similar vein that education, and especially its universalization, may play a decisive role in building control of corruption, although the statistical evidence is ambiguous, with only education in the 1900s playing a strong role.

In the framework of the same paradigm, political modernization is a rather distinct hypothesis. The proponents of this view follow Seymour Martin Lipset (1960) in believing that the increase in individual autonomy and its spread to larger groups in society (due to education, industrialization, urbanization or land reform) leads to an increased demand for inclusive institutions, and implicitly greater pressure on rulers to reduce rents. The advent of 'enlightened citizens', as Robert Dahl (1973) used to call them—as shown for instance in the newspaper readers at the turn of the twentieth century or the Internet users of the twenty-first century, additionally armed with social media as enhanced tools of association and coordination—leads to better control of corruption by pressing governments into necessary reforms through collective action.

Clearly, at least education is necessary to bring this development about, but education is not sufficient; neither are any of the modernization components unless a critical mass exists which is made up of active participating citizens and not, for instance, of consumers (Przeworski and Limongi

1997). This is the problem of how to achieve 'strong and sustained citizen involvement', in other words how to solve the collective action problem inherent to corrupt societies where incentives are for free-riding and collusion, so the public good of integrity cannot be created (Johnston 2014, ch. 8) In our earlier work this hypothesis was treated in full as part of a "Tocquevillian" paradigm to explain deep democratization by the collective action capacity of a society (Mungiu-Pippidi 2015a, ch. 6), but lack of historical comparative data on the middle class and associations are major impediments for a full statistical test. A good account of what might be seen as a paradigmatic case is offered by Jeremy Boissevain (1977) on Malta, when he narrates how the decline of traditional associations based on patronage (around the parish church or landlords, for instance) and the increase in membership of trade unions and other secular associations led to a reduction in the vulnerability of individuals and a rise in their personal autonomy.

But whether economic development or political reform is at the start of the virtuous circle of full modernization, governance included, is a hotly debated topic. Control of corruption is seen as an unrealistic goal before a certain income threshold is reached—some researchers place it at 1800 USD/capita; but seeing the recent evolution of some sub-Saharan African cases, this may be insufficient. Only after sufficient income exists and reasonable salaries can be paid to the police, judges and civil servants, and when life expectancy is raised and enough people are educated can massive corruption be addressed, as until then bribes and connections are needed to make the state function, even if suboptimally. This was the classic approach of Samuel Huntington, who presumed that economic development could and did take place irrespective of the quality of governance. This approach is less popular today, when a significant number of economists argue that economic development cannot take place precisely due to poor institutional quality (Rodrik et al. 2004) and the intrinsic opposition of rent-seeking to free and fair competition (Mauro 1995; Ades and Di Tella 1999); but this approach is still strong, as can be seen for instance in Fukuyama's criticism (2012) of Acemoglu and Robinson.

The argument on the primacy of politics is itself not unitary, coming in various forms. The most popular in the literature concerns the decision of elites to increase political and economic rights due to the lack of sustainability of old privileges (Acemoglu and Robinson 2005), although their particular example can be further explained by a rise in demand from the masses, making it closer to the political modernization hypothesis (Mungiu-Pippidi 2015a). There is a long-running debate on the relation between democracy and corruption; but evidence points to the fact that, while autocracy is clearly less conducive to good quality of governance, the role of democracy is more paradoxical and complex than meets the eye, and what seems to deliver is participation of enlightened citizens over many decades—obviously in democratic settings, because otherwise such participation would not be possible at all (see Treisman 2007; Mungiu-Pippidi 2015a, ch. 6). Table 1.1 shows that the countries with the best control of corruption are mostly free countries, but the situation is far more balanced in the other groups.

Finally, can we identify a path where control of corruption has ever resulted as an unintended consequence, even in the presence of unfinished modernization (and, with the restrictions of our case selection, in the absence of top-down enlightened human action, as in Bhutan)? Human development predicts only about half of the countries in the world: outliers are strong over-performers (New Zealand, Chile, Botswana), as well as dramatic under-performers (Argentina, Italy, Greece). The modernization model that presumes that human development should result in a certain quality of governance seems therefore to leave considerable room for exogenous factors (Appendix II shows the estimates of corruption by human development and the negative and positive outliers). They can be policies meant for other targets with unintended positive consequences for corruption, massive cultural or institutional transfers across borders (due, for instance, to military occupation) or other agency-type factors. In the absence of the right context, would such changes (even if once induced) be sustainable? All our selected 'transitions' are actually doing better than they should, considering their human development.

What does the evidence tell us of the paths to good governance? The final chapter of this book will compare the results of process-tracing with the limited but more representative evidence that statistical trend analysis can bring.

REFERENCES

Acemoglu, D., and Robinson, J. (2005). *Economic Origins of Dictatorship and Democracy*. Cambridge: Cambridge University Press.

Acemoglu, D., and Robinson, J. (2012a). *Why Nations Fail: The Origins of Power, Prosperity and Poverty*. New York: Crown Business.

Acemoglu, D., and Robinson, J. (2012b). "Response to Fukuyama's review" [blog]. Available at: http://whynationsfail.com/blog/2012/4/30/response-to-fukuyamas-review.html [accessed December 12, 2016].

Ades, A., and Di Tella, R. (1999). "Rents, competition, and corruption." *American Economic Review*, **89**(4), pp. 982–93.

Beasley, W. (2000). *The Rise of Modern Japan: Political, Economic, and Social Change since 1850*. London: Macmillan.

Boissevain, J. (1977). "When the saints go marching out: Reflections on the decline of patronage in Malta." In Gellner, E. and Waterbury, J. (eds). *Patrons and Clients in Mediterranean Societies*. London: Duckworth.

Byrne, E. A. (2012). *Political Corruption in Ireland 1922–2010: A Crooked Harp*. Manchester: Manchester University Press, pp. 145–59.

Cracraft, J. (2009). *The Revolution of Peter the Great*. Cambridge, MA: Harvard University Press.

Dahl, R. A. (1973). *Polyarchy: Participation and Opposition*. New Haven, CT: Yale University Press.

Eisenstadt, S. N., and Roniger, L. (1984). *Patrons, Clients and Friends: Interpersonal Relations and the Structure of Trust in Society*. Cambridge: Cambridge University Press.

Fukuyama, F. (2011). *The Origins of Political Order: Vol. 1*. New York: Farrar, Straus and Giroux.

Fukuyama, F. (2012). "Acemoglu and Robinson on why nations fail." *American Interest* [online]. Available at: www.the-american-interest.com/2012/03/26/ace-moglu-and-robinson-on-why-nations-fail/ [accessed December 15, 2016].

Fukuyama, F. (2014). *Political Order and Political Decay*. New York: Farrar, Straus and Giroux.

Glaeser, E., La Porta, R., Lopez-de-Silanes, F., and Shleifer, A. (2004). "Do institutions cause growth?" *Journal of Economic Growth*, **9**(3), pp. 271–303.

Graycar, A. (2015). "Corruption in Australia: Making it less acceptable." Paper prepared for ANTICORRP project. Available at: www.againstcorruption.eu/wp-content/uploads/2015/05/Graycar-Virtuous-circles-Berlin-July-2015.pptx [accessed December 9, 2016].

Heidenheimer, A., and Johnston, M. (2002). *Political Corruption* (3rd ed.). London: Transaction.

Hellman, J., Jones, G., and Kaufmann, D. (2003). "Seize the state, seize the day: State capture and influence in transition economies." *Journal of Comparative Economics*, **31**(4), pp. 751–73.

Hofstede, G. (1999). "Problems remain, but theories will change: The universal and the specific in 21st-century global management." *Organizational Dynamics*, **28**(1), pp. 34–44.

Huntington, S. P. (1968). *Political Order in Changing Societies*. New Haven, CT: Yale University Press.

Husted, B. W. (1999). "Wealth, culture, and corruption." *Journal of International Business Studies*, **3**(2), pp. 339–59.

Jensen, Mette Frisk (2011). "The traditional monarchy path to good governance." In Mungiu-Pippidi, A. (ed.). *Contextual Choices in Fighting Corruption: Lessons Learned*. Oslo: Norwegian Agency for Development and Cooperation.

Johnston, M. (2005). *Syndromes of Corruption: Wealth, Power, and Democracy*. Cambridge: Cambridge University Press.

Johnston, M. (2014). *Corruption, Contention and Reform: The Power of Deep Democratization*. Cambridge: Cambridge University Press.

Kaufmann, D., and Vicente, P.C. (2011). "Legal corruption." *Economics and Politics*, **23**(2), pp. 195–219.

Kaufmann, D., Kraay, A., and Mastruzzi, M. (2006). "Measuring corruption: Myths and realities." *Development Outreach*, **8**(2), pp. 124–37.

Kaufman, D., Kraay, A. and Zoido-Lobatón, P. (1999). "Aggregating governance indicators." World Bank Policy Research Working Paper No. 2195.

Klitgaard, R. (2014). *Addressing Corruption Together* [online]. Paris: Organisation for Economic Co-operation and Development (OECD). Available at: www. oecd.org/dac/governance-peace/publications/FINAL%20Addressing%20corrup tion%20together.pdf [accessed December 22, 2016].

Knack, S. (2006). "Measuring corruption in Eastern Europe and Central Asia: A critique of the cross-country indicators." World Bank Policy Research Working Paper No. 3968.

Lambsdorff, J. Graf (2008). "Good governance and the invisible foot." In Kötschau, K. and Marauhn, T. (eds). *Good Governance and Developing Countries: Interdisciplinary Perspectives*. Bern: Peter Lang.

Lipset, S. (1960). *Political Man: The Social Bases of Politics*. Garden City, NY: Doubleday.

Mauro, P. (1995). "Corruption and growth." *Quarterly Journal of Economics*, **110**(3), pp. 681–712.

Mosse, W. E. (1992). Alexander II and the Modernization of Russia. London: Tauris.

Mungiu-Pippidi, A. (2006). "Corruption: Diagnosis and treatment." *Journal of Democracy*, **17**(3), pp. 86–99.

Mungiu-Pippidi, A. (ed.) (2011). *Contextual Choices in Fighting Corruption: Lessons Learned*. Oslo: Norwegian Agency for Development Cooperation.

Mungiu-Pippidi, A. et al. (2014). "Quantitative report on causes of perfor- mance and stagnation in the global fight against corruption" [online]. Berlin: ANTICORRP. Available at: http://anticorrp.eu/publications/quantitative- report-on-causes/ [accessed October 10, 2016].

Mungiu-Pippidi, A. (2015a). *The Quest for Good Governance: How Societies Develop Control of Corruption*. Cambridge: Cambridge University Press.

Mungiu-Pippidi, A. (2015b). *Government Favouritism in Europe: The ANTICORRP Project: Anticorruption Report*. Opladen: Budrich.

Mungiu-Pippidi, A., and Dadašov, R. (2016). "Measuring control of corruption by a new index of public integrity." *European Journal on Criminal Policy and Research*, **22**(3), pp. 415–38.

Nettl, J. P., and Robertson, R. (1968). *International Systems and the Modernization of Societies: The Formation of National Goals and Attitudes*. London: Faber.

North, D. C., Wallis, J., and Weingast, B. (2009). *Violence and Social Orders: A Conceptual Framework for Interpreting Recorded Human History*. Cambridge: Cambridge University Press.

North, D. C., Wallis, J. J., Webb, S. B., and Weingast, B. R. (eds). (2013). *In the Shadow of Violence: Politics, Economics, and the Problems of Development*. Cambridge: Cambridge University Press.

Nye, J. S. (1967). "Corruption and political development: A cost–benefit analysis." *American Political Science Review*, **61**(2), pp. 417–27.

Offe, C. (2004). "Political corruption: Conceptual and practical issues." In Rose- Ackerman, S. and Kornai, J. (eds). *Building a Trustworthy State in Post-Socialist Transition*. New York: Palgrave Macmillan, pp. 77–99.

Parsons, T. (1968). *The Structure of Social Action*. New York: Free Press.

Parsons, T. (1997). *Introduction to Max Weber: The Theory of Social and Economic Organization*. New York: Free Press.

Pritchett, L., and Woolcock, M. (2004). "Solutions when the solution is the problem: Arraying the disarray in development." *World Development*, **32**(2), pp. 191–212.

Przeworski, A., and Limongi, F. (1997). "Modernization: Theories and facts." *World Politics*, **49**(2), pp. 155–83.

Rodrik, D., Subramanian, A., and Trebbi, F. (2004). "Institutions rule: The primacy of institutions over geography and integration in economic development." *Journal of Economic Growth*, **9**(2), pp. 131–65.

Rose-Ackerman, S. (1997). "The role of the World Bank in controlling corruption." *Law and Policy in International Business*, **29**(1), pp. 93–114.

Treisman, D. (2007). "What have we learned about the causes of corruption from ten years of cross-national empirical research?" *Annual Review of Political Science*, **10**(1), pp. 211–44.

Uslaner, E. M., and Rothstein, B. (2016). "The historical roots of corruption: State building, economic inequality, and mass education." *Comparative Politics*, **48**(2), pp. 227–48.

Wallis, J. (1989). "Towards a positive economic theory of institutional change." *Journal of Institutional and Theoretical Economics (JITE)/Zeitschrift für die gesamte Staatswissenschaft*, **145**(1), pp. 98–112.

Wallis, J. (2006). "The concept of systematic corruption in American history." In Glaeser, E., and Goldin, C. (eds). *Corruption and Reform: Lessons from America's Economic History*. Chicago: University of Chicago Press, pp. 23–62.

Weber, M. (1991). *From Max Weber: Essays in Sociology*. London: Routledge.

2. The atypical achievers: Botswana, Qatar and Rwanda

David Sebudubudu, Lina Khatib and Alessandro Bozzini

This chapter presents three highly significant anti-corruption "success" stories, as they are nearly the only regional achievers in two difficult regions, the Middle East and sub-Saharan Africa. These cases are also highly promoted by the international anti-corruption community and their own governments. One is ranked as free (Botswana) and the others as not free (Qatar and Rwanda), but they have changed considerably in recent times. Comparing these cases with the transitions that we selected for process-tracing allows a better understanding of what a governance context based on ethical universalism is—and what it is not. It is also a good warning about the limitations of perception indicators driven mostly by bank analysts and the business environment more generally.

2.1 BOTSWANA

In 1998, when Transparency International compiled the first large-scale Corruption Perception Index (CPI), Botswana—a small sub-Saharan, landlocked country of 2 million people, independent since 1966—ranked higher than Japan and Belgium, and alongside Spain. In 2015 it still fared better than the whole of Mediterranean Europe, ranking as the 28th least corrupt nation out of 175 countries according to the 2015 CPI. Its 2016 ranking was based on six different sources, fairly convergent in their assessment (Transparency International 2016). As Botswana has become an upper middle-income country, after being one of the poorest countries in Africa—with a GDP per capita of about US$70 per year in the late 1960s, only to reach above $16000 as GNI PPP in the twenty-first century (and continuous growth)—the country is a favorite of scholars and development agencies, representing the only uncontroversial success story in Africa. Of course, Botswana's governance far outperforms its Human Development

Table 2.1   Botswana's public integrity framework

Components of Index of Public Integrity	Component Score	World Rank	Regional Rank	Income Group Rank
Judicial Independence	7.01	23/105	3/22	4/28
Administrative Burden	6.77	87/105	17/22	23/28
Trade Openness	6.53	69/105	3/22	22/28
Budget Transparency	6.99	66/105	13/22	19/28
E-Citizenship	3.18	72/105	2/22	26/28
Freedom of the Press	6.03	45/105	6/22	9/28

Source: Index of Public Integrity (IPI), www.integrity-index.org, 1–10 with 10 best.

Index (HDI). So what kind of success is this? A closer look at Botswana by means of the Index of Public Integrity (see Table 2.1) indicates that it is a regional leader in low red tape, fiscal transparency and trade openness, but nearly a global leader when independence of the judiciary and rule of law are concerned (it ranks 23rd in the world and 4th in its income group). In other words, Botswana is doing exceptionally well on rule of law, and this is what drives its good corruption scores, especially since its performance regarding freedom of the press is more mediocre, and on e-citizens it only scores 3 (which still makes it the 2nd best performer of 22 African countries in the index).

The modernization fit of Botswana remains poor. According to the World Bank (2015), the country has high poverty and inequality levels and low human development indicators, even as it continues to experience economic growth. While poverty rates have declined from 50 percent at independence to just over 19 percent today, significant pockets remain, especially in rural areas. Income inequality in Botswana is among the highest in the world due to high unemployment levels and poor health among a significant portion of the population, with an HIV/AIDS pandemic at 22 percent adult prevalence rate. The economy was boosted by the discovery of diamonds, but remains much too driven by commodity prices rather than skills of the labor force, despite continuous investment in education. So, clearly Botswana's state is more developed than its society would allow us to predict, a sufficient reason to make this country a poster child for anti-corruption promoters. If they could make it, why would others not follow in their footsteps?

Botswana is a clear case of the primacy of politics and top-down reforms. Its constitution, adopted in 1965, lays down an institutional framework that includes the parliament as a representative, law-making and supervisory organ intended to ensure that the executive, led by the president as the head of state, delivers on its mandate. The parliament also monitors the implementation of laws and the management of public resources by the executive and administrative arms of government. The executive in turn has a largely politically neutral civil service to implement all policies, plans and development programs. Apart from the parliament, the executive, judiciary and civil service, the country has an elaborate local government system, relatively new and therefore weak but complemented by non-governmental organizations (NGOs). There are both public and burgeoning private media. Even so, the executive dominates both the economy and society because of the powers bestowed on the presidency in relation to parliament (Republic of Botswana 1966, ch. 1).

Botswana is an electoral democracy, although an unusual one. Its first independence leader and president was a traditional tribal chief, Sir Seretse Khama. He founded the Botswana Democratic Party (BDP), sometimes referred to as "the Chief's party," which has won every election and been the dominant force in parliament since independence, drawing its base from the traditional Setswana communities. His ancestor, King Khama III (reigned 1875–1923), had completed Botswana's Christianization. His grandson, Ian Khama, became vice president in 1998 and Botswana's fourth president in 2008. Although the popular vote for the BDP has been declining gradually, from over 80 percent in the 1970s and 1980s to 37 out of the 61 seats in the current parliament after the 2014 elections, the party still enjoys a majority, and Ian Khama won a second term, after surviving a party split. Nevertheless, Botswana's opposition has often been more effective than its sheer numbers would suggest, especially on good governance, managing to pass its own proposals at times with the support of the BDP's backbenchers and endorsement from civil society, however small.

The evolution of Botswana does not match the profile of a transition. The first 15 years following Botswana's independence—from 1966 to 1980 under the leadership of Seretse Khama—can rightly be described as years of the democratization of society characterized by the lowest possible rate of corruption with a zero-tolerance approach. For instance, a Minister of Mineral Resources who fell into the trap of corruption decided to commit suicide before his misdeeds could become publicly known.[1] However, the discovery of rich diamond deposits and their immediate positive impact on government revenues, combined with increased development assistance from the mid-1970s on, eventually led to the type of corruption which has become inherent to Botswana today. A massive infrastructural development program in the form of the construction of roads, schools, health and water facilities and telecommunications opened the way for a culture of public procurement in construction services, which in turn gave birth to the emergence to the sub-culture of "tenderpreneurship," that is, businesses that survive by tendering for government works, and the corruption associated with it.

In other words, the country transited slowly from patriarchalism to a regime aspiring to ethical universalism under its enlightened founder, who can be seen as comparable to the "King of Denmark" at the beginning of the nineteenth century. Since then, corruption has in fact slightly increased, and not decreased, prompted by an increase in resources: first by the discovery of diamonds, then by the mass infrastructure program on both national revenue and aid funds. Also, the modernization of the society with the decline of traditional authority as Botswana moved from a rural to an urban society (63 percent urban residents presently) has not helped ethical universalism, leaving the transition incomplete. Under the second president, Quett Ketumile J. Masire (1980–98), Botswana witnessed a rise in corruption related to nepotism, land allocation, housing, mineral-related deals and foreign trade. Under its third president, Festus G. Mogae (1998–2008), corruption became evident in all sectors: student loans, purchase of textbooks, transport licenses, agriculture; even the mining company Debswana, which had been the world's most successful example in how to manage mineral resources to prevent resource curse. Finally, under Ian Seretse Khama, the latest president, corruption is reported to have spread to all sectors; but it is also being tracked down and prosecuted, so a number of "big fish" (including ministers) have been put on trial.

So where is Botswana, finally? According to the 2015–16 Global Corruption Barometer, only 1 percent of people in Botswana pay bribes to access some public service, and 54 percent appreciate positively the government's fight against corruption, versus 42 percent who are skeptical (Transparency International 2015). On the African continent only Mauritius has a comparably low level of bribery, which contributes to the impression of many foreign observers that Botswana is practically free of corruption. But bribery is not the only form of corruption, and favoritism, on the other hand, is reportedly rife. Most government tenders for the supply of goods and services from government are won by members of the "tenderpreneurs" group linked to the ruling party.[2] The secretary general of the ruling party stated on record that: "I always hear people complaining of how the BDP members win tenders but they seem to forget that we are in the ruling party. How do you expect us to rule when we don't have money? You should just live with it and accept that we are ruling."[3] This was never sanctioned by the party leadership or by the government, thus endorsing the reports that members of the ruling party are the greatest beneficiaries of government projects and tenders. Some local journalists are convinced that the system is patrimonial in essence: "the state is Khama and Khama is the state"[4] and "There is an informal group that is evidently favored by the system and is not accountable to anyone. The group has access to the state and benefits from it. Anyone who tries to emulate them is stifled by using the law."[5]

Using Table 2.1 we can further attempt to determine on what point of the continuum, so closer to what norm, the governance of this country lies. Power distribution is uneven, with a status group formed by rich foreign and indigenous businesspeople, ruling party senior politicians, local councilors and their favorite, constantly tender-winning company owners. Many of them own also large parcels of land, for instance office accommodation rented to government departments, often without following proper procurement procedures. These groups also occupy most senior positions in the public sector, and executive positions in state agencies and parastatal organizations. The composition of this status group is diverse—some are politicians, others businesspeople and executive managers of state agencies or even public universities. The group is relatively stable despite slight changes over the past two elections—some ministers lost elections and were appointed ambassadors, and some formerly influential senior party cadres with farming backgrounds have slowly given way to "tenderpreneurial" and "executive management" groups. Also, due to a struggle for dominance within the inner party circles, some of the "old guard" have given way to a more aggressive group of tenderpreneurs—tender-dependent business groups.

Public housing, land allocation and appointments to senior public service positions depend on political affiliation, according even to presidential commission findings. Politicians and bureaucrats are not well separated: 13 (87 percent) of the 15 most senior political offices (including president, vice president, Foreign Minister and Speaker of Parliament) were held by former senior public servants between 2008 and 2013. Presidential commissions and chairs of boards are headed by ruling party activists. Under Ian Khama, particularism seems to have grown, with quite a few members of his cabinet being family members or natives of the same village.

Botswana originally had few human resources for government, which were allocated from the top down, and therefore meritocracy had a good start. A merit-based bureaucracy has persisted, although merit has slowly been replaced by political appointments, where party activists who have lost elections are allowed back into public service. On the whole, and historically, the bureaucracy has been highly influential in policy formulation and implementation, largely because of the low policy capacity of the ruling party; but under the current president the bureaucracy's influence over policy has somewhat weakened since 2008. Bureaucracy politicization is not the monopoly of the governing party, however, with lower tiers belonging to an opposition party. Teachers, doctors and nurses, and local government workers have increased their unionization since 2011, and are generally critical of the current regime. This led to the maiden large-scale strike of 2011. In other words, although the state is not fully autonomous towards private interests, plural tendencies can manifest themselves and there is no evidence of discrimination in public service.

Public lobbying is not part of the system's culture. Those who use their public office to influence decisions in their favor are severely criticized and seen as corrupt. The moral code on corruption is very strong. Watchdog institutions such as anti-corruption bodies, police and the media are fairly effective.

Policy formulation and public spending are some of the most transparent aspects of Botswana's governance system. Budgeting and development planning and prioritizing times are extensively consultative, involving communities, local government structures, non-state actors and political institutions. The media and citizens are free to listen to the processes. Generally, the allocation process targets different groups and there are specific programs for poorer sections of the population such as inhabitants of remote areas—including indigenous San people—as well as self-help housing programs for the urban poor. The budget allocation is generally fair regardless of whether the council (local authority) or constituency is led/held by the ruling party or not. The audit system is taken very seriously, and its activity was recently further reinforced by the Parliamentary Public Accounts Committee (PAC). The latter holds its proceedings in public, and has drawn a great deal of public and media attention to public spending and the weaknesses of the system.[6]

Public–private separation is uneven, reflecting the lack of modernity of Botswana's society. Family continuity in politics, public service, the private sector and political office is quite common in Botswana. There was concern when the president appointed his own brother as a minister instead of a better-qualified member of parliament. Many children of the first MPs have succeeded their parents and are current MPs and ministers, for example from the Khama, Blackbeard, Masisi, Balopi, Mosinyi and Saleshando families. In other sectors some relatives of politicians are quite visible as leaders of public institutions—the army, police, parastatal organizations and strategic private sector businesses.

It is, however, highly uncommon for officials to use public funds to cover private expenses, and this would arouse public disapproval if it happened. The Directorate on Corruption and Economic Crime (DCEC) supports a law on the declaration of assets and liabilities, and would prefer to report to parliament rather than the executive to be more effective at its job.[7]

The dominant norm is much closer to the formal than informal institutions. For example, there was public outrage when funds earmarked for "disaster programs" were informally diverted by the Office of the President to intelligence activities without the approval of parliament during 2012/13. That action was strongly opposed in parliament and condemned in the private media. There is no general practice of subverting formal institutions by informal ones. The system is generally formal in every respect. As a general rule and practice, leaders are expected to follow established procedures and to be able to justify their decisions. There is also a clear and concerted effort to enforce formal and legal norms and high normative constraints inflicted by the media and civil society in case of failure.

The dominance of one party over 50 years of democracy has managed not to affect the rule of law in Botswana, but obviously has consequences. It resulted in an entrenched particularism, especially at the level of public contracts and top government offices. The first-past-the-post system has preserved this advantage over a growing opposition, which reached 46 percent of the votes by 2009, although with far fewer seats in parliament. The opposition political parties played an important role by introducing bills and motions on the declaration of assets, freedom of information and other matters in a bid to expand the democratic space and improve the reporting of corruption.

The weakness of the parliament compared to the executive completes the picture. Here is a state which transited from patriarchalism to the rule of law, and a society which modernized only partly. While its journey to ethical universalism is far from complete and this case does not fit the pattern of a successful transition, there are important lessons to learn from Botswana (on audits, courts and rationality of public spending). However, such lessons can be applied only in another country with high traditional authority, leaders committed to public integrity and a rule of law tradition, and not in the usual competitive particularism environment which is widespread in young democracies.

2.2   QATAR

Perhaps the most spectacular ascent in charts in recent years is that of Qatar, which Transparency International came to rank as 22nd out of 168 countries, scoring 7 on a 1–10 scale. In recent years Qatar's rankings have placed it above countries such as Belgium, France or the United Kingdom, and well above Israel and Cyprus. Qatar is also the world's richest country in terms of per capita income. However, as we define corruption in this book as the particular (non-universal) allocation of public goods due to

Table 2.2   Qatar's public integrity framework

Components of Index of Public Integrity	Component Score	World Rank	Regional Rank	Income Group Rank
Judicial Independence	8.74	10/105	1/9	10/36
Administrative Burden	8.99	26/105	2/9	19/36
Trade Openness	7.52	46/105	4/9	29/36
Budget Transparency	1	98/105	6/9	34/36
E-Citizenship	8.27	13/105	1/9	13/36
Freedom of the Press	3.34	85/105	6/9	33/36

Source: Index of Public Integrity (IPI), www.integrity-index.org, 1–10 with 10 best.

abuse of influence and control of corruption as the capacity of a society to constrain abuse of influence resulting in social allocation on the basis of ethical universalism (Mungiu-Pippidi 2006), Qatar's achievements and the capacity of corruption perception indicators to really capture governance both need checking. Is Qatar's transition to good governance really a transition to ethical universalism? Are there lessons to learn from Qatar for other countries?

The Index of Public Integrity (IPI) is more modest on Qatar, showing that the country is an outlier on many counts. Freedom of the press and budget transparency are practically non-existent; but red tape is low, courts work well and e-government flourishes, coupled with high usage of e-services by a population well endowed with broadband internet and connected through Facebook. These paradoxes deserve a closer look in order to understand what lessons can be learned from Qatar's achievement. Last, but not least, Qatar featured prominently in the FIFA World Cup corruption scandal (Fontevecchia 2015).

2.2.1   State of Governance in Qatar

Qatar is a neo-patrimonial absolute monarchy with extreme particularism (O'Donnell 1996) in which the Emir reigns, rules and has historically owned state institutions. The Al Thani family has ruled the country for decades, with the current Sheikh Tamim taking over from his father Sheikh Hamad in 2013, following Hamad's bloodless coup against his own father, Sheikh Khalifa, in 1995. The Al Thani family has institutionalized tribal and filial relationships through allocating government roles and resources to local tribal leaders and princes in return for their political backing. The districts of modern Qatar are also divided according to tribal boundaries (Fromherz 2012).

Qatar's wealth has enabled the ruling family to curb potential dissent. Domestically, wealth is distributed both to citizens at large and to tribes in the form of cash handouts and social and health services, and through the allocation of bureaucratic posts. Qataris enjoy free health services and education, a stipend of around $7000 per month per citizen and almost guaranteed employment in the public sector (the unemployment rate is 1 percent). Tribal leaders are appointed to well-paid public posts (Rathmell and Schulze, 2000). Wealth distribution has aided Qatar in avoiding the rise of popular discontent seen elsewhere in the Arab world.

However, the privileges given to Qatari citizens do not extend to the majority of the resident population. The country is home to only around 250 000 Qatari nationals, with 80 percent of the total population being composed of expats from a wide variety of countries who possess only limited personal and economic rights.

Although Sheikh Hamad bin Khalifa engaged in top-down reforms, those reforms have retained the absolute rule of the Emir. In 2000, Hamad established the Council of the Ruling Family, consisting of 13 family members, but he has often bypassed this council. In 2005, he implemented a new constitution, passed by popular referendum in 2003 with 96 percent approval, which calls for the establishment of a partially elected advisory council to pass legislation to replace the current advisory council whose members are appointed by the Emir. The current council has existed since the rule of Sheikh Khalifa, but it has been mostly filled by members of Al Thani and close allies of the Emir, and its role is largely ceremonial—to be informed of policies by the Emir rather than formulating its own policies. To date, there has not been an advisory council election in Qatar, despite repeated promises by Sheikh Hamad, the latest being that such elections would take place in 2013.

2.2.2 Governance Regime Mechanisms

Studies of patrimonial states show that personal and social connections, not bribes, are the main type of privileged allocation in such states (Mungiu-Pippidi et al. 2011). Qatar is no exception. Informal networks and *wasta* (social connections), mainly based on tribal lineage, dominate the functioning of Qatar's formal institutions (Fromherz 2012). Because informal networks are an integral part of Qatari society, they are not perceived negatively, but are taken as a given. The Qatar World Values Survey 2010 reveals that 29 percent of Qataris attribute success to luck and *wasta* only, with a further 15 percent attributing it to mostly luck and *wasta*. At the same time, 91 percent of respondents report that they have complete trust in their families, followed by 43 percent in the case of people they know personally and 35 percent in the case of neighbors, compared to only 8 percent in the case of other nationalities and 5 percent of those from other religions (see SESRI 2010). In this sense, one can safely conclude that privileged allocation on the basis of social connections is not seen as corruption; corruption is generally viewed as being about bribes, which is not a problem that Qatar suffers from in general.

2.2.3   Governance Trends

The type of governance regime in Qatar has been consistent over time. However, the tipping point came with the takeover by Hamad bin Khalifa. Hamad's father had handed his son the task of modernizing the economy in Qatar, while Khalifa himself was extracting money from the Qatari state and not firmly pushing for economic progress. Hamad's bloodless coup was partly motivated by his frustration with the trajectory of economic development that Qatar had been following and his recognition of untapped potential for the country's economic and political future (Kamrava 2009). Hamad worked on liberalizing the state and installing some top-down reforms, such as granting women's suffrage and holding regular municipal elections, which first took place in 1999 and saw the participation of female candidates (Barany 2013). Hamad also abolished the Ministry of Information and gave the press more freedom. The establishment of Al Jazeera in 1996 was a landmark for the Arab world, as it was the first pan-Arab channel engaged in open criticism of Arab governments and leaders—albeit never in the case of Qatari affairs.

The political openings installed by Sheikh Hamad are more to do with establishing legitimacy for the regime, and thus continuity, than with the desire for genuine political reform. They are also driven by the Emir's political ambitions to put Qatar on the map in international relations and economic affairs. This approach paid off, resulting in the formation of alliances between the state of Qatar and key actors in the international community from across the political spectrum. On the economic front, Sheikh Hamad directed a process of privatization that has sharply increased Qatar's international standing.

2.2.4   Detailed Governance Diagnosis

Power distribution

Power in Qatar is distributed in a top-down manner, that is, by the Emir who allocates key government, civil service and private company positions to members of his family and to tribal figures. Under Sheikh Hamad bin Khalifa, the Prime Minister, Hamad bin Jassim, was a cousin from the Al

Thani family. Seven of the 19 key ministers were from the Al Thani family, as are the governor of the Central Bank and the current director of Al Jazeera. Members of the family of Sheikha Moza, Al Missned, occupy key security positions, as do members of the family of Sheikh Hamad's mother, Al Attiyah (Economist 2010).

Qatar has a centralized local governance structure. As Jill Crystal explains (2011, p. 183), "Qatar is divided administratively into ten municipalities (baladiyat). However since the majority of the population lives in the capital, local government is of little practical importance." Centralization and top-down control, coupled with the disempowerment of sources of discontent and the lack of government elections, serve to keep the distribution of power in Qatar consistent.

State autonomy from private interest

In Qatar, there is no real separation between the state and the private interests of the ruling family. There are no lobbies, no government watchdogs, no independent civil society; and freedom of the press is restricted when it comes to addressing internal affairs. Instead, citizens air their grievances through a traditional *majlis* with tribal leaders, where people can submit petitions (Economist 2010). Fromherz (2012, p. 125) quotes Crystal's statement about Qatar under Sheikh Khalifa as being still relevant today: "power remains uninstitutionalized. There is no meaningful distinction, either political or legal, between the person of the Emir and the institutions of the state."

There is also no transparency in public procurement. There is an official procurement process in place, as well as regulations regarding conflicts of interest; however, foreign companies have reported vagueness in the actual implementation of the process.

Public allocation

Public allocation in Qatar follows a rentier system. State wealth is subject to distribution, with the existence of a welfare state that increases dependence on foreign expatriates to be the real work force, while Qatari nationals take state distributions for granted. While non-citizens pay for health care, electricity, water and education, those services, in addition to housing, are provided to citizens for free (US Department of State 2011). Fuel is subsidized for businesses as well as citizens, and Qatari businesses and agriculture also receive capital, electricity and water subsidies (Losman 2010).

The current Emir, Sheikh Tamim, is head of the board of directors of the Qatar Investment Authority (QIA) responsible for domestic and foreign investments. The previous Prime Minister and Minister of Foreign

Affairs, Hamad bin Jassim Al Thani, was also vice chairman and CEO of the QIA while he was in office, and has now been replaced by the Emir's half-brother, Sheikh Abdullah bin Hamad Al Thani (Middle East Online 2013). The QIA does not publish its holdings, making it unclear whether it handles royal investments or not. In this way the state is not autonomous from private interests. It is difficult to establish the extent of this due to the lack of public information.

Relation between formal and informal institutions

Qatar's formal institutions intermingle with informal ones, mainly tribes. A major challenge for formal institutions in Qatar is that they are not always taken seriously because they are subverted by informal institutions. As *The Economist* reports (1999b), in the 1999 municipal elections, "turnout for registration was so low that the government had to extend the deadline by a week to rustle up voters . . . Most of Qatar's leading families did not take the poll seriously enough to field any candidates of their own." Among those who voted, almost all respondents in a survey conducted shortly after the elections revealed that they did so mainly according to tribal affiliations. The current appointed Advisory Council is dominated by Al Thani family members and tribal representatives, who are used by the Emir to ensure their consensus (Fromherz 2012).

Accountability and rule of law

Part of Sheikh Hamad's reforms covered the judiciary. In 1999 a court of final appeal was added to the Qatari legal system (Rathmell and Schulze, 2000) following the establishment of the High Judicial Council "tasked with offering advice on judicial appointments and to propose legislation concerning the judicial system. In October 2004, long-promised court reform unified Qatar's dual court system (of Shari'a and civil courts). In 2007 an Administrative Court and a Constitutional Court were established" (Crystal 2011, p. 185). In 2008 a Supreme Court was added, although the Emir appoints all of its justices. Although the judiciary system has been perceived as efficient in its operations, it suffers from the same infrastructural problems as other state institutions. The Emir also appoints all judges, implying that Qatari judges are selected on the basis of social connections while non-Qatari judges are vulnerable to deportation (see Heritage Foundation 2013). Thus, court cases involving foreign nationals frequently discriminate in favor of Qataris (Langer 2009).

Courts in Qatar do not engage in checks on the ruler. Court orders against royals and tribal allies are rare, and have tended to revolve around failed coups: such as the case of the cousin of Sheikh Hamad who attempted a coup in 1996 and was arrested in 1999; and the case of the

Al Murrah tribe, connected to the same coup, who were stripped of their Qatari nationality until it was restored in 2006 (Economist 1999a; Crystal 2011). An exceptional case is that of Sheikh Ali bin Jassim Al Thani, who was sentenced to six years in prison for involuntary manslaughter in 2013. Normally, corrupt practices by princes are settled out of court as princes are granted immunity.

Qatari state institutions may engage in good practices but they do not have transparent infrastructures: State Audit Bureau reports are not made public, and the head of the Bureau is appointed by the Emir. The National Human Rights Committee (NHRC) has limited ability and refrains from reporting on corruption cases. The National Committee for Accountability and Transparency (established in 2007) does not have public information or contact details. A new organization was established in 2011, called the Administrative Control and Transparency Authority. Its mandate includes "probing the misuse of public funds and investigating complaints against government officials." However, the authority also does not publish public information.

Personal autonomy and collective action capacity
Qatar's wealth has contributed to sustaining a sense of political apathy by negating the drive for economic-based calls for political change (Coates Ulrichsen 2011). From the distractions offered by investments in sports and clubs to public sector employment, public services and distributions based on social connections, the country's economy has served to stifle interest in political participation. The Qatar World Values Survey 2010 shows that 64 percent of Qataris named economic growth as their highest priority for Qatar, with only 16 percent saying their top national priority is more participation in decision making in work and community matters; this is despite 69 percent of all respondents saying that they are either "very interested" (15 percent) or "somewhat interested" (54 percent) in politics (see SESRI 2010).

Interest in politics does not necessarily mean interest in engaging in political activities, and this is not helped by the state of political parties and civil society: the former are banned, and the latter is not independent and is reliant on state revenue (Fromherz 2012). All non-governmental associations—private, professional and cultural—must be registered with and are monitored by the state (Blanchard 2008), "and most groups . . . have had license requests refused" (Crystal 2011, p. 183).

At the same time, "The right to peaceful public assembly is restricted. Public demonstrations . . . are banned. Permission is still required for public gatherings and demonstrations, and the government grants these reluctantly" (Crystal 2011, p. 183). Among the migrant communities, demands for reform or participation in protests are therefore rare as foreign workers are concerned about retaining their residency and jobs (Barany 2013). Although Al Jazeera has gained a reputation as a daring news outlet, Qatari law restricts press freedom. For example, the 2002 media law states that journalists can be punished for "criticizing friendly governments" (Barany 2013, p. 28). Al Jazeera refrains from criticizing Qatari affairs, and has since 2011 been put under the directorship of a member of the Al Thani family (Crystal 2011). While the seven daily newspapers in Qatar are not state owned, they are owned by members of the royal family or have close ties to the government. Foreign newspapers and magazines brought into Qatar are subject to censorship, as is internet usage for political and religious content (US Department of State 2011). There are also indirect restrictions on reporting on corruption due to social conditions and the absence of a legal framework that can enable this reporting, such as whistle-blower protection.

2.2.5   Summary and Conclusions

The governance regime in Qatar is a solid neo-patrimonial, particularist one that places citizens as clients in a rentier state. As such, Qatar's system can be described as falling under the "official moguls" label in Michael Johnston's typology of corruption. He writes that in countries labeled as such:

> institutions are very weak, politics remains undemocratic or is opening up only slowly, but the economy is being liberalized at least to a degree. Civil society is weak or non-existent. Opportunities for enrichment and new risks for the already wealthy abound—but political power is personal, and is often used with impunity. (Johnston 2005, p. 46)

However, unlike the case of most neo-patrimonial states, Qatari citizens report a high degree of satisfaction and quality of life, driven by the state's support of most of their economic needs. Informal networks, mainly based on tribal relations, permeate state institutions and associational life. Public procurement is not transparent and is reliant on social connections. There are, however, no mechanisms to prevent this, as accountability and the rule of law are mostly dependent on who is the point of focus: the ruling family is above the law, as there are no accountability procedures, whether political (elections) or economic, that apply to it. Public information about state institutions, including anti-corruption organizations, is largely absent, and the media refrain from reporting on corruption due to self-censorship as well as to their close ties to the government. Migrants are too scared to speak up about corruption or human rights abuses due to their complete dependence on Qatari job sponsorship. The Qatari judiciary may operate efficiently, but judges discriminate against foreigners; and judges are not fully independent, as they are appointed by the Emir. Western countries have been largely silent about the shortcomings of the governance regime in Qatar because of their political, economic and security interests that are invested in the regime and its stability.

Despite these factors, Qatar has engaged in more reforms to fight corruption than other countries in the Middle East and North Africa, and its success can be attributed to making economic bureaucracies efficient, eliminating the temptation to engage in petty corruption. Its liberalization of the economy has also forced it to adhere to international standards in order to attract foreign investors and traders. There has been a move to better governance in Qatar, as demonstrated by the Emir's control of access to treasury money by the royal family, the facilitations offered to businesses and the increased exposure to global markets with strict anti-corruption requirements, which has forced Qatar to adhere to certain international standards. However, the reforms remain strictly top-down measures directed by the government, and exclude the ruling family and people in the business community with close ties to the government. As such, no matter its position in anti-corruption indicators, "good governance" in Qatar remains partial, not universal. Only when meaningful political reform and social change occur in Qatar can the country be seen as able to formulate comprehensive anti-corruption policies that are implemented transparently (Khatib 2014).

2.3   RWANDA

In spite of the dark image associated with Rwanda's 1994 genocide, the country has managed to improve its reputation in recent years and, thanks to sustained high growth rates, has increasingly been seen as a development model. Since the genocide, Rwanda has made remarkable progress in many areas. Its GDP has registered an average annual growth of 7–8 percent since 2003, making it the world's 10th fastest-growing economy of 2000–2010. Extreme poverty is reported to have decreased dramatically. The World Bank Doing Business reports indicate that Rwanda improved its world ranking by almost 100 positions, from 150th in 2008 to 52nd in 2013. A number of socio-economic indicators—including school enrolment, life expectancy, child mortality and prevalence of HIV—have significantly improved and the HDI has reflected such improvements (World Bank 2012). An important contribution to these achievements has been made

Table 2.3   Rwanda's public integrity framework

Components of Index of Public Integrity	Component Score	World Rank	Regional Rank	Income Group Rank
Judicial Independence	7.62	16/105	2/22	1/14
Administrative Burden	8.44	40/105	2/22	2/14
Trade Openness	5.78	81/105	9/22	5/14
Budget Transparency	2.29	93/105	21/22	11/14
E-Citizenship	1.72	96/105	13/22	5/14
Freedom of the Press	1.94	97/105	22/22	14/14

Source: Index of Public Integrity (IPI), www.integrity-index.org, 1–10 with 10 best.

by foreign aid, which has been injected in large quantities by donors in the aftermath of the genocide, making Rwanda a so-called "aid darling" due to the government's ability to use "donor-friendly language and positioning" and donors' "desire for African success stories" (Zorbas 2011).

Much of this development is credited to good governance. The CPI ranks Rwanda at 44 out of 168 countries, scoring 5.4. A Transparency International report says that only 1.5 percent of people aged above 18 years have encountered bribery in the past 12 months, while 1 out of 25 interactions with an institution ended in the payment of a bribe. This still amounts to 24.4 people who have demanded or have been offered bribes in Rwandan institutions in 2016, up from 1 to 7.5 percent the year before (TI Rwanda 2016). Therefore, is Rwanda—an 11-million strong, landlocked, former Belgian colony in Central-Eastern Africa—an achiever in good governance? The IPI does not confirm this, showing a score of only 4.6 and a modest rank of 90 out of 105 countries surveyed (Table 2.3). While its good marks seem justified by red tape reduction and some progress on judicial independence—in which it is the regional leader, despite the president changing the constitution to run for an extra term and a TI activist having been murdered by police in 2014—its performance on fiscal transparency, e-citizens and freedom of the press cannot be further from the profile of a society based on open access and ethical universalism. Still, lessons from Rwanda can be of interest both in terms of good practices and of limitations.

2.3.1   The Key to Rwanda's Perceived Success

One of the key reasons behind Rwanda's improvements in the last few years, as well as one of the elements that explain donors' willingness to provide high volumes of aid, is considered to be governance. This is usually understood in a way that focuses more on authority and decision-making than accountability: the Rwandan government is commended for its high degree of organization, its capacity to manage resources efficiently and its focus on delivering results. Most observers would say that a key reason behind Rwanda's progress is the government's "political will" to fight corruption, which has resulted in numerous new laws and institutions. The key legal document is law 23/2003 on the prevention and repression of corruption and related offenses, but other laws include commitments to the fight against corruption, particularly the penal code in articles 220–27, while Rwanda has also signed and ratified most international anti-corruption conventions. Institutionally, the government established the Office of the Ombudsman, the Rwanda Public Procurement Authority, the Office of the Auditor General, the Anti-Corruption Unit in the Rwanda Revenue Authority and the Public Procurement Appeals Commission. Moreover, a number of high-ranking national authorities must disclose their assets: in 2011 the Public Accounts Committee was established within the parliament; and in July 2012 the government approved the national policy to fight against corruption, which formalizes the so-called "zero tolerance" approach. A whistle-blower protection law was approved in September 2012, while many public institutions have codes of conduct. Furthermore, both politicians and civil servants have been prosecuted when allegations of corruption were brought against them, though some cite these cases as being used for excising political opponents.

2.3.2 Power Distribution

Power in Rwanda is unevenly distributed, and it is difficult to definitively identify which group or network is the most powerful. However, the ruling Rwandan Patriotic Front (RPF) does enjoy a dominant position. While the current government is formally a coalition and several parties are officially registered and functioning, there is little doubt that Rwanda is de facto a one-party state. Several interviewees indicated:

- that top politicians who are not from the RPF often have a party member as deputy to monitor their actions;
- that party membership is often considered helpful for recruitment in public administration;
- that other parties have limited resources, virtually no visibility and almost no presence in remote areas;
- the RPF's strong, and, in some sectors, dominant position in the economy;

- the limited space for other groups to express dissent, including from abroad;
- the RPF's widespread presence in the field, down to the most local level, through structures that "mimic those of the state ... with the result that the lines between ruling party and state are blurred" (Purdeková 2011); and
- the party's extremely large membership.

This situation does not change with elections, as in recent years the RPF has largely won them all: Paul Kagame, as RPF leader, won presidential elections in both 2003 and 2010 with massive scores (see IFES 2013). Interviewees expect this to continue. As several respondents put it, "the party and the Government are the same thing" in Rwanda (Bozzini 2014).

2.3.3   Accountability Bodies and Mechanisms

In the case of the five sources used for Transparency International's CPI score for Rwanda, the highest score is the World Economic Forum (WEF) executive opinion survey, which mostly looks at the likelihood of firms to make undocumented extra payments or bribes. However, the sources that look more at transparency and accountability give Rwanda significantly lower scores. The 2012 edition of the Mo Ibrahim Index, probably Africa's most important assessment on governance, shows Rwanda at the middle of its ranking—23rd out of 52 countries, with a score of 53.5 out of 100 (Mo Ibrahim Foundation 2012). All these assessments point to a potential contradiction: Rwanda is a country which has achieved good results in controlling corruption but whose accountability bodies and mechanisms are extremely weak. Indeed parliament, the media, civil society and the judiciary play limited accountability roles in Rwanda.

2.3.4   Parliament

The parliament is dominated by the RPF, which won the parliamentary elections in 2008 and 2013 by a large margin (see IFES 2013). Other parties are more allies than opponents, and all parties (except those which were not allowed to register; see Longman 2011) are constitutionally mandated to be members of a consultative forum which provides a framework to discuss and then agree on political proposals. The government claims that Rwanda's "consensual democracy" is a successful model to unify the country, avoid conflicts and agree on policies; but the absence of a formal opposition weakens the parliament's potential as an accountability institution. The parliament has strengthened its accountability role in the last few years: the recently created Public Accounts Committee is working hard to summon politicians, requesting them to explain alleged irregularities related to public funds. As an interviewee pointed out, parliamentarians are accountable to the RPF and to the president because they know they "owe" their position to the party and its leader.

2.3.5   The Media

The genocide-era government tragically used the infamous Radio Télévision Libre des Mille Collines (RTLM) as a tool to spread ethnic hatred and incite violence, and the current government is still reluctant to grant press freedom and accept open dissent in the media. This is consistently certified by a wide range of observers, such as Reporters Without Borders or Freedom House, which ranks Rwanda 97 out of 105 countries and the worst for media freedom in sub-Saharan Africa. Also, some journalists have been murdered in unclear circumstances, and many engage in self-censorship (Reporters without Borders 2012; Freedom House 2011a). Radio is the most popular media, and new stations have started broadcasting in recent years; but, while there are shows where people call in to report their problems, radio programs usually avoid controversial issues, let alone government criticism, and are closely monitored. As a result, the Rwandan media do not play a strong role in scrutiny and accountability, and individual cases of corruption often make headlines. However, politically sensitive issues or cases involving the top leadership of the country are completely missing, while investigative journalism is discouraged and virtually non-existent.

2.3.6   Civil Society

The situation in Rwanda regarding civil society is similar to that of the media. The government, despite granting formal registration to most national and foreign NGOs, is reluctant to consider civil society organizations (CSOs) as full political actors, seeing them as mere service providers and allowing them limited space to question and challenge public policies and programs. CSOs are generally weak, highly dependent on foreign donors and have little capacity. They also often have limited independence from the political power, to the extent that they "are almost unanimously tied into or legitimized by Government in some fashion" (Gready 2011); and even though some "independent CSOs and NGOs exist at national level [. . .] they react to the government's distrust with self-censorship and therefore make little impact" (ibid.). The Bertelsmann Transformation Index (2012) gave Rwanda's "civil society participation" a three out of ten.

Most local NGOs see themselves as partners of the government rather as than counterweights or watchdogs.

2.3.7   The Judiciary and the Ombudsman

Rwanda's accountability institutions also include an ombudsman: an office whose presence is positive in itself and which plays a visible role in sensitizing the population to the negative consequences of corruption. However, the fact that for many years the chief ombudsman's position was held by a "top ideologue" and founder of the ruling party raises doubt about the independence of the institution, in spite of his reputation as a person of integrity and high morals. Similar concerns of limited independence apply to the Office of the Auditor General and to the judiciary: they tend to track relatively minor issues and rarely tackle cases of major corruption involving high-level members of the ruling party, the government or the army (Cooke 2011, p. 13)—and when they do, there are often rumors that the main rationale is to punish those who fell out of line (Bertelsmann Foundation 2012, p. 26).

2.3.8   Independence of State Bureaucracy

Rwanda's often-praised ability to manage projects, programs and donor funds would not be possible without a skilled, merit-based bureaucracy. At the same time, there are also claims that influential positions are held by RPF members or loyalists. Both assertions are correct. The government has introduced many measures to improve transparency in recruitment, including guidelines on timing and modalities for publishing vacancies and holding job interviews, as well as a provision that candidates who feel they have been treated unfairly can report the case to the ombudsman or the public service commission. Despite limited technical capacity in some fields, the Rwandan public administration is relatively efficient: recruitment practices have improved over time; and most technical positions, as well as most low- to middle-ranking officials indeed seem to be recruited based on merit. However, top officials tend to be politically appointed, and some interviewees also mentioned cases of politically influenced recruitment.

2.3.9   Separation of Public and Private

Some private companies are closely linked to and intertwined with the RPF, and thus with the government. Today there are three holdings, or conglomerates, of "party-statals." The largest one, Crystal Ventures Limited (CVL), formerly known as Tri-Star Investments, is a private holding company fully owned by the RPF. The second conglomerate, Horizon Group Limited, is often referred to in Kigali (the Rwandan capital) as "the army's company": having received initial capital from the Military Medical Insurance (MMI) and the Military Micro Finance Cooperative Society (ZIGAMA-CSS), it is now a private firm but is considered the army's investment arm, and its CEO is seconded by the army. The third consortium is the Rwanda Investment Group (RIG), a holding company with public and private shareholders created in 2006 at the instigation of the government, whose purpose is to raise funds to invest primarily in the construction and energy sectors.

While most people in Kigali know that some companies are controlled by the RPF and the army, and while party officials say "it is no secret" that they run a number of companies and major investments (Kagire 2012), still the websites of the three holdings do not mention the RPF anywhere, so this is a transparency issue. The second issue is the potential favoritism that might benefit these companies. There is a general perception among many local and foreign entrepreneurs that CVL and Horizon companies enjoy preferential treatment when they compete for public contracts, to the extent that some entrepreneurs said that, when they see that one of these companies are bidding, they "do not bother bidding." RPF officials and observers who support the party's role in the private sector deny any favoritism, and point to several bids that their companies have lost as well as to the competition they face from local and foreign companies. It is true that Crystal Ventures and other RPF-controlled companies do not win all the contracts they bid for; that the RPF is very careful to avoid a "winner-takes-all" image; and that Rwanda has made progress in procurement practices and has a comprehensive legal framework in this field. At the same time, in a country where accountability bodies are weak and not fully independent, it is hard to believe that members of a public tendering agency (for example a district) who usually have strong links to the ruling party are not tempted to favor companies linked to the same ruling party.

Another area of potential favoritism is taxation: a researcher who was able to examine the list of top taxpayers in 2010 (no longer available on Rwanda Revenue Authority's website) reports that "only 11 party-statals (less than half of the 25) were among the top 307 large taxpayers in 2010," and that the CVL subsidiary in the food processing sector, Inyange, whose market share is over 85 percent, "is not among the top taxpayers" while "its two immediate competitors [. . .], which have smaller market concentrations, do appear on this list" (Gökgür 2012, p. 27).

To conclude this complex and controversial issue, it is safe to say that in

Rwanda the state, the government, the ruling party and the private sector are not entirely separate entities. They have obvious problems in terms of separation of powers, risks of favoritism and limited transparency; and such blurred lines between private and public are key features of patrimonialism.

2.3.10   Service Delivery

Corruption in service delivery is the subject of tight scrutiny by the government, of harsh sanctions and of calls for integrity as well as sensitization campaigns. Indeed, the widely cited "political will" of the Rwandan government to fight corruption is mostly visible in this field. Overall, despite the persistence of some petty corruption, services such as health, education and water supply, or the issue of documents are provided evenly and impartially, with corruption being the exception and not the rule. Fear of sanctions or of retaliation by authorities may lead to underreporting of corruption cases; but it is safe to say that corruption in this field is not institutionalized, and that the overall goal is to cater to everybody.

2.3.11   Transparency

On top of the limited role played by the accountability organs and bodies, the concept of transparency has yet to fully develop in Rwanda. Indeed, in spite of efforts to disclose more information about the authorities and their activities and a recently adopted access to information law, transparency of key issues remains limited. The Open Budget Survey 2012, developed by the International Budget Partnership in cooperation with a local NGO, gives Rwanda a score of 8, which is much lower than the global average of 43 for the 100 countries surveyed, and is also significantly worse than other countries in the region. Interestingly, the country which is usually ranked as East Africa's least corrupt (by far), appears in this survey as the region's least transparent.

Politicians have to disclose their assets to the ombudsman, but many believe that some top leaders do not include some of their assets in such declarations, knowing that they will not be investigated. Procurement and the mineral trade from bordering conflict-ridden Eastern Congo are also areas where transparency is somehow limited. Transparency in elections has also been questioned, and there are allegations that the government might have altered the proportions of votes received by some parties (Freedom House 2011b; Longman 2011, pp. 39–40).

2.3.12   Citizen Participation

Citizen participation is often considered another key element to preventing and reducing corruption. Again, Rwanda is a paradox, as the relatively low level of corruption is matched by an even lower level of citizen participation. Indeed, ordinary citizens are reluctant to engage in the public sphere, and the government itself has acknowledged this challenge, stating in official documents the objective of encouraging more participation. At the same time, citizen participation is often "directed and controlled" by the authorities (Bertelsmann Foundation 2012, pp. 22–3). It is still noticeable that the only public demonstrations in the last few years have been pro-government, raising doubts that they were actually organized by the government itself. Interestingly, some observe that limited participation is nothing new in Rwanda. This would be due to the fact that, as a consequence of civil war, exile and the genocide, other forms of constituency and shelter have weakened (traditional and family ties, regional and religious identities) and "historically therefore Rwandans have tended to revere political power and are passive in political matters" (Kayumba 2013).

2.3.13   Conclusion

A number of lessons can be learned from the analysis of the state of governance and corruption in Rwanda. First, corruption should be defined in broad terms as encompassing all its forms, including non-monetary ones, as a country might have low incidence of some forms and high incidence of others. Moreover, the case of Rwanda suggests that petty or administrative corruption can in some cases be a very different issue from grand or political corruption, as curbing the former does not necessarily mean reducing the latter. In addition, and perhaps most importantly, Rwanda shows that relative success in fighting bribery is not necessarily associated, as many would assume, with high levels of accountability, transparency and citizen participation. This confirms the need, when investigating corruption, to analyze the broader governance context of a country.

NOTES

1. "Minister Segokgo late." *Botswana Daily News*, 1 December 1976.
2. See the report on the Mayor of Lobatse's bakery winning almost all bread tenders to schools, prisons, and so on, *Botswana Guardian*, May 2013.
3. "It's our turn to eat." *The Voice*, 28 June 2013.
4. According to an interview with the deputy editor of the *Sunday Standard* in 2013; see Sebudubudu (2014).

5. According to an interview with the deputy editor of the *Sunday Standard* in 2013.
6. According to annual audit reports and PAC proceedings, as well as media reports.
7. Interview with senior DCEC official, 2013.

REFERENCES

Barany, Z. (2013). "Unrest and state response in Arab monarchies." *Mediterranean Quarterly*, **24**(20), pp. 5–38.

Bertelsmann Foundation (2012). *Bertelsmann Transformation Index 2012: Rwanda Country Report*. [online] Available at: www.bti-project.org/country-reports/esa/rwa [accessed 21 February 2014].

Blanchard, C. M. (2008). *Qatar: Background and US Relations*. Washington, DC: Congressional Research Service. Available at http://wlstorage.net/file/crs/RL31718.pdf [accessed 4 March 2014].

Bozzini, A. (2014). "Background paper on Rwanda." [online] Berlin: ANTICORRP. Available at: http://anticorrp.eu/publications/background-paper-on-rwanda/ [accessed 16 March 2014].

Coates Ulrichsen, K. (2011). "Repositioning the GCC states in the changing global order." *Journal of Arabian Studies*, **1**(2), pp. 231–47.

Cooke, J. G. (2011). *Rwanda: Assessing Risks to Stability*. Washington, DC: Center for Strategic and International Studies.

Crystal, J. (2011). "Eastern Arabian States: Kuwait, Bahrain, Qatar, United Arab Emirates and Oman." In Long, D. et al. (eds.), *The Government and Politics of the Middle East and North Africa*. Boulder, CO: Westview, pp. 161–204.

Economist (1999a). "Royal jigsaw in Qatar," 29 July. [online] Available at: www.economist.com/node/228095 [accessed 31 January 2014].

Economist (1999b). "Voting fun," 11 May. [online] Available at www.economist.com/node/319329 [accessed 31 January 2014].

Economist (2010). "Qatar and its emir: He'll do it his way," 27 May. [online] Available at: www.economist.com/node/16219226 [accessed 27 February 2014].

Fontevecchia, A. (2015). "FIFA corruption scandal: Follow the money to Qatar." *Forbes*, 29 May. [online] Available at: www.forbes.com/sites/afontevecchia/2015/05/29/fifa-scandal-follow-the-money-to-qatar/#5ad42df22e44 [accessed 23 January 2016].

Freedom House (2011a). "Freedom on the Net 2011: Rwanda." [online] Available at: www.freedomhouse.org/sites/default/files/inline_images/Rwanda_FOTN2011.pdf [access 5 March 2014].

Freedom House (2011b). *Freedom in the World: Rwanda*. New York: Freedom House. [online] Available at: https://freedomhouse.org/report/freedom-world/2011/rwanda [accessed 5 March 2014].

Fromherz, A. J. (2012). *Qatar: A Modern History*. Washington, DC: Georgetown University Press.

Gökgür, N. (2012). *Rwanda's Ruling Party-Owned Enterprises: Do They Enhance or Impede Development?* Antwerp: Institute of Development Policy and Management.

Gready, P. (2011). "Beyond 'You're with us or against us': Civil society and policy-making in post-genocide Rwanda." In Straus, S. and Waldorf, L. (eds.) *Remaking*

Rwanda: State Building and Human Rights after Mass Violence. Madison: University of Wisconsin Press, pp. 87–102.

Green, E. (2011). "Patronage as institutional choice: Evidence from Rwanda and Uganda." *Comparative Politics*, **43**(4), pp. 421–38.

Heritage Foundation (2013). *Index of Economic Freedom: Qatar*. [online] Washington, DC: Heritage Foundation. Available at: www.heritage.org/index/country/qatar [accessed 14 April 2014].

International Foundation for Electoral Systems (IFES) (2013). *Election Guide: Rwanda*. [online] Washington, DC: IFES. Available at: www.electionguide.org/countries/id/180/.

Johnston, M. (2005). *Syndromes of Corruption: Wealth, Power, and Democracy*. Cambridge: Cambridge University Press.

Kagire, E. (2012). "Our businesses are clean, says RPF." *The East African*, 12 October [online] Available at: www.theeastafrican.co.ke/Rwanda/News/Our-businesses-are-clean-says-RPF/-/1433218/1532008/-/7j64skz/-/index.html [accessed 22 April 2014].

Kamrava, M. (2009). "Royal factionalism and political liberalization in Qatar." *Middle East Journal*, **63**(3), pp. 401–20.

Kayumba, C. (2013). "In Rwanda, you toe the official line, or live and die a pauper or in exile." *The East African*. [online] Available at: www.theeastafrican.co.ke/Rwanda/Opinion/In-Rwanda-toe-official-line-or-live-die-a-pauper-or-in-exile----/-/1433246/1912628/-/4bo83b/-/index.html [accessed 30 April 2014].

Khatib, L. (2014). "Background paper on Qatar." [online] Berlin: ANTICORRP. Available at: http://anticorrp.eu/publications/background-paper-on-qatar/ [accessed 14 January 2017].

Langer, N. (2009). Global Integrity Report 2009: Qatar. [online] Washington, DC: Global Integrity. Available at: http://report.globalintegrity.org/Qatar/2009/notebook [accessed 4 February 2014].

Longman, T. (2011). "Limitations to political reform: The undemocratic nature of transition in Rwanda." In Straus, S. and Waldorf, L. (eds.) *Remaking Rwanda: State Building and Human Rights after Mass Violence*. Madison: University of Wisconsin Press, pp. 25–47.

Losman, D. L. (2010). "The rentier state and national oil companies: An economic and political perspective." *Middle East Journal*, **64**(3), pp. 427–45.

Middle East Online (2013). "No surprise as Qatar dismisses Hamad Bin Jassim from investment authority." [online] Available at: www.middle-east-online.com/english/?id=59847 [accessed 5 March 2014].

Mo Ibrahim Foundation. (2012). *Ibrahim Index of African Governance 2012*. [online] London: Mo Ibrahim Foundation. Available at: www.moibrahimfoundation.org/iiag [accessed 15 January 2017].

Mungiu-Pippidi, A. (2006). "Corruption: Diagnosis and treatment." *Journal of Democracy*, **17**(3), pp. 86–99.

Mungiu-Pippidi, A. et al. (2011). *Contextual Choices in Fighting Corruption: Lessons Learned*. Oslo: Norwegian Agency for Development Cooperation.

O'Donnell, G. (1996). "Illusions about consolidation." *Journal of Democracy*, **7**(2), pp. 34–51.

Purdeková, A. (2011). "'Even if I am not here, there are so many eyes': Surveillance and state reach in Rwanda." *Journal of Modern African Studies*, **49**(3), pp. 475–97.

Rathmell, A., and Schulze, K. (2000). "Political reform in the gulf: The case of Qatar." *Middle East Studies*, **36**(4), pp. 47–62.

Reporters Without Borders. (2012). *World Press Freedom Index 2012*. [online] Paris: Reporters Without Borders. Available at: http://fr.rsf.org/IMG/pdf/classe ment_2013_gb-bd.pdf [accessed 5 March 2014].

Republic of Botswana. (1966). *Constitution of Botswana*. Gaborone: Government Printer.

Sebudubudu, D. (2014). *Botswana Background Report*. [online] Berlin: ANTICORRP. Available at: http://anticorrp.eu/publications/background-paper-on-botswana/.

Social and Economic Survey Research Institute (SESRI). (2010). *Qatar World Values Survey 2010*. [online] Ann Arbor, MI: SESRI. Available at: http://xn- -mgbeh7c1c.xn--wgbl6a/sesri/documents/QWVS_English_press_release__Final. pdf [accessed 17 January 2017].

Transparency International. (2015). *Africa Survey 2015: Global Corruption Barometer*. [online] Berlin: Transparency International. Available at: www.trans parency.org/whatwedo/publication/people_and_corruption_africa_survey_2015 [accessed 19 January 2017].

Transparency International. (2016). *Corruption Perceptions Index 2016: Botswana*. [online] Berlin: Transparency International. Available at: www.transparency.org/ country/BWA [accessed 19 January 2017].

Transparency International Rwanda. (2016). *Rwanda Bribery Index 2016*. [online] Kigali: Transparency International Rwanda. Available at: https://tirwanda.org/ resources/researches-and-publications?lang=en [accessed 22 January 2017].

US Department of State. (2011). *2010 Human Rights Report: Qatar*. [online] Washington, DC: US Department of State. Available at: www.state.gov/j/drl/rls/ hrrpt/2010/nea/154471.html [accessed 13 March 2014].

World Bank. (2012). *World Development Indicators 2009–12*. [online] Washington, DC: World Bank. Available at: http://data.worldbank.org/counry/rwanda [acces sed 14 January 2017].

World Bank. (2015). *Botswana Overview*. [online] Washington, DC: World Bank. Available at: www.worldbank.org/en/country/botswana/overview [accessed 21 January 2017].

Zorbas, E. (2011). "Aid dependence and policy independence: Explaining the Rwandan Paradox." In Straus, S. and Waldorf, L. (eds.) *Remaking Rwanda: State Building and Human Rights after Mass Violence*. Madison: University of Wisconsin Press, pp. 103–17.

3. The Uruguayan path from particularism to universalism

Daniel Buquet Corleto and Rafael Piñeiro

3.1 INTRODUCTION

Uruguay's present international reputation is one of a non-corrupt country. Even though clientelism as a discretionary practice to distribute goods, public employment and preferential treatment in exchange for electoral support has been a common political practice for much of the twentieth century, the phenomenon of corruption as "the misuse of public office for private gain" (Rose-Ackerman, 2008: 551) has never been pervasive in Uruguay. The introduction of comparative instruments of measurement across countries—such as Transparency International's Corruption Perception Index (CPI) and the Control of Corruption (CoC) indicator of the Worldwide Governance Indicators (WGI) project—has only confirmed this intuitive positive image. Furthermore, diverse comparative political studies of public opinion, such as those published by the Latinobarometer and Latin American Public Opinion Project, also place Uruguay in a position of regional good governance leadership. Finally, recent comparative academic works on corruption also place Uruguay, along with Costa Rica, among developed countries where corruption is not pervasive, reduced to a marginal "use of wealth to seek influence within strong political and administrative institutions" (Johnston, 2005: 60) and as a clear exception to the norm of public integrity (Mungiu-Pippidi, 2015: ch. 5).

Nevertheless, considering corruption in a broader sense, Uruguay shows a long history of political particularism. The way in which most of the citizenry related to the state had a significant discretional component until the 1960s. The intermediation of political brokers was the norm in order to obtain state services, and patronage defined the logic of recruitment to public sector jobs. Although corruption in the strict sense of the word was never a pervasive practice, Uruguayan public policy in the twentieth century belonged more with particularism than the ethical universalism model of governance. Nevertheless, significant changes in institutions and political competition occurring gradually between the sixties and the nineties made clientelism increasingly ineffective or directly non-viable in a way that transformed the country into an open-access regime.

The simple teleological view of modernization theory associates the processes of modernization with the end of particularism and the adoption of universal criteria. However, many countries in the world have experienced economic development without achieving significant improvements in terms of universalism. North et al. (2009), Fukuyama (2014) and Mungiu-Pippidi (2015) have stressed the complexities involved in this kind of transition, in particular for the late modernizers.

In the Uruguayan case the political elites associated with the traditional parties competed for votes since 1916 through open, free and fair elections. However, over time their electoral support increasingly came to depend on their ability to deliver public resources in a clientelistic manner. Therefore, the discretionary use of state resources became the norm. By the end of the fifties the limits of this political strategy to remain in power had become apparent. The gradual exhaustion of the efficacy of the clientelistic strategy led to the rise of a new challenger (outside the old traditional parties), the Frente Amplio (FA). More importantly, it led to to a change in mentality by the younger members of the traditional political elites that would govern the country during the eighties and nineties (among them Jorge Batlle, Julio María Sanguinetti and Luis Alberto Lacalle). This mentality change, which emerged in the sixties, was reinforced after the re-democratization in the eighties by the fear of dictatorship as an answer to politicians' incapacity to deal with economic and fiscal crisis. They realized the need to change the allocation of state resources towards more efficiency and equity in order to remain in power. In an incremental fashion, the transformation in electoral competition pushed leaders of traditional parties to commit to Uruguay's transformation into a regime of universal access, where particularism and corruption were the exception and not the rule.

This chapter outlines the process of change from particularism to universalism in Uruguay, departing from the socio-economic challenges the political system faced between the fifties and sixties and the political responses to these challenges. In particular, it shows how the changes in the way parties compete for votes (from a clientelistic to a programmatic manner) led to the more general transformation in the way that society grants rights and distributes and allocates public resources. The following section describes the historical departure point and the creation of the old bipartisan clientelistic equilibrium. Next, we propose a theoretical argument to explain the process of change. The fourth section describes the key political transformations and the political agency behind these processes of reform. The next section characterizes Uruguay as a "contemporary achiever" and, finally, the main lessons of the Uruguayan political and social process from particularism to universalism are discussed.

3.2 TIME ZERO: THE OLD BIPARTISAN CLIENTELISTIC EQUILIBRIUM

Uruguay has the longest democratic history of any Latin American country, and by the middle of the twentieth century had a very proud self-image that can be summarized with the sentence "Como Uruguay no hay" (There is nothing like Uruguay).[1] By that time, the country had a very wealthy socio-economic situation and a renowned democratic system. Wealth and democracy were closely connected. Setting aside the well-known literature in this regard (Lipset, 1959; Przeworski et al., 2000; Boix and Stokes, 2003), that specific connection was made in Uruguay through the state. During the first half of the twentieth century, Uruguayan traditional parties found a way not only to coexist peacefully through regularly conducted elections, but also to share government positions and the use of state resources. The latter, known in local politics as "co-participation," has been pointed out as one of the main features of the Uruguayan party system, and it originates from the pacts made between the two parties by which they distributed territorial authority by the end of the nineteenth century (Pérez Antón, 1988). The permanent growth of that partisan-shared state in functions and in personnel, but particularly in its increasing participation in economic activities, made for the economic development and the wealth distribution reached by the country.

Along with its early democratization, Uruguay developed a welfare state that implied a joint process of building political and social citizenry (Castellano, 1996). During the first decades of the twentieth century, under the leadership of José Batlle y Ordóñez of the Partido Colorado (PC), various political (universal and secret suffrage, free and fair elections), social (separation of church and state, eight-hour working day) and economic reforms were implemented. In the absence of strong contending actors, the state acquired a central role in the economy and in the provision of all kinds of public services. By these means the country forged a wealthy, integrated and modern society with a growing middle class during the first half of the twentieth century (Filgueira and Filgueira, 1994).

The cornerstone of the early democratization process in Uruguay is the 1917 constitutional reform. That constitution established the first set of electoral rules that allowed the traditional parties to reach a general agreement. It was an inclusive agreement that enacted not only all electoral guarantees (like universal and secret ballots) but also the instruments to obtain a fair distribution of power between the PC and the Partido Nacional (PN) and among their internal factions. In that vein the electoral system included the multiple simultaneous vote, proportional legislative representation and a very peculiar institution, the National Council of Administration (NCA), a collective organ of the executive power with one-third of its seats reserved for the minority. Additionally, that agreement gave constitutional status to different public companies and mandated that their directive boards must be appointed by the NCA, thus ensuring a formal share in the state apparatus for the opposition. That peculiar agreement, made at a particularly critical juncture in time, created a very strong inertia that restricted the characteristics of the subsequent reforms in a path-dependent way.

The two aspects of the reform—on the one hand the electoral system and, on the other, the co-participation between parties in governmental posts—are linked by an "electoral connection." The connection is made taking votes as a currency that is exchanged for positions. This exchange is direct and transparent in relation to elective positions, but it was also used increasingly over time to appoint all kinds of governmental authorities. The presence of a multiple simultaneous vote system was key to achieving that goal. The double and triple simultaneous vote (DSV and TSV) is one of the most particular or rare characteristics of the Uruguayan politics during the entire twentieth century. This system was developed by the traditional parties (PN and PC) to allow internal competition between party factions at the same time as they compete against each other. Citizens were able to vote for a party and then for a list or a candidate inside the party. For example, in a national election, citizens selected a party, then they could vote for any of the different presidential candidates running for that party, or any of the different lists the party had for the senate and for any of the party lists for representatives.

As the electoral supply—the combination of candidates between levels: President, Senate, and House of Representatives—was not restricted, every person who wanted to run was able to present a list of candidates. Therefore, the number of lists that competed inside each party started to grow. Nevertheless, the vast majority of the lists to the house were not able to elect a representative, even though they were useful anyway to collect votes. Party leaders and second-level politicians used the number of votes each list received as a measure of the effort made by a faction or a leader, and as a way to define the particularistic benefits allocation among lists (Aguiar, 1984).

The distribution of governing posts between the two parties and among the different factions inside parties was not problematic until the 1930s. But, "the Uruguayan Public Administration, after 1930 turned unconcerned with efficiency, facing the essential necessity to relieve the pressure exerted over the political system by those unemployed. For that reason, the distribution of public posts was made over clientelistic basis and not taking into account the qualities of the applicants" (Solari and Franco, 1983: 88). As a consequence of the 1929 international depression, the main factions of the two traditional parties made an agreement to use public employment as a means to alleviate the growing unemployment rate. In that pact they agreed to distribute public jobs over partisan bases. The opposing factions called that agreement the Pacto del Chinchulín (Chitterlings Pact) in order to discredit it, and they eventually took power by means of a coup in 1933. It was a civil coup that sought rapid re-institutionalization through constitutional and legal reforms, mainly eliminating the NCA and establishing the concurrence of all elections. However, the lack of legitimacy of the two elected governments (1934 and 1938) under these norms implied that effective democracy was only recovered in 1942, with a new constitutional reform.

The Conservative coalition that ruled the country during the 1930s made moderate use of public employment because they promoted economic growth and employment through public investments rather than public jobs (Filgueira et al., 2003). But when democratic competition was restored in 1942 the previously defeated factions regained power (in particular the Batllista faction of the PC led by Luis Batlle),[2] and from that point the generalized use of public jobs and the discretionary allocation of pensions came to be norms. During this period the PN, the PC and their different factions constructed their political bases over a clientelistic distribution of public resources. This equilibrium was based on institutions that assured easy access to goods to be distributed both for the party currently holding power and for the opposition. Álvarez Rivadulla points out that "Uruguay is a society with a strong tradition of statism and clientelism" (2012: 40). Using Schefter's (1994) categorization, both parties can be considered "internally mobilized" parties, those constructed from within the state apparatus.

If that practice did not become a fiscal problem while the economy was growing (during the forties and the beginning of the fifties), it increasingly turned into a significant problem as the economy stagnated by the mid-fifties. Complementarily, the system of co-participation was carried to an extreme by a new constitutional reform in 1952. Among other things, the reform reestablished a collegiate executive power with six seats for the majority and three for the minority. Additionally, the constitution stipulated that directive boards in all public companies and services must be appointed at the rate of three for the majority and two for the minority.

By that time the clientelistic use of the state had become apparent and was put at the center of all kinds of diagnoses of the country's problems. The scant literature that exists about the links between the state and politics refers to this problem without exceptions. Filgueira and Filgueira (1994), Solari (1988) and Rama (1971) say that public employees were recruited in exchange for party support. In the words of Solari and Franco (1983: 88), "the entry to public jobs was made by the intermediation of the traditional political parties. The 'political club' acted as an employment agency." And Filgueira and Filgueira (1994: 14) argue that in Uruguay state policies were not implemented by a bureaucratic organization under government orientation. For them, it was a state full of hidden party professionals serving as intermediaries between state and society. They add that political parties were able to capture the state apparatus due to the fact that social state consolidation was produced at the same time that the authority of the state was built and parties and the whole political system reached their modern configuration. This fostered clientelistic politics.

The particularistic application of universal norms was part of the political contest between parties, factions and politicians. Speeding up access to pensions implied being part of a political network. The same happened with subsidies, as in the case of access to milk at lower prices or the political distribution of cards to get access to public health care. In the same vein, Real de Azúa (2009) highlights that the power of political parties was based on electoral laws, on the distribution of public employment and on the brokerage to public services access. In particular, Real de Azúa argues that the key to the system was control over access to pensions. Political parties had the mechanisms to speed up or delay access to pensions. Thanks to this power, traditional political parties were able to reproduce their electoral support.

Not only academic literature agrees with the pervasiveness of clientelism. This feature of Uruguayan politics was also mentioned in technical reports, such as by the Commission of Investment and Economic Development (CIDE), the National Development Plan (PND) and even early on by a foreign consultant (Hall, 1954). The PND, an official report based on the CIDE work, states that "the relation between bureaucrats and professional politicians, in addition to leading to the proliferation of public posts based on particularistic loyalties, allows personnel with low levels of instruction, scarce vocation for public service, and mainly interested in a regular source of income, access to the bureaucracy." As it could be no other way, all our interviewees agreed with that characterization, particularly the elderly, including ex-presidents. As a piece of color, one interviewee, who was appointed director of a public oil company in 1985, told us that when he went to his office for the first time he was surprised by the size of the entrance hall, which is connected to the five directors' offices. One day, he asked the doorman, an old man who had worked for the company for a long time, why the hall was so large. The doorman answered: "You can't imagine how many people came to this hall in other times, bringing a card of a broker and asking for a job."[3] This anecdote vividly illustrates that the culture of clientelism was so pervasive that it was even translated into public architecture.

3.3 ECONOMIC STAGNATION, DISEQUILIBRIUM IN THE PARTY SYSTEM COMPETITION, AND THE LONG PROCESS OF REFORM

Following the Great Depression, the prosperity generated by the great performance of agricultural and cattle exports was associated with an "import substitution development model" which was intended to promote industrial development but which fell into crisis at the beginning of the 1950s as a consequence of a significant drop in commodity prices. As a result, a long period of economic stagnation and social turmoil followed (Thorp, 1998; Azar et al., 2009).

As can be seen in Figure 3.1, the total number of public employees, as well as the total number of pensions, grew systematically from the first decades of the twentieth century to the beginning of the 1970s. The period from the mid-fifties to the end of the sixties—when total pensions grew from 60 percent of people over 60 years old to double that figure, and the total number of state employees grew from 6 percent of people over 18 again to double that amount—coincided with the worst period of economic performance. This evolution partly explains why, during the 1960s, political and social conflict reached extraordinary levels of violence, and why political parties realized they needed to change their strategies to regain political support.

The first expressions of the political crisis were manifested in a systematic electoral turnover. After four consecutive electoral victories for the Batllista faction of the PC (1942, 1946, 1950, 1954) there were three consecutive changes in government. The PN came into office, for the first time in the twentieth century, after the 1958 election. In the following election, the PN retained office, but in the hands of its former minority faction; and in 1966 the PC came back to office, but led by the anti-Batllista faction. This is to say that, due to a worsening situation, the citizenry went through the whole political spectrum. Uruguayan voters subsequently elected the opposing factions of the two traditional parties. In a complementary way, during the same period the process of unification of minor parties took place. After two frustrated attempts in the 1962 and 1966 elections, the

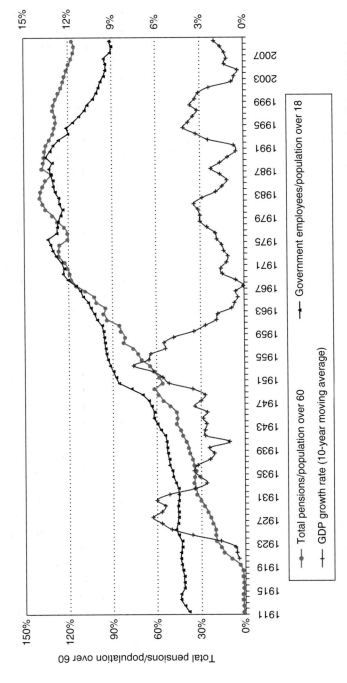

Source: Figure generated using data from Instituto de Economia, Facultad de Ciencias Economicas y de Administracion, Universidad de la Republica, Uruguay. Base de Datos: Series Históricas.

Figure 3.1 Government employment, pensions and GDP growth in Uruguay

64

launch of the third significant party, the FA, occurred in 1971 with a major electoral success. That fact implied the beginning of the new ideological configuration of the Uruguayan party system.

During the sixties, the traditional elites began to make subsequent attempts at reforming the government and functioning of the state. The first big project was the creation of the Commission of Investment and Economic Development (CIDE), an inter-ministerial organ coordinated by Enrique Iglesias and devoted to the elaboration of development plans and projects. The CIDE operated between 1960 and 1967, and made a complete diagnosis of the country situation and presented a significant number of projects in a wide range of areas. While most of the initiatives it presented were not put into practice, some recommendations were included in the constitutional reform of 1967, such as the creation of the Central Bank and the Planning and Budgeting Office.[4] In particular, a pamphlet with suggestions for reform written by Iglesias had significant influence over the new constitution.

That reform, which is still in force, could be considered the first step towards a more efficient government and more rational functioning of the state. The system came back to the one-person executive power, a president with more power than ever vis-à-vis the legislative branch. Among the most striking changes was the reinforcement of the exclusive initiative given to the executive in budgetary matters and the ban on the legislature increasing public spending. Representatives and senators lost room to bargain with the executive. That crucial reform totally altered the incentives for political careers, which in the House of Representatives had focused on pork barrel politics. The ex-president, Julio Sanguinetti (representative between 1962 and 1969 and leader of the constitutional reform process), said that "the expending initiative of the legislative, oriented by the voluntarism of legislators, led the system to an ungovernable nature."[5]

Additionally, the constitutional reform gave the executive more control over autonomous and decentralized entities such as public companies. Nevertheless, this change proved to be insufficient to limit the clientelistic practices that continued to be channeled preferentially through those institutions. The attempts to reform faced resistance from second-line politicians, who were supposed to exchange the votes they gathered for clientelistic benefits.[6] But, during the 1960s, the first rules limiting access to public jobs were enacted: in 1964 a system of open competition for state employment was established for the first time in the country's history; and in 1970 a ban on the incorporation of new civil servants until a certain date was approved.

Nevertheless, all attempts made by the political system during the 1960s and the beginning of the 1970s could not stop the deterioration. The economic, social and political crisis led to a coup in 1973 and a 12-year military regime that ended in 1985. The dictatorship was similar to others of the "bureaucratic–authoritarian" type that devastated the region at that time (O'Donnell, 1973), and was the only time in the twentieth century that the government was not elected and the traditional political parties were excluded from power. That period of authoritarianism represented the system's incapacity to include a new actor, the FA, which imposed a new competitive strategy based on a party platform rather than on clientelistic distribution.

When the constitution was restored in 1985, a double transition process took off (Lanzaro, 1993). On the one hand, the re-democratization was rapid and restored the rule of law— with the exception of the prosecution of human rights violations during the dictatorship— and the previous political and party system, with all its complexities. On the other hand, successive governments of the traditional parties gradually implemented a process of economic and state reform. But while the democratic transition was rapidly concluded, various attempts at privatization and state reform were blocked by a coalition between the leftist opposition (FA) and social organizations— mainly labor unions—frequently resorting to mechanisms of direct democracy.

The democratic restoration basically reestablished the same challenges that the country faced in the sixties, but with the 1967 constitution as an instrument and the traditional political elite more committed to the necessity of reforms because of the trauma suffered. Among political elites, many of those who were young politicians in the sixties and were involved in the above-mentioned reform projects were appointed to relevant governing posts.[7] By that means the reform proposals made by the CIDE and the PND reentered the agenda.

Nevertheless, the first democratic government, led by Julio Sanguinetti (1985–1990), could do little in that respect because it was more concerned with the tasks of political transition (like the restoration of the rights of those public employees dismissed by the military and the human rights violations under the dictatorship). However, a first attempt was made in order to orient public companies more technically. In President Sanguinetti's words, "The first major attempt was to transform the culture of state enterprises, [to] try to make politicians understand that the political directors had to run a business."[8] Differently from past traditions, some renowned technicians were appointed as directors instead of active politicians. As an example of that orientation, the appointment of the engineer Serrato as president of the electricity company or the accountant Slinger as president of the main public bank made for a more technical management of those public bodies. The former began an important process of reform in the management of the electricity company through a contract with a Spanish company, which was continued over time.

The reformist process gained momentum during the 1990s. In the Lacalle administration (1990–1995), the transition toward democracy was no longer the main issue, as it had been in the previous administration. Lacalle, the leader of the pro-market faction of the PN, tried to carry out different structural reforms in a neoliberal vein, such as privatization and economic openness. At the same time, he looked to reform the management of different public companies (for example the electricity company) and the Central Bank. As in the Sanguinetti government, not all appointments to the public companies' boards had the same high technical proficiency and commitment. Some of them were, as usual, politicians who did not have any special managerial capacity.[9]

Reducing the inflation rate was one of the main objectives of the Lacalle government. Therefore, public spending reduction was a major concern. In this regard, the government passed a law that prohibited the hiring of new public employees. This policy tied the government's hands from using public employment as an electoral resource. Nevertheless, this law did not cover all public administration, since public companies and local governments were not included under that restriction. Lacalle also promoted the appointment of "social directors" to the board of the Social Security Bank, as was mandated by the 1967 constitutional reform. Having on that board one representative of pensioners, one of active workers and one of businesspeople served as a control mechanism and made for a reduction in the discretionary allocation of pensions.[10]

Another strategy to reduce public spending was the Public Enterprises Law. This allowed the privatization of the main public companies and the de-monopolization of alcohol production and the car insurance markets.[11] After a referendum supported by the unions, the FA and the main faction of the PC led by Sanguinetti (the former PC president), the Public Enterprises Law was repealed. However, the process of de-monopolization remained, and was extended to the port services. Additionally, Lacalle's government launched the National Program of Debureaucratization (PRONADE), with the objective of cutting red tape. This initiative reduced paperwork and unified different procedures in public administration.

Economic and administrative reforms were more important during Lacalle's administration than in Sanguinetti's first government. However, most of the legislative initiatives during that period were not passed because his government soon lost parliamentary support (Chasquetti 1998). The main political leaders realized the necessity for state and administrative reforms in order to improve government performance. Since these reforms implied a good deal of electoral cost in the short run, the strong competitive character of the relation between the two traditional parties led to a lack of cooperation during that period, reproducing the "prisoner's dilemma" structure of the political game.

Lacalle's faction in the PN and Sanguinetti's faction in the PC were the favorites to win the next presidential election. Ex-president Lacalle explicitly recognized that his lack of legislative support from Sanguinetti's faction was due to the electoral interest of Sanguinetti, who was promoting his own presidential candidacy for the next term.[12] Putting aside the lack of legislative support, the interviewees who were involved in Lacalle's government stressed that they needed to improve state efficiency in order to gain electoral success, but recognized that the effort was not the same in the different state areas.

Surprisingly, the 1994 election result showed an almost triple tie among the PC, PN and the FA. In this scenario, the traditional parties (PN and PC) finally realized, on the one hand, that no significant reform would pass without the cooperation of both of them and, on the other hand, that the systematic growth in the FA's electoral support would throw them out of office in the near future. The natural vote-seeking strategy of both parties made it rational for the one that lost the presidency to oppose the initiatives of the other that were unpopular, like most of the needed reforms. But at that point this rationale became false inasmuch as the credit for opposing unpopular measures was increasingly turning to the advantage of the FA. The political interaction between the traditional parties turned at this point into a "game of chicken" where the non-cooperative strategies no longer led to equilibrium and resulted in worse payoffs for both.

Without cooperation between them, the incumbent traditional party cannot claim credit for any achievement; and nor can the opposition be electorally rewarded for opposing. This diagnosis made for a radical change in the strategies of the traditional parties, which from that moment began to lead the government within the framework of a formal and explicit coalition. From this point on, the PN gave the PC the legislative support that the latter denied the former during the previous administration.

The basic agreement to form a coalition between all the traditional parties' factions was led by the PC President Sanguinetti and Alberto Volanté, the then leader of the PN who acquired particular prominence during that period. That agreement had two cornerstones: reform of the pension system and electoral reform.[13] The former was done in order to solve the country's main fiscal problem in the long run, the social security huge and increasing deficit. The latter was done in order to create an institutional environment that facilitates electoral coordination among traditional parties. Different sectorial reforms continued to be carried out in different areas;[14] but both the above-mentioned reforms are keys to understanding the new ideological equilibrium of the Uruguayan party system.

On the one hand, pension reform could solve the fiscal problem of social security for the future (the country's main fiscal problem), but it immediately cut the use of pensions as the main clientelistic resource in the hands of politicians. The reform introduced private pension funds, creating a mixed public–private system that preserved the pay-as-you-go pillar for low wages, and introduced a personal savings account pillar for higher wages. It was a moderate change that preserved the state presence in the system and the interests of the current pensioners in order to be the least unpopular; but it introduced a rigorous system of registry (the labor record) and paperwork that prevents the discretionary allocation of pensions.

On the other hand, the electoral reform, introducing the majority runoff for the presidential election, worked as a double safeguard for the electoral future of the traditional parties. It not only made the electoral victory of one of them more likely, as traditional voters could gather their votes in the second round, but also prevented the strategic desertion from one of them in the first round causing disproportionate damage, especially in terms of legislative seats, since presidential and legislative votes are tied. Additionally, the electoral reform cut the triple simultaneous vote, reducing the possibility of political brokers claiming benefits on the basis of their own votes. Thus, the electoral reform promoted the cooperation between the traditional parties and, at the same time, concentrated party power in the hands of the main national leaders.

The traditional parties finally caught up with the needed reforms combining social security and electoral changes. Under the new system, if state reforms did not give them an electoral reward in the short term, they would likely have another five-year term to make the results apparent for the public. By that means, both traditional parties were placed together in the center-right of the ideological spectrum, as a consequence of their explicit moderated, pro-market orientation. The electoral system promoted such an ideological alignment since the electorate would face off in the second round, with one candidate of that block against the presidential candidate of the center-left, the pro state candidate of the FA, which increasingly assumed the role of a defender of state-owned enterprises (SOEs) along with the rights of the workers and the poor.

Even though the agreement reached its primary goal, things did not work out as expected. The PC's candidate, Jorge Batlle, won the presidency in the 1999 election due to the support of PN voters in the second round. But very soon a financial crisis arose when the system almost collapsed following a run on the banks, and a deep recession started. As a consequence, with a drastic devaluation of more than 100 percent and inflation rising to 26 percent, Uruguay reached its highest levels of fiscal deficit and external debt in more than a decade. But the reform process did not stop and, during that period, two other important reforms began—of the customs and tax offices—at least in part due to the state's extreme need for revenue.

In 2004 the FA won the presidential election in the first round and obtained an absolute majority in congress. Tabaré Vázquez (FA) took office with a strong mandate for change. The first FA administration (2005–2010) maintained previous reforms and promoted new ones in the same vein of efficiency and rationality. The FA is an exterior party; its electoral bases had not been built around the particularistic distribution of state resources because it had not been in office before. Therefore, reforms that reduced discretional use of governmental resources did not generate the same tensions between national leaders and sub-leaders as they did in the traditional parties.[15] Nevertheless, tensions emerged among the FA factions due to different ideological positions inside the party.

The FA governments (2005–2010 and 2010–2015) have shown a strong commitment to fighting tax evasion and informality. As Ignacio Otegui, president of the Uruguayan Chamber of Construction said, "I think there is an increasingly strong conviction in society and in government [to fight against informality], and that is a merit. I see it steadily increasing since the crisis and especially during the leftist governments. There is a militant attitude in seeking the formalization of the economy."[16] In particular, FA governments have made important advances in formalizing highly informal sectors such as domestic and rural work.

The FA governments promoted state reforms with a broader vision than the previous traditional parties' governments. Those reforms were led by the economics team, which pertains to the moderate wing of the party and has an institutional economics approach. That view could be found in the book that Mario Bergara (2003) published as an economic platform before the FA's victory. In an interview, Bergara claimed credit for the FA for almost all reforms; but he recognized that some reforms had been made or started before, only the FA reforms were based on a comprehensive reform program. This was in part due to the FA's condition of external party. So the FA could continue the process of reforms that were initiated earlier (such as of public companies); implement reforms previously approved (tax administration); and carry out its own initiatives such as tax reform, customs reform, a financial inclusion law, a new bankruptcy law and a competition promotion law.

3.4 A THEORETICAL EXPLANATION OF THE URUGUAYAN TRANSFORMATION

The Uruguayan case and its governance transformation cannot be explained by any modernization theory. Societal and economic transformations toward a more developed country are just the context, and neither the triggers nor the main causes of change. Moreover, in Uruguay particularism grew simultaneously with the middle class, and each fueled the other. Economic growth during the forties and fifties was the economic base that supported the expansion of the clientelistic manner of delivering public services and appointing public jobs. Citizens became more educated, and the middle class grew during those years; but at the same time educated middle-class citizens legitimized clientelism as the usual way parties compete for votes.

Exhaustion of the "import substitution industrialization model" since the end of the fifties made particularism unsustainable as a strategy of competition between the PC and the PN. It became increasingly expensive to reward the middle class through clientelism at the same time as public revenues became scarcer. While clientelistic competition was sustainable during the forties and fifties, the game between the Colorados and the Blancos can be represented as a "hunter dilemma," a game also called stag hunt or assurance game. Clientelism was the smaller prize for each, but both parties chose to pursue this strategy nevertheless, against cooperating for a market-based, impersonal development strategy that might have brought greater gains, thus increasing the payoffs for both.

Once the economic and fiscal crisis arose at the end of the fifties, the game changed and became the "prisoner's dilemma." The payoffs from clientelism decreased compared with those in times of economic growth. Additionally, the iteration until 1970 of the clientelistic strategy to compete for votes worsened the economic and fiscal situation, getting the system into a vicious circle. The deepening of the economic and social crisis at the end of the sixties made new parties more competitive because the traditional parties (PC and PN) and their particularistic strategies lost the support of the urban middle class. This situation led to the emergence of the FA, the first important challenger from the left.

In that context, the traditional parties increasingly clustered at the center-right of the ideological spectrum, since they jointly advocated and conducted pro-market reforms. Shifts in the party system strengthened after 1971 as the FA moved toward a more moderate ideological position and adopted state-oriented proposals that were being abandoned by the traditional parties. Once the FA appeared as a serious challenger to the traditional parties, the game between the PC and the PN changed again, taking the form of a game of chicken, with each party sticking to its old position in the hope that the other would be the first to let go. As both retained the clientelistic strategy, however, this left them in the worst scenario, leading to the 1973–1985 dictatorship caused by the same economic, social and political crisis.

The economic and fiscal crisis and the loss of legitimacy of the clientelistic system among citizens helped the FA break the domination of the traditional coalition and facilitated a change toward a more open regime in the terms of North et al. (2009). This new actor in the party system, without any access to public resources, competed only in programmatic terms and incrementally transformed the logic of political competition between parties in the whole system. Once the traditional parties returned to power after the dictatorship they needed to make state and electoral reforms in order to adapt the system to the new competitive equilibrium. This needed to cope with the new programmatic left–right electoral competition, so a second-round majority runoff was adopted to facilitate the gathering of the traditional parties' votes against the newcomers. The improvement in government performance was also driven by the increase in the competitiveness of the new political system after democratization and the long-term economic crisis.

The notion of equilibrium, as commonly used in game theory, suggests a situation in which outcomes are stable as the result of all players continuing to use their best strategies. But from a dynamic point of view, the question here is how that equilibrium is reached "by individuals interacting until they can find no position that would be better" (Levi, 2008: 128). The construction of the equilibrium mainly consists of the political process by which players come to the adoption of a set of rules to play the game. The search for the causes of the transformation requires a dynamic approach that begins identifying the critical junctures that led to a significant change of the rules (Collier and Collier, 2002). Those critical junctures are "often understood as periods of contingency during which the usual constraints on action are lifted or eased" and then "open up opportunities for historic agents to alter the trajectory of development" (Mahoney and Thelen, 2010: 7).

The critical juncture appeared as a consequence of the economic crisis and the political challenge mentioned above. The transformation of the system is the result of institutional reforms and elite behavioral changes made in the context of that critical juncture. The institutional reforms, mainly important reforms to the state apparatus and electoral reform in order to achieve a new competitive equilibrium that could accommodate the political interests of the main actors, were constrained by some path-dependency restrictions—for instance, preserving a strong state presence

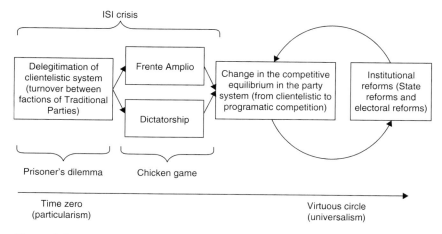

Figure 3.2   Process of transformation of governance in Uruguay

in the provision of different goods and services. The Pareto social welfare superior situation was the outcome of interest-based strategies of all players that generated a virtuous circle. Figure 3.2 represents the general idea of governance transformation, and the next section traces the process of that change.

3.5   URUGUAY AS A "CONTEMPORARY ACHIEVER"

In the past few years Uruguay has become an open-access regime. It is hard to find data, in particular quantitative data, which can be used to show the change in the governance regime that Uruguay underwent, due to the lack of statistics before 1973. Before and after regime change indicators are particularly important to understand if there have actually been any changes in the governance regime and their dimensions. But, Figure 3.1 shows that, from the 1990s on, the number of pensions and public employees in relation to the corresponding population shows a clear descending trend.

Another striking figure that shows an important change from particularism to universalism in Uruguay is the systematic improvement of tax-avoidance reduction. This stable pattern of progress in the development of state capacity implies significant changes oriented toward reducing the ability of economic agents to circumvent state control. Regarding informality, state capacity to collect taxes increased substantially since 2008. Tax reforms and institutional improvement of the tax-collection agency resulted in tax collection growing systematically more than GDP since

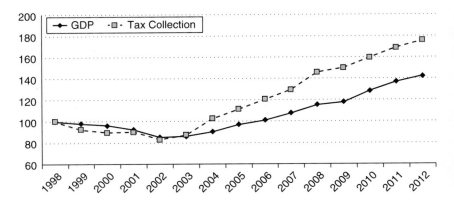

Source: Figure generated using data from Dirección General Impositiva: Aseosría Estadística.

Figure 3.3   *Uruguay's GDP evolution and gross tax collection, 1998–2012 (1998 5 100)*

2003 (DGI, 2013). The office in charge of collecting taxes in Uruguay, Dirección General Impositiva (DGI), was reformed in 2000 in terms of its bureaucratic capacities. The reform was initiated in the first year of Jorge Batlle's administration (PC) and was aimed at increasing tax collection. In 2007 Uruguay implemented a tax reform that included an income tax. This reform also simplified all tax systems and put an end to exemptions that favored different economic and social sectors.

Figure 3.3 shows that, since 2003, the evolution of the level of tax revenue collection at constant prices has been systematically bigger than GDP growth. At the same time, the number of people regularly contributing to social security increased by 62 percent after 2004 (BPS, 2013). The coverage of the Uruguayan social security system grew from 50 percent of the economically active population in 2003 (the post-crisis year) to 67 percent in 2010. These figures are outstanding in the Latin American context and comparable only to those of Costa Rica and Chile (Rofman and Oliveri, 2012). This process was driven not only by economic growth but also by specific policies oriented to formalize former highly informal activities such as domestic servants or rural workers. In that respect it is telling to observe that coverage in the primary sector grew from less than 45 percent in 2000 to more than 70 percent in 2010, while in the secondary and tertiary sectors the increase was just over 10 percentage points (Rofman and Oliveri, 2012). Additionally, other policy reforms encouraged labor formalization, like the health reform, which, by extending health coverage to relatives of formalized workers, created incentives for workers' formalization. These figures show an important process of economic formalization and a substantive improvement in the state's capacity to fight tax evasion.

Public allocation of services and goods is no longer discretionarily distributed. It is very difficult to observe any serious bias in the design or execution of public policies. For example, Vázquez's first administration (2005-2010) made important reforms in safety networks, especially increasing money transfers for the poor and expanding health coverage. The "equity plan" (Plan de Equidad), a classic conditional cash transfer (CCT) program, covers all children below the poverty line with a "family allowance" (Asignaciones Familiares) of about $50 per child. These kinds of plan open up opportunities for particularistic allocation; but in this regard there is no evidence of any political bias, even though the government party obtained some electoral profit among the targeted population (Queirolo, 2010).

Since the 1990s' reforms, traditional parties have strived to tackle an oversized and inefficient state by reducing the number of state employees and privatizing SOEs. Additionally, the Frente Aamplio (FA) governments—first at the capital's city hall (Intendencia Municipal de Montevideo) since 1990 and then in national government since 2005—made significant changes, introducing more competitive recruiting procedures without completely removing political influences. Thus, in general terms, it could be said that government currently makes efficient use of most available human, financial and organizational resources.

Change in the competitive strategy between parties from clientelism to programmatic offers led to this process of reforms that reinforces at the same time programmatic competition through the restriction of available resources to distribute in a particularistic manner. Therefore, in this process institutional changes constitute a virtuous circle (Mungiu-Pippidi, 2016).

3.6   THE URUGUAYAN PATH AND WHAT CAN WE LEARN FROM IT

Uruguay is a "contemporary achiever," a country that only recently could be considered an open-access regime and that has registered modest economic achievements since the mid-1980s. Uruguay shows how a change in the competitive equilibrium of the party system (from a system based on clientelistic competition to one grounded in programmatic competition) transformed the country into an open-access regime. In this context, the political, administrative and economic reforms mentioned in this chapter can only be fully explained because of a simultaneous transformation in the structure of party competition. Agency matters, since the will of the leaders is a necessary condition for reform; but agency needs institutional incentives to work.

Although corruption was never pervasive in the past, the former governance regime in Uruguay was built around particularistic distribution of benefits and public services. Rama (1993) shows how organized interest and individual citizens were prized or penalized in a discretionary manner. The Uruguayan transition from particularism to universalism since 1985 is a transformation which can be best understood in the context in which clientelistic competition became unsustainable, a change that was driven in large part by the transformation of the party system from one in competitive equilibrium between two traditional parties to another that had to incorporate a third party challenger. This process of change consolidated a system of political competition between two blocs that are ideologically opposed: the FA on the center-left and both traditional parties on the center-right. This highly institutionalized party system, which demonstrated once again its ability to adapt, is the key to this political transformation which is a cause and not an effect of the reform process in Uruguay.

Reforms in Uruguay were possible because the country met a set of conditions that made them viable. As Geddes argues, "reforms occur when the larger parties in a political system are approximately equal and thus control approximately equal amounts of patronage" and when "legislators have some additional incentive to eschew patronage, such a widespread pressure for reform from constituents" (1994: 21, 99). Also, reforms can advance and consolidate when a newcomer (from outside the two traditional parties) gets into office because his or her political support does not depend on the particularistic use of public resources. The successful trend of reforms in Uruguay took advantage of the sequence of both processes, which created a virtuous circle.

Economic and political crisis led to a change in the Uruguayan governance order. As Mungiu-Pippidi (2016: 104) says: "change will occur gradually and punctuated equilibria will be the rule." In Uruguay, this severe crisis removed the clientelistic barriers that had prevented programmatic challenges to traditional parties. Nevertheless, institutional changes were not the product of displacement of the traditional elite, but rather the transformation in its political strategy to remain in power in the face of a threat. Particularism was not an option for newcomers from the FA or for the younger leaders of the traditional parties.

The Uruguayan case shows how particularistic practices could be overtaken due to an institutionalized party system which could adapt its electoral strategies when an exogenous economic and financial crisis arises and produce the entry of a new challenger. In this chapter we tried to argue how the joint effect of a fiscal crisis and a new political challenger can create incentives for the elite to stop clientelistic practices. As on the one hand, a crisis leaves old parties with fewer resources and persuades voters to look for an alternative and, on the other hand, a new party poses a successful programmatic offer, the old parties must adapt to programmatic competition trying to show their capacity to govern in an efficient way. These were the political drivers of the Uruguayan transformation to an open-access regime.

NOTES

1. The slogan was coined in the 1950 election by the Batllista faction of the incumbent PC.
2. The nephew of José Batlle y Ordóñez.
3. Interview with Conrado Hugues (former director of the Planning and Budgeting Office, PN) on 11 March 2015.
4. Enrique Iglesias was appointed as the first president of the Central Bank.
5. Interview with Julio M. Sanguinetti (Uruguayan president 1985–1990, 1995–2000, PC) on 30 April 2015.
6. The continuity of these kinds of practices can be indirectly verified by the growing number of lists for the chamber of representatives that occurred during that period and were recorded by the entire academic research on the matter (see, for example, Aguiar, 1984).
7. Chief among them, Enrique Iglesias was appointed as Foreign Affairs Minister. But another good example is Agustín Cannessa, who authored the administrative reform chapter of the PND and was appointed vice-director of the Planning and Budgeting Office in 1985.
8. Interview with Julio M. Sanguinetti (former Uruguayan president 1985–1990, 1995–2000, PC) on 30 April 2015.
9. Interview with Conrado Hugues.
10. Gabriel Lagormasino (vice-president of the Social Security Bank) called our attention to this point in a personal interview on 7 July 2015.
11. The insurance market was a public monopoly since 1911, as was alcohol since 1931.
12. Interview with Luis A. Lacalle (former Uruguayan president 1990–1995, PN) on 9 October 2015.
13. As Alberto Methol Ferré, a prominent PN intellectual, stated, electoral reform was Sanguinetti's priority, but social security reform was the Volonté's condition to form the coalition: "it was the cornerstone of the coalition" (quoted in Podetti, 2003: 243).
14. During that period the most outstanding sectoral reform was the achievement of 100 percent digitalization of fixed telephone lines. This allowed new lines to be connected immediately and without restrictions in such a way that a former generalized clientelistic resource was eliminated for political brokers. Ricardo Lombardo, the then president of the telephone company, said in a personal interview that he received a lot of calls from second-line political leaders complaining about such a decision.
15. Again, as indirect evidence, the lower number of lists for the chamber of representatives that the FA always had confirms such an idea.
16. Interview with Ignacio Otegui (president of the Uruguayan Construction Chamber) on 23 March 2015.

REFERENCES

Aguiar, C. (1984). *Elecciones y partidos*. Montevideo: CIEDUR.

Álvarez Rivadulla, M. (2012). "Clientelism or something else? Squatter politics in Montevideo." *Latin American Politics and Society*, **54** (1): pp. 37–63.

Azar, P., et al. (2009). *De quiénes, para quiénes y para qué? Las finanzas públicas en el Uruguay del siglo XX*. Montevideo: Fin de Siglo.

Bergara, Mario (2003). *Las reglas del juego: El entorno institucional y los problemas económicos*. Montevideo: Ediciones Trilce.

Boix, C. and Stokes, S. (2003). "Endogenous democratization." *World Politics*, **55** (4): pp. 517–49.

BPS. (2013). *Boletín Estadístico 2012 del Banco de Previsión Social* (BPS) [online]. Montevideo: Instituto de Seguridad Social. Available at: www.bps.gub.uy/1920/boletin_estadistico.html# [accessed 3 March 2013].

Castellano, E. (1996) "Uruguay: un caso de 'Bienestar de Partidos.'" *Revista Uruguaya de Ciencia Política*, **9**: pp. 107–26.

Chasquetti, D. (1998). "Compartiendo el gobierno: multipartidismo y coaliciones en el Uruguay." *Revista Uruguaya de Ciencia Política*, **10**: pp. 25–45.

Collier, D. and Collier, R. (2002) [1991]. *Shaping the Political Arena: Critical Junctures, the Labor Movement, and Regime Dynamics in Latin America*. Notre Dame, IN: University of Notre Dame Press.

DGI (2013). *Boletín Estadístico 2012 de la Dirección General Impositiva (DGI)*. Montevideo: Dirección General Impositiva. Available at: www.dgi.gub.uy/wdgi/afiledownload?2,4,864,O,S,0,29320%3BS%3B2%3B108 [accessed 6 May 2013].

Filgueira, C. and Filgueira, F. (1994). *El largo adiós al país modelo: Políticas Sociales y Pobreza en el Uruguay*. Montevideo: Arca.

Filgueira, F., et al. (2003). "Los dos ciclos del Estado uruguayo en el siglo XX." In: Nahum, B. (ed.), *El Uruguay del siglo XX: La Política*. Montevideo: Banda Oriental, pp. 173–208.

Fukuyama, F. (2014). *Political Order and Political Decay: From the Industrial Revolution to the Globalization of Democracy*. New York: Farrar, Straus and Giroux.

Geddes, B. (1994). *Politician's Dilemma: Building State Capacity in Latin America*. Berkeley: University of California Press.

Hall, J. (1954). *La administración pública en Uruguay sugerencias para una reforma administrativa*. Montevideo: Instituto Nacional del Libro.

Johnston, M. (2005). *Syndromes of Corruption: Wealth, Power, and Democracy*. Cambridge: Cambridge University Press.

Lanzaro, J. (1993). "La 'doble' transición en el Uruguay: Gobierno de partidos y neopresidencialismo." *Nueva Sociedad*, **128**: pp. 132–47.

Levi, M. (2008). "Reconsiderations of rational choice in comparative and historical analysis." In: Lichbach, M and Zuckerman, A. (eds.), *Comparative Politics: Rationality, Culture, and Structure*. New York: Cambridge University Press, pp. 117–33.

Lipset, S. (1959). "Some social requisites of democracy: Economic development and political legitimacy." *American Political Science Review*, **53**: pp. 69–105.

Mahoney, J. and Thelen, K. (2010). *Explaining Institutional Change*. New York: Cambridge University Press.

Mungiu-Pippidi, A. (2015). *The Quest for Good Governance: How Societies Develop Control of Corruption*. New York: Cambridge University Press.

Mungiu-Pippidi, A. (2016). "Learning from virtuous circles." *Journal of Democracy*, **27** (1): pp. 95–109.

North, D., Wallis, J. and Weingast, B. (2009). *Violence and Social Orders: A Conceptual Framework for Interpreting Recorded Human History*. Cambridge: Cambridge University Press.

O'Donnell, G. (1973). *Modernization and Bureaucratic: Authoritarianism*. Berkeley: University of California Press.

Pérez Antón, R. (1988). "Cuatro antagonismos sucesivos: la concreta instauración de la democracia Uruguaya." *Revista Uruguaya de Ciencia Política*, **2**: pp. 41–59.

Podetti, R. (2003). *La política entre la cooperación y el conflicto: un balance del cogobierno blanco entre 1995 y 1999*. Montevideo: Ediciones de la Plaza.

Przeworski, A., et al. (2000). *Democracy and Development: Political Institutions and Well-Being in the World, 1950–1990*. Cambridge: Cambridge University Press.

Queirolo, M. (2010). "El rol de las transferencias monetarias en la reelección del Frente Amplio en 2009." In: Buquet, D. and Johnson, N. (eds.), *Del cambio a la continuidad: ciclo electoral 2009–2010 en Uruguay*. Montevideo: Fin de Siglo.

Rama, G. (1971). *El Club Político*. Montevideo: Arca.

Rama, M. (1993). *Rent-Seeking Trade Policy: A Time Series Approach*. Washington, DC: World Bank.

Real de Azúa, C. (2009) [1964]. *El impulso y su freno: Tres décadas de Batllismo y las raíces de la crisis uruguaya*. Montevideo: Ministerio de Educación y Cultura.

Rofman, R. and Oliveri, M. (2012). "Pension coverage in Latin America: Trends and determinants." Social protection and labor discussion paper, 1217. Washington, DC: World Bank.

Rose-Ackerman, S. (2008). "Corruption." In: Rowley, C. and Schneider, F. (eds.), *Readings in Public Choice and Constitutional Political Economy*. New York: Springer.

Schefter, M. (1994). *Political Parties and the State: The American Historical Experience*. Princeton: Princeton University Press.

Solari, A. (1988). *Uruguay, Partidos Políticos y Sistema Electoral*. Montevideo: El Libro Libre/FUCCYT.

Solari, A. and Franco, R. (1983). *Las empresas públicas en el Uruguay: Ideología y política*. Montevideo: Fundación de Cultura Universitaria.

Thorp, R. (1998). *Progress, Poverty and Exclusion: An Economic History of Latin America in the 20th Century*. Washington, DC: Inter-American Development Bank.

4.   Georgia: breaking out of a vicious circle

Alexander Kupatadze

4.1   INTRODUCTION

In the literature on political transitions it has been argued that post-transition countries may become trapped in a 'grey zone' when 'transitions get stuck' (Przeworski 1991; Carothers 2002). Similarly, empirical evidence suggests that despite economic transformations or political developments, many such countries become trapped in vicious cycles of malfeasance and corruption. Besides a few notable exceptions, cases of highly corrupt countries becoming less corrupt are strikingly rare (Damania et al. 2004).

Georgia demonstrates transition from a neo-patrimonial governance regime based on particularism to ethical universalism. In other words, from a hierarchical monopoly of central power in a state captured by private interests with distribution of resources done for the benefit of privileged individuals to a system of impartial governance based on the norms of fairness and citizen equality in a state which is autonomous and not beholden to private interests (Mungiu-Pippidi 2011, 2013). The transition is especially remarkable for a country previously infamous for corruption, for even in Soviet times Georgia was especially notorious for its levels of graft, corruption and bribery (Clark 1993). Between 1958 and 1972 180,000 people were tried for abuse of office and looting of state-owned property in Georgia (Gerber 1997, in Christophe 2003, p. 197). However, that was only the tip of the iceberg, for rampant bribery continued in post-Soviet Georgia in the 1990s. This led to dysfunctional state institutions and permanent economic crises, so that in 2003, on the eve of the Rose Revolution, Georgia could safely be categorized as a 'failed state' (Wheatley 2005). Ranked number 124 of 133 countries surveyed by Transparency International's (TI) Corruption Perceptions Index (CPI) in 2003 Georgia (together with Tajikistan, Azerbaijan and Angola) was found languishing at the bottom of the table.

The change in corruption levels happened in November 2003, immediately after the Rose Revolution which brought to power a team of young

Table 4.1   Georgia's public integrity framework

Components of Index of Public Integrity	Component Score	World Rank	Regional Rank	Income Group Rank
Judicial Independence	5.88	36/105	1/12	4/27
Administrative Burden	9.44	8/105	3/12	1/27
Trade Openness	9	13/105	1/12	1/27
Budget Transparency	8.85	18/105	2/12	1/27
E-Citizenship	5.26	54/105	7/12	2/27
Freedom of the Press	5.56	52/105	2/12	7/27

Source: Index of Public Integrity (IPI), www.integrity-index.org, 1–10 with 10 best.

politicians led by US-educated lawyer Mikheil Saakashvili. The new authorities immediately initiated radical reform of the public sector, often referred to as the 'big bang' approach. They cut red tape and brought in deregulation, dismissed vast numbers of staff from public institutions and employed new recruits, as well as radically reforming the tax laws and improving public services among other things. The result was a dramatic reduction in bribery, especially in the sectors where state and citizenry interact, such as policing of the streets, licensing laws, public services and so forth. Table 4.1 highlights the progress Georgia has made.

Ranked 48 out of 168 countries in the 2015 CPI and 30 out of 105 countries in the Index of Public Integrity (IPI, Table 4.1), Georgia is an absolute leader in its income group and region, and some of its reforms are seen as best practices around the world. However, those achievements have remained controversial because some of the practices of particularism survived and have become even more ingrained in the governance regime. Georgia therefore remains a borderline case overall (Mungiu-Pippidi et al. 2011) where ethical universalism has not yet emerged and elements of patrimonialism have remained.

This chapter looks at Georgia's path to reform from 2004 to 2012, beginning with a timeline of changes followed by a discussion of the political actors of change and their backgrounds, before considering internal and external factors regarded as significant in bringing about change.

4.2   AN ERA OF RADICAL REFORM (2004–2008)

The reforms began immediately in November 2003 after the Rose Revolution that removed the corrupt regime of Eduard Shevardnadze and opened up the path to a young team of reformers headed by Mikheil

Saakashvili. During that time the state was financially broken and institutionally dysfunctional to the extent that it was ungovernable (King
2004). 'We had no other choice . . . there was no budget . . . institutions
were dysfunctional . . . we had to function somehow', said a former high-
ranking official in the Ministry of the Interior, Shota Utiashvili.[1] The
authorities decided to capitalize on their popular mandate and implement
radical and swift reform. 'You need to make changes freshly as soon as
you build public confidence in the government', said Kakha Bendukidze
(2009), the author of Georgia's neoliberal reforms. Such a window of
opportunity provided by a revolution is usually short, as was acknowledged in one of Saakashvili's speeches in 2004. Quick results showing that
reform was possible were crucial to building the government's credibility
in the eyes of the public (Zguladze in Pomerantsev et al. 2014), and a key
aspect of it was the ability to demonstrate to all stakeholders that change
was imminent. The new measures were soon reflected in restored public
confidence in the government's anti-corruption efforts, so that in 2004 60
per cent of survey respondents expected that corruption would decrease
over the coming three years (TI 2004).

Reforms developed in all directions. The executive branch was reorganized and streamlined, and cabinet government was introduced. New
legislation was adopted to introduce a zero-tolerance policy and plea bargaining, while the idea of a 'minimalist state' was carried out in the practice of a simplified regulatory framework, with unnecessary bureaucracy
eliminated and the management of public finances improved (Anderson
and Gray 2006, p. 19). Just a year after the revolution 17 per cent of private
sector turnover had emerged from the shadows (Chamber of Control of
Georgia 2006, pp. 24–5).

By 2004 a campaign of arrests of former officials was in full swing,
and large fines were being imposed for past malfeasance. Prime Minister
Zurab Zhvania said during a press conference in late 2004 that 'all those
who are responsible for misappropriation of the people's property will be
held accountable' (Civil Georgia 2003). In 2004 alone, 50 million USD
was confiscated from corrupt Shevardnadze representatives (IWPR 2004),
while property worth EUR 40 million was reclaimed (Council of Europe
2006, p. 9). Many businessmen had made 'voluntary gifts' to the state,
which were in fact forms of organized extortion through systematic pressure and harassment from law enforcement structures (Macfarlane 2011;
Kupatadze 2012). A proportion of the business shares and property was
to be transferred back to the state and then re-privatized, while part was
to be registered in the names of the most loyal allies of the incumbents
(Welt 2009). According to the prosecutor's office, from 2004 to 2012
approximately 9,500 private properties were handed over to the state free

of charge, which naturally raised concerns as to how 'voluntary' those donations really were (Hammarberg 2013).

At the same time the government clearly signalled that corruption, even in its petty forms, would not be tolerated and that any public employee convicted of such crimes would go to prison. The zero-tolerance policy was officially announced in 2006 when Saakashvili stated that 'there will be no probation sentences . . . everyone who commits these crimes will go to prison'. According to Georgia's Justice Ministry in 2003–10, roughly 1,000 public officials faced charges of corruption, including six MPs, 15 deputy ministers and 31 deputy chairpersons of city councils. However, the zero-tolerance policy legitimated more powers for the police and the prosecutor's office, which resulted in occasional tolerance of police misconduct. It brought an increase in the prison population too, as well as regular breaches of human rights – including the mistreatment of detainees and disrespect for property rights. Anti-corruption policies were frequently based on quasi-legal practices with little respect for the rule of law, and there was also the use of excessive force (US Department of State 2006; Amnesty International 2007). Many allegations were made of violations of criminal procedure such as arrest without warrant (GYLA 2011; RFE/RL 2013); but in response the Tbilisi procurator once told reporters that because many suspects attempted to flee or might feign illness to avoid arrest, law enforcement was sometimes forced to detain individuals without too much regard for legal niceties. However, disregard for the rule of law led to serious criticism from human rights watchdogs and other non-governmental organizations (NGOs), who reported that at times police had been involved in extrajudicial killings, torture and other violations of the law.[2]

Despite such shortcomings it was clear that the government had managed to achieve significant success against petty bribery. According to a survey, only 3.8 per cent of Georgians in Tbilisi paid a bribe to a public official in 2005, compared to 17 per cent who had done so in 2000 (Bonvin 2006). According to European Bank for Reconstruction and Development (EBRD) enterprise surveys, the number of firms expecting to give gifts to public officials 'to get things done' decreased from 74.2 per cent in 2002 to 14.7 per cent in 2008. Achievements began to consolidate once a neoliberal agenda had become a unifying ideological platform for the government, which coincided with Kakha Bendukidze's return to Georgia in 2005 to take up a ministerial position.[3] 'Everything is on sale except our conscience,' said Bendukidze upon his arrival at Tbilisi airport, signalling a wave of large-scale privatization and deregulation. Before Bendukidze's entrance on the political scene, the economic thinking of the political elite had been rather vague, with Vakhtang Lezhava for instance, at the time an important member of the economic policy team, recalling that a dominant idea in early 2004 was to pass legislation imposing higher taxes on wealthy individuals. The idea was rejected due to administrative considerations rather than on ideological grounds.[4] Bendukidze became the key ideologue and masterminded deregulation, reform of taxation and optimization of the bureaucracy.

There was a large-scale overhaul of the staff in public institutions. Overall, the number of public sector employees fell by almost half from 120,000 in 2003, while the salaries of the remaining civil servants increased roughly 15-fold. Some government institutions and procedures that had been generating illicit rents had been cancelled, including for example the anti-monopoly agency, the food security agency and technical checking of private cars. They were replaced by general economic liberalization policies that both reduced red tape and eliminated opportunities for bribery (Lezhava 2010; Engvall 2012). In 2005 a new tax code was adopted for a greatly simplified tax system, with the number of separate taxes decreasing from 22 in 2004 to six in 2008. Coupled with strict enforcement, the simplification resulted in higher sums collected so that, as a proportion of GDP, the tax take approximately doubled from 11.7 per cent in 2003 to 24.5 per cent in 2009 (Burakova 2011, pp. 187–8).

As a consequence of the reforms, corruption has been substantially reduced in the sectors where citizens and state agencies have the most contact, which includes the police, property registration offices, licensing of businesses and tax administration. The distribution of public resources became fairer, and it appeared that the state had become more capable of delivering services. The general progress was consequently acknowledged in numerous surveys and reports. The 2005 EBRD BEEPS survey identified Georgia as the transition country with the largest reduction in corruption in the period 2002–2005, while the World Bank's Doing Business Survey of 2007 ranked Georgia as the number one reformer globally. The country became increasingly attractive to foreign investment, so that foreign direct investment (FDI) had increased from 340 million USD in 2003 to 1.56 billion in 2008,[5] which had an important impact in what is a resource-poor country.

The period of radical reform shows clear signs of movement from particularism to ethical universalism; however the depth and sustainability of change is debatable, as became even more apparent in Saakashvili's second term in government – although there had been some signs of it even earlier.

The team that initially took office was a broad coalition of democratic forces, but the dominance of Mikheil Saakashvili within the team was obvious from the beginning as he emerged as the clear leader. Capitalizing on his victory with 96 per cent of the votes in the 2014 presidential elections, Saakashvili moved Georgia to an even more highly concentrated system of power than before, leading some researchers to describe it as 'hyperpresidentialism' (Fairbanks 2004). As Henry Hale (2006, p. 312) observes, Saakashvili might have decided that 'necessary reforms are best promoted by the decisive actions of the chief executive rather than by sharing power'. Even though power had been highly concentrated, the political system allowed upward mobility of gifted individuals from lower ranks to the top levels of management in public institutions, so that while it did not completely disappear, nepotism was reduced.[6] The number of survey respondents reporting that personal connections were important for obtaining a job decreased from 39 per cent in 2007 to 21 per cent in 2012.[7] New legislation on self-governance was passed in 2005, and reforms of the civil service were implemented to limit incentives for nepotism (George 2009); however employment in some public institutions continued to be influenced by considerations of political loyalty rather than merit (Siradze 2004). In addition some researchers have observed strong vertical integration in centre–periphery relations and clientelism-based handlings of local political appointments (Timm 2010).

4.3 REVERSAL OF ACHIEVEMENT? CONTROVERSIAL OUTCOMES IN THE SECOND TERM (2008–2012)

While legal deregulation was implemented swiftly, Georgia did not turn into the 'the Switzerland of the Caucasus' as the incoming leaders had wished for on the eve of the Rose Revolution (EurasiaNet 2010). As the re-privatization process neared completion in 2007–08 a new class of oligarchs emerged which included former cabinet ministers and close friends of Saakashvili. They co-existed with certain older oligarchs to fund the United National Movement (UNM) after the Rose Revolution (Rimple 2012);[8] and in comparison with the parliament elected in 2004 the UNM faction elected in 2008 included a number of wealthy businessmen (TI Georgia 2013; Wilson 2013). That therefore indicates that state autonomy had begun to decrease and that a state–business nexus was re-emerging.

Pyramid-type corruption schemes might have disappeared, but other types of corruption more along the lines of clientelism and patrimonialism emerged, where the state would often use discretionary powers to distribute resources to benefit specific groups and individuals. The government was believed to have awarded public contracts to 'friendly' companies in exchange for political support. The owners of such companies would be found among key financial contributors to the ruling UNM (TI Georgia

2013). It has been alleged that a company's contribution to UNM party coffers might have been among the reasons why the prosecutor's office would show no interest in investigating large-scale fraud involving the company in question (TI Georgia 2012).

Concerns over 'elite corruption', that is distribution of public resources on a particularistic basis, have been voiced by numerous observers. The key indication of vested interests is the transformation of certain members of the political elite into some of Georgia's wealthiest individuals. That was not the usual 'revolving door' enrichment of a succession of officials because it involved the establishment of permanent near-monopolies in various markets and the illicit takeover of businesses through blackmail and misuse of the criminal justice system. Interestingly, the World Economic Forum's 2012 Global Competitiveness report ranks Georgia in the lowest tier in terms of effective anti-monopoly policy (141st out of 144) and for property rights (131st).

Practices of that kind also subverted key developments relating to transparency, such as e-government, because many of the deals related to public procurement were negotiated 'offline'. Large infrastructure projects meant that the construction sector became one of the key business sectors that were quickly captured by oligarchs close to the UNM (Wilson 2013), although it appears the drive to establish a monopoly of rents was motivated more by a wish to consolidate political power than for a simple desire for private profiteering. In 2013 Tbilisi's Mayor Gigi Ugulava was charged with misspending 28.2 million USD of public funds from the capital city's development fund in 2011–12. He was accused of illegally channelling money to finance the UNM and its activists by creating fictitious jobs (Civil Georgia 2013). Government favouritism and corrupt practices at higher level had long been perfected, and it seemed now that old interest groups had been replaced by new ones; however, petty corruption and bribery remained relatively low. In a 2010 survey 78 per cent of Georgians, a higher proportion than in any other country in the world, said that they believed corruption had decreased over the last three years (TI 2010).

Importantly, public support for the Saakashvili government had been decreasing since 2007. The government had failed to address the problems of unemployment and poverty, while mass dismissals and zero-tolerance policies had alienated many groups throughout society and the people eventually took to the streets. After the violent breakup of one such rally Saakashvili was obliged to announce an early presidential election, which he won with only 53 per cent of votes cast. However, political opposition had been gaining ground against the background of the increasingly unpopular UNM, and was exacerbated in August 2008 when Georgia was defeated in a five-day armed conflict with its de facto independent territories of Abkhazia and South Ossetia, which were now being formally recognized by Russia.

Arguably, the authorities since 2007–08 had increasingly resorted to the use of the criminal justice system to clamp down on political dissent and consolidate control. After the change of government in 2012 evidence emerged that under Saakashvili officials of the Ministry of the Interior and Ministry of Defence had engaged in illegal video recordings of the private lives of citizens and representatives of political opposition (US Department of State 2013). Evidence released by the prosecutor's office showed how key branches of the Interior Ministry were working to discredit and undermine political opposition through surveillance, eavesdropping and unsanctioned telephone tapping (Democracy and Freedom Watch 2013; RFE/RL 2013). The investigation also built up a well-documented case of how the state law enforcement apparatus had been manipulated to attack and bankrupt financial institutions owned by the political opposition leader (Civil Georgia 2013). In a sense, such policing driven by private or regime interests can qualify as another form of particularism if 'particularism' is defined broadly enough to include the use of official resources for private ends.

To be sure, during this period the reforms did not stall and the Saakashvili government continued to deliver in terms of public service efficiency. By 2010, 92 per cent of citizens were satisfied with procedures for delivery of official documents (EBRD 2010); but the highest similar achievement came in 2011 when the concept of public service halls began to come to life. The first service hall opened in Batumi and brought into one space more than 250 services, ranging from business and property registration to passports and ID cards. The innovation won the United Nations Public Service Award in 2013 and is regarded as a major achievement by local and international observers.[9] After that and other changes the perceived role of connections, gifts and informal payments in dealings with formal institutions decreased substantially, according to EBRD surveys.

Such an increase in the efficiency of public service delivery should have resulted in greater trust and cooperation with public institutions, but some surveys suggest that that might not have been the case. For example, Georgians were still reluctant to report crime to the police (Van Dijk and Chanturia 2011) and remained suspicious of institutionalized cooperation. In addition, links based on kinship still prevailed over formalized relationships (CRRC 2011), suggesting great resilience within informal institutions that were highly resistant to the changes taking place in the formal environment.

4.4 KEY ACTORS: WINNERS AND LOSERS

Most of the reform-related decisions were made within a small group comprising Mikheil Saakashvili, Ivane Merabishvili, Giga Bokeria, Kakha Bendukidze and Gigi Ugulava. They were the core of a group that remained influential throughout the whole period from 2004 to 2012 while other key decision-makers were continuously reshuffled. For instance, Minister of Defence Irakli Okruashvili, one of Saakashvili's closest allies, went into political opposition in 2006. Most of the reformist initiatives belonged to the individuals in the team, such as Ivane Merabishvili, who came up with the idea of heavily glazed transparent buildings to house the police, or Kakha Bendukidze, who was the author of most of the initiatives for reducing red tape.

Importantly, this was a team of young and well-educated individuals who demonstrated a great structural and ideological cohesiveness. Most were in their 20s and 30s, with Saakashvili (2011) later saying that his team was 'nothing more than a group of young men and women from student organizations, opposition parties and civil society groups'.[10] The core of the team had experience of working in Tbilisi-based NGOs, in particular the Liberty Institute, which had been founded in 1996 and was a prominent critic of the Shevardnadze government. In the late 1990s the Liberty Institute was both a shelter for liberally minded young and dynamic individuals and a key actor in campaigning for human rights and anti-corruption. Giga Bokeria (MP in 2004–08, Secretary of the State Security Council in 2010–13), Gigi Ugulava (Tbilisi's mayor in 2005–12), Givi Targamadze (influential MP, chairman of the Defence and Security Committee in Parliament) and some of Saakashvili's closest associates were among the founders and employees of the organization.

Saakashvili himself used the platform of anti-corruption while Minister of Justice (2000–2001) in Shevardnadze's government when his own popularity owed much to his anti-bribery drive (Freizer 2004, p.4). Saakashvili was seen as an 'island of honesty' at the heart of a corrupt system. The Georgian public remembered well Shevardnadze's meeting with the government when Saakashvili (as Minister of Justice) showed photographs of the impressive mansions owned by corrupt officials, some of whom were present at the meeting. Saakashvili demanded immediate action against them. Certainly his rhetoric did not go unheard. His resignation as minister was seen as 'the hopeless single-handed effort' of a brave 'corruption-crusader' against the whole machinery of state bribery. Saakashvili himself said that his departure had been 'caused by the impossibility of reforming the government from within'.[11]

After the Rose Revolution an anti-corruption campaign of incoming elites immediately targeted most of the corrupt bureaucrats of the Shevardnadze era, as well as other entrenched interest groups. Several key groups of losers can be identified as having lost both economic power and political leverage in the aftermath of the revolution. They included corrupt officials in Shevardnadze's bureaucracy, so-called oligarchs and powerful mafia structures led by mafia bosses called *kanonieri qurdebi* ('thieves-in-law'). We should now consider certain conditions if we are to explain why those 'losing' groups failed in their attempts to oppose reform. First there was a revolution, which provided a window of opportunity. That window of opportunity was then used by incoming elites, seen as highly legitimate, to launch a radical break with the past and a clean-up of the bureaucracy. They could then sweep away the stragglers and carry-overs from an old guard seen to have lost their legitimacy.

Arguably, legitimacy is the most important aspect to consider here. The incoming authorities had a clear mandate to address corruption, and had early established their credibility to be able to do so. At the same time the old guard had used up all their legitimacy during ten years of decay, unfairness and inefficiency in public institutions and widespread and unpunished crime. As a result the old interest groups had been disempowered by their own past failures and had acquired a bad reputation, until corrupt officials could not find support even among the medium and lower bureaucratic ranks. As Utiashvili comments, 'most of the corruption schemes were organized in a pyramid and hence mostly benefited the top leadership of the government institutions' while the lower ranks had only been 'getting peanuts'.[12] Most of those officials were dismissed from public office and replaced by younger and more motivated individuals.

The oligarchical class who on the eve of the Rose Revolution in Georgia had been the wealthiest businessmen consisted of Eduard Shevardnadze's friends and family. Three main groupings can be distinguished. First was the group headed by Guram Akhvlediani, father-in-law of Shevardnadze's son, Paata. He was the chairman of the Chamber of Commerce and his business interests were in minerals, oil and aircraft. He controlled the port area of Poti, which directly or indirectly dominated the city's infrastructure. The second group, that of Shevardnadze's son-in-law, Gia Jokhtaberidze, owned Magti, one of the two major mobile telephone companies in Georgia, and held interests in the state nitrogen plant of Rustavi as well as in the non-ferrous metallurgy plant in Zestafoni. The third sub-group was led by Eduard Shevardnadze's nephew, Nugzar Shevardnadze, and played a major role in the import of consumer goods, chiefly fuel (Chiaberashvili and Tevzadze 2005, p. 191).

By appointing close friends and relatives to government positions all three groups made sure that their private interests would be guarded by the state. For instance Deputy Interior Minister Zurab Urotadze had been a childhood friend of Nugzar Shevardnadze, while the best man at Jokhtaberidze's wedding, Gia Kakuberi, had become Deputy Minister of Communications. However, as the power base of the government changed, those individuals were undermined. Some had their businesses claimed back by the state, while others, such as Jokhtaberidze, were forced to buy their freedom by paying large amounts of money into the state budget. Again those interest groups had no capacity to counteract the state because they lacked any legitimacy as far as the people were concerned.

Other major losers from the post-revolutionary changes included the so-called 'thieves-in-law'. They were professional criminals from the Soviet and post-Soviet era who had become influential wielders of power throughout the 1980s and 1990s. They simply engaged in wide-ranging criminal activities, including extortion, racketeering and smuggling. They also provided protection for businesses, and even acted informally as judges and arbiters. The state largely tolerated them, and in fact frequently enlisted them to provide a number of services. The most influential thieves maintained friendly relations and ran businesses jointly with law enforcement officials and well-known politicians (Kupatadze 2012; Slade 2013). But after the Rose Revolution the state response changed from tolerance and cooperation to antagonism when Saakashvili initiated an anti-crime campaign. Various strategies of legislative change were integrated, for example the US Racketeer Influenced and Corrupt Organizations (RICO) and Italian anti-mafia legislation, law enforcement personnel were refreshed with new blood, and there were educational campaigns. The new policies played an important role in the demise of the thieves, who lost nearly all political and financial leverage in post-revolutionary Georgia (Kupatadze 2012). However, as Slade shows, their demise should not be explained by state policies alone, for disintegrative processes within the thieves' own world created internal pressures among them. The intra-group competition between different factions in the thieves' world and inter-group competition with other violent actors together created further pressures to expand the network. That expansion came at the expense of lowered entry standards so that substandard individuals had to be recruited. Those trends certainly had a detrimental effect on the status and reputation of the group, and therefore on its overall resilience. Along with the general commercialization of the thieves' status the commitment-inducing mechanisms and disincentives for exit became similarly weakened. Some rules were discarded, such as the one forbidding members from owning private property. Increasing linkage of their status with wealth and power was instrumental in undermining the reputation and popular legitimacy of the thieves (Slade 2013).

So it was that the losers from the reforms had actually undermined themselves and lost legitimacy long before the reforms began. That is something that should be considered together with the great popularity of the incoming elites and their willingness to pursue anti-corruption and anti-crime policies, and their subsequent commitment to them. I shall discuss that further in the next section.

4.5 ACCOUNTING FOR CHANGE: INTERNAL FACTORS

In Georgia a number of internal and external conditions converged that made change possible. In the following sections I shall briefly outline them and discuss how they had an impact on levels of corruption.

As we have seen, under Shevardnadze's rule Georgia matured into a dysfunctional state with very weak institutions. A popular movement was triggered by fraud at the parliamentary elections with facilitating conditions that included perceived decay of the state, malfeasance by its rulers and the incapacity of political elites to deliver public goods. Many of the revolution's leaders had been part of Shevardnadze's government, and those individuals then became known as 'reformers' and anti-corruption crusaders. The uprising itself was largely described by experts and politicians alike as an 'anti-corruption revolution' because anti-corruption slogans dominated the popular movement and corruption was perceived to be a major cause of the public uprising (Shelley and Scott 2003; Nodia 2005, p. 99; Kandelaki 2006, p. 3). By mid-November 2003 the 'revolutionary situation' was defined by Charles Tilly (2006, pp. 163–77) as 'incapacity or unwillingness of [incumbent] rulers o suppress the alternative coalition and/or its popular support'.

The revolution was an important factor in anti-corruption reform because it provided a crucial window of opportunity. It removed from power the patrimonial regime of former Soviet Foreign Minister Eduard Shevardnadze and opened the way for young reformers. However that condition was not sufficient by itself because similar revolutions have occurred elsewhere but largely failed to follow up on the anti-corruption front, examples being Ukraine's Orange Revolution (2004) and Kyrgyzstan's Tulip Revolution (2005). The crucial differences were to be found in the influence of the old guard in the aftermath of each of the so-called Coloured Revolutions. In Georgia the political leadership was not constrained by the existence of reform 'spoilers'. The changeover to the radical elite distinguished the Rose Revolution in Georgia from those in Ukraine and Kyrgyzstan, where the transitions were 'pacted' and the 'old guard' managed to retain significant power. Our explanation here therefore needs to be complemented by reference to a number of different internal conditions which included a radical break with the past. There was also the cohesiveness of the incoming political elites, their great popularity and the mandate they had for change and reform. In turn, the new elite showed willingness and commitment to change. I will now go through each factor separately.

Although Saakashvili and other members of his core team had held senior positions in the previous government, they were not part of the entrenched and corrupt interest groups of Shevardnadze's regime. Initially at least, Saakashvili's team were only peripherally connected with Georgia's large businesses and had only one or two financiers, for example natural-gas trader David Bezhuashvili. Most economic resources – legal and illegal – were monopolized by members of Shevardnadze's family (Chiaberashvili and Tevzadze 2005) so that the incoming elite were less beholden to big private economic interests while the most radical reforms took place (2004–07). Georgia's elected parliament in 2004 was overwhelmingly dominated by the young activists of Saakashvili's UNM, with only a few businessmen to be found among them. Although that changed as re-privatization proceeded with a number of new incumbents developing vested interests, the temporary breakdown of the state–business nexus and loosening of links between Saakashvili's team and the *ancien régime* eliminated the impact of reform spoilers and limited the opportunities of entrenched interest groups to oppose reform.

The break with the past was related to another variable, namely the cohesiveness of the elite. The two reinforced one another, and a radical break with the past was possible because new and existing elites were equally cohesive. A cohesive political elite was in turn the outcome of the radical break with the past. The incoming political elite comprised a structurally and ideologically cohesive group of long-time friends which allowed quick and efficient responses to challenges. As predicted by the 'weak government hypothesis' (Roubini and Sachs 1989; Ashworth et al. 2005; Coffé and Geys 2005), that lack of fractionalization increased the decision-making capabilities of the Saakashvili government.

Significantly, there was a generational change in Georgia's ruling elites.[13] Saakashvili was 37 years old when he came to power and many of his cabinet members were even younger, in their late 20s or early 30s. By significantly reducing bureaucracy and increasing the salaries of the staff remaining in public institutions the new government succeeded in attracting young and educated personnel for middle and lower levels of the bureaucratic apparatus. The new young recruits too wanted the opportunity to be part of the imminent change in the bureaucracy, and many of them were highly motivated, full of new ideas and, most importantly, zealously committed to institutional integrity (World Bank 2012). The impact of the 'age variable' on corruption can be related to strategic time horizons, when the younger leaders are more interested in curbing corruption for the sake of 'establishing the brand name' and ensuring a safer exit strategy (Manow 2005). More research is needed on the causal mechanisms of how the age of elites influences anti-corruption policies, but it is still safe to argue that the young team's cohesion and shared radical thinking were important factors in making reform possible.

This new political elite enjoyed high levels of legitimacy and could afford radical and often unpopular reforms. In 2004 Saakashvili was elected with 96 per cent of the votes cast (Election Guide 2015), which gave him a clear mandate for unconstrained action. Such popularity converged with the electorate's support for strong measures against corruption. For example a survey from June 2003, just before the revolution, indicated that corruption was perceived as one of the gravest problems facing the country, with more than 60 per cent of the population convinced that all public institutions were engulfed by it. Another survey immediately after the revolution suggested that a decrease in corruption ranked highest on the agenda for ordinary people as some 64.3 per cent of respondents were optimistic that the political change would lead to a decrease in corruption (Sumbadze 2009).[14] Anti-corruption policies would therefore be highly popular, and the incumbents elected by so large a margin of votes saw that they had the necessary mandate to implement them.

Capitalizing on its mandate, Saakashvili's team demonstrated an impressive level of dedication and commitment to anti-corruption reform. In fact the new government garnered large political dividends from its fight against crime and corruption (Macfarlane 2011; Slade 2013). Arguably, the need to 'legitimize' did not provide the initial impetus. Rather it was the success of the government's anti-corruption measures that was effectively used to establish its credibility in the eyes of both its domestic public and the international community.

The fight against corruption and organized crime became a key element of Saakashvili's state-building project from the very beginning in late 2003. It became clear that the new government would not tolerate the existence of rampant bribery which would have undermined the legitimacy of the new ruling elite and would have had the effect of distorting the political system. In general, the new administration concentrated on state-building rather than democratizing (Mitchell 2006, pp. 674–5). Saakashvili's role models were strong men and state-builders like Mustafa Kemal Atatürk or Charles de Gaulle rather than democratizers like Vaclav Havel and Thomas Jefferson (Cornell 2013). In a highly symbolic gesture just before his inauguration as president in January 2004, Saakashvili visited the tomb of the Georgian king David the Builder and swore there an oath to build 'a united and strong state'. Saakashvili's concept of a 'strong state' comprised efficient public institutions, low levels of organized crime and corruption, and aspects of a 'minimalist state' such as reducing red tape and instituting deregulation. It should be borne in mind, however, that internal factors like those had to be complemented by crucial external dynamics in order to further account for the change.

4.6 ACCOUNTING FOR CHANGE: EXTERNAL FACTORS

The drive by the new Georgian elite to clean up their ranks was significantly delineated by antagonism towards Russia and willingness to escape any notions of 'post-Sovietness'.[15] The new Georgian political elite had chosen policies explicitly to divert the country from the developmental path being followed by Russia. Saakashvili often said that the Georgian leadership was building an 'alternative governance model in post-Soviet Eurasia', meaning government marked by low levels of corruption and in contrast to the way Russia was then functioning – and still is (Saakashvili 2013). Concerns about the co-opting of Georgian security forces established strong incentives to crack down on corruption in law enforcement structures, which partially prompted a major 'decontamination' of the Georgian police and security forces (Light 2014; Slade 2013).

The effect of antagonism towards Russia regarding corruption has been exacerbated by Georgia's drive to move closer to the European Union (EU) and NATO. The majority of the respondents from all Georgian political parties interviewed in 2010 looked favourably on the idea of EU integration (AIR 2010) and the orientation towards the West was thought of as a national mission in Georgia (Saakashvili 2013). Symbolically, EU flags have often been displayed on government buildings and in the offices of senior officials, as well as during important events such as the president's inauguration in 2004. Rhetorically meanwhile, various members of the ruling party have repeatedly emphasized their foreign policy priority of 'Euro-Atlantic integration'. As Giga Bokeria put it, Georgia had no other choice: 'There is no other environment. There is no other family we can move to' (quoted in De Waal 2011, p. 33). That attitude promoted strong ties between the Georgian political elite and European leaders which perhaps contributed to a more reformist stance as predicted by the model offered by Way and Levitsky (2007). The reforms are also believed to have been an attempt to compensate for the geographical ambiguity of Georgia's place in Europe. Georgian government minister Thornike Gordadze made reference to Georgia's relative distance from EU borders compared to those of the Balkan states. As he said in 2011 to the Croatia summit of senior European and North American leaders, in its efforts to get closer to the EU, 'Georgia is fighting geography with successful reforms'. The first successful example of the reforms was 'the elimination of corruption and organized crime'.[16]

However, as Carnegie Endowment analyst Thomas de Waal argues (2011), the rhetoric about foreign policy goals was often controversial. The models of emulation have been diverse, with confusing and contradicting references to Estonia, Singapore, Switzerland and a host of European countries. Saakashvili's reference to Singapore goes as far back as 2007 and was based on the belief that Georgia finds itself in a similarly difficult geopolitical environment. In 2011 Saakashvili said that, unlike the Baltic countries, Georgia borders neither Norway nor Finland, and that is why Georgia must be innovative and look to countries like Singapore for inspiration.

Due to such ambiguity it is difficult to assess the cumulative impact of Georgia's emulation of different models, especially as the impact of foreign expertise has varied from one sector to another. For instance Mart Laar, formerly Prime Minister of Estonia and appointed as an advisor to the Georgian government in 2006, 'gave many useful recommendations regarding deregulation and tax reform'.[17] Foreign expertise was instrumental too in drafting crucial legislation with, for example, the US RICO Act and Italian anti-mafia legislation serving as models for laws with similar effect in Georgia. Nevertheless the overall antagonism towards Russia was a more powerful driver than were more ambiguous ideas concerning emulation. As Light has argued, the foreign policy objective of rapprochement with NATO and the EU was not a primary impetus, but the Georgian government had successfully promoted reform with those objectives in mind. It is not entirely clear therefore whether the impact of the EU goes much beyond a symbolic role and an influence on change at the legislative level, such as ratifying the Council of Europe's Civil and Criminal Law Conventions, or the accession to the Group of States against Corruption (GRECO) in 2004.

At the operational level Georgian government officials often went against the advice of European advisors and institutions. Interviews with certain of the decision-makers suggest that the advice of European experts often emphasized a more moderate approach, while the Georgians had been in favour of quick and radical action. For example the mass dismissals in 2003 were undertaken against Western counsel (Burakova 2011). Shota Utiashvili, a former official of the Interior Ministry, said in an interview that European experts 'mainly wanted us to write plans and strategies' and 'strongly favoured a slow pace of reform'.[18] Another respondent, former Deputy Economic Minister Vakhtang Lezhava, said that despite little regard in the Georgian political establishment for the need for an anti-corruption strategy on paper, finally 'the government decided to write it due to the West's obsession with it.'[19]

4.7   CONCLUSION

Despite continuing problems, Georgia represents a remarkable case of transformation from a particularistic regime to ethical universalism, even though it is still a 'borderline case'. This chapter has outlined the timeline of change, discussed actors and looked at internal and external factors to account for it. Most radical reforms happened between 2004 and 2008, when a structurally cohesive young elite with similar ideology seized their chance and initiated 'big bang' reform. As time passed the new incumbents too developed vested interests, as became clear during 2008–12 when a state–business nexus re-emerged and the new elite began to manipulate the state themselves for their own group and even private interests. While Mikheil Saakashvili was in power those new particularistic interests undermined market competition as the new elite networks used state power to control economic and political structures. Nevertheless, although it is true that concerns remain over government favouritism and particularistic practices, petty bribery at least has decreased substantially.

NOTES

1. Interview with Shota Utiashvili, former head of analytical department, Ministry of Interior, 2015.
2. The climax of alleged official disregard for the law was the assassination of Sandro Girgvliani, a banker kidnapped and assassinated in 2006, allegedly by high-ranking police officials. The case led to a major uproar in Georgian society and greatly damaged the public standing of the police.
3. Businessman active in Russia in the 1990s: Minister of Economic Development in 2004–05, State Minister for Reforms Coordination in 2005–08 and then the Head of State Chancellery in 2008–09.
4. Interview with Vakhtang Lezhava, former Deputy Minister of Economy, 2015.
5. See the 2003 figure in data from Investment Guide for Georgia (available online at www.investmentguide.ge/index.php?sec_id=145&lang_id=ENG) and for 2008 figure see Civil Georgia (2010).
6. Examples would include Giorgi Vashadze, who started his career in the Tbilisi district branch of the Ministry of Justice and rose to the post of Deputy Justice Minister; and Davit Sakvarelidze, who began as a specialist in the Legal Expertise Department of the Ministry of Justice and has since risen to the post of first Deputy General Prosecutor.

7. Caucasus Research Resource Centers (CRRC) Barometer surveys. No data is available for the pre-Rose Revolution period.
8. Re-privatization had other negative consequences as well. Since the change of government in October 2012 numerous complaints have been filed. More than 1,000 persons claimed that prosecutors had played a central role in the illegal seizure of their property, forcing them to 'donate' it to the state (see Hammarberg 2013).
9. Another internationally acclaimed reform initiative was the launch of a system of online submission for asset declaration in 2010 by the Civil Service Bureau (www.dec larations.gov.ge) that replaced paper-based declarations and contains data from 1998 onwards.
10. Initially the so-called reformers were divided into two camps: one united in 2001 under the banner of the political National Movement party and headed by Mikheil Saakashvili; and another led by parliamentary speaker Zurab Zhvania, who resigned to found the United Democrats party, also in 2001 (Nodia and Scholtbach 2006). The two groups converged only during the Rose Revolution when Saakashvili, owing much to his personal charisma, emerged as an unequivocal leader of a popular movement. Consequently the two parties merged in 2004 and adopted the name National Movement-Democrats.
11. BBC Monitoring Former Soviet Union, 19 September 2001.
12. Interview with Shota Utiashvili, former head of the analytical department, Ministry of Interior, 2015.
13. By 2000 more than 50 per cent of the Georgian state officials consisted of former *nomenklatura* members (Stefes 2006)
14. These hopes were associated with an anticipated diminution of corruption (64.3 per cent), economic development (55.8 per cent), restoration of territorial integrity (46.6 per cent), rule of law (42.9 per cent), good governance (40.9 per cent), the fostering of close relations with the West (40.4 per cent) and improving relations with Russia (23.8 per cent).
15. Because of its Moscow-backed breakaway republics, Georgia had few alternatives to the West (that is, the US and the EU) as sources of support. Since the mid-1990s Georgia has pursued integration with NATO and has drifted away from the Russian orbit. Georgia and Russia fought a short war in August 2008, and there are still no diplomatic relations between them. Its conflict with Russia left Georgia with little foreign policy choice.
16. Gordadze's address is available online at www.youtube.com/watch?v=sD5oAXG_nOc [accessed 13 March 2013].
17. Interview with Shota Utiashvili, 2015.
18. Ibid.
19. Interview with Vakhtang Lezhava, 2015.

REFERENCES

Amnesty International. (2007). *Georgia Profile*. London: Amnesty International.
Anderson, J. H., and Gray, C. W. (2006). *Anticorruption in Transition 3: Who is Succeeding . . . and Why?* Washington, DC: World Bank.
Ashworth, J., Geys, B., and Heyndels, B. (2005). Government weakness and local public debt development in Flemish municipalities. *International Tax and Public Finance*, **12**(4), pp. 395–422.
Association for International Relations (AIR). (2010). *Looking through the Party Lenses: A Comparative Study of Georgian Political Parties' Views on Foreign and National Security Policies*. Tbilisi: AIR and Friedrich Ebert Stiftung.
Bendukidze, K. (2009). Interview by Andrew Schalkwyk, 5 May. Innovations for

Successful Societies, Bobst Center for Peace and Justice, Princeton University. Available at: http://successfulsocieties.princeton.edu/interviews/kakha-bendukidze [accessed 15 May 2017].

Bonvin, B. (2006). *Public Security in Georgia: Crime Victimisation, Fear of Crime, Fraud, Corruption, and Policing.* Geneva: TC Team Consult.

Burakova, L. (2011). *Pochemu u Gruzii poluchilos.* Moscow: United Press.

Carothers, T. (2002). The end of the transition paradigm. *Journal of Democracy,* **13**(1), pp. 5–21.

Caucasus Research Resource Centers (CRRC). (2011). *Social Capital in Georgia: Final Report and Recommendations.* Tbilisi: CRCC.

Chamber of Control of Georgia. (2006). *Report on Economic Activity in 2005.* Tbilisi: Chamber of Control.

Chiaberashvili, Z., and Tevzadze, G. (2005). Power elites in Georgia: old and new. In: Fluri, P., and Cole, E. (eds) *From Revolution to Reform: Georgia's Struggle with Democratic Institution Building and Security Sector Reform.* Vienna: Austrian Ministry of Defence.

Christophe, B. (2003). Bringing culture back into a concept of rationality, state–society relations and conflict in post-socialist Transcaucasia. In: Zurcher, C. and Koehler, J. (eds) *Potentials of Disorder: Explaining Conflict and Stability in the Caucasus and in the Former Yugoslavia,* pp. 193–207.

Civil Georgia. (2003). New leadership pledges fundamental reforms [online]. 1 December. Available at: www.civil.ge/eng/article.php?id=5721&search [accessed 24 June 2015].

Civil Georgia. (2010). FDI down to USD 759 mln in 2009 [online]. 16 March. Available at: www.civil.ge/eng/article.php?id=22090 [accessed 24 June 2015].

Civil Georgia. (2013). Ex-justice minister and five others charged over 'plot against Cartu Bank' [online]. Available at: www.civil.ge/eng/article.php?id=25660 [accessed 24 June 2015].

Clark, W. A. (1993). Crime and punishment in Soviet officialdom, 1965–90. *Europe-Asia Studies,* **45**(2), pp. 259–79.

Coffé, H., and Geys, B. (2005). Institutional performance and social capital: an application to the local government level. *Journal of Urban Affairs,* **27**(5), 485–501.

Cornell, S. E. (2013). *Getting Georgia Right,* Brussels: Center for European Studies.

Council of Europe. (2006). Evaluation report on Georgia. Group of States against Corruption (GRECO).

Damania, R, Fredriksson, P., and Mani, M. (2004). The persistence of corruption and regulatory compliance failures: theory and evidence. *Public Choice,* **121**(3–4), pp. 363–90.

De Waal, T. (2011). *Georgia's Choices: Charting a Future in Uncertain Times.* Washington, DC: Carnegie Endowment for International Peace.

Democracy and Freedom Watch. (2013). Interior minister found his own phone had been trapped. *Democracy and Freedom Watch* [online]. 6 February. Available at: http://dfwatch.net/interior-minister-found-his-own-phone-had-been-tapped-689 37 [accessed 12 January 2013].

Election Guide. (2015). *Georgia* [online]. Washington, DC: US AID. Available at: www.electionguide.org/countries/id/81/ [accessed 1 July 2015].

Engvall, J. (2012). *Against the Grain: How Georgia Fought Corruption and What It Means.* Washington, DC and Stockholm: Central Asia-Caucasus Institute/Silk Road Studies.

EurasiaNet. (2010). Georgia: Saakashvili says Switzerland will meet Singapore in Tbilisi [online], 9 March. Available at: www.eurasianet.org/departments/news/articles/eav031010.shtml [accessed 13 September 2011].

European Bank for Reconstruction and Development. (2010). *Life in Transition Survey* [online]. London: EBRD. Available at: www.ebrd.com/what-we-do/economic-research-and-data/data/lits.html [accessed 13 October 2011].

Fairbanks, C. H. (2004). Georgia's Rose Revolution. *Journal of Democracy*, **15**(2), pp. 110–24.

Freizer, S. (2004). The pillars of Georgia's political transition. Caucasus: regional fractures [online]. Available at: https://www.opendemocracy.net/democracycaucasus/article_1732.jsp [accessed 28 March 2014].

George, J. A. (2009). The dangers of reform: state building and national minorities in Georgia. *Central Asian Survey*, **28**(2), pp. 135–54.

Georgian Young Lawyers Association (GYLA). (2011). *Legal Analysis of Cases of Criminal and Administrative Offenses with Alleged Political Motive*. Tbilisi: GYLA.

Hale, H. E. (2006). Democracy or autocracy on the march? The colored revolutions as normal dynamics of patronal presidentialism. *Communist and Post-Communist Studies*, **39**(3), pp. 305–29.

Hammarberg, T. (2013). *Georgia in Transition: Report on the Human Rights Dimension: Background, Steps Taken and Remaining Challenges* [online]. Available at: www.sida.se/globalassets/global/countries-and-regions/europe-incl.-central-asia/georgia/georgia-in-transition-hammarberg.pdf [accessed 28 March 2014].

Institute for War and Peace Reporting (IWPR). (2004). Georgia in the black, for once. Caucasus Reporting Service no. 245, 4 August.

Kandelaki, G. (2006). *Georgia's Rose Revolution: A Participant's Perspective*. Washington, DC: United States Institute of Peace.

King, C. (2004). A rose among thorns: Georgia makes good. *Foreign Affairs*, **83**(2), pp. 13–18.

Kupatadze, A. (2012). *Organized Crime, Political Transitions and State Formation in Post-Soviet Eurasia*. Basingstoke: Palgrave Macmillan.

Lezhava, V. (2010). Fighting corruption, history of success: Georgia's experience in combating corruption: eligibility for Ukraine. Open Ukraine Arsenyi Yatseniuk Foundation [online]. Available at: www.openukraine.org/en/programs/young-generations/anticorruption [accessed 5 June 2010].

Light, M. (2014). Police reforms in the Republic of Georgia: the convergence of domestic and foreign policy in an anti-corruption drive. *Policing and Society*, **24**(3), pp. 318–45.

Macfarlane N. (2011). *Post-Revolutionary Georgia on the Edge?* London: Chatham House.

Manow, P. (2005). Politische Korruption und politischer Wettbewerb: Probleme der quantitativen Analyse. In: von Alemann, U. (ed.), *Dimensionen politischer Korruption: Beiträge zum Stand der internationalen Forschung*. Wiesbaden: VS Verlag für Sozialwissenschaften, pp. 249–66.

Mitchell, L. A. (2006). Democracy in Georgia since the Rose Revolution. *Orbi*, **50**(4), pp. 669–76.

Mungiu-Pippidi, A. (2011). Becoming Denmark: understanding good governance historical achievers. In: Mungiu-Pippidi, A. et al. (eds) *Contextual Choices in Fighting Corruption*. Oslo: Norwegian Agency for Development and Cooperation.

Mungiu-Pippidi, A. (2013). Controlling corruption through collective action. *Journal of Democracy*, **24**(1), pp. 101–15.

Mungiu-Pippidi, A. et al. (eds) (2011). *Contextual Choices in Fighting Corruption: Lessons Learned*. Norwegian Agency for Development Cooperation.

Nodia, G. (2005). Breaking the mould of powerlessness: the meaning of Georgia's latest revolution. In: Karumidze, Z., and Wertsch, J. (eds) *Enough! The Rose Revolution in the Republic of Georgia 2003*. New York: Nova.

Nodia G., and Scholtbach, A. (2006). *The Political Landscape of Georgia: Political Parties: Achievements, Challenges and Prospects*. Delft: Eburon Uitgeverij BV.

Pomerantsev, P. et al. (2014). *Revolutionary Tactics: Insights from Police and Justice Reform in Georgia*. London: Legatum Institute.

Przeworski, A. (1991). *Democracy and the Market: Political and Economic Reforms in Eastern Europe and Latin America*. Cambridge: Cambridge University Press.

Radio Free Europe/Radio Liberty (RFE/RL). (2013). Illegal surveillance recordings destroyed in Georgia [online]. 6 September. Available at: www.rferl.org/a/georgia-illegal-recordings/25096623.html [accessed 17 October 2015].

Rimple, P. (2012). *Who Owned Georgia 2003–2012*. Tbilisi: Transparency International and Open Society Georgia Foundation.

Roubini, N., and Sachs, J. (1989). Government spending and budget deficits in the industrial countries. *Economic Policy*, **4**(8), pp. 99–132.

Saakashvili, M. (2004). Speech delivered at the parade for the independence celebration, 26 May 2004 [online]. Available at: www.president.gov.ge/?l.E&m.0&sm.3&st.190&id.151 [accessed 16 December 2007].

Saakashvili, M. (2006). President's Office of Georgia State of the nation address [online]. Available at: www.president.gov.ge/index.phplang_id_GEO&sec_id_228&info_id_2686 [accessed 8 June 2009].

Saakashvili, M (2011). From popular revolutions to effective reforms: the Georgian experience. Speech to the Brookings Institution, Washington, DC, 17 March [online]. Available at: www.brookings.edu/wp-content/uploads/2012/04/20110317_saakashvili_transcript.pdf.

Saakashvili, M. (2013). Speech at the UN General Assembly, 25 September. *Civil Georgia* [online]. 26 September. Available at: www.civil.ge/eng/article.php?id=26491 [accessed 10 March 2014].

Shelley, L. and Scott, E. (2003). Georgia's 'Revolution of Roses' can be transplanted. *Washington Post* [online]. 30 November. Available at: www.washingtonpost.com/archive/opinions/2003/11/30/georgias-revolution-of-roses-can-be-transplanted/9918f7da-b483-4365-bfa2-5d94e6cafe86/?utm_term=.e4cd12c71aaf [accessed 1 December 2003].

Siradze, G. (2004). *Corruption in the Ministry of Internal Affairs of Georgia: Transnational Crime and Corruption in Georgia*, TraCCC-GO [online]. Available at: www.traccc.cdn.ge/pulications (in Georgian) [accessed 22 March 2007].

Slade, G. (2013). *Reorganizing Crime: Mafia and Anti-Mafia in Post-Soviet Georgia*. Oxford: Oxford University Press.

Stefes, C. H., (2006). Understanding Post-Soviet Transitions: Corruption, Collustion and Clientelism, Palgrave Macmillan, London.

Sumbadze, N. (2009). Saakashvili in the public eye: what public opinion polls tell us. *Central Asian Survey*, **28**(2), 185–97.

Tilly, C. (2006). Regimes and Repertoires. University of Chicago Press, Chicago, IL.

Timm, C. (2010). Neopatrimonialism by default: state politics and domination in

Georgia after the Rose Revolution. Paper presented at the Neopatrimonialism in Various World Regions workshop, GIGA German Institute of Global and Area Studies, Hamburg, 23 August.

Transparency International. (2004). *Global Corruption Barometer* [online]. Available at: www.transparency.org/research/gcb/gcb_2004 [accessed 7 June 2010].

Transparency International. (2010). *Global Corruption Barometer 2010/2011* [online]. Available at: http://gcb.transparency.org/gcb201011/ [accessed 21 April 2013].

Transparency International Georgia. (2012). *Center Point Group: Georgia's Biggest Construction Scandal*. Tbilisi: Transparency International Georgia.

Transparency International Georgia. (2013). *Businessmen in Politics and Politicians in Business Problem of Revolving Door in Georgia*. Tbilisi: Transparency International Georgia.

US Department of State. (2006). *Country Reports on Human Rights Practices: Georgia*. Washington, DC: US Department of State.

US Department of State. (2013). *Georgia 2013 Human Rights Report* [online]. Available at: www.state.gov/documents/organization/220492.pdf [accessed 2 March 2015].

Van Dijk, J. J. M., and Chanturia, T. (2011). *The Remarkable Case of Georgia: Georgian Crime Trends in an International Perspective: Secondary Analysis of the 2010/2011 Crime and Security Survey*. Tbilisi: Ministry of Justice.

Way, L. A. and Levitsky, S. (2007). Linkage, leverage, and the post-communist divide. *East European Politics and Societies*, **21**(48), pp. 48–53.

Welt C. (2009). Still staging democracy: contestation and conciliation in post-war Georgia. *Demokratizatsiya*, **17**(3), pp. 196–227.

Wheatley, J. (2005). *Georgia from National Awakening to Rose Revolution*. Burlington, VT: Ashgate.

Wilson, A. (2013). Background paper on Georgia. Work Package: WP3, Corruption and governance improvement in global and continental perspective.

World Bank. (2012). *Fighting Corruption in Public Services: Chronicling Georgia's Reforms*. Washington, DC: World Bank.

5.   The world's smallest virtuous circle: Estonia

Valts Kalniņš

5.1   INTRODUCTION

By a number of measures, Estonia is the most successful country of the former Soviet area, although its level of wealth lags behind Western European countries. Estonia was forcefully incorporated into the Soviet Union in 1940 and regained its independence in 1991. In 2004, the country acceded to NATO and the European Union (EU). In 2011, it introduced the Euro. Estonia is still relatively poor compared to the average level of wealth in the EU, with a GDP per capita of EUR 14,200 in 2013 compared to EUR 26,600 for the EU 28 (Eurostat 2014a). Estonia's population was only 1.3 million in 2014 (Eurostat 2014b). Ethnic Estonians made up approximately 70 percent of the population in 2011 (Statistikaamet 2014, p. 54). The majority of the rest of the population are Russian speakers, many of whom are Soviet-era immigrants or their descendants.

Already in 2000, the European Commission (EC) admitted that "corruption is a relatively limited problem in Estonia. Only isolated cases can be reported, mainly in the local administrations where business and officials are more closely interconnected" (European Commission 2000, p. 17). Since 2000, Estonia's score on the Control of Corruption (CoC) indicator has risen to the 88th percentile (World Bank 2015). This lies well above the other ten EU members with a former socialist background (hereafter EU-FS countries),[1] which were between the 75th percentile (Slovenia) and the 49th percentile (Bulgaria) in 2014. The data attest to an exceptional position for Estonia among other former socialist states. Estonia does even better in the Index of Public Integrity (IPI), where it enjoys the spectacular rank of 11th out of 105 states (Table 5.1). The country is a global leader in red tape reduction and administrative simplicity, and performs very well across all categories, especially considering that it is compared not against the region it comes from (the Soviet Union) but against the EU that it joined in 2004, the group with the highest standards of rule of law possible.

This process-tracing study focuses largely on Estonia's spectacular

Table 5.1   Estonia's public integrity framework

Components of Index of Public Integrity	Component Score	World Rank	Regional Rank	Income Group Rank
Judicial Independence	8.38	13/105	11/29	13/36
Administrative Burden	9.67	3/105	1/29	2/36
Trade Openness	9.53	5/105	4/29	5/36
Budget Transparency	8.07	32/105	14/29	17/36
E-Citizenship	7.97	18/105	14/29	17/36
Freedom of the Press	9.3	8/105	8/29	8/36

Source: Index of Public Integrity (IPI), www.integrity-index.org, 1–10 with 10 best.

break from the Soviet political and economic system at the end of the 1980s and beginning of the 1990s. The chapter aims to show how a new ruling political elite replaced the old communist nomenclature in the early 1990s. It also provides insights into some of the reforms undertaken, and explores the roles of their proponents. A systematic review of these processes shows peculiarities that accompanied the changes and made them possible. The pace of reforms varied, just as the ruling powers changed several times during the 1990s. The chapter reviews the developments of the 1990s, paying attention to how the changes and their anti-corruption effects turned into a lasting equilibrium rather than withering away among various vested interests under governments run by quite different political leaders and parties. Only a few events from periods after the turn of the twenty-first century are described to illustrate the longer-lasting trends in countering corruption.

The research for this case study relied on a review of existing publications and official documents, as well as on 24 qualitative interviews with former and current politicians, civil servants and experts. The interviews were carried out between June 2014 and February 2015.[2] The chapter benefited a great deal from comments on and analysis of the Estonian context by the sociologist Aare Kasemets.[3]

5.2   THE SOVIET-ERA BACKGROUND

It is common to consider corruption and particularistic distribution as endemic under the Soviet regime. Fine-tuning this view is somewhat difficult because corruption was not systematically studied in the Soviet Union. Although the distribution of control over state resources was clearly particularistic until 1990, it remains unclear exactly how corrupt the practices were at the administrative level in Estonia. However, the so-called *blat* relationships did exist, and not only for obtaining personal consumer goods but also for gaining resources for industrial plants, collective farms or even public agencies. Also in Estonia, foodstuffs, the liqueur Vana Tallinn or invitations to the sauna were among the means used to influence bureaucrats who could award resources to particular enterprises, collective farms or *sovkhozes* (state-owned farms) (Kurvits 2007; Soodla 2006).

Serious corruption cases, even when detected, were usually not covered in the media directly (except for a few cases). For example, Vladimir Käo, who had occupied a number of top economic and political positions in Estonia's industrial sector since the 1940s and became the first Vice-Chairman of the Council of Ministers of the Estonian Soviet Socialist Republic (ESSR, 1983–85), was removed from office because of serious corruption (Misiunas and Taagepera 1993, p. 279). In reaction to the case of Käo, the Soviet Estonian humor and satire magazine *Pikker* published a popular satirical poem, "Pink Elephant," by Uno Laht (Viivik 2000). Soviet satirical publications quite often criticized lower and middle management for waste of resources, *blat* or other kinds of misdeeds. However, the targets of such criticism were individual black sheep rather than the political or economic system more generally. Targeting criticism as high up as a member of government was an utmost rarity.

It remains unknown exactly how significantly corruption levels differed among various regions of the Soviet Union. Estonia was the most developed republic of the Soviet Union by some key wealth indicators and, in many ways (together with the other Baltic republics of Latvia and Lithuania) was viewed within the Soviet Union as the Soviet West. What this meant for corruption is hard to say with precision. Estonian experts and politicians commonly argue that the Estonian people had less tolerance for corruption than in many other parts of the former Soviet Union, especially for corruption in the form of bribery, in particular bribery in monetary form. An anecdotal story tells of Georgian students who had come to study at the Tallinn Polytechnic Institute during the Soviet era. They came to Estonia because there they could get their diplomas by actually studying, while at home they would have had to buy their diplomas and they were too poor to do so (Meel 2012). Starting in the 1960s, Estonia was home to organized networks of intellectuals that became far more developed than those in Latvia and Lithuania. Li Bennich-Björkman (2007, p. 340) argues that they paved the way for the morally and socially integrated counter elite, which came to power in 1992.

Estonia was unique among the Soviet republics because of the exposure of a large part of its population to Western (Finnish) television starting in the 1970s. Due to the similarity of the Estonian and Finnish languages, people in the northern part of Estonia could absorb Western ways of thinking through news, films and other TV shows (Kasemets 2012, pp. 32, 51). To sum up, Estonia was by and large the wealthiest Soviet republic, with the most developed elements of autonomous civil society and considerable exposure to Western information.

5.3   HOW THE ELITE WAS REPLACED

In 1985 Mikhail Gorbachev became Secretary General of the Communist Party of the Soviet Union. Gradually he started initiating a number of liberalizing reforms widely known by the Russian words *glasnost* (openness) and *perestroika* (restructuring). In 1987, the civic activism of various groups became openly visible in Estonia. At the end of the 1980s, the reformist political groups in Estonia stemmed from rather different sources. In the administrative and economic management circles of the ESSR, a considerable number of people realized the need to carry out reforms, and eventually also became increasingly supportive of the idea of an independent Estonia. In parallel, other groups became increasingly active: people who, throughout the Soviet era, were either dissidents resisting Soviet rule chose walks of life that had as little connection as possible with the Soviet power structures, or mainly confined themselves to the pursuit of academic careers. Additionally, Estonians in exile started participating in Estonia's public life. The variance in the distance from the Soviet power structures left a significant imprint on Estonia's political spectrum at the beginning of the 1990s.

Important pushes for reforms stemmed from people working in official structures. In September 1987, the Head of Department of the State Planning Committee of the ESSR, Edgar Savisaar, Deputy Editor of the Estonian Communist Party newspaper *Rahva Hääl Siim Kallas* and two other individuals published a proposal for the economic autonomy of Estonia, which was a daring idea in the unitary Soviet Union and also invoked connotations of political autonomy. On 13 April 1988, during a television show, Savisaar, who by then had become the Scientific Director of Mainor (a think tank of the Ministry of Light Industry of the ESSR), proposed the idea to form the Popular Front. Initially announced as an organization to help in carrying out *perestroika*, it turned into a mass movement struggling to achieve the independence of Estonia (Dobbs 1988; Liivik 2010–12).

Other organizations stemmed from less official areas. The Estonian Heritage Society was established in December 1987. The correspondent of the weekly culture magazine *Sirp ja Vasar* and translator Trivimi Velliste

(Minister of Foreign Affairs 1992–94) was the main initiator of the new organization and became its chairperson. In April 1988, Heritage Days became the first time during the Soviet occupation that the Estonian national blue-black-white tricolor was broadly demonstrated in Tartu. In December 1988, the Estonian Students' Society was re-established. The organization's members included many people who later became important political actors, for example, Prime Minister Mart Laar and the Minister of Foreign Affairs and Defense Jüri Luik (Muuli 2012),[4] also the President of Estonia, Toomas Hendrik Ilves (Eesti Üliõpilaste Selts 2015).

In parallel to the creation of the Popular Front (founded in October 1988), smaller political organizations developed and were much more distanced from the ESSR establishment. At the beginning of 1988, an initiative was formed to establish the first new party—the Estonian National Independence Party—which gained 10 out of 101 seats in parliament in 1992 and joined the government of Mart Laar. The party included a number of prominent dissidents who had suffered under Soviet repression, such as Mati Kiirend, Viktor Niitsoo, Lagle Parek (later Minister of the Interior), Vello Salum and Erik Udam.

In December 1988, the Estonian Christian Union was established, which later changed into the Estonian Christian Democratic Union. The party's leaders included the pastor Illar Hallaste (leader of the ruling Pro Patria parliamentary faction in 1992–93) and Mart Laar. It merged into the Pro Patria National Coalition Party after the parliamentary elections of 1992. Three further constituents of the Pro Patria party were the Christian Democratic Party of Estonia (established in July 1988), the Conservative People's Party of Estonia (established in June 1990) and the Republican Coalition Party (established in September 1990). The Estonian Liberal Democratic Party was the fifth member of the Pro Patria election list, but it did not merge with the Pro Patria party in the post-election period. Many of the leaders of these five parties were people whose Soviet-era careers were outside the political *nomenklatura* (Kaido Kama, Paul-Eerik Rummo), dissidents (Enn Tarto) or young people who had recently graduated from university or just started scientific careers (Kalle Jürgenson, Heiki Kranich, Indrek Kannik, Daimar Liiv, Jüri Luik, Mart Nutt). Two additional parties that became part of the parliamentary coalition of Mart Laar's government were the Estonian Social Democratic Party and the Estonian Country Centre Party, which had a common election list called the Moderates and also had leaders from academic and scientific circles, such as Marju Lauristin of the social democrats and Ivar Raig and Liia Hänni of the country centrists.

The period between 1987 and 1990 saw a fundamental shift towards competitive politics. A distinctive feature of Estonia's transition was the existence of two bodies with a claim to be the highest political authority. In 1989, the movement of citizens' committees started with the aim of registering citizens of Estonia (those who had Estonian citizenship until 1940 and their descendants) and electing a representative body of the Estonian citizenry that would be able to legitimately restore Estonia's independence. The Estonian Heritage Society, the Estonian National Independence Party and the Estonian Christian Union supported the initiative. The position of these organizations was to insist that the new independent Estonia rest on the principle of legal continuity from the republic of 1918–40. In February 1990, the Congress of Estonia was elected by almost 600,000 voters (a surprisingly high turnout for the election of an "unofficial body"). Candidates of the Popular Front gained 107 seats, the Estonian Heritage Society 104 seats and the Estonian National Independence Party 70 seats out of 499. More than 30 political and civic groups were represented in total. However, party affiliations were rather vague and fluctuating at the time (Pärnaste 2000). The Congress of Estonia became a center of political power unrelated to the state structures of the ESSR (in contrast, a similar institution in Latvia remained by and large marginal throughout its operation in 1990–93).

On the official political level, the Communist Party's state power monopoly lasted until March 1990, when the first multi-party elections of the ESSR parliament (the Supreme Council) took place. Until then, state institutions coexisted with party structures and the latter exercised non-accountable control over the state apparatus. The Popular Front gained the plurality of votes but fell short of an absolute majority—its faction initially had 43 members in the 105-seat legislature (Mõttus 2013, p. 118). However, there was stable majority support (over two-thirds) for Estonia's independence. Some representatives in the Congress of Estonia and the Supreme Council viewed each other cautiously, although the two institutions were not antagonistic and a sub-set of politicians was elected to both of them. On 30 March 1990, the Supreme Council declared Soviet rule in Estonia illegal and launched the transition to the restoration of the Republic of Estonia. Leaders of the Committee of Estonia (the executive body of the Congress of Estonia) agreed to support the government led by Edgar Savisaar in the Supreme Council as long as this government adhered to the principle of legal continuity. On 20 August 1991, the Supreme Council declared Estonia fully independent and made an historic agreement with the Committee of Estonia to create the Constitutional Assembly with an equal number of representatives from both bodies. The relationship between the two bodies reflected diverse attitudes as to whether Soviet state structures could be used as the basis for the new Estonian institutions. The relatively heavy political weight of the Congress of Estonia also reflected the potential within Estonian society to radically replace the political elite.

Both in the Supreme Council (1990–92) and the first post-independence parliament, the Riigikogu (1992–95), the share of MPs who were involved in communist politics was lower than in the other Baltic states of Latvia and Lithuania. (Matonytė 2009, pp. 30, 31) Elite replacement was facilitated by the decision in 1992 to limit Estonian citizenship to those who had it before the Soviet occupation and their descendants. This decision was in line with the doctrine of legal continuity of the Estonian state and non-recognition of the legality of Soviet rule in Estonia. This formed the basis for the partial political exclusion of the Russian-speaking minority who had immigrated to Estonia during the Soviet period—a factor occasionally cited as favorable for anti-corruption. Only 68 percent of Estonia's population were citizens of Estonia in 1992 (Estonia.eu 2015). Vello Pettai, Professor of Comparative Politics at the University of Tartu, described some of the implications of this exclusion:

> All of these people were cut out really effectively, very quickly. They could no longer come into the state civil service, they couldn't vote, at least on the national level. [. . .] It kind of purified or cleansed the Estonian elite. It took away all of the Soviet era ethos.

In the parliamentary elections on 20 September 1992, the Pro Patria coalition gained 29 out of 101 seats.[5] The main pre-election slogan of the coalition was "Clean the Place!" The slogan resonated well with demands for change among large parts of Estonian society. Although this message did not focus explicitly on corruption, but rather more generally on the remnants of the Soviet past, both anti-communism and anti-corruption were probably mentally linked in popular perceptions. Aare Kasemets (2012, p. 44) states that: "After Gorbatshov's [sic] perestroika and Estonian 'singing revolution' 1987–1991 it was quite a common thinking that the corruption and other unethical things are directly related to the Soviet political regime." In the pre-election period, Pro Patria was also one of the favorites of several Western partner parties, which provided support through training of politicians and perhaps also money for the campaign (Muuli 2012). Foundations of German political parties and ideologically related parties of the Scandinavian countries used to provide support to several Estonian parties. Questions regarding equal opportunities could arise, since not all of the political forces in Estonia had such supportive partners.

On 21 October 1992, Riigikogu approved the government of Mart Laar. The governing coalition included the Pro Patria coalition together with the Moderates (the Social Democratic Party and the Country Centre Party) and the Estonian National Independence Party.

The replacement of the communist elite manifested itself strongly in the composition of this cabinet, which consisted of 14 members. The Minister of the Interior, Lagle Parek, an architect by education, was imprisoned from 1983 to 1987 for dissident activity, and one of the founders of the Estonian National Independence Party in 1988. Three other ministers (Minister of Social Affairs Marju Lauristin, Minister of Culture and Education Paul-Eerik Rummo and Minister of Environment Andres Tarand) had signed the so-called "Letter of 40 Intellectuals" expressing concern about Russification and other policies of the Soviet regime in Estonia on 28 October 1980.[6] The open letter, sent to several official media outlets (but never published in the Soviet Union), was a reaction to the repression of several youth demonstrations in Tallinn and elsewhere in Estonia. The signatories were prominent writers, artists and scientists. Most of them were not dissidents. Marju Lauristin (Estonian Social Democratic Party) had (and still continues) an academic career at the University of Tartu in the fields of journalism and sociology, and was one of the founders of the Popular Front in 1988 (since 2014 she has also been an MEP). Paul-Eerik Rummo is a prominent Estonian poet and was the leader of the Liberal Democratic Party. Andres Tarand, educated in climatology and geography, was a researcher at the University of Tartu and the Director of the Tallinn Botanical Gardens in 1988–90. Several other ministers came from humanitarian and/or scientific careers. Mart Laar himself studied history, was a history teacher from 1983 to 1985 and worked for the Heritage Protection Board of the Ministry of Culture in 1986–90. The Minister of Justice, Kaido Kama, had a rather unusual background: with an education in architecture, he was a forest guard from 1982 to 1990 and became one of the most important Estonian politicians of the early 1990s. Three ministers had lived abroad during the Soviet rule. Only three ministers had had long-term careers in the economic or administrative structures of the ESSR. Nine members of the cabinet had previously been members of the Congress of Estonia.

It is impossible to review the background of all the key ruling politicians, but people with no Soviet nomenclature roots played a large role in the parliament. The Chairman of the Legal Committee 1992–93 and 1999–2002, and Minister of Justice 1993–94, Jüri Adams (Estonian National Independence Party), was a dissident, used to work as a teacher, forest guard and fireman, and was one of the principal authors of Estonia's new constitution. Daimar Liiv, who played an important role as Chairman of the Legal Committee from 1994 till 1999, had no substantial work experience from the Soviet era.

Overall the strong anti-communist/Soviet and nationalist moods of Estonians appear to be a key driving force behind the high degree of replacement of the ruling elite, which culminated in 1992. Moreover, a remarkable feature of Estonia was a large pool of people who had qualifications appropriate for elite positions but who had kept their distance from Soviet power structures. The relatively high degree (in comparison with, for example, Latvia) of passive and sometimes also active resistance against Soviet rule facilitated the accumulation and maintenance of human capital outside the Communist Party system. Estonia was the only one of the three Baltic countries where the rather more anti-communist and nationalist groups created an alternative formal authority—the Congress of Estonia (1990–92), which insisted on basing the citizenry on the law of the pre-war Estonian republic and ensuring legal continuity also in other respects. This body turned into a key political player rather than becoming a marginalized organization like in Latvia. All of this resulted in a pool of ruling elite that included many individuals who bore strong idealistic commitments to particular ideological principles such as non-recognition of the legality of Soviet rule in Estonia, the rule of law and a free market economy. Within that group, the former dissidents, who had been prepared to give up a great deal of personal comfort for the sake of their ideological struggle, formed a significant minority. Also, political luck in the elections of 1992 helped, attested to by the rather slight majority enjoyed by the government of Mart Laar (approved with a mere 54 votes in a parliament of 101 members).

5.4   HOW THE VIRTUOUS CIRCLE STARTED

The year 1991 marked the beginning not only of regained statehood but also of radical reforms. Even before the first truly post-Soviet elections, the Supreme Council, the governments of Edgar Savisaar (April 1990–January 1992) and Tiit Vähi (January–October 1992) and the Constitutional Assembly (August 1991–April 1992) embarked on a course of change.

Among the earliest key decisions was the adoption of judicial reforms. On 23 October 1991, the Supreme Council adopted the Courts Act and the act "On the Status of Judges." These laws envisaged the establishment of a three-tier court system, which was also embedded in the new Constitution adopted in a referendum on 28 June 1992. The new system created a whole new tier of courts and was based on a newly established Supreme Court rather than a reformed Supreme Court of the ESSR. Such a design of the reform meant that all the judges had to be appointed anew. Supreme Court judges had to be selected anew because it was a new court. The rest of the judges had to be nominated by the Supreme Court and appointed by the President of Estonia. Hence, all the Soviet-era judges who wanted to continue their careers had to be reappointed.

Possible involvement in corruption was not the key concern during the reappointment of judges. The actual appointment process started after the parliamentary elections of 1992. The Riigikogu appointed Assistant Professor of Law Rait Maruste to the post of President of the Supreme Court on 8 December 1992. The ideological mood of the parliamentary majority meant that the key political criterion for the approval of Supreme Court judges was their lack of involvement in political cases during the Soviet era. Minister of Justice Kaido Kama (1992–94) recalls:

> We did not let for the positions of judges people who, as lawyers say, "sat" in political cases in the Soviet time. [. . .] Judges asked me—why are we guilty, we simply applied laws, which were in force. I then said if tomorrow there is the Soviet rule again and we have Soviet laws in force again, you will try me. I think my article will be state treason. And then they kept silent. (Maruste 1994)

The Riigikogu rejected three candidates to the Supreme Court (ibid.).

In addition to the reappointment process, the nature of the judiciary changed considerably because the number of judicial positions increased radically. There were 83 judges in Estonia before the reform. As of 1 May 1994, the President of Estonia had appointed 154 judges, and even then a number of vacancies still remained (Maruste 1994). In an interview, the then chairman of the Legal Committee of the Riigikogu, Daimar Liiv, described the influx of new judges and the loss of the dominant position of the Soviet-era judges:

> We brought in quite a big number of new people. [. . .] Most of these newcomers were not top lawyers. They were quite a big number of mainly female judges who came from the former Soviet enterprises and had worked there as lawyers, personnel office women and so on. These new judges were mainly middle-aged, having no other career perspectives. They someway worked out. They did not have very big private business career possibilities. Because of quite normal or, let's say, not low salary initially, also compared to their former positions, and the lifetime appointment, they were very motivated to stay in this system. [. . .] I suppose by the end of 1995 maybe a half of [former Soviet judges] stayed. The idea was that they were not establishing the culture for the judiciary. The culture was established by the Supreme Court.

In a short period of time, Estonia had established a new court system which, both institutionally and in terms of personnel, had as little continuity from the Soviet system as was reasonably possible. In most other parts of the public sector, the replacement of cadres was not as radical, and by default civil servants continued working. However, less systematic replacement or sidelining of Soviet-era cadres in many institutions was common.

In order to adjust the structure of the executive branch of government to the principles of the new constitution, the Riigikogu had to adopt the Government of the Republic Law to allow the new coalition government to start working. The new law was adopted on the day after the approval of the Mart Laar government. It was done hastily because the new government coalition had agreed to reduce the number of ministries from 18 to 11, subordinate various bodies to the ministries and reduce the public sector by one-third (Sarapuu 2012, p. 812). The approved composition of the cabinet corresponded to the yet to be adopted law. A working group established by the Supreme Council and led by Illar Hallaste had already developed the draft. In addition to the reduction of the public service, a key change was the introduction of non-political top managers of ministries, *kantslers*, and a clear distinction between the political leadership and administrative management (Muuli 2012). As Külli Sarapuu has described, the whole politico-administrative system was deinstitutionalized. The transformation proceeded hastily under strong ideological imperatives to dismantle the Soviet system and maintain Estonia's continuity from the pre-war state.

The political context strongly influenced recruitment in the public administration. The public administration expert and professor Tiina Randma-Liiv explained how the old civil servants gave up their positions:

> First it was a very clear political message that they have no future in the civil service and that was given from the very top politicians, from the Prime Minister. And also the President Lennart Meri [in office 1992–2001] was very much on the same line. So some of the old *nomenklatura* stayed but in small numbers. By that time the Soviet nomenklatura people were quite old, some just retired or were very close to retirement, some left to Russia and some, especially the younger crowd, just made use of the transition time labor market with so many new opportunities around in the private sector. Actually some became very successful businessmen as well.

On 25 January 1995, the Public Service Act was adopted (in force from 1 January 1996). It established a merit-based approach to recruitment and also favored the replacement of incumbent civil servants with new cadres with a modern education. However, according to Randma-Liiv, even before the adoption of the Public Service Act the share of young officials increased rapidly as "the Soviet civil service experience conflicted with the needs of the democratic government." In 1994, the number of staff under the age of 30 was 31 percent in the Ministry of Finance, 28 percent in the Ministry of Justice and Ministry of Defense, and 48 percent in the Ministry of Foreign Affairs (Randma 2001). In 2002, a Sigma assessment found that "merit-based, open competition is in general used in the recruitment of civil servants" and that "selection based on candidates' qualifications and professionalism" was ensured, although exceptions existed (Sigma 2002, pp. 5–6). By and large, public employment was no longer a resource to be grabbed by cronies of corrupt cliques. Both the ideological context of 1992–95 and subsequent implementation of merit-based practices facilitated the development of a professional civil service. The reformed judiciary and public administration constitute important elements for constraining corruption.

If reforms of state institutions facilitated the development of legal constraints of corruption, privatization was a process that released major resources. In approximately 1990–92, uncoordinated siphoning of assets of state companies took place, as similarly occurred in other countries in the region during the collapse of the socialist system. Managers of state-owned enterprises (SOEs) tapped into resources of these companies (Brown 1993, p. 498). The first major steps towards the transformation of property ownership were made by the Supreme Council in 1991. However, this chapter does not aim to map all of the key decisions in this area. The success of Estonia in containing corruption is commonly linked to the country's decision to carry out most of the privatization of enterprises in a transparent auction-based procedure. In 1992, Estonia set up the Privatization Enterprise, modeled on the example of the Treuhand agency, which privatized enterprises of Eastern Germany. According to a book by the journalist Kalle Muuli (2012), the Minister of Economy, Olari Taal (enterprise director in the Soviet era and later a major Estonian business-man), planned to create Estonia's own Treuhand to manage the massive, centralized privatization of enterprises mostly for money. The Supreme Council approved the establishment of the Privatization Enterprise in August 1992. Andres Bergmann, who returned to Estonia from Germany in 1989, became the head of the enterprise.

Later Bergmann had to leave his post, but the Treuhand model was kept and privatization was carried out mostly through direct sale open to foreign bidders. A key person in the implementation of the privatiza-tion process was Väino Sarnet, the General Director of the Privatization Agency between 1993 and 1999. A member of the Pro Patria council, Sarnet had an education in agronomy and psychology. Between 1980 and 1991 he was a scientific fellow at the Estonian Land Cultivation and Land Improvement Institute, and between 1989 and 1993 a local politician in Lääne-Viru county (Eesti Entsüklopeedia 2000–13). Sarnet described foreign consultants paid by international donors as a key element in the implementation of privatization:

> At the best time during 1994 we had 20 percent of our staff foreign consultants. They negotiated deals, prepared drafts for the board, participated in board

meetings, visited enterprises. This educated our people and also helped us keep this process fair. It was much more difficult for Estonian interest groups to approach these foreign consultants. There were no connections. Estonia is a very small country where everybody knows everybody, they say. But foreign consultants didn't speak Estonian, many Estonian managers did not manage in English then and this helped us greatly. [. . .] The foreign consultants actually favored foreign consultants. But this was in our interest.

In 1996 the privatization of non-infrastructure enterprises was 90 percent complete (OECD 2001, p. 60).

Another way to reduce the flow of resources for corruption was the stance of the government against handing out subsidies and money for bailouts. This was an important element in the ideology of the Mart Laar government which, even if not a direct anti-corruption measure in itself, reduced opportunities for corruption. Laar wrote about this policy (2007, p. 5):

As part of this momentum, subsidies for state owned companies were identified as poor policy, and they were cut. This was important for the development of new private companies because subsidies preserve old and often outdated production structures and hamper structural change in the economy. Cutting subsidies sent the Soviet industrial dinosaurs a simple and clear message: Start working or die out. As was shown by subsequent developments, the majority chose to start working.

On 1 January 1994, a flat-rate personal income tax was introduced. The policy of open trade (reduction of trade tariffs and non-tariff barriers, elimination of export controls) was painful for many sectors of domestic industry and agriculture, but also furthered a level playing field for all business regardless of political connections (see Laar 2007, p. 6).

The judicial, property and other reforms show that the Supreme Council had already laid the groundwork for fundamental change. The Laar government maintained the reform drive, ensured sustainability of the changes and added new reforms. Individual integrity of particular politicians in the Riigikogu and the government clearly played a role in getting corruption under control. The withdrawal of the state from economic operations reduced the amount of material resources available for corruption, while the acute anti-communist position (which associated among other things nepotism and clientelism with the Soviet/Russian type of rule) gave a boost to the normative constraints of corruption. Moreover, this new elite group (just like many in their electorate) did not have any inhibitions against excluding non-Estonians and former Soviet officials from political power and administrative structures. Meanwhile the new elite were inviting and open to the rich supply of advice given and practical work done by Western consultants.

However, in the period between 1992 and 1995, elements of crony business and political collusion continued to develop, as in all post-socialist/communist countries. There were instances of privatization that proceeded outside the general, transparent procedures run by the Privatization Agency, that is, privatization of banks by the Bank of Estonia. Despite overall success, Estonia did not stay free from suspicion of unethical or illegal privatization practices (Bennich-Björkman 2001, p. 21). Business structures were used directly to support political developments such as the creation of the Reform Party in 1994.

Nevertheless, it seems plausible to argue that the foundations of the new state laid in 1991–95 changed the state apparatus as well as the relationship between the state and society to such an extent that a certain path dependency emerged for Estonia's further evolution towards universalistic governance.

5.5   WHY THE ANTI-CORRUPTION TREND SURVIVED

The scope and depth of the reforms of 1991–95 alone do not reveal how and why exactly the presumed path dependency maintained its effects in the long term. The political developments in the mid-1990s might suggest that Estonia should have stabilized at the same particularistic "normality" as the average EU-FS country.

The parliamentary elections of 5 March 1995 led to the first major shift of political power after the founding post-independence elections. In part due to the economic hardships and uncertainty inflicted by reforms upon many social groups (for example, pensioners and the rural population), the previous governing center-right parties were defeated. The principal winner (41 out of 101 seats) was the electoral union "The Coalition Party and Country People's Union," which contained the Coalition Party, three agrarian parties and the Association of Pensioners and Families. On 17 April 1995, the government of Tiit Vähi (Coalition Party) was approved and included members from the Coalition Party and the Estonian Country People's Party (which was a part of the winning electoral union), plus the Centre Party of Edgar Savisaar.

The Coalition Party of Tiit Vähi was established in 1991 and was largely composed of people from the urban establishment of the ESSR. Managers of the Soviet-era collective farms dominated the rural parties. A review of Vähi's second government shows that two-thirds of the members of the new government had belonged to the Communist Party (Mänd 2008). Tiit Vähi came to his first political position still in the ESSR as Minister of

Transportation in 1989, even before the first competitive elections of 1990. The only politician from the Estonian Country People's Party in the government was the Minister of Environment, Villu Reiljan, who had spent a considerable part of his Soviet-era career as the director of a forestry school. The leading representative of the Centre Party was its chairman, Edgar Savisaar, as the Minister of Interior. According to Vello Pettai:

> The mid-nineties, the second half of the 1990s, was not necessarily a strong continuation of this right/centre-right pro-Western thing. [. . .] They were not the young very ferocious right-wingers. Mart Laar clearly gave up power in 1995 and sat in opposition for four years. It was a tilt from a very strong Western [orientation] but it did not go to the East either. The way that a lot of Estonian political scientists see the Tiit Vähi crowd is that they weren't ex-communists but they were potentially problematic because they were very much an oligarchic group, [. . .] strongly pro-business and perhaps less than fully above the board group had they stayed in power. But interestingly they kind of faded. [. . .] They were allied with the agricultural parties and that was always a very weird mix because you have the old Soviet enterprise directors allied with the old Soviet *sovkhoz* directors.

The two consecutive governments of Tiit Vähi (1995 and 1995–97) did not have the same zeal for reform of the previous governments. Neither was Vähi perceived as an anti-corruption champion; on the contrary, he was subject to certain corruption suspicions. Revelations of unethical privatization in Tallinn during Vähi's tenure in the City Council in 1993–95 led to his resignation from the Prime Minister's post in February 1997 (Smith et al. 2002, p. 100). In hindsight, apparently Villu Reiljan was also not an anti-corruption champion, being one of the highest Estonian officials ever convicted for corruption more than a decade later. On the face of it, the new coalition could be expected to provide more opportunities for well-connected business groups to tap into state resources and return Estonia to the higher corruption levels typical of post-socialist transition countries. Still, in the long term, it seems obvious that Estonian tycoons did not gain the kind of control over politics that such groups have enjoyed elsewhere in Eastern Europe (Huang 2002, pp. 4–5). Why did this not happen after the change of power in 1995?

Two political characteristics are important with regard to Vähi's governments and the government of the next Prime Minister of the Coalition Party, Mart Siimann (1997–99): there was no intent to fundamentally reverse course; and the governments were politically quite fragile, with shaky majorities in the parliament. The majority of the members of the governments, and Tiit Vähi personally, were not intent on reversing the liberal economic policies of the previous period, since economic results were by then positive and benefited them, and they remained committed to Estonia's integration into the EU and NATO. Privatization was by and large complete, with the important exception of several large (mainly infrastructure) enterprises, such as the Estonian Railway. There was no majority will to fundamentally reverse policies. The international monitoring of Estonia's policies, together with the first solid signs of economic success in 1995, further weakened incentives for any reversal (Lauristin and Vihalemm 2009, pp. 11–12). Also, the historical fear of Russia felt by many Estonians encouraged Estonia's adherence to the standards and rules of Western organizations in economic, administrative, judicial and other policy areas.

The demise of parties with social roots in Soviet-era management was marked by the parliamentary elections of 7 March 1999. The previously ruling Coalition Party suffered a major loss, gaining just seven seats in the legislature, and was disbanded altogether a few years later. There is no proof that the governments of 1995–99 were fundamentally more corrupt than those immediately preceding and succeeding them, although some could see it as suspicious that, for example, Vähi gained control over the rare earth processing company Silmet, which was privatized during Siiman's government. By 1999 a portion of the electorate was disillusioned due to corruption suspicions about politicians of various parties (not just the government) (Smith et al. 2002, p. 100). Additionally, for some businesspeople the new liberal Reform Party of Siim Kallas represented a more attractive alternative than the weakened Coalition Party. On 25 March 1999, the second government of Mart Laar took office, based on the coalition of the Pro Patria Union, the Reform Party, the People's Party and the Moderates.

The governments of 1995–99 were probably too short-lived, too weak and indeed not quite revisionist enough to reverse many of the positive effects of the reforms of 1992–95. However, some more general characteristics of the relationship between politics and economic heavyweights in Estonia have to be considered as well. Top officials of the ESSR who became businessmen never returned to the political elite as politicians. Those who wanted to play a role in politics tended to confine themselves to the role of supporters and donors. Additionally, important political parties retained a noticeable degree of autonomy from their sponsors and vested economic interests.

The rather effective exclusion of individuals with Communist backgrounds (or with reputation problems) from political life, or at least from the more visible part of it, was a recurring topic in the interviews.[7] According to the common narrative they were not able to exert anything close to decisive influence in politics, although some managed to gather significant economic resources, including through privatization. For example, the last Prime Minister of the ESSR, Indrek Toome, participated in privatization and became a wealthy person, but since 1992 has never made any attempt to return to political activity (Ammas 2003; Kaio 2012). Mehis Pilv, the former Chairman of the Planning Committee and the Deputy Minister of Economy under the Toome government, also became an entrepreneur. The former First Secretary of the Tartu City Committee of the Communist Party, Tõnu Laak, became a major businessman in several important companies (Bloomberg Business 2015). Neither of them attempted a public political career in the independent Estonia.

Of course, the 1990s also saw the growth of the entrepreneurial elite, including people who were not top officials in the ESSR. In 1993 the Taxpayers' Club, established by 13 influential businesspeople and officials, ended up in a conflict with several Pro Patria politicians, including Kaido Kama. A key episode was the privatization carried out by the Bank of Estonia of one-third of the Savings Bank to Hansabank without an auction and for what seemed to Kama a very low price. The crony image of the deal was strengthened by the fact that the President of the Bank of Estonia, Siim Kallas, the Chairman of the Board of the Savings Bank, Olari Taal, and the Chairman of the Board of Hansabank all belonged to the Taxpayers' Club (Muuli 2012). Eventually the sale remained in force, but Kaido Kama still concludes that "the danger of new oligarchy was sufficiently high."

There was consensus among the interviewees that a corrupt oligarchy did not become established in Estonian politics. A number of instances show that major donations to ruling parties did not always translate into control over political decisions. An example was Olari Taal, who even as a major sponsor of the Res Publica party was unable to consolidate his financial contribution into political control. The party was established in 2001 based on the long-existing youth organization related to Pro Patria and became one of the winners of the 2003 election. Res Publica leader Juhan Parts was Prime Minister in 2003–05. Despite securing millions of kroons for the party, Taal was nominated but not elected Vice-Chairman of the party (Muuli 2013). On many occasions the political parties have felt the need to maintain a degree of autonomy in decision making, apparently often under media influence.

The way this influence worked can be seen through the role of the media. Already during the parliamentary period of 1992–95, the media exerted strong pressure. Väino Sarnet claims that, before the elections of 1995, the Coalition Party and the Centre Party had informally agreed to remove him from the post of General Director of the Privatization Agency, and it was the positive approval and support in the media that prevented the removal:

The Estonian media rescued me. If you look at the media in the summer of 1994, there were only positive articles considering me. This was very exceptional because privatization as such is not a very positive thing for media usually and not for the general public. [. . .] Mr. Vähi once said that this was a very exceptional situation to carry on with privatization when the general public and media support the privatization chief and you must not remove this man this time.

There is consensus among Estonian experts that most media enjoy editorial independence from their owners. The presence of Nordic owners has been a factor encouraging editorial independence. For example, the Norwegian media group Schibsted owned the largest quality daily, *Postimees*, and other media of the Eesti Media concern from 1998 till 2013.

One of the hallmarks of the second Laar government was the adoption and implementation of various transparency provisions. It can be surmised that the virtuous circle is perpetuated by the interplay between, on the one hand, pressures of public opinion (largely through the media) requiring more efficient and universalistic governance and, on the other hand, initiatives from governments in response to public needs (for example, by providing more transparency). More transparency, in turn, added yet more opportunities for public oversight.

5.6   OTHER FACTORS

One paradox of Estonia lies in the fact that the cleanest of the EU-FS countries has not officially prioritized anti-corruption policy quite to the extent that some other countries of the region have done, at least in words. Estonia does not have a dedicated, autonomous anti-corruption body, and its first comprehensive anti-corruption strategy was adopted as late as 2004. Estonia slightly resembles Scandinavian countries, where corruption is rare but the formal anti-corruption framework limited. This does suggest that explanations for Estonia's ability to keep corruption under control lie in the way the political system has changed and performed more generally. However, once the dominant ideologies, constellations of political groups and public demands had exerted their thrust for universalistic governance, the effects of rather mainstream anti-corruption activities should not be neglected.

Estonia has a framework of legal constraints on corruption which started developing in the early 1990s. In 1991, the Security Police Bureau was created within the Police Board. In 1993, the parliament made the decision to establish the Security Police as an independent institution (Security Police of the Republic of Estonia 1999, p. 10). The head of the

Security Police, Jüri Pihl, enjoyed the confidence of the ruling political parties despite his career in the interior system of the ESSR since the 1970s. With hindsight, it can be argued that the detection of the offer of a bribe by former ESSR Prime Minister Indrek Toome to an officer of the Security Police in November 1994 attested to the appearance of effective restraints on corruption (ibid., p. 37). The case did not challenge the ruling elite, as Toome was no longer active in politics and there was no political pressure on the Security Police to halt the investigation. Quite to the contrary, Kaido Kama, who was Minister of Interior at the time, remembered: "Jüri Pihl called me—Toome wants to give, what do we do? Catch! That's all."

In the 1990s, the activity of the Security Police clearly represented a constraint on middle and higher administrative level corruption in national and local government institutions (see, for example Security Police of the Republic of Estonia 1999, p. 38; Freedom House 2003). In 2006, for the first time the Security Police launched a criminal investigation into corruption by ruling national government politicians, which ended in convictions. This can serve as an indication of established capacity to counter corruption by members of the political elite. Estonia also developed a high degree of judicial independence. Overall it seems fair to say that encouraging the development of relatively impartial institutions has been a stronger anti-corruption factor than an explicit anti-corruption policy as such. Articulated anti-corruption policy emerged in Estonia in 1994–95 and, on 19 January 1995, the first Anti-Corruption Law was adopted, introducing incompatibilities and declarations of economic interests for public officials.

The official start of Estonia's EU membership bid was on 24 November 1995, when the country presented its application. The EU membership application evidenced the fact that the suspected political backlash exemplified by Tiit Vähi's government did not affect the fundamentals of Estonia's geopolitical orientation. The experts and actors interviewed provided differing opinions as to the particular role of EU accession vis-à-vis Estonia's anti-corruption achievements. Some assert that most of the significant reform steps were adopted without EU conditionality and therefore the EU's role with regard to Estonia's control of corruption was minimal. According to Mart Laar, EU conditionality was not a factor explaining Estonia's ability to control corruption. On the other hand, the EU's role is acknowledged in the strengthening of the general framework of public administration, thus entrenching universalistic principles therein and helping to "clean up the system." All in all it does seem that the logic of EU accession served as a safeguard against possible reversals in a number of areas and ways. The European integration process also facilitated exchange of information and socializing with EU countries such as, for example, the Nordic countries Finland, Sweden and Denmark.

In the context of international integration, Estonia's special closeness to Finland and other Nordic countries deserves particular mention. In addition to such factors as the Soviet-era exposure to Finnish television and the general cultural proximity of Estonians and Finns, rapidly developing links with Nordic (particularly Finnish) economies arguably influenced the business and indirectly also the political environment of Estonia. Out of all former Soviet countries, Estonia was the most exposed to foreign investment from some of the most universalistic states of the world. In 1994 direct investment from Finland amounted to 637.4 million Estonian kroons, followed by Sweden (531.6 million), and only then Russia (422.6 million) (Bank of Estonia 2002, p. 65).

Even after reviewing a great amount of empirical data and a reasonable degree of understanding of how changes happened in the 1990s, one may be left wondering why many Estonian politicians were seemingly unwilling to exploit all of the opportunities for personal enrichment that the environment of the post-Soviet transition offered. Culture is one factor which could provide some additional explanation. This study did not particularly focus on mapping cultural traits. However, some interviewees did provide insights into cultural factors. There was a recurrent mention of certain traits of the Estonian mentality (allegedly Nordic type) as a possible explanatory factor: for example, distance in personal relations except for a narrow circle; inclination towards rules-based and transparent behavior in public life; and a high level of intolerance towards particularistic gains of public figures. A study focusing on the legacy of the political culture of Estonia in the inter-war period reached a finding which is compatible with the above statement, and notes "strong expressive individualism, which saw the individual as the source of his or her own fortune but who also held the right to claim reward for his or her achievements" (Bennich-Björkman 2007, p. 337). This individualism is coupled with a particular type of egalitarianism akin to the principle of equality of opportunity. Both of these characteristics may be factors that prompt individuals to organize their relations based on rules and not so much on personal loyalties and group ties. In addition, Bennich-Björkman highlights a civic culture emphasizing solidarity and cooperation. According to the World Values Survey, Estonia is among those societies of the world exhibiting the most rational-secular values, a factor that tends to limit corruption, at least moderately (Sandholtz and Taagepera 2005, pp. 113–14). Another theme which threads through the interviews is intolerance towards visible signs of corrupt gains.

5.7   SUMMARY AND CONCLUSIONS

Despite overall success, episodes of particularistic acts (in legally punishable or other forms) are recurrent in Estonia. By 2003, the public had become so upset about perceived corruption that the new challenger party, Res Publica, could win elections with the slogan "Incorruptible!" Political patronage and shady party finance deals continue to rock Estonian politics to this day. Let us recall, for example, the revelations of the former MP Silver Meikar in 2012, who was allegedly given cash to pass on to the ruling Reform Party in 2009–10. The Secretary General of the Reform Party, Kristen Michal (Minister of Justice at the time of the revelations), allegedly initiated this financial intermediation scheme. Eventually Meikar was expelled from the Reform Party and Michal resigned from his ministerial post (Pettai and Mölder 2013, pp. 225, 226). Also, the practically unchallenged dominating position of the Reform Party in the government since 2005 probably favors political corruption and particularism. The media has used the term "oligarch" to describe the entrepreneur, politician and key sponsor of the Reform Party, Neinar Seli, fined in a conflict of interest case by the court of first instance in 2014 (Hõbemägi 2012; Err.ee 2014).

Nevertheless, Estonia is probably the least corrupt of all former socialist countries, even though anti-corruption has rarely been at the top of the country's political priorities. A peculiar mixture of cultural traits inherited from pre-war times survived in parts of the population, and featured individualism coupled with cherishing equality of opportunity, solidarity and cooperation.

The radical reforms in 1990–95 (and especially in 1992–95) and gradual strengthening of the legal constraints on corruption in the period prior to Estonia's accession to the EU and afterwards have led to the current relatively universalistic state of governance.

The strong anti-communist and nationalist mood of Estonians appears to be a key driving force behind the drastic replacement of the ruling elite, which culminated in the 1992 parliamentary elections. The rather large pool of people who had qualifications for elite positions but had kept their distance from Soviet power structures became politically active and created reforms that had defining effects for several decades in the future. At least in the first years of regained independence, many members of the new ruling elite had strong idealistic commitments to ideological principles such as the non-recognition of the legality of Soviet rule in Estonia, rule of law and a free market economy. Several of the new parties also benefited from support by ideologically close partner parties from Germany and Scandinavian countries.

The coming to power of the Mart Laar's government maintained the already pre-existing drive for reform, ensured sustainability of the changes and added new reforms. The withdrawal of the state from economic operations reduced material resources available for corruption, while the acute anti-communist position (which associated among other things nepotism and clientelism with socialist rule) gave a boost for the normative constraints on corruption. Moreover, this new elite group and many of their voters did not have any inhibitions against excluding non-Estonians and former Soviet officials from political power and administrative structures. On the other hand, they were inviting and open to the rich supply of advice given and practical work done by Western consultants generously paid for by international donors. The foundations laid in 1991–95 changed the state apparatus as well as the relationship between the state and society to such an extent that a certain path dependency emerged for Estonia's further evolution towards universalistic governance.

The ruling groups changed in 1995, but the governments of 1995–99 were probably too short-lived, too weak and indeed not quite reactionary enough to reverse many of the positive effects of the reforms of the previous period. New legal guarantees of public access to information and broad access to online public services came after 1999 to serve as a new layer of constraints on corruption.

NOTES

1. The former socialist members of the EU are Bulgaria, Croatia, the Czech Republic, Estonia, Hungary, Latvia, Lithuania, Poland, Romania, Slovak Republic, and Slovenia.
2. Interviews were conducted with the following: Jüri Adams, MP 1992–2003, Minister of Justice 1994–95; Kaido Kama, MP 1990–94, Minister of Justice 1992–94, Minister of Interior 1994–95; Priit Kama, civil servant since 1993, Undersecretary of the Ministry of Justice responsible for the Prison Service; Mart Laar, MP 1992, 1994–99, 2002–11, 2012–13, Prime Minister 1992–94 and 1999–2002, Minister of Defense 2011–12, Chair of the Board of the Bank of Estonia; Daimar Liiv, MP 1992–99, judge; Uno Lõhmus, judge of the European Court of Human Rights 1994–98, President of the Supreme Court 1998–2004, judge of the European Court of Justice 2004–13; Peeter Mardna, Chief Inspector of the Health Board; Elmar Nurmela, former long-time police officer, adviser to the Police and Border Guard College of Estonian Academy of Security Sciences; Vello Pettai, Professor of Comparative Politics at the University of Tartu (lecturer since 1995); Aive Pevkur, adviser at the Government Office 2004–09 and the Ministry of Finance 2010, teacher and researcher at Tallinn University of Technology (TTÜ); Jüri Pihl, Director General of the Security Police 1993–2002, Attorney General 2003–05, Minister of Interior 2007–09; Ivar Raig, MP 1989–95, professor at the University of Tallinn; Tiina Randma-Liiv, professor at TTÜ; Jüri Saar, Professor of Criminology at the University of Tartu; Leno Saarniit, lecturer in governance at TTÜ, member of the Public Service Ethics Council at the Ministry of Finance; Külli Sarapuu, researcher at TTÜ; Väino Sarnet, Director General of the Estonian Privatization Agency 1993–99; Anneli Sihver, adviser at the Public Administration and Public Service Department of the Ministry of Finance; Mari-Liis Sööt, Director of the Criminal Statistics and Analysis Division of

the Criminal Policy Department of the Ministry of Justice; Rein Taagepera, Professor Emeritus at the University of Tartu; Ivar Tallo, MP 1999–2001, founder and Research Director of the e-Governance Academy; Tarmu Tammerk, editor and writer since 1990, Media Ombudsman at the Estonian Public Broadcasting Company, board member of TI-Estonia; Raivo Vare, State Minister 1990–92, Minister of Roads and Communication 1996–99, Chairman of the Council of the Estonian Railway; and Tiit Vähi, Minister of Transportation 1989–92, MP 1997, Prime Minister 1992, 1995–97.

3. Aare Kasemets is a researcher with the Estonian Academy of Security Sciences and has been an observer of many of the covered events in his past employment, having worked in the parliament of Estonia (1993–2003) and the Ministry of Environment (2004–08).
4. According to Muuli, other members of the Estonian Students' Society who became known political actors included Indrek Kannik, Sulev Kannike, Margus Kastehein, Margus Kasterpalu, Margus Kolga, Eerik-Niiles Kross, Tõnis Lukas, Tiit Pruuli, Tiit Riisalo, Ivo Rull, Marek Strandberg, Indrek Tarand, and Lauri Vahtre.
5. In addition to the four parties described earlier in this chapter, the Estonian Liberal Democratic Party participated in the Pro Patria election coalition but did not merge with the Pro Patria National Coalition Party in November 1992.
6. "Letter of 40 Intellectuals" (trans. Estam, J. and Pennar, J.). The full text of the letter in English is available at: www.sirjekiin.net/40%20Letters.htm [Accessed 28 February 2015].
7. With some important exceptions, for example, the former Chairman of the Presidium of the Supreme Council of the ESSR, Arnold Rüütel, became President of Estonia in 2001.

REFERENCES

Ammas, A. (2003). Indrek Toome: poliitikarattalt maha astunud mees. *Eesti Päevaleht*, 8 February. Available at http://epl.delfi.ee/news/melu/indrek-toome-poliitikarattalt-maha-astunud-mees?id=50946316. [Accessed 05 March 2015].

Bank of Estonia (2002). *Estonian Balance of Payments Yearbook 2001*. [online] Tallinn: Bank of Estonia. Available at: www.eestipank.ee/en/publication/balance-payments-yearbook/2001/estonian-balance-payments-yearbook-2001. [Accessed 01 October 2014].

Bennich-Björkman, L. (2001). State formation and democratic consolidation in the Baltic states: a political perspective on the EU membership. Uppsala University. Available at: www.snee.org/filer/papers/25.pdf. [Accessed 02 March 2015].

Bennich-Björkman, L. (2007). The cultural roots of Estonia's successful transition: how historical legacies shaped the 1990s. *East European Politics and Societies*, **21**(2), 316–47.

Bloomberg Business (2015). Company overview of AS Cresco. [online] Available at: www.bloomberg.com/research/stocks/private/person.asp?personId=107456858&privcapId=21010694&previousCapId=21010694&previousTitle=AS%2520Cresco. [Accessed 05 March 2015].

Brown, W.S. (1993). Economic transition in Estonia. *Journal of Economic Issues*, **27**(2), 493–503.

Dobbs, M. (1988). Radical program adopted by Estonian Popular Front. *Los Angeles Times*. [online] Available at: http://articles.latimes.com/1988-10-03/news/mn-2409_1_popular-front. [Accessed 02 May 2015].

Eesti Entsüklopeedia (2000–2013). *Sarnet, Väino*. [online] Available at: http://entsyklopeedia.ee/artikkel/sarnet_v%C3%A4ino. [Accessed 02 March 2015].

Eesti Üliõpilaste Selts (2015). *Liikmed* [online]. Available at: www.eys.ee/liikmed. php. [Accessed 02 May 2015].

Err.ee (2014). Olympic Committee president fined in conflict of interest case. *News.err.ee.* [online] Available at: http://news.err.ee/v/6a2319c7-98cb-4493-a568-c1d45d90d27f. [Accessed 02 May 2015].

Estonia.eu (2015). Citizenship. [online] Government of Estonia. Available at: http://estonia.eu/about-estonia/society/citizenship.html. [Accessed 28 February 2015].

European Commission (2000). *2000 Regular Report from the Commission on Estonia's Progress towards Accession.* [online] Luxembourg: European Commission. Available at: http://ec.europa.eu/enlargement/archives/pdf/key_documents/2000/es_en.pdf. [Accessed 01 October 2014].

Eurostat (2014a). *Gross Domestic Product at Market Prices.* [online] Luxembourg: European Commission. Available at: http://ec.europa.eu/eurostat/tgm/table.do?tab=table&init=1&language=en&pcode=tec00001&plugin=1. [Accessed 27 February 2015].

Eurostat (2014b). *Population on 1 January.* [online] Luxembourg: European Commission. Available at: http://ec.europa.eu/eurostat/tgm/table.do?tab=table&init=1&language=en&pcode=tps00001&plugin=1. [Accessed 27 February 2015].

Freedom House (2003). *Estonia: Nations in Transit 2003.* [online] Washington, DC: Freedom House. Available at: www.freedomhouse.org/report/nations-transit/2003/estonia#.VCwnW_mSwqI. [Accessed 01 October 2014].

Hõbemägi, T. (2012). Neinar Seli, Estonia's own oligarch. *Baltic Business News.* [online] Available at: http://balticbusinessnews.com/article/2012/11/8/neinar-seli-estonia-s-own-oligarch. [Accessed 02 May 2015].

Huang, M. (2002). *Wannabe Oligarchs: Tycoons and Influence in the Baltic States.* Camberley: Conflict Studies Research Centre.

Kaio, H. (2012). Jõukust nautiv Indrek Toome. *Eesti Päevaleht.* [online] Available at: http://epl.delfi.ee/news/lp/joukust-nautiv-indrek-toome?id=65408758. [Accessed 05 March 2015].

Kasemets, A. (2012). The long transition to good governance: the case of Estonia. Looking at the changes in the governance regime and anti-corruption policy. Working paper no. 32, European Research Centre for Anti-Corruption and State-Building, Berlin. Available at: www.againstcorruption.eu/wp-content/uploads/2012/09/WP-32-Long-Transition-Estonia1.pdf. [Accessed 28 February 2015].

Kurvits, T. (2007). Reiljaana. *Kultuur & Elu,* 4. [online] Available at: http://kultuur.elu.ee/ke490_toimetajaveerg.htm. [Accessed 02 May 2015].

Laar, M. (2007). *The Estonian Economic Miracle.* Washington, DC: Heritage Foundation.

Lauristin, M. and Vihalemm, P. (2009). The political agenda during different periods of Estonian transformation: external and internal factors. In Lauristin, M. and Vihalemm, P. (eds) *Estonia's Transition to the EU: Twenty Years On.* London: Routledge.

Liivik, O. (2010–12). The Popular Front. *Estonica: Encyclopedia about Estonia.* [online] Available at www.estonica.org/en/The_Popular_Front/. [Accessed 02 May 2015].

Mänd, A. (2008). Valega ei saa taastada Eesti Vabariiki. In: *Nõmme valitsus.Tiit Vähi valitsuse ja Riigikogu 2. koosseisu kuritegu eesti rahva vastu.* Available at:

www.nommevalitsus.org/index.php?option=com_content&view=article&id=1
25:aegumatu-kuritegu&catid=62:a_vasak&Itemid=109&lang=et. [Accessed 01
October 2014].

Maruste, R. (1994). Kohtureform: kas lõpu alguses või alguse lõpus? *Juridica*, **5**, 103–5.
Available at: www.juridica.ee/juridica_et.php?document=et/articles/1994/5/28749.
SUM.php. [Accessed 02 March 2015].

Matonytė, I. (2009). Ex-nomenklatura and ex-dissidents in the post-communist
parliaments of Estonia, Latvia, Lithuania, and Poland. *Viešoji politika ir admin-
istravimas*, 29, 28–39.

Meel, M. (2012). Poliitilisest võimust on saanud kaan ettevõtja kaela peal. *Äripäev*,
4 June. Available at: www.aripaev.ee/uudised/2012/06/03/poliitilisest-voimust-
on-saanud-kaan-ettevotja-kaela-peal. [Accessed 02 May 2015].

Misiunas, R. and Taagepera, R. (1993). *The Baltic States: Years of Dependence,
1940–1990*. London: Hurst & Co.

Muuli, K. (2012). *Isamaa tagatuba. Mart Laari valitsus 1992–1994*. Tallinn:
Tulimuld.

Muuli, K. (2013). *Vabariigi sünnimärgid. Varjatud murdehetki Eesti poliitikas
1987–2007*. Tallinn: Tulimuld.

Mõttus, A. (ed.) (2013). *Eesti NSV / Eesti Vabariigi Ülemnõukogu XII koos-
seis. Statistikat ja ülevaateid. 29.03.1990, 29.09.1992*. Riigikogu Kantselei,
Eesti Rahvusraamatukogu. Available at www.riigikogu.ee/wpcms/wp-content/
uploads/2015/02/Eesti_NSV_Eesti_Vabariigi_Ulemnoukogu_XII_koosseis_29
.03.199029.09.19921.pdf. [Accessed 02 May 2015].

OECD (2001). *OECD Reviews of Foreign Direct Investment: Estonia*. Paris:
Organisation for Economic Co-operation and Development.

Pärnaste, E. (2000). *Eesti Kongress: siis ja praegu*. Eesti Vabariigi Riigikantselei.
Overview. Available at: www.sirjekiin.net/Eesti/Eesti%20Kongressi%20ajalugu.
htm. [Accessed 28 February 2015].

Pettai, V. and Mölder, M. (2013). Nations in transit: Estonia. Freedom House.
[online] Available at: www.freedomhouse.org/report/nations-transit/2013/
estonia. [Accessed 04 July 2013].

Randma, L. (2001). A small civil service in transition: the case of Estonia. *Public
Administration and Development*, **21**(1), 41–51.

Sandholtz, W. and Taagepera, R. (2005). Corruption, culture, and communism.
International Review of Sociology, **15**(1), 109–31.

Sarapuu, K. (2012). Administrative structure in times of changes: the development of Estonian ministries and government agencies 1990–2010. *International
Journal of Public Administration*, **35**(12), 809–19.

Security Police of the Republic of Estonia (1999). *Annual Review 1998*. [online]
Tallinn: Kaitsepolitseiamet. Available at: www.kapo.ee/cms-data/_text/138/124/
files/aastaraamat-1998-eng.pdf. [Accessed 05 March 2015].

Sigma (2002). *Estonia: Public Service and the Administrative Framework Assessment
2002*. Paris: Support for Improvement in Governance and Management.

Smith, D.J. et al. (2002). *The Baltic States: Estonia, Latvia and Lithuania*. London:
Routledge.

Soodla, H. (2006). Halinga kolhoosist on järel parem tiib ja vorstilõhn. *Pärnu
Postimees*. [online] Available at: www.parnupostimees.ee/2131873/halinga-kol
hoosist-on-jarel-parem-tiib-ja-vorstilohn. [Accessed 02 May 2015].

Statistikaamet (2014). Eestistatistika aastaraamat 2014. [online] Tallinn:
Statistikaamet. Available at: www.stat.ee/72571. [Accessed 27 February 2015].

Viivik, A. (2000). Pikri pealik kõndis noateral. *Õhtuleht*, 19 February. Available at: www.ohtuleht.ee/71134/pikri-pealik-kondis-noateral. [Accessed 28 February 2015].

World Bank (2015). *Worldwide Governance Indicators*. [online] Washington, DC: World Bank. Available at: http://info.worldbank.org/governance/wgi/index.aspx #reports. [Accessed 20 December 2015].

World Values Survey (1981–2014). *Findings and Insights*. Stockholm: World Values Survey. Available at: www.worldvaluessurvey.org/WVSContents.jsp. [Accessed 02 May 2015].

6. South Korea: the odyssey to corruption control

Jong-sung You

6.1 INTRODUCTION

Various indicators of corruption show that when compared to other Asian countries South Korea has been relatively successful in controlling corruption. However, the country's performance remains below Organisation for Economic Co-operation and Development (OECD) standards (You 2015: 47–55). In particular, according to Transparency International's Global Corruption Barometer surveys, the level of petty bureaucratic corruption is among the lowest in Asia, along with those of Japan, Hong Kong and Singapore. Petty electoral corruption and vote-buying practices have almost disappeared, although corporate and political corruption are still of considerable concern (Kalinowski and Kim 2014). The country's rank in the Corruption Perception Index (CPI) is 37 out of 168, but the fact-based Index for Public Integrity (IPI) shows Korea as an undisputable achiever, at rank 16 of 105 (Table 6.1), a regional leader and a medium performer in its income group in nearly all categories.

The country's reasonably good performance in controlling corruption indicates that the norms of ethical universalism largely prevail over

Table 6.1 Korea's public integrity framework

Components of Index of Public Integrity	Component Score	World Rank	Regional Rank	Income Group Rank
Judicial Independence	5.4	47/105	8/17	26/36
Administrative Burden	9.34	17/105	3/17	13/36
Trade Openness	9.63	3/105	1/17	3/36
Budget Transparency	8.93	15/105	3/17	10/36
E-Citizenship	8.14	15/105	2/17	15/36
Freedom of the Press	7.31	30/105	2/17	28/36

Source: Index of Public Integrity.

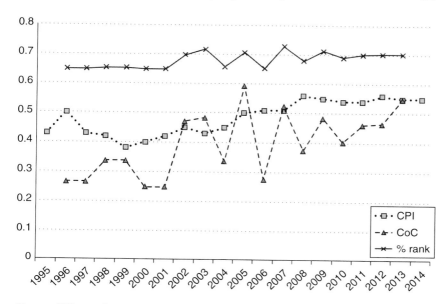

Notes: CPI score formerly ranged from 0 (most corrupt) to 10 (least corrupt), but the scale changed to 0–100 in 2014. I have normalized the CPI scores to range between 0 and 1. Control of corruption (CoC) score has a standardized normal distribution, with a mean of 0 and standard deviation of 1. Percentile rank (% rank) is denoted in terms of CoC score.

Sources: Transparency International, WGI Control of Corruption.

Figure 6.1   Trends of CPI and CoC in Korea, 1995–2014

particularism, although particularism is still significant in some areas, for example corporate governance and relations between business and government (Figure 6.1).

While South Korea today is widely recognized as a rich and robust democracy with relatively good governance, in the 1950s many Western observers considered the country a poor and hopelessly corrupt autocracy. However, since independence in 1948, South Korea has been transitioning – even if it has not yet completed the job – from particularism of the limited-access order to ethical universalism of the open-access order (North et al. 2009; You 2012).

- How has that been happening?
- Is the development of good governance, based on ethical universalism, a natural by-product of economic development?
- Was good governance established by a benevolent dictator or has it been achieved by the efforts of the people?

- How have governance norms developed over time?
- Who has been responsible for the changes and what factors have been behind those changes?

Those are the questions I shall attempt to address in this chapter.

First, I shall assess the political, economic and social bases of contemporary control of corruption in South Korea, focusing on how norms of ethical universalism prevail over particularism. Then, I shall look at the early period of post-independence, when Syngman Rhee was the first president (1948–60), a time when particularism was still dominant. A comparison of the political, economic and social bases of control of corruption in those two periods indicates that it was not just the level of economic development but also the broader political economy that differentiated them, which suggests that the changes in governance norms were indeed more than a by-product of economic development. In order to identify the causes of the changes I shall conduct process-tracing, or causal process observation, of the broad political economy of the norms of governance; and, while not neglecting the effects of structural factors, I shall focus on the role of human agency in changing them.

My process-tracing of dynamic sequences of events has distinguished four periods with different norms in the equilibrium between particularism and universalism, each period defined by major political events. The first, from 1948 to 1960, began with the establishment of two separate governments on the Korean peninsula. The second began with the Student Democratic Revolution of 19 April 1960, followed by the military coup of 16 May 1961 and lasted until 1987. The third began with the democratic transition of 1987 and continued until the financial crisis of 1997. The fourth, from 1997 onwards, since when ethical universalism has become dominant, was ushered in with the first transfer of power to the opposition and accompanying sweeping reforms of the corporate and financial sectors in the aftermath of the financial crisis.

I also identify a number of critical reforms that have contributed to the changes in norms of governance. From 1948 to 1950 came the dissolution of the landed aristocracy and sweeping land reform which led to a relatively equal distribution of wealth. Rapid expansion of education laid the structural foundations for the growth of ethical universalism, and a gradual expansion of civil service examinations which began in the 1950s and carried on into the 1990s promoted norms of ethical universalism, as did democratization movements which went on from 1960 to 1987. Since the democratic transition of 1987 have come good governance reforms and economic reform following the financial crisis of 1997–98. I shall explore how those reforms were carried out, who were the main actors, what made them possible and what impact they had on the norms of governance.

6.2   POLITICAL, SOCIAL AND ECONOMIC BASES OF CONTEMPORARY CONTROL OF CORRUPTION

In this section I shall examine the broad political economy of Korea as it affects opportunities and constraints for corruption. My particular focus has been on features of ethical universalism as against particularism within the bureaucratic structure, and I have looked closely too at the question of political competition, and have considered underlying socio-economic conditions such as the distribution of power resources and the strength of civil society.

In contemporary South Korea, meritocracy is well established in bureaucratic appointment and promotion, the manner of public administration is largely impartial, and Korean politics is largely defined by programmatic competition rather than clientelistic competition. Corruption scandals still occur frequently, but many corrupt politicians are prosecuted, albeit not all of them in all circumstances – and they are punished at the polls. While particularism is still significant in certain political, social and economic spheres, ethical universalism and the rule of law largely prevail in Korean society today.

Bureaucratic Structure

Empirical studies have shown that Weberian bureaucracy, particularly meritocratic recruitment, is closely associated with lower corruption (Rauch and Evans 2000; Dahlström et al. 2012). Meritocratic recruitment is considered an important feature of universalism, while the prevalence of patronage appointments in many developing countries is an important manifestation of particularism. South Korea has been widely recognized for its autonomous, meritocratic and competent, or Weberian, type of bureaucracy. According to Evans and Rauch's (1999) 'Weberianness' score data for 35 developing countries in the period from 1970 to 1990, South Korea was among the best, with a score of 13. That figure is much higher than the sample mean of 7.2 and behind only Singapore with its score of 13.5. The Quality of Government Institute at Gothenburg University has recently conducted a survey of bureaucratic structures for 105 countries throughout the world (Teorell et al. 2011). South Korea scored 5.05 in terms of 'professional bureaucracy' or absence of patronage, much higher than the sample mean of 3.93, and leaving it ranked 12th (just behind Canada) of the 105 countries. South Korea scored 0.71 in terms of 'impartial administration' or absence of bureaucratic corruption, much higher than the sample mean of -0.11, and ranked 19th, just behind the United States.

Party System and Electoral Mobilization

Political competition is an important distinction between universalism and particularism, while electoral mobilization is significant for the relative prevalence of programmatic competition vs. clientelistic competition. While programmatic competition and mobilization take place in a world of distinct political parties which offer differing policies to be applied equally to everyone who meets certain criteria or to the whole population, clientelistic competition and mobilization take place where the norm is that particularistic benefits are exchanged for political support. Clientelism increases petty corruption both at electoral level and in high-level politics because individual politicians need clientelistic resources. Clientelism increases bureaucratic corruption too because it provides jobs in the bureaucracy by means of patronage. Moreover, clientelism means that voters are unable to punish corrupt politicians at the polls (You 2015: 23–7).

In today's South Korean politics, clientelistic competition based on particularistic provision of constituency services and favours done in return for political support is still significant, but actual vote-buying practices have all but disappeared. Elections are increasingly defined by programmatic competition between major parties with different ideological orientations and policy programmes (You 2015: 105–14). While major parties frequently change their names and reshuffle, and sometimes split or merge with others, there are always at least two major parties – one more conservative and the other more liberal – both clearly identified and recognized by the electorate. There have been two peaceful transfers of power, first from a conservative government to a liberal one in 1997 and back to a conservative one in 2007. Smaller parties too, on the political left, have been clearly recognized by the general public. Regional politics is no less significant than ideological politics at national level, with the main conservative and liberal parties enjoying strong support in different regions of the country. Regional politics is substantially intertwined with ideological politics (Moon 2005), and the importance of ideological and generational cleavages has been growing rapidly (Kang 2008; Seong 2015). All the same, while clientelistic practices designed to exchange votes for particularistic benefits have become substantially less frequent than in the early years of post-democratic transition, clientelistic relations with business are still an important reason for continuing corruption scandals.

Distribution of Power and Power Resources

As Alina Mungiu-Pippidi (2006) has noted, particularism mirrors the vicious distribution of power, which in turn is affected by the distribution of power resources. In authoritarian regimes, where power is concentrated and access to it is limited to privileged individuals and groups, particularism prevails. In democracies, voting rights are in principle distributed equally to every citizen, although skewed distribution of income, wealth, knowledge (via education), social networks and other power resources can undermine political equality and the norms of ethical universalism. High economic inequality not only increases the risks of elite capture, but also encourages clientelism (You 2015: 30–34).

While South Korea's president still enjoys strong constitutional power, checks and balances too have been strengthened since the democratic transition. In particular, frequent occurrence of divided government often placed strong constraints on the executive from an increasingly assertive legislature. However, the conservative governments of Lee Myung-bak (2008–12) and Park Geun-hye (2013–17) have enjoyed comfortable majorities for their party in the National Assembly. With little constraint from the legislature, both presidents were able to fill vacancies in the Supreme Court, Constitutional Court and National Human Rights Commission with very conservative people loyal to them, causing concern that the independence of the courts and the commission had been compromised. In consequence too, there are growing concerns about the politicization of prosecutions, and about the suppression of free speech (You 2014a; Haggard and You 2015).

South Korea has been recognized as a success story for 'growth with equity' (World Bank 1993; Rodrik 1995). With an unusually equal distribution of income and wealth and a high level of human capital (You 1998), South Korea has been seen to have created favourable structural conditions for state autonomy and good governance. On the other hand, there have been concerns about economic concentration in the hands of large *chaebol*s and about crony capitalism (Kang 2002; Kalinowski 2009). Recent studies have shown that both income inequality and *chaebol* concentration have indeed been rising rapidly. Kim (2011) shows that *chaebol* concentration, although it declined for a number of years after the post-financial crisis reform, has been rising again. Kim and Kim (2014) show that the top 1 per cent's share of national income has been increasing rapidly since the late 1990s, and there is evidence that increasing income inequality has been translated into a widening gap in educational opportunity (Kim 2014).

While increasing concentration of wealth and income among the few is eroding the structural foundations for good governance, a vibrant civil society in Korea functions as an important check on corporate malfeasance as well as on the abuse of public office. Highly trusted and respected, civil society organizations (CSOs) exert considerable political influence in South Korea. According to the 2015 Edelman Trust Barometer, non-governmental organizations (NGOs) are more highly trusted in Korea (68) than in other countries (global mean=63), while government and business are less trusted there (33 and 36, respectively) than in other countries (global mean=48 and 57, respectively).

6.3   POLITICAL, SOCIAL AND ECONOMIC BASES OF CONTROL OF CORRUPTION DURING THE FIRST REPUBLIC AND THE SUBSEQUENT DEVELOPMENT OF GOVERNANCE NORMS

South Korea during the First Republic, or Syngman Rhee period (1948–60), was a poor country with rampant corruption. Clientelism dominated politics, patronage was common in bureaucratic appointments and, to a great extent, favouritism and nepotism were the norm in much of both the making and implementing of policy. Overall, particularism prevailed and corruption was part of everyday life from the top to the bottom of society. However, the dissolution of the landed aristocracy, a relatively egalitarian socio-economic structure and a rapid expansion of education provided favourable conditions for the future development of civil society, and with it the norms of ethical universalism.

Distribution of Power and Power Resources during the Rhee Period

Although the country was a democracy in formal terms, President Syngman Rhee became increasingly authoritarian. He amended the constitution twice in irregular ways to remove the limited term of office for himself as the first president of the country. Power was concentrated in the office of the president, so that the National Assembly lost its capability to check abuses of power by the executive. The police and the bureaucracy effectively became the political machinery of the president's Liberal Party.

Civil society was weak, with leftist political parties and left-leaning political and civil groups completely suppressed. Government-organized and government-sponsored right-wing organizations (including some violent youth groups), trade unions and women's groups dominated civil society, leaving little room for autonomous civil action.

While almost everyone was poor, an emerging class of industrialists sought lucrative business opportunities from the government's distribution of former Japanese-owned enterprises, and from import licences. Large amounts of US aid made up another important source of rents, for aid was neither administered nor distributed impartially, with favouritism and nepotism both commonly occurring. The ruling Liberal Party and bureaucrats therefore had plentiful resources to distribute to their supporters, clans and cronies. Business success was dependent more on political connections than on productivity or competitiveness.

However, there was no dominant class in a position to capture the state after the landed aristocracy had been dissolved under the land reforms mentioned above. With the introduction of universal primary education, enrolment in primary education rose rapidly and reached almost 100 per cent by the end of the 1950s, while secondary and tertiary education too expanded tremendously (McGinn et al. 1980). However, such structural conditions, although clearly favourable to the development of state autonomy and the norms of ethical universalism, did not automatically foster the development of either of them.

Clientelistic Politics during the Rhee Period

Young democracies are prone to clientelism because it takes time for political parties to build policy reputations (Keefer 2007; Keefer and Vlaicu 2008). Small wonder then that in South Korea too, personalistic and clientelistic competition did indeed dominate National Assembly elections in the early years. The proportion of independent candidates elected in the 1948, 1950 and 1952 legislative elections ranged between 40 and 60 per cent, as major political parties showed no substantial differences in their policy directions, apart from the opposition party's criticism of the current government's increasingly authoritarian style. The two-party system was first established in the 1956 and 1958 elections, after which national elections became contests between the authoritarian ruling party and the pro-democracy opposition party (You 2015: 106).

Although the two-party system gradually became the norm and there emerged a certain degree of programmatic competition surrounding democratization, the ruling Liberal Party's reliance on clientelistic mobilization was strengthened as President Rhee's popularity with the electorate waned over time. Thus clientelism and vote-buying became increasingly prevalent not only in legislative and local elections but in presidential elections too. Major corruption scandals broke during every presidential election year, as the government dispensed favours to the incipient *chaebol* in return for illicit political contributions (You 2015: 131).

Bureaucratic Patronage during the Rhee Period

Competitive examinations to enter the civil service were first implemented in 1949. However, during the Syngman Rhee period most civil servants were recruited not via civil service examinations but by special appointment, many to patronage jobs dispensed by powerful politicians and senior bureaucrats. The rampant practices of patronage appointment led to endemic bureaucratic corruption, as bureaucrats who landed their jobs via patronage sought to repay their patrons and then obtain promotion by bribing powerful officials. The insignificant role of the civil service examinations in establishing a meritocratic bureaucracy stemmed from at least two problems.

First, the bulk of civil servants were hired before the establishment of the examinations. Since the South Korean state was in the process of creating a new bureaucracy, it was to a certain extent inevitable that the bulk of civil servants would be recruited from the pool of Korean officials who had previously been serving in the American Military Government from 1945 to 1948. Indeed, many of them had worked for the previous Japanese colonial government.

Second, while the civil service examinations were set up during the Syngman Rhee period, they were for only the higher-entry level (Grade III-B) and middle-entry level (Grade IV-B), not for the lower-entry level (Grade V-B). Consequent on the recruitment of such a large number of officials via special appointments during the first few years, demand was not great for new recruits at the higher- and middle-entry levels, although the number recruited annually at the lower-entry level was much higher. There was therefore ample scope for patronage appointments. Even among new recruits at the higher- and middle-entry levels, during the 1950s fewer than half had passed the civil service examinations, with similar results in the high number of patronage appointments.

Development of Governance Norms in South Korea

As we have seen above, governance norms during the Syngman Rhee period were radically different from those in today's South Korea. How have those norms changed? Process-tracing of changes in governance norms suggests that there were four distinct periods, each with a different equilibrium in its norms of particularism and universalism. Between the first period from 1948 to 1960 during which norms of particularism were dominant and the still-running fourth period, which began in 1998 when ethical universalism became dominant, there were two intermediate periods. Table 6.2 summarizes governance norms, critical reforms, major actors and context variables for each period.

Table 6.2 *Development of governance norms in South Korea*

Period	Governance Norms	Critical Reforms	Actors	Context Variables
1948–60	Particularism, with formal institutions of universalism • Clientelistic politics • Bureaucratic patronage • Favoritism, nepotism • Business, relying on political connections	Land reform (1948, 1950) Formal democracy • Universal suffrage (1948) • Universal primary education (1948) • Civil service exam (1949)	• Popular demand • US • National Assembly • President Rhee Opponents: • Landlords • Korea Democratic Party	• North Korea's radical land reform (1946) • Korean War (1950–53) • Poor • Inequality, reduced • Landed aristocracy, dissolved • Educational expansion
1960–87	Particularism, with some development of universalism • Meritocratic bureaucracy • Business, relying on exports (efficiency) and government favors	Democratization movements • Student Revolution (1960) • Civil service exam, expanded (1960–) • Military coup (1961) • Spring of Seoul and military crackdown (1980)	• Students • Professors and religious leaders • Urban, educated middle class • Working class Opponents: • Military • Chaebol • U.S. support of the military regimes	• Security threat from and economic competition with North Korea • Rapid, export-oriented Industrialization • Chaebol concentration • Growing middle class and working class

Table 6.2 (continued)

Period	Governance Norms	Critical Reforms	Actors	Context Variables
1987–97	Particularism and ethical universalism, in conflict • Rule of law • Clientelistic politics • Capture by chaebol	Democratic transition (1987) Transparency and anti-corruption reform (1993–95)	• CSOs (CCEJ, PSPD, TI-Korea) • Popular demand • President Kim Young-sam Opponents: • Chaebol • Clientelistic politicians	• Empowerment of civil society • Growing political influence of chaebol
1998–	Ethical universalism, with some particularism • Programmatic politics • Corporate governance, ups and downs	Corporate and financial reform (1998–99) Transparency and anti-corruption reform (1998–)	• CSOs • Popular demand, esp. younger generation • Presidents Kim Dae-jung and Roh Moo-hyun Opponents: • Chaebol • Clientelistic politicians	• Financial crisis and IMF bailout (1997) • Change of governing parties (1998) • Transfer of power back to the conservatives (2008)

The first period (1948–60), a time of new state-building, began with the establishment in 1948 of two separate states in the Korean peninsula. There was then a devastating civil war which lasted from 1950 to 1953 and developed into the first international armed conflict of the Cold War era. Although the period was characterized by the norms of particularism, there were important reforms that had long-lasting effects on the subsequent development of the norms of ethical universalism. First of all, formal institutions of democracy were implemented, and then came far-reaching land reform, which by dissolving the landed aristocracy had a particularly fundamental effect in that it changed the class structure of Korean society. Land reform contributed to the rapid expansion of education too by making it affordable to the new class of tenants turned owner-cultivators.

The second period (1960–87) was the time of democratization movements which began with the Student Democratic Revolution of 19 April 1960 and was followed in due course by the military coup of 16 May 1961. The period saw an important development: civil service reform, meaning the development of a meritocratic bureaucracy. It was also a period of state-led industrialization and growth of the *chaebol*.

The third period, representing the early period of democratic consolidation, began in 1987 with transition to democracy and ended with financial crisis ten years later. The period was marked by conflicts between the norms of particularism and those of ethical universalism, for although President Kim Young-sam carried out certain important reforms to enhance transparency and combat corruption, he never managed to put a stop to his party's clientelism and collusion with the *chaebol*.

The fourth period (from 1998 to the present) began with the first transfer of power to the opposition and sweeping economic reforms in the aftermath of the financial crisis, and saw democracy consolidated. Programmatic competition between political parties developed, while clientelism and vote-buying declined. Political finances became more transparent as corporate governance improved and markets became more competitive; all this despite some regressions in recent years.

6.4 THE POLITICAL ECONOMY OF GOVERNANCE REFORMS

In this section, I shall explore the political economy of five critical reforms in South Korean history: land reform; reforms to the civil service; general democratization; reforms to ensure good governance; and the economic reforms which came after the financial crisis. Although land reform is strictly speaking not a governance reform but a redistributive reform, nevertheless it laid the structural foundations for future reforms of governance. My analysis here will focus on who (actors) and what (context variables) were mainly responsible for those reforms, how the reforms were carried out and what impact they had on changes to governance norms.

Land Reform (1948, 1950)

At independence, South Korea inherited a system of land distribution which was both skewed and deeply unequal. The richest 2.7 per cent of rural households owned two-thirds of all land under cultivation, while 58 per cent owned no land at all (You 2015: 68). However, the sweeping land reform implemented in 1948 and 1950 completely changed that pattern of distribution.

The redistribution of land in South Korea was carried out in two stages, first by the US Military Government (USMG) in 1948 and then by the South Korean government in 1950. In March 1948, the USMG distributed 240,000 hectares of formerly Japanese-held land, amounting to 11.7 per cent of the total arable land, to its tenants. That land was sold to tenant-cultivators who were to pay three times the annual harvest, in instalments over 15 years (Mitchell 1949).

When the first election was held in the southern part of the Korean peninsula in May 1948, all parties pledged to implement land reform and the constitution included a commitment to it, and Syngman Rhee's government did implement agrarian land reform in 1950, just before the Korean War broke out. Restricting the upper ceiling of landownership to 3 hectares per household, the government redistributed 330,000 hectares of excess farmland and land owned by absentee landlords. As compensation, the landlords received from the government 1.5 times the annual value of all crops, and their former tenants, now the owners of the land, were to pay the same amount to the government in five years. The implementation of land reform was expediently done, effectively completed before 30 May 1950, when the second National Assembly elections were held. In anticipation of the reform, many landlords voluntarily sold their lands directly to their tenants, the bulk of such transactions occurring in 1948 and 1949. Direct sales covered about 500,000 hectares of farmland (Hong 2001).

In total, ownership of 52 per cent of the total cultivated land, or 89 per cent of the land that had been cultivated by tenants, was transferred to them, and the principle of 'land to the tiller' was effectively realized. As a result, by 1956 the top 6 per cent owned only 18 per cent of the cultivated lands, while tenancy dropped from 49 per cent to 7 per cent of all farming households as the area of land cultivated under tenancy fell from 65 to 18 per cent (Ban et al. 1980; Lie 1998). So it was that South Korea fundamentally transformed its rural class structure by implementing one of the most radical land reforms in the non-communist world (You 2015: 68–75).

That effective policy of land reform profoundly transformed Korean society as the traditional *yangban* (aristocracy) landlord class was dissolved and peasants became farmers (Lie 1998). Reform also made room for state autonomy from the dominant class, because immediately after it was done there was no longer a privileged class. The redistribution of the land and then the destruction of large private properties during the Korean War produced an unusually equal distribution of assets and income (Mason et al. 1980; You 1998). In fact, according to Kim and Kim (2014), the top 1 per cent's share of income fell from approximately 20 per cent during the 1930s to roughly 7 per cent after the reform.

Land reform facilitated the expansion of education by making it affordable for more people. Land reform also encouraged large landowners to donate their land to educational institutions, because such institutions were exempt from the expropriation of land (Park 1987; Oh 2004). At the time of independence, about 80 per cent of Koreans had received no public schooling of any kind, fewer than 2 per cent had more than primary education and only 0.03 per cent had experienced a university education (McGinn et al. 1980). Between 1945 and 1960 the number of schools almost doubled, the number of teachers almost quadrupled and there were more than three times as many pupils, while by 1960 primary education had become virtually universal in Korea. Enrolment in secondary schools increased from 3 per cent of children in 1945 to 29 per cent in 1960, with tertiary enrolment increasing during the same period from 4 persons per 10,000 of the whole population to 41 (McGinn et al. 1980). Considering that the government's budgetary commitment to public education was minimal during that period, educational expansion would have occurred more slowly without land reform, so it is clear that land reform and the expansion of education together laid the foundations for rapid industrialization and economic growth with greater equity (Rodrik 1995; Lie 1998; You 2012, 2014b).

Why did the USMG and the South Korean government implement such radical land reform? And what made that reform so successful? Certainly the landowners resisted; their representatives continually tried to delay reform and to water it down. However, as reform was favoured by both external and internal factors, their resistance proved ineffective.

Both the threat of communism from North Korea and US policy played important roles (You 2014b, 2015). In March 1946, in the Soviet-occupied north of Korea, the Provisional People's Committee implemented its own land reform based on uncompensated confiscation and free redistribution, a radical approach which compelled US policymakers as well as the South Korean political leaders to embrace some form of land reform themselves in order to prevent a majority of the peasant population from seeing the attractions of the communist propaganda emanating from the north. In 1946 the USMG changed its initial conservative position, instead pursuing liberal land reform, and in 1948 the Americans redistributed formerly Japanese-held land before the South Korean government was established. Moreover, the US continued to advise the newly formed South Korean government to carry out a liberal land reform quickly as an effective tool in the fight against communism.

Domestic politics too did not favour the landowning class. After liberation, they were put on the defensive because they had collaborated with the Japanese colonial government. Immediately after independence peasant movements and leftist political parties were initially strong, although the USMG quickly suppressed them. When in May 1948 elections were held for South Korea's Constitutional National Assembly, the leftists and some prominent nationalists boycotted them because they were opposed to the establishment of two separate governments on the peninsula. As a result, the Korea Democratic Party (KDP) representing landlords became the largest party in the Assembly.

Syngman Rhee forged a conservative coalition with the KDP and was elected president by the National Assembly. However, President Rhee began to distance himself from the KDP and surprisingly appointed Cho Bong-am, a former communist, as Minister for Agriculture. Although the KDP attempted to increase compensation to three times annual yield, the assembly passed the land reform Bill, with compensation set at 150 per cent of yield. When President Rhee signed the Bill into law on 10 March 1950, he urged the administrators to implement the redistribution of lands quickly, apparently because he wished to weaken his main opposition, the landlord-dominated KDP, in the approaching 30 May elections (Kim 1995). Furthermore, as an opponent of communism, President Rhee was also motivated in favour of land reform because he agreed with the Americans that such reform would negate what would have been an effective propaganda tool for communist North Korea (Kim 2009).

Civil Service Reform (1950s–1990s)

Previous developmental state literature exclusively credited Park Chung-hee with the establishment of a meritocratic and autonomous bureaucracy, and with overhauling the patronage-ridden bureaucracy of the Syngman Rhee period (Kim 1987; Cheng et al. 1998; Evans 1995). However, my own research has revealed that meritocracy developed gradually over time and that the short-lived Chang Myon government (1960–61) made a no less important contribution than did Park (You 2015: 149–57; You 2017).

Previous studies have focused on the proportion of special appointments as against appointments arising from competitive civil service examinations for higher entry-level positions (Grade III-B level). Byung-kook Kim (1987: 101) has argued that the proportion of higher entry-level positions filled by candidates who had taken higher civil service examinations 'quintupled' from 4.1 per cent to 20.6 per cent between the Rhee and Park periods, and his study has been cited many times by other scholars. However, Kim's comparison was based on the average for the whole Rhee period (1948–60) but the average for only the last three years of Park's rule (1977–79). That is misleading because there were large differences between the first few years of building the new bureaucracy and the later years of the Rhee period, just as there were between the earlier and later years of the Park period.

In fact, the proportion of meritocratic recruitment through competitive civil service examination for higher entry-level positions (Grade III-B) increased from 4.7 per cent during the first few years of new bureaucracy building (1948–52) to 48.3 per cent during the later years of the Rhee period (1953–59). The proportion actually dropped slightly to 35.6–38.3 per cent in the early period of Park Chung-hee (1964–65), but then increased again to 55.0 per cent (1966–73) and to 65.2 per cent in the last three years of his presidency (1977–79). It further increased to 70.4 per cent after the transition to democracy (1988–95).

That all rather contradicts the myth that Park established a meritocratic bureaucracy early in his rule. The proportion of recruitment through competitive civil service examinations for Grade III-B was in fact reduced during the early years of Park's regime. That seems to reflect the sizable number of appointments given to former military individuals, as Park apparently compromised the principle of meritocracy in order to secure the loyalty of the military, which he seems to have hoped to do by rewarding them with bureaucratic posts. He perhaps also wished to control the bureaucracy by employing military men-turned-bureaucrats (Ha and Kang 2011). The practice of appointing former members of the armed forces to bureaucratic posts continued under another military dictator, Chun Doo-hwan (1980–87), but was finally abolished in 1988 after democracy was adopted (Bark 1998; Ju and Kim 2006: 262).

In fact, a more important indicator for the development of meritocratic bureaucracy can be found in the recruitment of lower entry-level officials (Grade V-B). A significant development in that regard took place after the Student Revolution; civil service examinations for Grade V-B were first administered in 1960 by the short-lived democratic government led by Prime Minister Chang Myon (1960–61). There was a pressing need to recruit a large number of lower-level civil servants at Grade V-B through open and competitive examination because many had been promoted to higher ranks relatively quickly during the 1950s and 1960s. Until 1959, civil service examinations were restricted to the recruitment of a small number of highly coveted elite bureaucrats at Grades III-B and IV-B. But, beginning in 1960 after the Student Revolution, civil service examinations became widely accessible to thousands of young applicants every year, opening up a wide road to posts in the bureaucracy (You 2017).

The above discussion suggests the gradual development of a meritocracy during the later years of Rhee (1953–60), democratic Chang (1960–61), Park (1961–79) and post-Park periods, and even more after the democratic transition in 1987. In addition, a series of reforms were implemented to advance professional bureaucracy. They included the assurance of political neutrality, the legalization of public unions and the introduction of parliamentary hearings for the appointment of ministers (Ju and Kim 2006).

What was it, then, that made it possible for South Korea to develop meritocracy over time? Some scholars have emphasized the influence of a Confucian tradition of bureaucracy in Korea (Cumings 1984; Evans 1995; Kim 1987; Lie 1998; Woo-Cumings 1995), while others have mentioned the positive effect of Japanese colonial bureaucracy. However, former Japanese colonial bureaucrats had a negative influence on the development of meritocracy because they did not want the rapid expansion of meritocratic recruitment through civil service examinations, as that would have reduced their own opportunities for promotion (Bark 1966; Lee 1968).[1]

I believe that the rapid expansion of education increased pressure for meritocratic recruitment; and certainly during the 1950s and 1960s such pressure did indeed come mainly from university students and their professors, who often complained about the small number of recruits through competitive civil service examinations (You 2015: 156–7, 166–7). As the number of graduates grew, it became increasingly difficult for them to find work, for jobs in the private sector were neither plentiful nor very attractive. At the same time, there were too few public sector jobs open to candidates in competitive examinations to absorb the new glut of graduates. The Student Democratic Revolution of April 1960 further increased pressure for the expansion of civil service examinations. The Chang Myon government of 1960–61 was the first to introduce examinations for Grade V-B (lower entry-level) civil servants to cater to the new university students (Lee 1996: 111–12). However, even the military junta that seized power by overthrowing the legitimate government could not ignore the students' demand for meritocracy, so the Park regime continued the civil service examinations for Grade V-B and implemented the reforms planned by the Chang Myon government to professionalize the civil service (You 2017).

Land reform too contributed to the development of a meritocratic bureaucracy, even if indirectly, because it gave impetus to the rapid expansion of education. Unlike in the colonial period, opportunities for higher education were no longer restricted to the upper classes. More higher education then led to increased pressure for meritocracy and democracy. Land reform dissolved the landed elite, and thereby helped forestall penetration of the new bureaucracy by a powerful cadre – something often found in societies dominated by a landed elite (Ziblatt 2009). Land reform therefore, by insulating the bureaucracy from powerful societal interests, afforded breathing space for state autonomy to grow (Amsden 1989; Cumings 1984; Evans 1995; Lie 1998; Rodrik 1995; You 2017).

The gradual advance of meritocracy in recruitment and promotion helped spread the norms of impartiality and universalism and reduce corruption within the bureaucracy. The ratio of public officials indicted for corruption to public officials indicted for all crimes has steadily declined from 36.8 per cent in the 1950s under President Rhee to 17.2 per cent in the 1960s and 16.1 per cent in the 1970s under President Park. Since then that figure has been reduced to 14.3 per cent under President Chun in the early 1980s and then 3.6 per cent in the 2000s under President Roh Moo-hyun (You 2015: 170–71). In the 1950s, if a public official were indicted the probability would have been more than 1 in 3 that the charges would have related to corruption. In the 2000s, that probability would be only 1 in 30. It is noteworthy that development of meritocracy and reduced relative numbers of bureaucrats prosecuted for corruption are highly correlated.

Democratization (1960, 1987)

South Korea's constitution introduced democratic institutions, and the country was an electoral democracy from 1948 to 1961 and again from 1963 to 1972. However, South Korea was never a liberal democracy until the democratic transition of 1987, except for the one-year period after the Student Revolution of 19 April 1960. Basic rights as well as universal suffrage were granted under the 1948 constitution, but President Rhee became increasingly authoritarian throughout his 12-year presidency. The Rhee regime was quick to suppress opposition, conveniently abusing the National Security Law; neither did Rhee hesitate to amend the constitution unlawfully or manipulate elections to perpetuate his rule.

However, popular demand for democracy steadily increased, and the expansion of education too produced anti-authoritarian forces among students and intellectuals. Student demonstrations against an enormous amount of electoral fraud during the 1960 presidential election escalated into the Student Democratic Revolution of 19 April 1960, which led to the resignation of Syngman Rhee. But the democratic period did not last long, for Chang Myon's democratic government was overthrown in May 1961 by a military junta led by General Park Chung-hee.

Park Chung-hee ruled Korea from 1961 to 1979 as a formally civilian president for most of the time, but he packed both the ruling party's leadership positions and the bureaucracy with military men, and it was his regime that established the Korean Central Intelligence Agency (KCIA), which became notorious for its persecution of dissidents and violations of human rights. When Park found no constitutional path beyond his third term, he declared martial law, disbanded the National Assembly and tore up the existing constitution in the name of *Yushin* (reform) in October 1972. The Yushin Constitution abolished direct presidential elections, effectively guaranteeing Park the presidency for life. However, the anti-dictatorship student movement continued to grow in spite of harsh suppression, and popular support for the authoritarian Park regime declined.

After Park's assassination by KCIA chief Kim Jae-kyu in 1979, there was another short period of democratic opening, called the 'Seoul Spring'. Then in 1980 a military junta led by General Chun Doo-hwan seized power through a two-stage coup and by bloody suppression of the Kwangju democratization movement. Meanwhile, in spite of all this democratization movements continued to grow. Industrialization and economic growth meant that the middle and working classes increased in number, and their organizations grew and their voices became louder. When in 1987 hundreds of thousands of citizens including students and blue- and white-collar workers came out onto the streets all over the country in support of democracy, President Chun could do nothing but accede to their key demands, including those for direct presidential elections.

What then led to the eventual success of democratization movements in 1987, when earlier efforts had failed? University students constituted the core of the organized forces in the movement for democratization which confronted the military–*chaebol* coalition. A growing educated urban middle class played an important role, particularly in the large demonstrations of 1987 demanding direct presidential elections. It is clear too that the security threat from North Korea was by now perceived to have declined, and the new confidence created more favourable conditions for democratization than had existed earlier.

While both the earlier democratic episode (1960–61) and the Seoul Spring after the assassination of Park Chung-hee in 1979 were short-lived, and both were brought to an end by military intervention, they nevertheless had some constraining effects on the subsequent authoritarian regimes of

Park Chung-hee and Chun Doo-hwan. Both Park and Chun were obliged to publicize their efforts to punish corruption as well as demonstrate their commitment to economic development in order to fill their 'legitimacy deficit'. They also had to accommodate the demands of university students and professors, such as the expansion of the system of examinations for civil service applicants. However, it was inevitable that the reliance of both those authoritarian regimes on clientelistic strategies increased not only petty electoral corruption but high-level political corruption too, and collusion between the government and *chaebol* (Schopf 2004).

Democratic Consolidation and Deepening: Good Governance Reforms (1987–)

Unlike the earlier democratic episodes in 1960–61 and 1979–80, the democratic transition of 1987 was more resilient and proceeded towards democratic consolidation and deepening. Democratic consolidation required first and foremost the establishment of firm civilian control over the armed forces, followed by entrenchment of the rule of law and empowerment of civil society. Civil society organizations pushed for governance reforms to embrace ethical universalism, and governments implemented various reforms to improve transparency and fight corruption.

In fact, the armed forces did restrain themselves during the democratic transition in 1987. Between 1993 and 1997 President Kim Young-sam, the first civilian president since Syngman Rhee, successfully purged a group of politically ambitious military officers, while the former presidents Chun Doo-whan and Roh Tae-woo were prosecuted for treason and corruption and convicted in 1996. That sent a strong message to the military that the leaders of even successful coups would eventually be punished; not a single coup has been attempted since the democratic transition. Democracy also provided checks on arbitrary state violence, while at the same time militant social movements declined and lost their influence, allowing peaceful movements to become more influential. The rule of law was strengthened and improved, with the Constitutional Court in particular playing an important role in protecting human rights and, importantly, property rights.

During the authoritarian period, policy processes were closed and opaque and the powerful executive dominated both the making and implementing of policy practically without constraint from either the legislature or the judiciary. The reverse was true after democratization, as policy processes became increasingly transparent and open. The power of the legislature and the independence of the judiciary were steadily strengthened.

During the Kim Young-sam administration a number of new laws such

as the Freedom of Information Act and Administrative Procedures Act
contributed to enhancing the transparency and openness of the government. In particular, the passing of the Real Name Financial Transaction
Act enhanced the transparency of finance flow by outlawing accounts in
false or 'borrowed' names. President Kim Dae-jung (1998–2002) implemented far-reaching reforms to increase transparency in both public and
corporate sectors. He and his successor, President Roh Moo-hyun (2003–
07), put in place a series of reforms to enhance the openness of the government, particularly e-governance, and to ensure the transparency of the
budget (You and Lee 2013). Indeed, South Korea's e-governance systems,
including its online procurement system and online public engagement
system, are now internationally recognized as models of good governance
(Kalinowski and Kim 2014). Consolidated central government fiscal data,
budget and audit reports approved by the National Assembly and the data
for each local government are all available online. Participatory budgeting
was first introduced by certain leftist local governments in 2002 and has
since been rolled out to all local governments. During the conservative
Lee Myung-bak government (2008–12) there was some regression, such
as the circumvention of feasibility studies for the controversial Four River
Projects (Lee and You 2014). However, South Korea is regarded as one
of the top performers in budget transparency in the Asia-Pacific region,
according to the Open Budget Index (IBP 2012). In the 2012 OBI, the
country ranked eighth of 100 countries surveyed, and was second in the
Asia-Pacific region behind only New Zealand.

President Kim (1993–97) also launched an aggressive anti-corruption
campaign. He declared that he would receive no money from business
during his presidency, while introducing mandatory disclosure of the personal assets of senior public officials. He also oversaw the prosecution of a
number of powerful politicians on corruption charges, which culminated
in the prosecution of the two former presidents (You 2003).

The Anti-Corruption Act, which includes a code of conduct for civil
servants, was passed into law in 2001 during Kim Dae-jung's government,
which was in office from 1998 to 2002. The law also provides protection
and rewards for whistle-blowers in the public sector; protection of whistle-
blowers was expanded in 2011 to cover those in the private sector too.
The Korea Independent Commission Against Corruption – renamed the
Anti-Corruption and Civil Rights Commission after a merger with the
Administrative Appeals Commission and the Ombudsman of Korea in
2008 – was created in 2002. The independent anti-corruption agency pre-
pares an annual evaluation of the anti-corruption activities of government
agencies and makes recommendations (Lee and Jung 2010).

Surprisingly, and for the first time in Korean history, President Roh

Moo-hyun encouraged the prosecution service to conduct a thorough investigation of illegal presidential campaign funds – with shocking results (You 2015: 110–11). It was found that a number of *chaebol* had delivered lorry-loads of cash to the conservative opposition candidate, Lee Hoi-chang. Lee's illegal fundraising totalled 82.3 billion *won*, while Roh's had amounted to 12 billion *won*. The prosecution of illegal presidential campaign funds had a heavy impact on the behaviour of political parties, politicians and the *chaebol*. In addition, there was further reform of political and campaign finance that required more transparent fundraising and expenditure. Thanks to a series of reforms under Kim Young-sam, Kim Dae-jung and Roh Moo-hyun, the *chaebol*'s practice of routinely delivering billions of *won* to the president seems to have disappeared. Although corporate and political corruption scandals still occur, they have tended to be of smaller scale than before.

After the Sewol Ferry accident of March 2014, which revealed the problem of entrenched regulatory capture and corruption, the need for additional anti-corruption laws has been debated (You and Park 2017). An Act for Banning Illegitimate Solicitations and Gifts was passed in March 2015 to strengthen ethical requirements for public officials by criminalizing receipt of monetary or material benefits of more than a million *won* (roughly equivalent to $1,000) even if not as quid pro quo for a specific favour.

Democratization facilitated the growth of civil society generally, and an empowerment of civil society that encourages universalism has been an important factor in contemporary control of corruption in South Korea. Civil society actions have been behind a number of transparency and anti-corruption laws and programmes (You 2003). NGOs such as the Citizens' Coalition for Economic Justice (CCEJ) and the People's Solidarity for Participatory Democracy (PSPD) have fought for broad political, economic and social reforms to promote the norms of ethical universalism. Good governance organizations such as Transparency International-Korea have focused their work on monitoring political and corporate corruption and advocating government transparency and openness. These organizations' enduring legislative campaigns were largely responsible for the enactment of the real-name financial transaction system, freedom of information and anti-corruption laws. Moreover, the prosecution of the two corrupt former presidents would not have happened without the actions of organized civil society, considering that President Kim Young-sam was initially reluctant to prosecute them.

Civil society groups played an important role in reducing vote buying and clientelism as well as promoting programmatic politics. They established a wide coalition of fair-election campaigns, beginning with the 1991 local elections (You 2003). They created a coalition of anti-money politics in 1996, pressuring politicians to regulate campaign finance transparently. In 2000, before the upcoming National Assembly elections, the CCEJ released a list of unfit candidates, most of whom had been convicted or accused of corruption. Subsequently, a large civil society coalition demanded that political parties should not nominate them, and indeed the political parties then decided not to nominate many on the list. Of 86 blacklisted candidates who did receive party nomination or stood as independents, 59 were defeated at the polls. At the 2004 National Assembly elections, 129 of 206 candidates blacklisted by the civil society coalition went on to lose their election (Kim 2006). The negative campaigns therefore demonstrated the effectiveness of the concerted action of civil society. Political parties repeatedly had to take measures to remove corrupt elements, including the reform of nomination criteria and procedures.

Civil society organizations played a role in promoting programmatic competition too. In 1992, the CCEJ first published a book on the '54 reform agenda', which included the real-name financial transaction system and the Freedom of Information Act (You 2003), and pressed the presidential candidates to state their positions on the agenda. Many organizations followed suit in subsequent national elections. Recently however, the conservative governments of Lee Myung-bak and Park Geun-hye have been less accommodating to civil society demands and have increased suppression of critics, abusing the criminal law of defamation (Haggard and You 2015; You 2014a). However, the now established and vibrant civil society in Korea is likely to remain an important constraint on the abuse of executive power.

Democratic Deepening: Reform of Crony Capitalism (1998–)

Although sweeping land reform in South Korea dissolved the landlord class and created reasonably egalitarian socio-economic structures, Park Chung-hee's choice of a *chaebol*-centred industrial policy increased economic concentration and collusion between government and business. Park's idea of emulating Japanese pre-war conglomerates, or *zaibatsu*,[2] coupled with the launch of the drive to develop heavy industry led the government to concentrate the award of its favours to the large *chaebol*. At first the government could control the *chaebol*, but in time rather too-cosy relations developed between them. The government in fact often bailed out the troubled *chaebol* at the taxpayers' expense, until the authoritarian rulers came increasingly to rely on the *chaebol*'s illicit political contribution to supply their clientelistic resources. The result was that the latter became more and more able to capture the former (Kang 2002; Schopf 2004).

As the size and power of the *chaebols* grew, the Chun Doo-hwan government (1980–87) began to take measures to promote gradual economic liberalization. The Monopoly Regulation and Fair Trade Act was introduced to counter the market power of the *chaebols*, but the law was not vigorously enforced. The *chaebols* grew even bigger and concentration increased. Combined sales of the top ten *chaebols*, as a percentage of GDP, grew from 15.1 per cent in 1974 to 32.8 per cent in 1979 to 67.4 per cent in 1984 (Amsden 1989: 116, 134–7).

Democratization provided both opportunities and constraints for reform of the *chaebol*-dominated economy (Kalinowski 2009). On the one hand, popular demand rose for the reform of the *chaebol*'s abuse of both market and non-market power. On the other hand, major political parties and politicians were forced to rely on the *chaebols*' illicit contributions in order to be able to finance their electoral campaigns. Hence, the *chaebols*' political influence grew and the policy-making process was increasingly captured by them. At the time, political and social organizations that might have been able to counterbalance *chaebol* influence simply were not yet strong enough. The government was therefore unable to contain the *chaebols*' moral hazard, and their belief that they had become 'too big to fail' (TBTF) led to overinvestment and over-borrowing, including a build-up of excessive short-term foreign debt. As a result, the Korean economy fell victim to the East Asian financial crisis of 1997 after a series of bankruptcies of over-leveraged *chaebols*.

The breakthrough for reform in fact came with the financial crisis. The conditions attached by the International Monetary Fund (IMF) to the bailout loan acted as strong external pressure, but in any case newly elected and reform-minded president Kim Dae-jung launched a comprehensive reform programme that went beyond the IMF-mandated reforms. President Kim pursued a policy of 'parallel development of democracy and market economy' and declared the end of collusion between government and business, or 'crony capitalism' (You 2010).

The sweeping economic reforms of the Kim government increased both openness and competition in the economy (Mo and Weingast 2013), and with 16 of the 30 largest *chaebol* groups disappearing in a restructuring process market discipline was significantly strengthened. There was substantial improvement in the transparency and accountability of corporate governance and the protection of minority shareholders. Korean financial markets have been completely restructured, reducing the scope for rents originating from bank loans, while many new economic players such as banks, foreign investors and institutional investors began to act independently of the government and the *chaebols*. Such economic reform both weakened the collusive links of government–*chaebol*–banks and increased the transparency of *chaebol* management.

Chaebol concentration, which peaked in 1998, declined in the subsequent years. However, the reform was not as thorough as was originally intended and *chaebol* concentration rose again. The ratio of *chaebol* assets to GDP fell from 90 per cent in 1998 to approximately 50 per cent in 2002, but by 2010 it had again reached the pre-crisis level (Kim 2011). Income inequality increased too; in particular, the top 1 per cent's income share rose rapidly, surpassing 12 per cent in 2011, and has continued to rise since (Kim and Kim 2014). Corporate governance deteriorated again during the business-friendly government of Lee Myung-bak (2008–12) when, according to the Asian Corporate Governance Association (2015), South Korea's corporate governance score declined from 55–58 in 2003–04 to 45–49 in 2010–12. In 2012 Korea ranked not only behind Japan, Taiwan, Singapore and Hong Kong, but also behind Thailand, Malaysia and India. The poor corporate governance in the country indicates that crony capitalism is still alive and well.

Why, then, was Kim Dae-jung able to implement substantial reform of the corporate and financial sectors, and why has that reform been regressing recently? For one thing, Kim Dae-jung was less constrained by the influence of *chaebol* than his predecessors had been. Plus, the timing was right. Because of the grave financial crisis and the humiliating IMF bailout, the *chaebol* were on the defensive, and civil society organizations that had been pushing for reform of *chaebol* corporate governance were able to gain the upper hand. In particular, the PSPD organized a minority shareholder movement to hold *chaebol* chairmen and CEOs to account (Jang 2001). The Kim government's tacit coalition with civil society groups then proved powerful enough to overcome *chaebol* resistance, at least for the first two years or so of his term.

However, the *chaebol* soon regained their political influence and the reform coalition lost power as the worst of the crisis passed. One important reason for the decline of the coalition for reform was the alienation and weakening of organized labour. The Kim government's 'IMF-plus' reform package included measures to increase flexibility in the labour market, which eventually led to a breakdown of the Tripartite Commission that President Kim himself had formed to push for the comprehensive reform programme. On the other hand, the top *chaebol* groups such as Samsung, Hyundai and LG, having survived the crisis, became even more dominant players in the market, and their political influence was strengthened. It is commonly believed that both Hyundai and Samsung had close ties with the Kim Dae-jung and Roh Moo-hyun governments. Moreover, when Lee Myung-bak, formerly CEO of a Hyundai company, became the president of Korea in 2008 his government almost created a *chaebol* republic. Not surprisingly, Lee retreated from some of the important reforms of the previous governments, relaxing the regulations on *chaebol* corporate governance and domination of the financial sector. Lee also granted tax cuts to both the *chaebol* and the wealthy.

During the 2012 legislative elections and presidential election, all the major parties and major presidential candidates pledged to introduce significant reform of the *chaebol* in the name of 'economic democracy'. However, President Park Geun-hye failed to make any significant progress towards it. Instead, she was impeached due to her involvement in a corruption scandal involving the *chaebol*. It remains to be seen if South Korea will be able to implement significant reform for *economic democracy* in the near future or will fall into a *captured democracy*, using Acemoglu and Robinson's term dating from 2008.

6.5   CONCLUSION

During the second half of the twentieth century South Korea transformed itself from a poor and corrupt country into a rich and democratic country enjoying relatively good governance. It is regarded as one of the three East Asian countries which, like Japan, have either completed the transition from a 'limited access order' to an 'open access order' or, like Taiwan, have moved a long way towards it. In an open access order, governance of the polity and economy is based on equality and impartiality, or norms of ethical universalism (North et al. 2009). The process-tracing of the transition, albeit incomplete and even fragile, indicates that the transformation of governance norms was more than just a by-product of economic development, for it took place within a broader context of change in the political economy of the country.

In particular, I have identified five critical reforms:

1. the radical land reform that took place in two stages in 1948 and 1950, which dissolved the landed elite and produced favourable conditions for state autonomy as well as rapid expansion of education;
2. the gradual process of civil service reform, which improved meritocracy in bureaucracy and thereby reduced bureaucratic corruption;
3. democratization (1960, 1987), which required long struggles by civil society led by student movements and supported by the growing middle and working classes;
4. good governance reforms intended to enhance transparency and control corruption, particularly under presidents Kim Young-sam (1993–97), Kim Dae-jung (1998–2002) and Roh Moo-hyun (2003–07);

5. reform of the corporate and financial sectors by Kim Dae-jung's government in the aftermath of the financial crisis of 1997, which was aimed at ending crony capitalism and enhancing the transparency of *chaebol* governance and market competition.

None of the reforms just happened of their own accord; nor was any simply gifted to the people by a benevolent dictator. Each reform was achieved at least partly by the concerted efforts of civil society, and in turn helped empower civil society. The historical experiences of South Korea show the importance of both structural conditions and human agency. However, even favourable structural conditions like the dissolution of the landed elite and the development of an egalitarian socio-economic structure did not occur 'naturally'. Instead, human agency was essential, along with the capacity of politicians and civil society actors to overcome the collective action problem.

However, South Korea's recent records on corruption and corporate governance, as well as some backsliding in freedom of speech and civil liberties, have raised concerns about the stalling of further progress towards ethical universalism, if not of a reversion to particularism of a 'limited access order'. The recent political corruption scandal that involved President Park Geun-hye (2013–17) and the country's largest conglomerates, including Samsung, shows the weaknesses in this regard; but the peaceful candlelight rallies of millions of people that led to the impeachment of the president indicates that there are very high normative constraints stemming from the civil society. South Korea's vibrant civil society provides grounds for optimism at the prospect of the eventual completion of transition to an open access order with ethical universalism, but there is a degree of uncertainty about whether and how the country will move forward.

NOTES

1. Author's interview with an old retired bureaucrat corroborates this argument.
2. Both the Korean word *chaebol* and the Japanese word *zaibatsu* share the same Chinese characters, 財閥.

REFERENCES

Acemoglu, D., and Robinson, J. (2008). Persistence of Power, Elites, and Institutions. *American Economic Review* **98**(1), pp. 267–93.

Amsden, A.H. (1989). *Asia's Next Giant: South Korea and Late Industrialization.* New York: Oxford University Press.

Asian Corporate Governance Association. (2015). CG Watch. [online] Hong Kong: ACGA. Available at: www.acga-asia.org/content.cfm?SITE_CONTENT_TYPE_ID=19#cg [accessed 15 June 2015].

Ban, S., Moon, P., and Perkins, D. (1980). *Rural Development: Studies in the Modernization of the Republic of Korea, 1945–1975.* Cambridge, MA: Harvard University Press.

Bark, D. (박동서). (1966). 신규채용과 승진: 인사행정상의문제점(New Recruitments and Promotions: Problems in Personnel Administration).*사법행정* (*Judicial Administration*) **7**(7), pp. 9–11.

Bark, D. (박동서). (1998). 고급 공무원의 성분 변화 (Changes in Social Background of the Higher Civil Servants). *행정논총* (*Korea Journal of Public Administration*) **30**(1), pp. 181–201.

Cheng, T., Haggard, S., and Kang, D. (1998.) Institutions and Growth in Korea and Taiwan: The Bureaucracy. *Journal of Development Studies* **34**(6), pp. 87–111.

Cumings, B. (1984). The Origins and Development of the Northeast Asian Political Economy: Industrial Sectors, Product Cycles and Political Consequences. *International Organization* **38**(1), pp. 1–40.

Dahlström, C., Teorell, J., and Lapuente, V. (2012). The Merit of Meritocratization: Politics, Bureaucracy, and the Institutional Deterrents of Corruption. *Political Research Quarterly* **65**(3), pp. 658–70.

Edelman. (2015). 2015 Edelman Trust Barometer. [online] Available at: www.edelman.com/2015-edelman-trust-barometer-2/trust-and-innovation-edelman-trust-barometer/global-results/ [accessed 21 June 2015].

Evans, P. (1995). *Embedded Autonomy: States and Industrial Transformation.* Princeton, NJ: Princeton University Press.

Evans, P., and Rauch, J. (1999). Bureaucracy and Growth: A Cross-National Analysis of the Effects of 'Weberian' State Structures on Economic Growth. *American Sociological Review* **64**(5), pp. 748–65.

Ha, Y., and Kang, M. (2011). Creating a Capable Bureaucracy with Loyalists: The Internal Dynamics of the South Korean Developmental State, 1948–1979. *Comparative Political Studies* **44**(1), pp. 78–108.

Haggard, S., and You, J. (2015). Freedom of Expression in South Korea. *Journal of Contemporary Asia* **45**(1), pp. 167–79.

Hong, S. (행정논총). (2001). 농지개혁 전후의 대지주 동향 (Responses of the Landlords before and after the Land Reform). In: Hong, Song-Chan (홍성찬) (ed.), *농지개혁 연구* (*Studies of Agrarian Land Reform*). Seoul: Yonsei University Press.

International Budget Partnership. (2012). *Open Budget Index.* [online] Available at: http://survey.internationalbudget.org/ [accessed 21 May 2013].

Jang, H. (2001). Corporate Governance and Economic Development: The Korean Experience. In: Iqbal, F. and You, J. (eds), *Democracy, Market Economics, and Development: An Asian Perspective*, Washington, DC: World Bank.

Ju, G., and Kim, M. (주경일 김미나). (2006). *Understanding of Personnel Administration System in Korean Bureaucracy* (*한국관료제 인사행정체제의이해*). Seoul: Gyongsewon (경세원).

Kalinowski, T. (2009). The Politics of Market Reforms: Korea's Path from Chaebol Republic to Market Democracy and Back. *Contemporary Politics* **15**(3), pp. 287–304.

Kalinowski, T., and Kim, S. (2014). *Corruption and Anti-Corruption Policies in Korea*. Hamburg: GIGA.

Kang, D. (2002). *Crony Capitalism: Corruption and Development in South Korea and the Philippines*. Cambridge: Cambridge University Press.

Kang, W.T. (2008). How Ideology Divides Generations: The 2002 and 2004 South Korean Elections. *Canadian Journal of Political Science* **41**(2), pp. 461–80.

Keefer, P. (2007). Clientelism, Credibility, and the Policy Choices of Young Democracies. *American Journal of Political Science* **51**(4), pp. 804–21.

Keefer, P., and Vlaicu, R. (2008). Democracy, Credibility and Clientelism *Journal of Law, Economics and Organization* **24**(2), pp. 371–406.

Kim, A. (2006). Civic Activism and Korean Democracy: The Impact of Blacklisting Campaigns in the 2000 and 2004 General Elections. *Pacific Review* **19**(4), pp. 519–42.

Kim, B. (1987). *Bringing and Managing Socioeconomic Change: The State in Korea and Mexico*. PhD dissertation, Harvard University, Cambridge, MA.

Kim, H. (2014). Intergenerational Mobility and the Role of Education in Korea. Korea Development Institute paper. [online] Available at: www.kdi.re.kr/upload/10152/Paper_14.pdf [accessed 14 May 2017].

Kim, I. (김일영). (1995). 농지개혁, 5.30 선거, 그리고 한국전쟁 (Agrarian Land Reform, May 30 Elections, and the Korean War). 한국과 국제정치 (*Korea and International Politics*) **21**, pp. 301–35.

Kim, N., and Kim, J. (2014). Top Incomes in Korea, 1933–2010: Evidence from Income Tax Statistics. Naksungdae Institute of Economic Research Working Paper 2014-03.

Kim, S. (2011). Concentration of Economic Power by Korean *Chaebols*: Engines of Growth or Threats to Democracy? Working paper, Hansung University, Seoul, Korea.

Kim, S. (김성호). (2009). 이승만과 농지개혁 (Syngman Rhee and Land Reform). 한국논단 (*Hanguknondan*) 9, pp. 174–7.

Lee, H. (1968). *Korea: Time, Change, and Administration*. Honolulu: East-West Center Press.

Lee, H. (1996). *Lee Han-Been's Memoir: Working and Thinking* (이한빈 회고록: 일하며 생각하며). Seoul: Chosunilbosa.

Lee, S.Y., and Jung, K. (2010). Public Service Ethics and Anticorruption in South Korea. In: Berman, E., Moon, M., and Choi, H. (eds), *Public Administration in East Asia: Mainland China, Japan, South Korea, Taiwan*. Boca Raton, FL: CRC Press, pp. 401–25.

Lee, W., and You, J. (2014). Budget Participation in South Korea. Paper delivered to International Budget Partnership.

Lie, J. (1998). *Han Unbound: The Political Economy of South Korea*. Stanford, CA: Stanford University Press.

Mason, E., et al. (1980). *The Economic and Social Modernization of the Republic of Korea*. Cambridge, MA: Harvard University Press.

McGinn, N., et al. (1980). *Education and Development in Korea*. Cambridge, MA: Council on East Asian Studies, Harvard University.

Mitchell, C. (1949). Land Reform in South Korea. *Pacific Affairs* **22**(2), pp. 144–54.

Mo, J., and Weingast, B. (2013). *Korean Political and Economic Development: Crisis, Security, and Institutional Rebalancing*. Cambridge, MA: Harvard University Asia Center.

Moon, W. (2005). Decomposition of Regional Voting in South Korea: Ideological Conflicts and Regional Interests. *Party Politics* **11**(5), pp. 579–99.

Mungiu-Pippidi, A. (2006). Corruption: Diagnosis and Treatment. *Journal of Democracy* **17**(3), pp. 86–99.

North, D., Wallis, J., and Weingast, B. (2009). *Violence and Social Orders: A Conceptual Framework for Interpreting Recorded Human History.* New York: Cambridge University Press.

Oh, S. (오성배). (2004). 사립대학 팽창과정 탐색: 해방후 농지개혁기를 중심으로 (Exploration of Private University Expansion Process: Based on Land Reform after the Liberation). *KEDI 학술마당 (KEDI Research Reports)* KD 2004-31-03: 1–20.

Park, S.D. (박석두) (1987). 농지개혁과 식민지 지주제의 해체: 경주 이씨가의 토지경영 사례를 중심으로 (Agrarian Land Reform and the Dissolution of Colonial Landlord System: The Case of Gyungjoo Lee Family's Land Management). *경제사학 (Studies in Economic History)* **11**, pp. 187–281.

Rauch, J., and Evans, P. (2000). Bureaucratic Structure and Bureaucratic Performance in Less-Developed Countries. *Journal of Public Economics* **75**(1), pp. 49–71.

Rodrik, D. (1995). Getting Interventions Right: How South Korea and Taiwan Grew Rich. *Economic Policy* **20**, pp. 55–107.

Schopf, J. (2004). *Corruption and Democratization in the Republic of Korea: The End of Political Bank Robbery.* PhD dissertation, University of California, San Diego.

Seong, K.R. (성경륭) (2015). Emergence of the Dual Cleavage Structure and Changes in Voting Mechanisms: Focusing on the 18th Presidential Election (이중균열구조의 등장과 투표기제의 변화 : 1 8 대 대통령선거를 중심으로). Draft.

Teorell, J,. Dahlström C., and Dahlberg, S. (2011). *The QoG Expert Survey Dataset.* University of Gothenburg: Quality of Government Institute. Available at: www. qog.pol.gu.se [accessed 24 November 2014].

Woo-Cumings, M. (1995). The Korean Bureacratic State: Historical Legacies and Comparative Perspectives. In: Cotton, J. (ed.), *Politics and Policy in the New Korean State: From Roh Tae-Woo to Kim Young-Sam.* New York: St. Martin's Press, pp. 141–69.

World Bank. (1993). *The East Asian Miracle: Economic Growth and Public Policy.* New York: Oxford University Press.

You, J.I. (1998). Income Distribution and Growth in East Asia. *Journal of Development Studies* **34**(6), pp. 37–65.

You, J.I. (2010). Political Economy of Economic Reform in South Korea. Working paper.

You, J.S. (2003). The Role of Civil Society in Combating Corruption in South Korea. Paper presented at the International Anti-Corruption Conference, Seoul, May.

You, J.S. (2012). Transition from a Limited Access Order to an Open Access Order: The Case of South Korea. In: North, D., et al (eds), *In the Shadow of Violence: The Problem of Development for Limited Access Order Societies.* Cambridge: Cambridge University Press, pp. 293–327.

You, J.S. (유종성). (2014a). Korean Democracy and Freedom of Expression: Crisis of Liberal Democracy (한국민주주의와 표현의 자유: 자유민주주의의위기). *Trends and Prospects (동향과 전망)* **90**, pp. 9–44.

You, J.S. (2014b). Land Reform, Inequality, and Corruption: A Comparative Historical Study of Korea, Taiwan, and the Philippines. *Korean Journal of International Studies* **12**, pp. 191–224.

You, J.S. (2015). *Democracy, Inequality, and Corruption: Korea, Taiwan, and the Philippines Compared.* Cambridge: Cambridge University Press.

You, J.S. (2017). Demystifying the Park Chung-Hee Myth: Land Reform in the Evolution of Korea's Developmental State. *Journal of Contemporary Asia.* Advance online publication. DOI: 10.1080/00472336.2017.1334221.

You, J.S., and Lee, W. (2013). Budget Transparency and Participation in South Korea. In: Khagram, S., Fung, A., and de Renzio, P. (eds), *Open Budgets: The Political Economy of Transparency, Participation, and Accountability.* Washington, DC: Brookings Institution, pp. 105–29.

You, J.S., and Park, Y.M (2017). The Legacies of State Corporatism in Korea: Regulatory Capture in the Sewol Ferry Tragedy. *Journal of East Asian Studies* **17**(1), pp. 95–118.

Ziblatt, D. (2009). Shaping Democratic Practice and the Causes of Electoral Fraud: The Case of Nineteenth-Century Germany. *American Political Science Review* **103**(1), pp. 1–21.

7. Tracing Taiwan's road to good governance

Christian Göbel

7.1 INTRODUCTION

In 1997, when the World Bank and Transparency International first rated Taiwan in its Corruption Perception Index (CPI), the country was in the upper tercile on both scales. In 2016 it ranked 30 out of 168 countries on the CPI and its percentile rank with the World Bank was as high as 82. Taiwan is not rated by the Index of Public Integrity (IPI), as some indicators are missing, but the Bertelsmann Transformation Index (BTI) gives it the highest possible score for 'protection of abuse of office' (Bertelsmann Foundation 2013). At the same time, the number of people who report that they have themselves experienced corruption is low – on par with countries such as Germany, France and Austria (Transparency International 2011). Although the overwhelming majority of people have not experienced corruption directly, some pessimism persists in Taiwan's population.

The negative perceptions of Taiwan's corruption might in fact be shaped by the very instances where anti-corruption worked well, such as the arrest of politicians and businessmen – and ultimately their convictions. While it is regrettable that a number of high-level officials, judges, legislators and even a former president have been found to be corrupt, there is reason for optimism that they were indicted by their own governments. That these are obviously not cases of political revenge implies that ethical universalism, in other words equal and fair treatment of everyone by the government, is on the rise in Taiwan. No matter how widespread corruption might be in fact, the likelihood that corrupt activities are detected, investigated and punished has increased significantly since the mid-1990s.

Since Taiwan became a democracy in 1992, and especially after the change in ruling parties in 2000, the passage of new laws and reform of existing ones has defined more clearly than ever what constitutes 'corrupt' behaviour, and legal changes have followed international norms. Moreover, since the change in ruling parties judicial independence has been guaranteed and anti-corruption agencies have been strengthened considerably.

Despite the fact that there is still corruption, and that the institutional configuration of Taiwan's anti-corruption agencies is far from the optimum, those are major achievements.

This chapter explains those achievements by analysing the impact on agency in Taiwan's anti-corruption reforms felt at the two turning points in Taiwan's history, which occurred first with democratization and then with the change in ruling parties. It does so by applying the methodology of process-tracing, which investigates the historical developments around those two 'critical junctures' in Taiwan's history while taking into consideration certain enabling and constraining factors 'inherited' from the authoritarian era.

The main findings are as follows: first, as implied above, there was not one but two critical junctures on Taiwan's road towards ethical universalism. Second, although most breakthroughs in the fight against corruption were achieved with the change of ruling parties, I will show that a distinction needs to be made between how parties as collective actors and how individuals within those parties behaved. That might seem a trivial point, but the importance of agency can be seen from attempts by influential individuals in both parties to change or subvert their party's dominant strategy. Added to that, arguably the inability to distinguish between systematic and individualized corruption is the cause of many misconceptions in the general population. Third, and relatedly, I will show that agency matters in that the strengths and weaknesses of the various ministers of justice had a large impact on the development of Taiwan's anti-corruption policies. Perhaps most important is the fourth point, that control of corruption is inseparable from improvements in the rule of law. Indeed, the professionalization and independence of Taiwan's judicial system has probably been the single most important achievement in Taiwan's anti-corruption reforms. Although that point too might seem of lesser importance, few previous studies on Taiwan's anti-corruption have taken it into consideration.

This chapter proceeds as follows. After an introduction to key terms and previous findings, I shall go on to examine the historical factors that had a crucial influence on the development of democratization and the change in ruling parties, before examining those two phenomena in detail. My analysis draws on interviews with present and former ministers and vice-ministers of justice and the director-general of the new Agency Against Corruption (AAC), as well as with legislators, chief prosecutors and assistant prosecutors, investigators, judges and experts, some of whom were already experts in the law when Taiwan became democratized.

7.2   THEORETICAL FRAMEWORK AND METHOD

7.2.1   Studying Anti-Corruption in Taiwan

Corruption and anti-corruption in Taiwan together amount to an enigma. On the one hand indicators that measure corruption based on the perceptions of professionals and ordinary citizens suggest that anti-corruption in Taiwan has been on a roller-coaster. For example the Control of Corruption (CoC) indicator in the World Bank's Worldwide Governance Indicators (WGI) has fluctuated wildly. Within a possible range of −2.5 and +2.5, Taiwan's score rose from 0.59 to 0.86 between 1996 and 2004, fell to 0.48 in 2008, peaked at 0.86 in 2011 and declined again to 0.68 in 2013 (World Bank 2013). Even when taking measurement errors into consideration, results suggesting that corruption lessened, increased and then lessened again remain statistically significant – and is indeed a gloomy picture, which is perpetuated by journalists and scholars alike. Newspapers lash out at the persistence of 'black gold', a term that denotes the twin evils of organized crime and money politics (Chin 2003); and they complain about vote-buying, private sector corruption and the continued influence on national politics of 'local factions', by which they mean family-based clientelist networks (Göbel 2004).

Scholars echo that sentiment. In an earlier contribution (Göbel 2014), I characterized the fight against corruption in Taiwan as an attempt to 'behead the hydra', the mythical creature which, when one of its head is chopped off immediately grows two more in its place. In his insightful monograph, John Quah (2010) shows that Taiwan is plagued by low salaries, red tape and low probability of detection and punishment for corrupt offenders and particularist behaviour like *guanxi*, gift-giving and vote-buying. Quah reveals too that a 'lack of political will in curbing corruption' has pervaded every government with the sole exception of the one under Ma Ying-jeou's presidency, which began in 2008 and ended in 2016. He also points to a good deal of dysfunction in Taiwan's corruption control apparatus, in that anti-corruption is not the task of a single independent agency but is overseen by a number of institutions with overlapping responsibilities, of which the most important are the Ministry of Justice Investigation Bureau (MJIB), the Department of Government Employee Ethics and the Public Prosecutor's Offices. To them should be added the Black Gold Investigation Center (BGIC), which was created in 2001 but later disbanded, and the AAC, which was set up in 2011, the year after Quah's book was published (Göbel 2014).

As one anti-corruption investigator confirms, that diffuse arrangement is far from effective because 'the AAC and the MJIB now snatch away each others' cases'.[1] Although competition can benefit efficiency, it is unlikely to do so for those two organizations because they are obliged to cooperate in investigating corruption. Quah rightly points out that although the AAC is a specialist anti-corruption agency, it has only a fraction of the budget and the manpower of the MJIB, for which anti-corruption is just one of nine major tasks.

Other scholars are more optimistic in their assessments. In a later publication (Göbel 2013), I argued that things had improved as a result of the transition of power from the former ruling party Kuomintang (KMT) to the Minzhu jinbu Dang (Democratic Progressive Party, DPP). For the DPP, which defeated the KMT in the presidential elections in 2000, fighting corruption was a matter of survival, simply because it was used by the KMT to control its supporters. Under DPP rule important legal changes were made, such as the establishment of an anti-corruption task force, and there were frequent crackdowns on corruption and vote-buying. In a recent report for the European Union (EU)-sponsored ANTICORRP project, I (Göbel 2014) showed that indictments and convictions for corruption have increased since 2000, apparently following electoral cycle and perhaps indicating that the DPP abused anti-corruption as a campaign tool. However, at the time I was not able to substantiate his assumption; nor could I answer the question of whether KMT politicians were especially likely to be convicted.

In another important study, Chung-li Wu provides some insight into the question. After analysing nearly 2,400 court decisions in vote-buying cases between 2000 and 2010, Wu was able cautiously to assert that 'there is not necessarily a causal relationship between court verdicts and partisan effects, whether the defendant wins the election or not, the type of election [. . .], or the level of the court' (Wu 2012, p. 802).

As this brief summary of the main positions shows, scholars are deeply divided about how successful Taiwan has been at fighting corruption. Existing scholarship has provided valuable insights into the institutional sources of corruption in Taiwan, as well as legal and organizational changes designed to target political corruption, and the outcomes of crackdowns on it. Since we can only ascertain that corruption continues – but not if it has increased, decreased or stayed the same – opinions must remain divided. In this contribution, I suggest another approach. Instead of asking if corruption has been reduced or not, I would inquire whether or not it has been made more difficult.

It might be that continuing corruption is the result of a 'collective action problem'. Perhaps politicians are unwilling to fight corruption because they are afraid that they will simply lose out to others who continue to line their pockets (Persson et al. 2013) It might be the result of risk-taking, too, for it is conceivable that culprits do it because they believe they can get away with it, even though politicians are now fighting corruption seriously.

The conviction of the former president and a number of other high-level politicians by their own administration in fact makes the second scenario more likely, and indeed a certain prison warder who is in frequent contact with numerous incarcerated politicians confirms it. According to him, power made them so self-centred that they miscalculated the consequences of their actions.[2] It is difficult to find out why individuals take the risk of engaging in corrupt behaviour, but investigating whether the authorities are serious in combating corruption is more feasible. However, to do so requires an examination of an aspect of anti-corruption that has been neglected in previous studies, that is to say how corrupt behaviour is investigated. In particular, we know very little about the degree of political influence on prosecutors and investigators in Taiwan (Wu 2012, p. 786), if it has changed over time and, if so, how any changes have been brought about. The present study will shed light on the subject by examining the events around two critical junctures in Taiwan's recent history.

7.2.2   Critical Junctures

The two most critical junctures were democratization and the first change in the ruling parties. The concept of a 'critical juncture' is based on the assumption that it is difficult to change institutions, to alter the formal and informal rules that govern people's behaviour. People adjust their behaviour to conform to the rules; they become accustomed to them and, in many cases, even profit from them. Adjusting to another set of rules is always difficult because new rules first have to be made and then learned. As Ruth Berins and David Collier point out, however, under certain conditions institutions do undergo fundamental changes. Major institutional change is especially feasible during serious social conflicts or an economic or political crisis. Most notably, conflicts and crises frequently discredit existing institutions and bring new actors to power. The conditions for institutional change are especially likely to be created if those new actors see no advantage in the persistence of the old arrangements and would profit from their obliteration (Collier and Collier 1991). According to Paul Pierson, such critical junctures are characterized by 'the presence or absence of a specified causal force push[ing] multiple cases onto divergent long-term pathways, or push[ing] a single case onto a new political trajectory that diverges significantly from the old' (Pierson in Slater and Simmons 2010, p. 888). Given their disruptive character, 'critical junctures are typically moments of expanding agency' (Slater and Simmons 2010, p. 890) where actors can forge new paths, such as determinedly fighting corruption.

7.2.3 Process-Tracing

Information about what transpired around the two critical junctures in Taiwan's recent history is gleaned from interviews with actors who played important roles in drafting anti-corruption laws, who decided on anti-corruption policies, who investigated corrupt behaviour, who imposed the verdicts and who were positively or negatively affected by anti-corruption. By means of snowball sampling I was able to obtain interviews with two former ministers of justice; a former vice-minister of justice; the deputy-general of Taiwan's Agency Against Corruption; the previous speaker of the DPP, a close associate of former Minister of Justice Chen Ding-nan who passed away in 2006; and a former member of the BGIC. I was also able to interview the head prosecutor of a district court; one section chief from both the anti-corruption division and the office of budget, accounting and statistics of the MJIB; two prosecutors subordinated to the Department of Prosecutorial Affairs in the Ministry of Justice and one prosecutor in the high prosecutor's office; and a head of department in Taiwan's Judges' Academy. I received considerable support and information from Chilik Yu and Kevin Yeh, the current and former executive directors of Taiwan's Transparency International chapter; from Chen Ming-tong, a Professor of Political Science at National Taiwan University; and from Chang Kun-sheng, Professor of Law at Cheng-chih University.

With most of those persons I carried out at least one (and in some cases two) interviews of 2–2.5 hours each, conducted entirely in Mandarin Chinese. In most cases I was given permission to record the conversation, but where I was not I took notes. I began by asking open questions about major achievements, obstacles and important actors in Taiwan's fight against corruption, to allow the respondents to express their opinions without being influenced by my own hypotheses. I asked respondents who had been part of the historical process that lies at the heart of this study to retrace their time in office, frequently interrupting them to ask for more information, perhaps to probe a particular point or even to suggest what I perceived to be inconsistencies. Finally, I asked them to comment on the hypotheses I had developed from the existing literature on anti-corruption in Taiwan.

Before analysing how expanded agency during the two critical junctures benefited institutional change, it is important to examine the status quo ante. As will be seen in the next section, many of the very factors that enabled the KMT to rule Taiwan in an authoritarian fashion eventually turned out to benefit anti-corruption.

7.3   ENABLING CONDITIONS

Various elements in the particular nature of the authoritarian regime that ruled Taiwan from 1947 to 1992 actually benefited anti-corruption, of which elements two were especially important. First, it is nearly impossible to fight corruption where development levels are low, bureaucrats uneducated and untrained, and politicians and civil servants dependent on bribes to make a living. All of that, however, had not been the case in Taiwan, which counts as one of Asia's 'developing states' where politicians guided developments and corruption took the more benign forms of rent-seeking or dividend-collecting.

The recruitment of bureaucrats was strictly regulated both in the numbers and quality of recruits. Beginning in 1950 the government carried out annual civil service examinations which 'provided the aspirants in society with a regular route to social and economic mobility and infused the bureaucracy with new blood' (Liu 1985, p.11). The specialized and standardized examinations were conducted by a government organ called Examination Yuan specially established for the purpose, and had to be undertaken by all civil servants. Higher-level bureaucrats had to pass additional examinations (Tien 1989, p.121).

In addition the administration was reformed frequently. In 1958 an ad hoc Committee for Administrative Reform was formed under the Presidential Office to 'help construct a more modern administrative system, through which the authoritarian regime could enhance its ability to control every aspect of Taiwanese society' (Wang and Shih 2010) and, it should be added, steer economic development. Reforms were implemented in that year and in 1966, 1967 and 1969 to improve administrative procedures, the civil service and management (Wang and Shih 2010).

Skilful economic planning by well-educated technocrats in the Ministries of Finance, Economic Affairs, the Central Bank and the Council for Economic Planning and Development contributed significantly to the sustained economic growth Taiwan has enjoyed since the 1950s – along with equal distribution and social welfare perhaps the most important component of output legitimacy (Meyer 2004).

The second element is the cleavage between 'Mainlanders', the part of Taiwan's population who arrived on the island in 1947–49, and the 'Taiwanese'. However, the relationship is not straightforward. On the one hand this cleavage benefited corruption because clientelism served to co-opt influential local families into the minority Mainlander government. On the other hand urban Taiwanese intellectuals, many of whom had studied law, resented the KMT and its way of governing Taiwan. That requires some explanation.

The Taiwanese consist of indigenous minorities as well as Han Chinese who settled on Taiwan in the eighteenth century, so that in effect a government representing 20 per cent of the population dominated a resentful 80 per cent majority. Given that the KMT government had little infrastructural power at its disposal, it initially quelled dissent by political terror disguised as an anti-communist movement. Approximately 3,000 people were executed and 8,000–10,000 imprisoned (Meyer 1996). By no coincidence, that period of 'white terror' ended in 1954 when Chiang Kai-shek had begun to consolidate his autocracy by taking over and reforming the provincial bureaucracy and, perhaps more importantly, overhauling the KMT. Martial Law and 'Temporary Provisions in the Period of Mobilization against Communist Rebellion', both announced in 1948, as well as some other draconian laws continued to remain in place until at least the late 1980s. Enforced with the help of a number of police and security organs, the regulations enabled the regime to use violence to discourage opposition, and to disregard the Constitution (Chao and Myers 1998, ch. 2).

Besides suppressing dissent the KMT upheld stability by co-opting clientelist networks into the regime, centred on influential Taiwanese families. Their method was to implement local elections in which two or more 'local factions', as the networks were called, competed against each other. Because other parties were outlawed, local candidates had the choice of either becoming KMT members, and thereby gaining access to a formidable campaign machine, or standing as independents. The chances of winning an election as an independent were very low, so local elites chose to apply for KMT membership, thereby giving the party legitimacy (Göbel 2012). In return, commissioners, mayors and parliamentarians gained access to public service providers as well as small credit institutions, which allowed them to distribute favours and line their pockets. While the central government was reasonably clean, bribery, embezzlement, nepotism and organized crime went nearly unchecked at the local level (Chao 1997, p. 68).

At another level, however, sub-ethnic cleavage proved beneficial to anti-corruption. Many Taiwanese were not affiliated to any local faction – or, if they were, resented them. They strove for equal access to education and government jobs or envisioned a political system that was democratic and free of corruption. As the next section will show, many young Taiwanese studied law, and fighting for reform of the legal and judicial systems came naturally to them. As we shall see, the presence of an elaborate bureaucratic apparatus, established norms of good governance in the central government and the activities of Taiwanese students all helped the fight against corruption in Taiwan. On the other hand, however, the local factions had become so powerful that the KMT leadership continued to rely on them to win the first democratic elections. The next sections examine how those opposing forces played out.

7.4   DEMOCRATIZATION

The first critical juncture in Taiwan's anti-corruption history was the transition to democracy. In the late 1980s Martial Law and other provisions that restricted democratic freedoms were repealed, and in 1991/92 representatives to the two 'houses' of parliament – the National Assembly and the Legislative Yuan – were chosen in free and fair elections. Democratization had both enabling and constraining effects on anti-corruption. Among the enabling effects was that Taiwan's population embraced their new freedoms. They successfully demonstrated against vestiges of authoritarianism in Taiwan's public institutions, for example the presence of KMT officers in Taiwan's universities; they subjected politics to close scrutiny and formed professional associations.[3] One such organization, the Prosecutors' Reform Association, is of particular interest to this study because it was a significant force in the fight for judicial independence. Among the constraining effects was that democratization not only fostered accountability but also provided incentives for electoral candidates to work together with local factions in order to mobilize votes. Lee Teng-hui, the first democratically elected president, used the factions to reach out to the Taiwanese majority to garner support against his opponents in the KMT (Chen 1995).

7.4.1   The Prosecutors' Reform Association

Most of Taiwan's judges and prosecutors at national level had studied at National Taiwan University (NTU). NTU has long been considered the country's best university, and one of the best in Asia. Peter Evans (1995, 50–51) famously argued that socialization in elite universities has contributed to the diffusion of meritocratic values and professionalism in the bureaucracy to form the backbone of the 'developing state'. In very similar manner, NTU has become the place where not only Taipei's bureaucrats but also national-level lawyers, prosecutors and judges are groomed.

During the time of autocracy the KMT rigorously controlled education, ensuring for example that teachers had a main event background and supported the KMT. Moreover, a quota system heavily discriminated against people of Taiwanese descent who wished to obtain higher education. Although the Taiwanese were the overwhelming majority of the population, they formed the minority of students, especially so in NTU's law faculty.[4]

The situation changed with Taiwan's transition to democracy in 1991–92, as the quota system was abolished and access to university places was regulated through entrance exams. That led to a rapid increase in the number of ethnic Taiwanese students in Taiwan's university, and the law faculty at NTU was no exception. Taiwanese law students were unhappy with the KMT's continued political dominance, especially because the 1990s saw the diffusion of particularist politics from the localities to the central government. Studying law made many Taiwanese aware of the glaring difference between the ethical universalism that must always be inherent in the rule of law and Taiwan's political reality. Many therefore believed that legal reforms were needed in order to improve Taiwan's democracy, and, according to a prosecutor who had studied law at NTU in the 1990s, 'The majority of those studying at NTU's faculty of law leaned towards the Dangwai [which would later become the DPP].'[5] Quotas favouring Mainlanders in Taiwan's civil service examinations were also abolished, with the consequence that it was now possible for students with a 'Taiwanese' background to become prosecutors or judges.

According to a number of interviewees, among them a former Minister of Justice and a senior prosecutor, the establishment of the 'Prosecutor's Reform Association' (PRA, *jianchaguan gaige xiehui*) by reform-minded prosecutors in 1998 was a milestone in Taiwan's transition to ethical universalism.[6] The establishment of the PRA was motivated by news reports of politicians repeatedly trying to interfere in prosecutorial investigations. Such reports brought to public attention the problem of the lack of independence of judicial organs and provided the reformers with a platform from which to voice long-held grievances (Minjian sixiang gaige jijinhui 2005). Perhaps as important as publicly advocating judicial reforms was the formation of an easily identifiable group of prosecutors who were willing to challenge the KMT's interference in legal affairs.

When Chen Ding-nan became Minister of Justice in 2000 he appointed PRA members to key positions in the prosecutorial system.[7] Chen, who quickly became known as 'Mr Clean', had planned to follow the examples of Singapore and Hong Kong and establish an independent Anti-Corruption Agency. However, due to the KMT's continued domination of the legislature he failed to gain the necessary majority in the Legislative Yuan. Instead, he established a 'Black Gold Investigation Centre' (*chaji heijin zhongxin*), which he staffed with members of the PRA.[8]

7.4.2 Parties, Identities and Clientelism

In Taiwan's first democratic elections there were two serious contenders for power, the KMT and the Democratic Progressive Party. The DPP was founded in 1986 but really has a much longer history, for as early as the 1960s Taiwanese contenders for seats in local elections had united under the label 'Tang-wai', which translates as 'outside the party' and essentially means 'non-KMT'. However, the main competition at that time was not between KMT and DPP but between 'Mainlanders' and 'Taiwanese'. Lee Teng-hui became KMT chairman in 1988 in the face of resistance from powerful Mainland politicians. Lee was closer to moderates in the DPP than to the conservatives in the KMT, and in essence the so-called 'Mainstream Faction' of Lee and his supporters was more engaged in a struggle against the KMT's own conservatives than against the DPP (Chao and Myers 1998). It is instructive to see that Lee was in contact with leading DPP politicians, and that two formal meetings were held with them to discuss Taiwan's future.

The local factions were another factor the new KMT leadership had to consider. Their clientelist nature meant that profits were deemed more important than democratic values, but previous attempts to weaken their power over local society had failed and resulted in electoral losses for KMT candidates (Chen 1995). Given the high number of elections after democratization and that Taiwan's peculiar electoral system required the political parties to know their share of votes before an election and to entice voters to cast their ballots for particular candidates, the former leadership correctly assessed that local elections could not be won without cooperating with local factions. Factional power was so strong that not even a change to the electoral system would have weakened their hand (Göbel 2012).

With the removal of the constraints imposed by the KMT during Martial Law the local factions managed to extended their influence beyond their places of origin and were able to enter national politics. In that, they were aided by a legal system without provisions to deal with behaviour that is today considered to be corrupt, and so were readily enough accepted as a partner in keeping the KMT's Mainstream Faction in power. Their clientelist nature and frequent involvement in organized crime gave rise to a phenomenon that was later dubbed *heijin* (black gold), a term denoting the infusion of organized crime and money politics into Taiwan's political process (Chin 2003). In dealing with the side effects of the party's alliance with local factions the Lee Teng-hui government steered a middle course. It did little to abolish clientelism in 1996, but launched crackdowns against vote-buying and organized crime (Chin 2003). While previous literature has described that as a strategy of 'selective persecution' designed to rid the KMT of its image as a corrupt party while at the same time continuing to rely on local factions (Göbel 2004), it seems more likely that Lee Teng-hui selected as ministers of justice individuals of great integrity to whom he then gave carte blanche. However, he reined them in them when their actions were met with too much resistance from the local factions.

Hence, as the following sections will show, it would be wrong simply to equate the KMT with the fostering of particularism and the DPP with the promotion of ethical universalism. It is true that the institutional political structure during the KMT's rule did encourage particularism and that, after they came to power, DPP politicians fought against particularism and championed ethical universalism. All the same, that did not mean that all relevant authorities within both parties accepted those alternative directions. Important contributions to the process of engineering Taiwan's transformation to ethical universalism were made not only during the DPP era but also by KMT ministers of justice such as Ma Ying-jeou and Liao Cheng-hao. On the other hand, corrupt activities of the DPP president and his family severely hurt the DDP's image as an anti-corruption party. In both parties certain individuals tried very hard to fight corruption, but in both they eventually found their efforts undermined by their own superiors. It is very unfortunate that extreme partisanship in Taiwanese politics makes it enormously difficult to trace the dynamics of anti-corruption. In interviews KMT politicians belittled even the most obvious achievements made under DPP rule, while for their part most DPP politicians refused to recognize any efforts made during the KMT era, although they did admit that the DPP's anti-corruption policy was facilitated by individuals within the KMT who were not content with their party's alliances with local factions and organized criminals.

Before examining how much impact each minister's character and approach had on anti-corruption it is necessary to specify exactly how the critical junctures of democratization and change in the ruling parties strengthened the hands of particular ministers of justice, and how the resilience of particularist institutions constrained the scope of what they could do.

7.4.3   Fighting Corruption under the KMT

One example is Ma Ying-jeou, president of Taiwan from 2008 to 2016 who previously served as Minister of Justice between 1993 and 1996. During his tenure he cracked down on Taiwan's drug trade and on vote-buying. Most notably, 341 of 883 councillors elected in 1994 were indicted for vote-buying. The KMT councillors allegedly complained that Ma 'shook the party to the foundations', and Lee Teng-hui is rumoured to have accused him of using criticism of the KMT to raise his own profile, saying that Ma, 'nearly ruined the party'. To the general public Ma became recognized for his efforts to clean up Taiwan's politics, but various sources point out that many in the KMT considered that he went too far. Whatever the reasons, Ma was dismissed from office less than three months after Lee was re-elected in Taiwan's first direct presidential elections, to be replaced by Liao Cheng-hao, who since February 1995 had served as the head of the MJIB.[9]

Liao took a conciliatory stance against local factions 'as long as they did not violate the law'. In an interview with the author Liao remarked that the laws at the time had been too sketchy and evidence too difficult to come by to move effectively against local factions.[10] In fact he did not consider them Taiwan's biggest problem:

> Many local factions do not have an organized crime background. At that time, I was of the opinion that the government should take a neutral position. We should lead them towards the right path. Those who take the right path can be given guidance [*fudao*], those who do bad things, you punish. They need to be shown the line between what is legal and what is illegal.

In any case Liao had already devoted his life to fighting organized crime, which he saw as a much bigger problem: 'The population suffered a lot. All trades and professions had been swallowed by organized crime. So I wanted a radical rectification of the situation.' Shortly after assuming office Liao had spear-headed operation 'Chih-ping', which between August 1996 and June 1998 led to the arrest of 675 alleged organized crime figures (Ministry of Justice 1998).

While media reports state that Lee Teng-hui ordered the crackdown because the public was shaken by a number of gang-related abductions and murders that year, Liao claims that the campaign was his own initiative:

> I did not report this case with the Executive Yuan and did not inform the president. [. . .] It was very clear to me: if I perform well, if my superiors support me, then I will be able to continue. If I don't perform well or if my superiors do not support me, then it is over.

According to Liao, the support of Lee Teng-hui and premier Lien Chan was tacit:

> He [Lee] did not tell me what I could or what I could not do. That is a kind of support. Lee and Lien never told me whom I could and whom I could not arrest. I told them, very simply, 'I cannot make even one exception. As soon as there are exceptions, I will resign'.

Liao was as single-minded in his investigation of organized crime as was Ma in his anti-corruption activities. He recalled being aware that many in the KMT resisted his actions, but knew that he had strong backing from the public: 'I did not dwell on the question of whether people were against me. If you do that, then things become difficult'.

The importance of agency becomes obvious in the strategies chosen by Liao. First of all, in his efforts against criminals he involved not only investigators and prosecutors who fell under his own direction as Minister of Justice, but also the police and the armed forces. However, believing that coordinating his actions with the Ministers of the Interior and the Minister of Defence would certainly lead to debilitating conflicts, Liao discovered a legal loophole that meant he was able to avoid having to do so. He found out in fact that the Law of Procedure and the Criminal Law allowed the prosecutor to detail forces from both the civil and military police without seeking permission from other executive organs. Following that, he opened channels for whistle-blowers, then abolished the principle whereby the police were restricted to operating in 'administrative regions', because 'allowing the police of one locality to investigate officials of the same locality was unworkable in the light of strong professional and personal relationships'.

After that reform Taipei-based agents were permitted to investigate anywhere in Taiwan, which Liao considers a very important reform. Liao then established a 'unit for special cases' (*zhuan'an xiaozu*), a small task force that orchestrated crackdowns. The task force met on Wednesday nights, decided on a target and raided the private and business premises of suspects at the earliest legally allowed time shortly after sunrise the next day, so leaving suspects with little time to destroy evidence. Liao confirmed that MJIB agents were embedded in local governments as 'secretaries', and offered that as one of the reasons why suspects often received advance warnings. He pointed out finally that anti-corruption should not be restricted to the police and only those organs of the state concerned with legal matters, but must involve all ministries. As an example he cites underground banks run by criminal gangs that charged crippling levels of interest and did not hesitate to murder any who failed to repay loans on time. Two particularly gruesome cases motivated Liao to suggest that banks hand out microcredits. Another example is cooperation with the tax authorities in tracing irregular income, with another being education against corruption. Eventually Liao resigned in 1998 after failing to receive backing from Hsiao Wan-chang over a row with MJIB acting director Cheng Chuan, who had replaced Lien Chan as prime minister in 1997 (Chen 1998).

7.5 THE CHANGE IN RULING PARTIES

Process-tracing provided important insights into the difficulties of implementing anti-corruption policies, and of how they were overcome in Taiwan. One difficulty was passing laws to define corruption and thereafter allowing the authorities to punish corrupt behaviour; the other difficulty was implementing them. Agency was important for both processes. The passage of anti-corruption laws hinged on overcoming the resistance of the KMT-dominated legislature, while implementation depended on neutral investigators, prosecutors and judges. Anti-corruption laws were passed by mobilizing public opinion – any legislator's open resistance to the fight against corruption might have come at the cost of a failed attempt at re-election. Political corruption has long been perceived as one of the major political ills in Taiwan, and the DPP's electoral campaign had centred on its promise to rid the country of it. Accordingly, much of the party's energy was devoted to creating a legal basis to begin the fight against corruption after it came to power. However, it should be kept in mind that the KMT was a broad church. Anti-corruption legislation had already been initiated by individual KMT legislators in the 1980s, and not all KMT legislators came from local factions. As DPP-related interviewees recalled, some progressive KMT legislators sympathized with the DPP's anti-corruption agenda.

Implementation was more difficult because, in following up corruption cases, investigators and prosecutors had been guided by political considerations. Most notably prosecutors and investigators had to clear their actions with their superiors, many of whom had been part of the very clientelist networks that anti-corruption forces were now supposed to fight.[11] Democratization certainly greatly facilitated the overcoming of resistance within the legislature, but was not enough to improve the process of investigating and persecuting corrupt behaviour, which is so opaque and specialized that it is difficult even for specialists to judge whether an indictment or verdict is justified or not. The change in ruling parties created genuine political interest in improving not only legislation but also implementation. Since clientelist networks worked against the DPP and, being tailor-made for the KMT could not be simply co-opted by DPP politicians, DPP leaders had a strategic interest in weakening the KMT's mobilization machine by taking the matter of implementation seriously (Göbel 2013).

7.5.1 Limitations

Chen Shui-bian appointed Chen Ding-nan as Minister of Justice. Chen Ding-nan had obtained a law degree from NTU in 1966 and entered politics after the KMT's crackdown on a pro-democracy demonstration in 1979. He was part of the Dangwai alliance of politicians opposed to the KMT, and later became a member of the DPP. Before assuming office he had served as a county commissioner and later as a legislator. His considerable experience in local politics was cited by all interviewees as one reason why he was chosen to head the MoJ. When he served as commissioner, Cheng became famous for his incorruptibility. A contemporary described him as manically obsessed with order; for example whenever he called a meeting he even specified where the pens had to be placed. He was also feared for his on-the-spot investigations. After public infrastructure projects in his county had been completed he would personally inspect the construction site to check that no building materials had been misappropriated and that the material used matched the legal quality standards.[12]

Although Chen had an incentive to obliterate the KMT's political machine, he was faced with the problem that the legal system was still controlled by people who were closely connected with the KMT. As one interviewee describes it, head prosecutors and chief investigators were tied to politicians and made their careers together with them. If the head of such a network received a promotion then others would be promoted along with him.[13] The bureaucratic culture at that time was one where personal relationships trumped the law and leaders in the prosecutorial system were defined by their allegiance to influential politicians. As pointed out in the previous section, before investigations happened local politicians were warned by MJIB personnel embedded in local administrations, perhaps as secretaries or even secretaries-general of the commissioner or the mayor.[14] Apart from the MJIB the prosecution was allowed to search public officials too, but there were too few local prosecutors to collect evidence if several raids were planned to coincide. As the interviewee put it, Chen had 'weapons, but no troops'.[15] The interviewee, who at the time had himself been a prosecutor, remarked that it was easy to obtain evidence only when there was some internal strife.

Another problem pertained to ordinary prosecutors and investigators, who were used to clearing every investigation with their superiors. The interviewee characterized them as 'foot-soldiers without initiative', people who were used to following orders but not to taking the initiative in dealing with cases. There were exceptions, but the norm during the KMT regime had been to collect 'just enough' evidence to justify a conviction. However, with the professionalization of prosecutors, lawyers and judges that was no longer enough. Lawyers became skilled at discovering holes in indictments, and prosecutors would appeal the decisions of judges.[16]

7.5.2 Anti-Corruption as a Political Campaign

Chen had travelled to Hong Kong and Singapore, and decided to establish an independent and specialized anti-corruption agency based on the blueprint of Hong Kong's ACA.[17] His plan was to disband the MJIB's anti-corruption unit and merge it with the MoJ Government Ethics Department (Göbel 2004). However, the creation of a new government agency required a legislative majority that Chen did not have, and the head of the MJIB, Wang Kuang-yu, who had been retained from the previous administration, fiercely resisted Chen's interference. The conflict between Chen and Wang ended when Wang, along with the Prosecutor-General, was replaced by presidential order. Yeh Sheng-mao was that replacement, a man whom journalists have described as fiercely loyal to President Chen Shui-bian.[18] Under Yeh changes in personnel became possible, and chief investigators with an obvious loyalty to the KMT were replaced by individuals willing to part company with the old ways. In addition Yeh established the BGIC, a task-oriented agency that he staffed with only ten persons, all of whom had been active in the Prosecutors' Reform Association.[19] Because the prosecutorial system was still dominated, as Chen's contemporary put it, by 'the people of the others' (*biede ren de renma*), the BGIC was incorporated into the High Court Prosecutor's office.[20] These changes encouraged MJIB personnel who disliked clientelism and had been repressed by the KMT.

In the course of a year Chen had built up a coalition of prosecutors and investigators who were loyal to him, and they formed the backbone of his crackdowns on vote-buying and corruption.[21] In 2002, when Chen had consolidated his position, a 'Special Investigation Unit' (*tezhenzu*) intended to target high-ranking politicians was established under the High Court.[22] In contrast to the BGIC, however, the unit's highest official had to be confirmed by the legislature, which reduced resistance somewhat.[23] Furthermore, 'ethics units' (*zhengfengsi*) in 1992 under the jurisdiction of the MJIB had already been established in every functional department. In practice that meant that investigators were embedded in departments and were able to prevent and, should the need arise, quickly investigate corrupt behaviour.

Nearly half of all corruption cases now are reported by those units (Ministry of Justice 2014). Critics say that their functionality is hindered by the fact that they are embedded in departments, and because opportunities for promotion have been few for these so-called 'ethics investigators'.[24] There is little evidence to suggest this, but the question does deserve further inquiry. Finally, Chen reduced the influence of head prosecutors over the promotion of ordinary prosecutors, thereby giving the latter more freedom to disobey their superiors if those superiors sought to exert undue influence. Previously promotions had to be recommended by the superior, but as things are now they are decided by a panel composed of officials, some of whom are selected by the minister and some elected from within the prosecution service.[25]

Chen's measures were successful in changing the Taiwanese bureaucratic culture despite that fact that only leadership positions had been re-staffed. A former chief prosecutor pointed out that the replacement of key individuals in the judicial system is generally sufficient to inspire a change in bureaucratic culture because their subordinates must follow their instructions. 'Taiwan has almost 1,000 prosecutors. It doesn't matter who governs, the prosecutors will always be there. Chen thought, if I influence a couple of hundred, the atmosphere will change completely'.[26] As one of the ten members of the BGIC recalls, the team was specifically instructed not to take party affiliation into consideration when conducting investigations.[27] At first, given that the DPP had held executive positions no higher than county level, it was mostly KMT lawmakers who were investigated. As time went on, however, a number of high-ranking DPP politicians too succumbed to the temptations of power. High-level DPP politicians – including the commissioner of Nantou county (who was a close friend of Chen Ding-nan), the vice-minister of internal affairs and the head of the government's High Technology Commission – were convicted of corruption.[28] One of the BGIC prosecutors even appealed a 'not-guilty' finding on one of the anti-corruption charges brought against President Chen Shui-bian.[29]

7.5.3   Resistance from Without and Within

Nevertheless, the KMT-dominated legislature wanted to abolish the BGIC, which investigated cases not only of corruption but of vote-buying too. Since they could not legislate the BGIC out of existence they simply threatened to cut the budget of the MoJ.[30] In Taiwan at that time the budgets of the individual ministries were decided by functional commissions in the Legislative Yuan, and a position as convener in the Law Commission was sought after among members of local factions and organized crime – and was frequently granted to them. Indeed, at one time even Taiwan's most notorious crime boss held the position (Göbel 2004). However, after mobilizing public opinion by organizing a hearing and publicly criticizing the KMT for supporting black gold, and asking them what alternative organization they would support, the legislators were forced to withdraw their motion.[31]

With the DPP demonstrating that they were serious about eradicating corruption the KMT party-central could no longer afford to block efforts aimed at reducing corruption, but themselves became obliged to project a 'clean' image. It was for that very reason, and the fact that there were also 'idealist' legislators in the KMT caucus, that the Conflict of Interest Avoidance Law could be passed in 2001.[32] Two more laws were passed in 2004 and 2008, but critics argue that they are toothless. The Political Donations Law can allegedly be avoided by establishing a foundation and employing 'consultants' at high, tax-exempt salaries, while the Lobby Law is simply not observed. Since its implementation in 2008 not a single registration has reached the Ministry of Interior Affairs, despite the fact that lobbying continues unabated.[33]

Despite his apparent success and popularity Chen Ding-nan did not see out the second term of the DPP administration. As one contemporary remarked, his campaign-style, output-oriented politics 'offended many people', by which he meant particularist KMT politicians as well as 'a minority' of DPP politicians.[34] First, Chen was an outsider to the legal profession, and because of this he did not always communicate well with them. He could never be sure if the perceived inefficiency was due to formalities that had to be observed, as the prosecutors claimed, or to foot-dragging, as he suspected. Second, as already mentioned, some DPP politicians, once in power, also engaged in corrupt acts. In addition, even some of those who did not themselves engage in corruption needed the support of the local factions in their campaigns. Such legislators and commissioners allegedly pressured the DPP's party-central to rein in Chen lest the DPP's support basis was undermined. As one contemporary of Chen remarked of him, 'He reached the limit of what he could achieve'.[35]

7.5.4 Institutionalizing Anti-Corruption

Chen Ding-nan was succeeded by Shih Mao-lin, who had studied law together with Minister of Justice and later President Ma Ying-jeou. When he was appointed Minister of Justice Ma remarked to the prime minister that he did not have the political background to head the Ministry of Justice, and the premier famously answered: 'That is why I chose you.' As adviser to the Ministry of Justice, Ma appointed Shih, who had excelled in his legal studies and had experience both as a local judge and a local prosecutor. Shih is one of the few politicians who command respect from people in both parties. A former head prosecutor and veteran DPP politician remarked that Shih was indeed a good choice.[36]

In contrast to Chen, who was impulsive and wanted to see changes immediately, Shih would 'take it slower, but also be successful'. Shih seems to agree when he says that Chen was the right man at the right time, and that there were a number of problems he could not solve that demanded an intimate knowledge of the politics in Taiwan's legal institutions:

When I was appointed Minister I had studied Chen's achievements closely and knew where progress had been made, and where problems remained. For example, prosecutors and investigators have become more and more skilled, but so have the criminals. I learned from this experience and used my knowledge about the legal system to initiate some reforms.

In particular Shih introduced four distinct changes: 'follow the money flows' instead of investigating transactions; make prosecution more efficient; focus on big corruption cases; and shift from punishment to prevention.[37]

First, Shih shifted the focus of the investigation from politicians to entrepreneurs:

> I was interested in the sources of corruption money. How do entrepreneurs give the money to public officials? Organized crime and money politics are interrelated. For example, we got to Lo Fu-chu [Taiwan's most notorious gang leader, who fled to Mainland China after his indictment] not by investigating his crimes, but the illicit money flows. It is difficult to hide large amounts of money; you can't just put it in the bank.

Shih remarked that finding proof of a financial crime was often easier than finding evidence for gang murders, especially if the suspect holds political office.[38]

Second, when asked about what he had done differently from Chen, Shih also remarked that he 'led prosecutors as an insider' instead of 'using authority and strong force'. He recalls that he spent much time with prosecutors and investigators to see how they dealt with cases. Based on that and his own experience, he would 'show them how to conduct an investigation, how to follow up on evidence. If their method is not effective they will not be successful in investigating vote buying and corruption. They knew I was an insider and that they could not fool me.' Besides providing training in methods of investigation, Shih put pressure on local prosecutors by imposing quotas: 'Every person had to solve 30 cases. Let's not discuss if this was good or not, but at that time that is what we did. Of course, we respected human rights – if you can't find evidence then you have to let a suspect go'.[39]

Third, he professed to have been dissatisfied with the low conviction rate for high-level officials:

> The conviction rate was not even 20 per cent. Before, the investigators could not obtain enough evidence to convict high-level politicians so they spared the tigers and went after the flies. I did it the other way round. Once they had completed their vote-buying investigations [of the 2004 legislative and presidential elections] I got them to investigate big corruption cases. We rewarded confessions and evidence that led to the conviction of others with reduced sentences.[40]

Finally, after some years of campaign-style crackdowns on corruption, Shih shifted the focus from prosecution to prevention. He became interested in management studies and initiated the development of risk-assessment systems. Departments were rated according to how likely it was that a particular line of work might offer incentives for corruption. According to Shih, those facilitating 'collective crimes' like customs inspections or public construction projects were especially risk-prone, as were the police.[41]

7.5.5   Outcomes

Legal statistics for 2005 show that the measures did have an impact. The fluctuation of indictments, convictions and investigations seemed to follow electoral cycles, leading to the suspicion, which I have referred to elsewhere, that these measures served as a campaign tool (Göbel 2014). However, recent findings have led me to revise my opinion. More convincing now is the alternative explanation that the figures reflect personnel changes in ministers of justice. In addition, the learning curve of investigators and politicians influenced the choice of cases for indictment and how many people were indicted in each case. For example, slightly fewer cases were lodged with local prosecutors when Chen was minister, but the number of people indicted for each case rose steeply. As pointed out above, corrupt officials had become more careful; but if the prosecutors managed to collect the necessary evidence, then usually not only the immediate parties but also their accessories were charged, which led to the increase in the number indicted per case.[42]

Similarly, the increase in asset-declaration lawsuits after 2005 is probably the result of the concentration on money flows after 2005. Finally, the increase in convictions for violating the Conflict of Interest Prevention Law, which had been passed in 2001, can be explained by the fact that 'people had to learn how to investigate these cases'. According to Shih:

> [T]his law is really convenient. It is very simple, the most efficient of all Sunshine laws. As only administrative punishments are meted out, the process is very quick. As opposed to other cases, which are decided by courts of law and take three to five years, depending on whether verdicts are appealed, there is a decision within the year.[43]

7.6   CONCLUSION

In Taiwan it has become far more risky than it was in the mid-1990s to engage in acts of corruption. Although there is certainly still much room for improvement there have been far-reaching legal and organizational changes that have severely restricted what is permissible, and those changes have made it more likely that corrupt behaviour will be discovered. Furthermore, it is now much more difficult for senior politicians to intervene in an investigation or to influence a court case. Investigators, prosecutors and judges have become far more professional and independent, and less likely to be swayed by influence or money.

The present analysis is an enquiry into the factors that made such far-reaching changes possible. It has shown that expanded agency during critical junctures does indeed account for many of the observed changes, but the impact of factors such as democratization or party affiliation is not clear-cut. On the one hand, democratization removed the restrictions that had kept corruption largely confined to local political institutions, although that is not to say that democratization caused corruption. Rather, while corruption did exist during authoritarianism, non-democratic constraints restricted it to the local level. Once those constraints were lifted corruption flourished. On the other hand, democratization unleashed the forces that are necessary to promote universalism, including equal access to political office, the formation of professional associations and media freedom.

As for political parties, the KMT under Lee Teng-hui readily embraced particularism and even cooperated with organized criminals in order to remain in office, but at the same time appointed two men as ministers of justice who weakened those same foundations. Similarly, the DPP government, which had credibly fought corruption after taking office, itself became involved in major corruption scandals. The very politician who delivered on his promise when he was appointed Minister of Justice, to fight corruption in Taiwan resolutely, was among those who were not included in the cabinet after the DPP's re-election in 2004, allegedly because he had 'offended too many people in the party'.

Given the now-obvious political risk, why did those individuals pursue anti-corruption reforms so actively? One explanation is rooted in the political context of the time. Both Ma and Chen assumed office shortly after major political changes, namely democratization and the change in ruling parties; and their superiors gave them carte blanche. As institutionalization set in, however, interests diversified and leading politicians decided that anti-corruption must take a back seat to more 'conciliatory' approaches. Both parties remained or became dependent on social and political forces of which the operational logic clashed with a radical understanding of anti-corruption. Idealism was therefore sacrificed on the altar of political pragmatism. As the ministers had built their reputations on precisely such idealism they were at a disadvantage when the political winds shifted. They were expendable, as all politicians are or should be, and it had probably already been decided who their successors would be. That those individuals believed in their own political vision and would rather taste defeat than compromise is another, equally plausible explanation.

Among the problems that continue to restrict ethical universalism are old-boy networks that are remnants of the authoritarian era and the politicization of society today, which many believe influence the verdicts of judges. Those phenomena should not be confused as, while protecting members of a clientelist network certainly constitutes corruption, for a judge to impose a higher or lower penalty on some convicted politician with whom the judge might not agree politically, while perhaps unprofessional, does amount to corruption if there is no material gain.

Further problems complicating the fight against corruption are of an institutional nature, examples being cases ranging from legal money laundering in foundations and temple societies to the unclear relationship between Taiwan's confusing array of anti-corruption organizations. The fact that political resistance prevents the resolution of such matters is a problem in itself and testifies to the fact that, the major achievements described in this chapter notwithstanding, particularism remains a significant problem in Taiwan.[44]

NOTES

1.   Interview with MJIB section chief in the anti-corruption division, Taipei, 08 November 2014.
2.   Prison guard in group interview, Taipei, 29 October 2014.
3.   Interview with participant in student democratization movement, Taipei, 04 November 2014.
4.   Ibid.
5.   Interview with former member of the Black Gold Investigation Center (BGIC), Taipei, 06 November 2014.
6.   Interview with former head prosecutor, Taipei, 25 October 2014.
7.   Interview with associate of Chen Ding-nan, Taipei, 25 October 2014.
8.   Ibid.; see also Göbel 2004.
9.   *Apple Daily*, 23 March 2008, available at: www.appledaily.com.tw/appledaily/article/headline/20080323/30379953/.
10.   Unless otherwise noted, the information in this section is based on the author's interview with Liao Cheng-hao, Taipei, 30 October 2014.
11.   Interview with associate of Chen Ding-nan, Taipei, 25 October 2014; interview with MJIB section chief in the anti-corruption division, Taipei, 08 November 2014.
12.   Interview with associate of Chen Ding-nan, Taipei, 25 October 2014.
13.   Ibid.
14.   Ibid. Interview with Liao Cheng-hao, Taipei, 30 October 2014.
15.   Interview with associate of Chen Ding-nan, Taipei, 25 October 2014.
16.   Interview with Shih Mao-lin, Taichung, 03 November 2014.
17.   Interview with associate of Chen Ding-nan, Taipei, 25 October 2014.
18.   Yeh was later sentenced to ten years in prison because he had conveyed confidential information to Chen Shui-bian.

19. Interview with former member of the BGIC, 06 November 2014.
20. Interview with associate of Chen Ding-nan, Taipei, 25 October 2014.
21. Interview with former member of the BGIC, 06 November 2014.
22. Interview with associate of Chen Ding-nan, Taipei, 25 October 2014.
23. Ibid.
24. Ibid.
25. Interview with Shih Mao-lin, Taichung, 29 October 2014.
26. Ibid.
27. Interview with former member of the BGIC, 06 November 2014.
28. Interview with Shih Mao-lin, Taichung, 29 October 2014.
29. Interview with former member of the BGIC, 06 November 2014.
30. Interview with Shih Mao-lin, Taichung, 03 November 2014.
31. Ibid.
32. Interview with former legislator, Taipei, 25 October 2014.
33. Interview with DPP spokesperson Huang Di-Ying, Taipei, 01 November 2014.
34. Interview with associate of Chen Ding-nan, Taipei, 25 October 2014.
35. Ibid.
36. Ibid.
37. Interview with Shih Mao-lin, Taichung, 29 October 2014.
38. Interview with Shih Mao-lin, Taichung, 03 November 2014.
39. Ibid.
40. Ibid.
41. Ibid.
42. Ibid.
43. Ibid.
44. I should like to thank all the individuals I interviewed for their time and enthusiasm; many of them were extremely busy because of an approaching election. I am especially grateful to Kun-sheng Chang and Vicky Wei-ya Wu for facilitating many of the interviews, allowing me to draw on their encyclopaedic legal expertise and supporting me in any way they could before, during and after the fieldwork stage of this research.

REFERENCES

Bertelsmann Foundation. (2013). Bertelsmann Transformation Index 2013. Country Report: Taiwan.

Chao, L., and Myers, R. (1998). *The First Chinese Democracy: Political Life in the Republic of China on Taiwan*. Baltimore, MD: Johns Hopkins University Press.

Chao, Y. (1997). *Taiwan Difang Zhengzhi De Bianqian Yu Tezhi* (*Change and Characteristics of Taiwan's Local Politics*). Taipei: Hanlu.

Chen, M. (1998). "Controversy Hits the Bureau of Investigation." *Taiwan Panorama* 23(8), p. 76.

Chen, M. (1995). *Paixi Zhengzhi Yu Taiwan Zhengzhi Bianqian* (*Factional Politics and Taiwan's Political Development*). Taipei: Yuedan.

Chin, K. (2003). *Heijin: Organized Crime, Business, and Politics in Taiwan*. Armonk, NY: M.E. Sharpe.

Collier, R., and Collier, D. (1991). *Shaping the Political Arena: Critical Junctures, the Labor Movement, and Regime Dynamics in Latin America*. Princeton: Princeton University Press.

Evans, P. (1995). Embedded Autonomy: States and Industrial Transformation. Princeton: Princeton University Press.

Göbel, C. (2004). "Beheading the Hydra: Combating Corruption and Organized Crime." *China Perspectives* **56**, pp. 14–25.

Göbel, C. (2012). "The Impact of Electoral System Reform on Taiwan's Local Factions." *Journal of Current Chinese Affairs* **41**, pp. 69–92.

Göbel, C. (2013). "Warriors Unchained: Critical Junctures and Anticorruption in Taiwan and South Korea." *Zeitschrift für Vergleichende Politikwissenschaft* **7**, pp. 219–42.

Göbel, C. (2014). "Anticorrp Background Paper on Taiwan." [online] Berlin: ANTICORRP. Available at: http://anticorrp.eu/publications/background-paper-on-taiwan/ [accessed 10 May 2014].

Liu, A.P.L. (1985). "The Political Basis of the Economic and Social Development in the Republic of China 1949–1980." *Occasional Papers/Reprint Series in Asian Studies, University of Maryland* 1.

Meyer, M. (1996). "Der Weiße Terror der 50er Jahre: Chancen und Grenzen der Bewältigung eines Dunklen Kapitels in der Geschichte Taiwans." In Schubert, Gunter, and Schneider, A. (eds), *Taiwan an Der Schwelle Zum 21. Jahrhundert.* Hamburg: Institut für Asienstudien, pp. 99–134.

Meyer, M. (2004). *Ideen und Institutionen: Die Historischen Wurzeln der Nationalchinesischen Industriepolitik.* Baden-Baden: Nomos.

Ministry of Justice. (1998). *Sao Hei Baipishu (The Whitebook on Fighting Organized Crime).* Taipei: Ministry of Justice.

Ministry of Justice. (2014). Lianzheng Anjian Banli Qingxing (The Status Quo of Anti-corruption Cases). [online] Available at: http://www.rjsd.moj.gov.tw/rjsdweb/common/WebListFile.ashx?list_id=1416. [accessed on 24 July 2017].

Minjian sixiang gaige jijinhui. (2005). *Li Yu Li: Shi Nian Fa Sheng, Shi Nian Si Bian (Reason and Force: 10 Years of Making Voices Heard, 10 Years of Speculation).* Taipei: Wunan tushu chuban gongsi.

Persson, A., Rothstein, B. and Teorell, T. (2013). "Why Anticorruption Reforms Fail: Systemic Corruption as a Collective Action Problem." *Governance* **26**(3), pp. 449–71.

Quah, J. (2010). *Taiwan's Anti-Corruption Strategy: Suggestions for Reform.* Baltimore, MD: University of Maryland School of Law.

Slater, D., and Simmons, E. (2010). "Informative Regress: Critical Antecedents in Comparative Politics." *Comparative Political Studies* **43**(7), pp. 886–917.

Tien, H. (1989). *The Great Transition: Political and Social Change in the Republic of China.* Stanford: Hoover institution Press.

Transparency International. (2011). *2010/11 Global Corruption Barometer.* [online] Berlin: Transparency International. Available at: www.transparency.org/gcb2013 [accessed 04 March 2012].

Wang, G., and Shih, M. (2010). "Entrenchment or Retrenchment? A Historical-Institutional Analysis of the Central Government Reorganisation in Taiwan." Symposium "Reform and Transition in Public Administration Theory and Practice in Greater China" (Hong Kong).

World Bank. (2013). *Worldwide Governance Indicators.* [online] Washington, DC: World Bank. Available at: http://info.worldbank.org/governance/wgi/index.aspx#home [accessed 22 May 2015].

Wu, C. (2012). "Charge Me If You Can: Assessing Political Biases in Vote-Buying Verdicts in Democratic Taiwan (2000–2010)." *China Quarterly* **211**, pp. 786–805.

8. Costa Rica: tipping points and an incomplete journey

Bruce M. Wilson and Evelyn Villarreal

8.1 INTRODUCTION

In contrast to many of the countries discussed in this book, where transitions from particularism to ethical universalism were swift and recent events, Costa Rica's journey followed a long, gradual and undulating arc towards ethical universalism. Until the start of the 20th century government corruption was systematic and widespread, yet in the contemporary period from 2000 to the present corruption scandals involving public officials have been sporadic, if spectacular and well publicized. In this chapter, to flesh out Costa Rica's progress in limiting corruption, we shall divide the historical developments into four 'tipping points,' each of which was followed by a period of increasingly democratic governance that saw breakthroughs in the fight against various forms of corruption, although there were differing levels of success. We then used a process-tracing method to revisit each of the tipping points to illustrate causality and links among different key events and the resulting reforms that ultimately steered the country to its current condition of ethical universalism.

Costa Rica is the only Central American country that can be seen as approximating ethical universalism; corruption is rife in the rest of the region. The head of Transparency International (TI) in Latin America, Alejandro Salas, notes that Costa Rica has always been ranked as the least corrupt in Central America because it has strong institutions rather than because of its relative wealth: 'It is not the poverty of a country which matters but the weakness of its institutions' (Luxner 2014). Nicaragua, the poorest country in Central America, is also the most corrupt; but Panama, the richest country in the region, experiences similarly high levels of corruption and is currently on the 'grey list', denoting it as a major money-laundering country.[1] The extent of Central America's ongoing corruption problem is reflected in recent events in Guatemala, Honduras and Panama, where charges have been brought against presidents and senior officials for operating complex and well-organized networks of government corruption. In Guatemala, for example, an investigation by the United Nations-initiated International Commission against Impunity in Guatemala (CICIG) resulted in the resignation and arrest of Vice-President Roxana Baldetti in August 2015 and President Otto Pérez Molina in September 2015 on corruption charges related to a conspiracy to defraud the state of millions of dollars in import duties (Ahmed and Malkinsept 2015; Lakhani 2015).

We argue that the origins of Costa Rica's contemporary anti-corruption success can be found in the early 20th century, after which came four major tipping points. Each of these tipping points, detailed in Table 8.1, enhanced corruption-free governance through the devolution of political power across the branches of government; the weakening of executive branch control over the national budget and state accountability agencies; the creation of new agencies whose actions expanded state anti-corruption capacity; and the increasingly important role of the established traditional and new social media as anti-corruption watchdogs (Caryl 2015). The balance of the chapter unfolds as follows: first, we describe the tipping points and place Costa Rica in its historical and regional context. Next we return to a detailed examination of the individual tipping points in chronological order, to better understand the underpinnings of the enhanced anti-corruption capabilities of the Costa Rican state. We present our conclusions in the final section.[2]

8.2   THE FOUR TIPPING POINTS

The first tipping point began with the overthrow of Costa Rica's last military dictator, Federico Tinoco (who ruled from 1917 to 1919), when the economic disruptions caused by World War I caused a major financial collapse, which in turn triggered a political crisis which then led to a period of patrimonialism. Although economic and political elites initially supported Tinoco's coup their support quickly evaporated as the dictator became increasingly despotic and attempted to eliminate political opposition and attack civil liberties; and he was tainted by numerous corruption scandals (Fernández 2010). A series of gradual democratic reforms were begun in the post-dictatorship period and lasted throughout the first half of the 20th century. They included major institutional changes, particularly to the judiciary, which laid the foundations for the separation of powers and the creation of new accountability agencies. As Figure 8.1 highlights, those anti-corruption reforms were introduced during a long period of economic crisis where GDP growth was stagnant for ten years and then negative for the following decade.

Table 8.1 Four tipping points in Costa Rica

Regime	Period	Characteristics	Institutions and legislation
Patrimonialism	Until first half of 20th century	Legal controls, entities within the Executive, beginning of the Rule of Law consolidation process	Judicial Branch independence 1871 Constitution 1879 and 1937 Ley Orgánica del Poder Judicial (organic law of the Judicial Branch)
Competitive particularism	1949 (end of civil war) to 1980s 1949 Constitution	Financial and legal controls Dependent on the executive for appointments and budget limited powers	Specialized anti-corruption agencies: Office of Comptroller General Office of Attorney General Banks Audit (within Central Bank) National Electricity Service (SNE)
Borderline	Transition period 1980s to the end of the 1990s	New legal framework More powerful mechanisms Significant expansion in subjects under control, from human rights to environment protection and corruption More independence, more technical appointments, etc.	Human Rights Office (1984); Constitutional Court (1989); General Audit of Financial Institutions (1988); National Committee in Defence of the Consumer Rights (1994); Regulator Authority of Public Services (1996); Ombudsman (1994); Superintendents (1995 and 1998); internal comptrollers (1996), etc.
Ethical universalism	Consolidation 2000 Constitutional Reform to current period Principle of accountability as a duty of all public servants	Consolidation of new institutional framework; efforts to enforce the legislation created in the previous period; increase in their budget and personnel Increased citizen participation and enhanced role of traditional and social media as anti-corruption watchdogs	Law of Financial Management and Public Budget (2002); Law of Internal Controls (2002); Law against Corruption and Illicit Enrichment in the Public Sector (2004); Fiscalía Penal de Hacienda y Función Pública; Public Ethics Office; enhanced press freedoms; civil society organizations (CSOs)

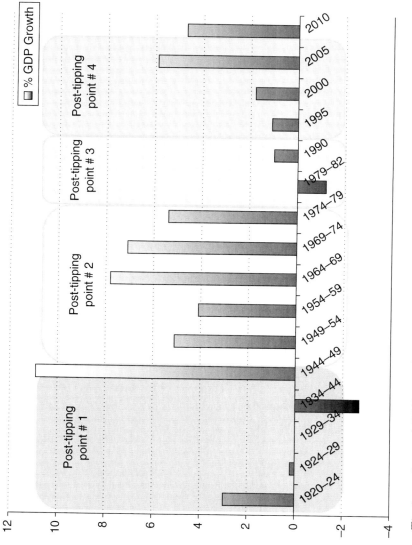

Figure 8.1 Tipping points and GDP growth rates in Costa Rica, 1920–2010

The second tipping point was the consequence of a short but bloody civil war in 1948 and the promulgation in 1949 of the current constitution. The war had many origins, chief among them rampant government corruption and cronyism, major electoral fraud and a perceived threat from communism. The two decades of economic crisis were followed by five years of rapid economic growth (see panel two in Figure 8.1), which facilitated the illicit enrichment of the governing coalition. The end of the civil war ushered in a new regime and promulgated a new constitution that reconfigured political power to create one of the weakest presidencies in the Americas. Moreover, electoral fraud was eradicated through the creation of what almost amounted to a fourth branch of government, called the Supreme Election Tribunal. The Tribunal guaranteed free and fair elections and removed the direct influence of politicians (Wilson and Rodríguez 2011).[3] The particularistic capacities and tendencies of the executive and other government officials were further curtailed with the creation of new audit agencies to investigate government expenditure and contracts, and a vast group of autonomous institutions financed from outside the executive budget. The new specialized institutions and financial controls marked a period of competitive particularism.

A third tipping point came during the 1980s and 1990s in response to major political and financial corruption scandals, which in our opinion delineate a 'borderline' period edging closer to 'ethical universalism'. The state's response was to create more audit and accountability agencies and situate them outside the control of the executive, thereby granting them more political and financial autonomy. Among the most significant of the new institutions was the Constitutional Chamber of the Supreme Court (Sala Constitucional, commonly called the Sala Cuarta or Sala IV), generally viewed as one of the most powerful superior courts in Latin America (Navia and Ríos-Figueroa 2005; Gloppen et al. 2010). Figure 8.1 depicts the major economic crisis of the late 1970s and 1980s, and the anaemic economic growth during the 1990s while the state was being reorganized and reformed, all of which provided the backdrop for the anti-corruption initiatives.

The fourth tipping point, sparked by a series of political corruption scandals that severely tested the capacities of existing anti-corruption agencies, saw two former presidents and many of their senior aides arrested, tried and sent to jail for corruption.[4] The subsequent period was marked by broader anti-corruption driven legal reforms and their more comprehensive implementation. It was also after this tipping point that the concept of 'accountability' was constitutionalized and the candidate from the anti-corruption Citizen's Action Party (PAC), Luis Guillermo Solís, was elected president.[5]

Our analysis suggests an institutional explanation that identifies a relationship between Costa Rica's progress in the fight against corruption and its decision to arrange the devolution of political power across government branches and agencies; the creation, funding and empowerment of accountability agencies; the freeing of the press (including social media); and the more recent rise of civil society organizations. Many of the changes were not in fact designed with the specific or primary intent of curtailing corruption, but nonetheless changed the institutional context in a way that severely limited the opportunities for corruption, and the reforms tended to take place prior to major periods of economic development and rising national income.

8.3   HISTORICAL BACKGROUND

Costa Rica is a small, middle-income developing country situated on the Central American isthmus between Nicaragua and Panama to the north and south respectively, and the Caribbean and Pacific Oceans to the east and west. Politically and economically Costa Rica is frequently considered an outlier in Central America. The country has had regular, competitive, fair and legally unchallenged executive and legislative elections without incident every four years since 1953 (Freedom House 2014). For much of the 20th century it was not just the only democracy in Central America, but the only country in the region not embroiled in internecine wars or state terrorism. The country has no standing army, enjoys the highest Human Development Index (HDI) and World Bank governance indicator rankings in the region (World Bank 2013), and is consistently classified by the Bertelsmann Index as one of the top developing countries (Bertelsmann Foundation 2014). It is the least corrupt country in Central America, and the third least corrupt in Latin America (Transparency International 2014). The IPI places it as number 18 out of 105 countries, a great achievement indeed (Table 8.2).

Many scholars of Costa Rican history and politics point to a purported 'exceptionalism' that afforded the country a long egalitarian economic and social history punctuated by democratic elections which began in the 1880s. However, more recent scholarship suggests its early development was similar to that of its Central American neighbours. Like the rest of Central America, during colonial times Costa Rica was part of the Spanish empire and was governed by the same highly centralized administrative structure where the separation of public office and private gain tended to be blurred. It was, for example, common practice for government officials to purchase their positions and recoup their 'investments' by skimming

Table 8.2   Costa Rica's public integrity framework

Components of Index of Public Integrity	Component Score	World Rank	Regional Rank	Income Group Rank
Judicial Independence	7.4	20/105	1/16	2/28
Administrative Burden	8.11	56/105	7/16	16/28
Trade Openness	8.21	30/105	5/16	6/28
Budget Transparency	8.85	18/105	3/16	5/28
E-Citizenship	6.13	40/105	4/16	6/28
Freedom of the Press	9.18	10/105	1/16	1/28

Source: Index of Public Integrity.

taxes and duties; Creedman (1991, p. 234), for example, notes that corruption was so widespread in Costa Rica that the jobs of the *regidores* (aldermen) 'usually went to the highest bidder'.

Post-independence governance did not deviate very far from this pattern; the newly created presidential office was the strongest branch, and most presidents took office not through the ballot box but through non-democratic means. Presidents regularly used their position to reward friends and family with government jobs or contracts – and to punish the losers. For example, Tomás Guardia Gutiérrez – Costa Rica's modernizing, if dictatorial, president from 1870 to 1882 – used his position to diminish the political power of the dominant coffee elite by dislodging them from high government office to replace them with members of his own family, and by expanding the franchise (Wilson 1998, p. 22). Using public office for personal enrichment was still common practice and rarely investigated. In 1873, for example, when Congress asked President Guardia to account for 100,000 pounds he received from Henry Meiggs, a railway builder, the president claimed it was a donation used to pay for a feasibility study for the railway. However, no documents were ever provided to support Guardia's claim (Peraldo and Rojas 1998).[6]

Although ostensibly the struggle for political control of the newly independent country was between the Conservative and Liberal parties, the battles are perhaps better understood as struggles between competing elite families rather than ideologically based political parties. The vast majority of presidents of Costa Rica from independence until the late 1880s represented the Liberal Party, yet many of them took office by removing other members of the same Liberal Party. Again, President Guardia presents a compelling example of political succession, for in 1882, when President Guardia Gutiérrez – who had himself come to power in the first place in a coup d'état against another Liberal president – died in office, he was replaced by his brother-in-law, Próspero Fernández Oreamuno (also of the Liberal Party). Three years later, when President Fernández too died in office, his son-in-law, Bernardo Soto Alfaro (Liberal Party), became president. Although such dynastic transfer of power was far from democratic, President Guardia Gutiérrez and his family's long control of the state facilitated an increasing separation of public and private interests, in part by breaking the coffee elite's historical grip on political power and opening up the franchise to a growing number of competing interests and voters.

The policies pursued by Guardia Gutiérrez and his family ushered in a new liberal constitution in 1871[7] and oversaw the watershed election in 1889 that was open, competitive, covered by a free press and an 'honest tabulation of results' (Rinehart 1984, p. 29).[8] The 1889 election marked the first time in Costa Rican history that a peaceful transfer of power had ever taken place from an incumbent president to a challenger, in this case one José Joaquín Rodríguez Zeledón. Social groups mobilized to demand the election results be respected in recognition that the opposition party had won (Salazar 1990; Salazar and Salazar 1992; Pérez 1997). Although that was a major step towards democratic government, real democracy continued to develop only slowly and with many setbacks, including numerous undemocratic transfers of power, a military dictatorship from 1917 to 1919 and short civil war in 1948.[9]

If the post-independence period was a political free-for-all for control of the state machinery, during the first half of the 20th century Costa Rica gradually became more democratic. It also saw the creation of the first mechanisms of control, including some accountability agencies that allowed the state to deal, even if only ineffectually, with matters considered corruption or the misuse of power. An important first step towards reducing routine political corruption was the gradual limitations placed on presidential powers brought about by a struggle gathering pace within the judicial branch for increased autonomy and professionalism. Since the 1880s Costa Rica's political discourse had included the idea of promoting a modern state with professional, impartial institutions, an independent judiciary and a legal culture similar to those found in Western industrialized democracies. The reforms were not to be an explicit attack on the power of the executive; nor were they part of any larger plan to restrict the particularistic behaviour of the president. The judicial sector reforms, for example, designed to insulate magistrates from the partisan politics of the day, produced the unintended consequence of enhancing the institutional autonomy and power of the judiciary to limit the self-serving actions of the executive. Congress, not the executive, appointed magistrates to their four-year terms and could remove them only in exceptional circumstances. To insulate them further from politics, all judicial personnel were prohibited from joining political parties or taking part in election campaigns,[10] and an 1898 reform decoupled magistrates' appointments from presidential elections by moving the appointment period to the middle of the presidential term.

Many governments in the post-independence period were led by enlightened if less than democratic leaders inspired by liberal ideas from Spain. They introduced policies and laws, such as free compulsory education in 1869, that laid the foundations of the modern Costa Rican state and facilitated the rise of an export economy based on coffee and bananas. Not least, they prepared the ground for a nascent welfare state in which the state would become the provider of key social goods.

8.4   TIPPING POINT #1: THE END OF DICTATORSHIP AND PATRIMONIALISM

The tipping point constituted by the overthrow of the Tinoco dictatorship in 1919 resulted in increased judicial independence and the creation of the first horizontal accountability controls.[11] High levels of corruption and concentration of political power during the dictatorship motivated the political elite's efforts to limit presidential control over public resources. Fernández (2010) details abuses of power by the president, including advance payments to family members appointed to diplomatic posts and renting the Fabrica Nacional de Licores (FANAL) to one of his friends for a nominal sum. Tinoco and his allies' wide-ranging illicit behaviour was made public as the opposition parties began to use a rising 'fourth estate', especially the newly founded anti-government newspaper *Diario de Costa Rica* (Cañas 2010). Shortly after the fall of the dictatorship an office of the Budget Comptroller (*Oficina de Control*) was created to audit government spending and contracts within the president's office.

The post-Tinoco government removed all magistrates appointed during the dictatorship and granted all new ones life tenure and a guaranteed salary structure. Employees in the judicial branch were well organized, and during the 1930s they successfully demanded a more professional judiciary as well as autonomy and freedom from interference from the executive.[12] The resultant reforms, including the 1937 *Ley Orgánica del Poder Judicial* (Organic Law of the Judicial Branch), facilitated the creation of a judiciary with distinct institutional cohesion and helped strengthen its institutional capacities and the formal separation of powers (Cascante 2014; PEN 2015). Taken together, the reforms enhanced the judiciary's identity as a cohesive and distinct branch of the state. The reforms also facilitated the judiciary's ability to exercise with less political interference its constitutionally mandated horizontal function to uphold the rule of law and provide accountability.

Although these reforms began a process of strengthening the de facto separation of powers and increased the extent to which presidents could be held accountable for their actions, other institutional designs undercut their effectiveness. For example, this newly discovered judicial independence was weakened by the retention of the Supreme Court as an administrative unit of the Ministry of Justice, which left it as part of the executive branch, which therefore remained in control of the judiciary's budget. Moreover, before 1935 most magistrates tended to come from political backgrounds; it was not until 1935 that for the first time a career judge became president of the Supreme Court. All the same, those institutional shifts had created a judiciary with a professional mind-set that understood its function as a body separate from politics, so the changes did indicate that steps were being taken towards imposing constraints on the overreach of power then routinely exercised by presidents.

In 1937 the *Ley Orgánica del Poder Judicial* introduced constitutional review for the first time, a first legal control to limit government decisions and which put in place a mechanism for checks and balance between branches. The law also introduced the *Inspección Judicial* (Judicial Inspection Office), a new internal but independent control mechanism for the oversight of all judicial workers, including judges. Since the adoption of that law the judiciary in Costa Rica has had complete control over both its budget and its employees, their recruitment, salaries and sanctions. It is important to note that the law was framed by magistrates and judicial employees; the judiciary was formally granted its prerogative of self-regulation by the 1949 Constitution.

During the same period of economic turmoil (see Figure 8.1) the first modern political parties were founded, among them the Reformist Party in 1923 (a product of the *Confederación de Trabajadores Costarricenses* labour union) and the Communist Party in 1931. With the expansion of the franchise and increased regularity of cleaner elections, political party platforms tended to focus more on 'social' questions rather than personalities. Simultaneously, new intellectual groups were founded, including the *Alianza Revolucionaria Costarricenses* (1929) and the *Centro para el Estudio de los Problemas Nacionales* (1940) and they began proposing broad political reforms to improve the functioning of the democratic regime, economic and social development models, and the creation of and intervention in a strong national state.

8.5   TIPPING POINT #2: ELECTORAL FRAUD, CORRUPTION, CIVIL WAR AND COMPETITIVE PARTICULARISM

The 1948 civil war marks the second tipping point in the fight against corruption, and represents perhaps the most significant juncture in Costa Rica's political history. Lack of space precludes a complete explanation here of the complex causes of the civil war, but it is important to note that government corruption, electoral fraud, expropriation of the property of the descendants of Germans and fear of communism were the principal arguments used by the insurrectionists to challenge the incumbent military government (Ameringer 1982; Molina and Lehoucq 2002). In the aftermath of the civil war a number of measures were codified and institutions created to prevent repetition of the political chaos, corruption and electoral fraud that had been a regular feature of the period before the war.

The civil war and its aftermath in fact helped change the country from a politically unstable democracy to a stable and consolidated democracy with competitive elections among ideas-based political parties as Costa Rica was transformed from a poor backwater to the most prosperous country in the region. The victorious forces in the civil war were an alliance between José Figueres, a small farmer affiliated with a small social democratic party, and his National Liberation Army on the one hand,[13] and the conservative National Unity Party (*Partido Unidad Nacional*, PUN) and the coffee elite. The PUN was led by Otilio Ulate Blanco, the presumed winner of the 1948 fraudulent election. During an 18-month interregnum Figueres governed the country with a junta and helped create a new constitutional order with the goal of preventing a return to the corrupt and undemocratic *caudillo* politics of the 1940s.

Figueres drew on many of the ideas espoused by the intellectual father of the modern Costa Rican state, Rodrigo Facio Brenes, perhaps the closest thing to a 'reforming hero' figure. Facio founded the *Centro de Estudio para los Problemas Nacionales*, CEPN, 1942) and the *Partido Social Demócrata* (PSD, 1945) and was an influential member of the Constitutional Assembly in the immediate post-war period.[14] He argued in favour of Uruguayan-style autonomous institutions,[15] a professional civil service and elected judges, and against a powerful presidential office, personalistic politicians and the traditional way of doing politics. Facio's ideas were informed in part by the huge corruption scandals during the pre-civil war governments of Calderón Fournier and León Cortés; but it would be an overstatement to suggest that he was driven by an anti-corruption agenda.

Facio's goal of replacing the 1871 Constitution was made more difficult because the CEPN and *Junta Fundadora* even together made up only a minority in the elected Constitutional Assembly. The drafting of the new constitution required negotiation and compromise with the conservative majority that wanted merely to update the 1871 Constitution. In a speech in the Constitutional Assembly, Facio declared that 'we want a democratic state, free, efficient, accountable, controlled with the division of functions and decentralization that guarantee citizenship against alleged disrespect of their rights' (cited by Castro 2003, p. 119).

The most significant change was the disbandment and constitutional prohibition of a standing army and the diminution of the powers of the executive that gave Costa Rica perhaps the weakest presidential office in its hemisphere (Shugart and Carey 1992). Perhaps surprisingly, in 1949, at the end of its agreed period of office, Figueres voluntarily dissolved the governing junta and allowed Ulate Blanco to assume the office of president (Acuña 1993; Cerdas and Contreras, 1988; Cerdas 1998).[16]

Electoral corruption was dealt a severe blow with the creation of a fourth quasi-governmental branch, the institution of a politically and financially autonomous *Tribunal Supremo de Elecciones* or Supreme Elections Tribunal (TSE 2014).[17] The magistrates of the TSE are doubly removed from the contemporary political life of the country. They are elected to six-year renewable terms by a two-thirds majority vote of the full Supreme Court, those magistrates being in turn elected by Congress using a super-majorities rule (Wilson 2003).[18] Congress may not alter or reduce the TSE's budget, so that the body enjoys effective financial autonomy, too. The TSE supervises and controls all aspects related to voting and the election process, including civil registry of births, marriages, deaths, citizenship, electoral rolls and identity cards. The TSE also trains polling station workers, designs and prints ballot papers and certifies all election results. Polling data show Costa Ricans tend to have a great deal of confidence in the work of the TSE and in electoral outcomes (Hernández 1977, pp. 76–9).

The post-civil war state maintained many of the social policies initiated by the defeated government, expanded the state's economic and social role by nationalizing many industries and public utilities, and augmented the existing emerging welfare state. The 1949 Constitution established the first generation of modern accountability mechanisms in Costa Rica and created institutions to control the administration of a more professional civil service. A series of new accountability agencies were created to prevent the re-emergence of pre-civil war corruption and to curtail particularism in state agencies and politicians. The most important of those agencies were the Comptroller General's Office (*Contraloría General de la República*, CGR), the Attorney General's Office (*Procuraduría General*

de la República, PGR) and the Bank Auditing Office, an audit agency for
the newly nationalized state agencies which included the new state banks.
Important too for public services was the National Electricity Service
(SNE) (Villarreal 2004).

Another effort to limit public corruption was articulated in one of the
earliest laws of the new republic – Law No. 1166 of June 1950, *Declaración
de bienes de los funcionarios públicos* (Declaration of Assets of Public
Officials). The law required senior public officials to list all their assets
every year, although in fact the utility of the exercise depended entirely
on the honesty of the individual public official, for there was no effective
agency that could realistically check the veracity of claims or corroborate
what was or was not reported. The number of public officials covered by
'declaration of assets' laws has been expanded over the years, most recently
to include judges. Nancy Hernández, a senior advisor to the Supreme
Court (now a magistrate in the Constitutional Chamber of the Supreme
Court), notes that the previous lack of requirement for such reporting
from judges created significant opportunities for corrupt politicians and
criminals to bribe judges.[19]

In 1973 the judiciary became responsible for the operations of the
General Prosecutor's Office (*Ministerio Público*, MP) and the criminal
police (*Organismo de Investigación Judicial*, OIJ), which had previously
reported to the executive branch. The goals of those reforms were to
increase job security and reduce political interference in the criminal
system by placing its agencies within the remit of the judicial branch. As a
consequence of the reorganization the *Fiscalía* was no longer controlled by
the executive,[20] and was for the first time able to pursue corruption cases
even when they involved high-level politicians. Simultaneous but unrelated
improvements in the checks-and-balances system included a gradual movement towards an increasingly professionalized civil service.[21] Although
during the first decades of this 'Second Republic' the governing party
controlled nearly all public appointments, the historical pattern of periodic
sweeping changes of civil service personnel was eventually ended.[22]

This first generation of accountability institutions were highly dependent on the executive for appointments and budgets, had limited powers
and experienced personnel shortages; they suffered too from an almost
non-existent level of citizen participation. For example, in 1977 the
Comptroller General's audit department was responsible for investigating over 80 municipalities and hundreds of other public institutions,
but employed only 25 civil servants. The consequence was an enormous
backlog, with most audit reports taking between two and four years: by
definition they were always out of date and were most probably ineffective as anti-corruption audit agencies (Hernández 1977; Vicenti 1977).

Their limitations were particularly serious considering the rapid growth of nearly all state sectors across the whole of Latin America. In Costa Rica in the 1950s public servants constituted 6 per cent of the economically active population (EAP), whereas by 1979 they made up more than 18 per cent (Vargas Cullell et al. 2001). The period 1950 to 1980 was not only one of democratic progress and political inclusion; for most of the population those years also held a success story of social and economic development, as evidenced by multiple indicators illustrated in Table 8.3.

8.6   TIPPING POINT #3: THE 1980S AND 1990S, A TWO-PARTY SYSTEM AND A BORDERLINE CONDITION

The decline of public trust in government (Alfaro and Seligson 2014), together with a major drug trafficking scandal in the middle of the 1980s, marked the third tipping point and the beginning of a second phase in the expansion of the accountability mechanism. The period was characterized by the creation of new institutions, expansion of the powers of existing ones and the criminalization of corrupt acts. All of that went hand in hand with increased media capacity to investigate and report corruption cases. Unlike the earlier periods of anti-corruption development, the period marks the first time international influences played a crucial role in both promoting anti-corruption legislation and in the creation of new accountability institutions in Costa Rica (Villarreal 2004; Uggla 2003).

The 1980s and 1990s witnessed the arrival of new mandated institutions and increases in the size of the state. The rest of the region too experienced the creation of similar new mandated institutions also with the support of international donors. A good example is the ombudsman office set up in the 1990s with European Union (EU) and Scandinavian assistance. Existing accountability institutions such as the CGR and the PGR underwent profound reforms that increased their political independence, because now a two-thirds majority was required in congress for the appointment of their directors and they gained enhanced budget autonomy. This institutionalization of accountability agencies resulted in a major expansion of their staff and budgets in Costa Rica unparalleled in other Central American countries (Figure 8.2).

During the same period a major transformation took place in the political arena. Various small conservative parties that had fought elections as an anti-PLN alliance now formally merged and became a single party, the *Partido Unidad Social Cristiana* (Social Christian Unity Party, PUSC), while the revolutionary left (banned since the civil war) returned to contest

Table 8.3 Costa Rica's major socio-economic indicators, 1940–2010

Indicator	1940	1950	1960	1970	1980	1990	2000	2010
Population (1,000)	656	812	1199	1758	2302	3050	3925	4509
Population in metropolitan area (1000)		190	320	475	647	843	1044	1199
Poverty (% households)			50.0	29.0	19.0	27.0	21.0	18.5
Life expectancy	46.9	55.6	62.5	65.4	72.6	76.7	77.7	79.3
Childhood mortality (1000)	123	90	68	61	19	15	10	9
Fecundity rate		7.0	7.0	5.0	3.6	3.2	2.4	1.9
Malnutrition under 6 years (%)			14	12	4	4	3	2
Social security coverage (%)		8	15	39	70	82	88	90
Illiteracy (+11 years) (%)	27	21	16	13	10	7	5	
Years of education (pop. + 24 years)		3.1	3.6	5.3	5.9	7.4	8.2	8.8
Drinking water at home (1000)			640	770	860	941	974	1000
Primary forest coverage (%)			56	51	29	22		
GDP per capita (US$)	702	847	1080	1501	2032	2301	4058	6492
EAP women (%)		15	16	19	28	29	35	38
Agriculture sector (%)	66	63	59	49	35	25	20	11
Women in congress (%)					5	12	19	39

Source: PEN (2014).

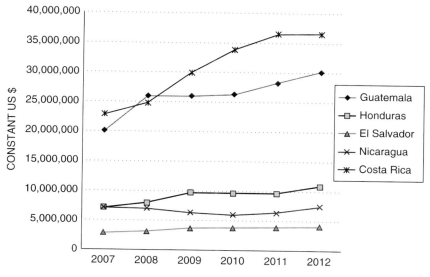

Source: MESICIC (2012).

Figure 8.2   *Annual budgets of supreme audit agencies in Central America,*
                2007–2012

general elections. In the 1990 general election the PUSC won majority control of the legislative assembly and the presidency; this marked only the second time since the civil war that a party other than the PLN had achieved a single-party majority government.[23] Historically it had been the PLN that had dominated Costa Rican politics, winning five of eight presidential elections between 1953 and 1986 as well as majority control of the Legislative Assembly on six occasions.

In October 1989, a constitutional amendment created a Constitutional Chamber of the Supreme Court (commonly called *Sala IV*), which is generally regarded as one of the most powerful superior courts in the Americas. Its decisions are binding on everyone;[24] it has extensive powers of judicial review both before and after a bill is passed into law; and it grants standing and access to even the most marginalized people. Indeed, since its inception Sala IV has played the most important accountability role in Costa Rica. Its open access and broad definition of standing has allowed anyone to bring a case to the court to challenge the constitutionality of the actions of any public or private official. However, in spite of its powers and the centrality of its role in the political and administrative life of the country, Sala IV was not expressly designed to take on an anti-corruption role. Nevertheless, as Wilson (2014) has shown, the court has acted as a referee of laws and regulations which, taken together, have limited the ability of politicians to engage in particularistic allocations of state funds, government contracts and jobs.[25]

During the 1980s, corruption stories appeared infrequently either in the national media or as any sort of concern in opinion polls. That might indeed have been due to the great deal of political turmoil that engulfed the isthmus during that decade. There was of course the revolution and counter-revolution in Nicaragua to the north, the US invasion of Panama to the south and, not least, a major economic crisis that brought the country's economic model into question. Despite apparent lack of public concern about corruption congress decided to pass a law against illicit enrichment in a public function in 1983 that compelled public servants to declare all their sources of income. But, as with the earlier laws of the kind, the CGR did not have the capacity to audit declarations, so the law was never used to initiate any investigation of financial impropriety by public servants.[26] In 1996, Costa Rica signed another international anti-corruption instrument, the Inter-American Convention against Corruption (OAS 1996).

Media denunciation of political corruption scandals rose in the context of this new institutional and legal framework. During the 1990s there were at least ten major corruption events involving presidents, vice-presidents or ministers being exposed by the media, including major scandals with the Emergency Funds, *Banco Anglo* (BAC), FODESAF and *Aviación civil* (Vargas Cullell et al. 2011; Raventós 2004).

Scandals even affected state institutions that had previously been believed impervious to corruption, such as the TSE. Despite the TSE's long history of successfully safeguarding democratic elections the scandals revealed its weak capacity to monitor private donations to political parties (Global Integrity 2007, p. 36). There is little transparency concerning any donations private companies or even drug cartels might make to political parties, and it is difficult to prove illicit enrichment. That was indeed the case with former president Abel Pacheco, who accepted $100,000 from Alcatel and $500,000 from a Taiwanese businessman apparently in return for government contracts (Global Integrity 2007, pp. 3–4). Similarly, Oscar Arias (PLN 1986–90) received a $20,000 cheque from the USA that he later acknowledged was money from an international drug cartel. On a separate occasion Arias's campaign attempted to take delivery of a suit-case stuffed with $750,000 and smuggled into the country (Reuters 1992). In response to all this, the Electoral Code (*Código Electoral Ley* 8765) was reformed in 2009 to empower the TSE to audit political parties' campaign expenses more closely. In the 2010 elections, the five best-supported parties were investigated for mismanagement and irregularities, and some of the resulting cases were referred to the Prosecutor's Office (PEN 2012, p. 239). Such cases included one of electoral fraud against a number of Libertarian party leaders; guilty verdicts and jail sentences were the result (Cambronero 2015).

Certain prevailing characteristics of corruption during that period are worth noting. First, in the rare cases where the press reported acts of corruption it targeted mainly high-level political corruption involving congressmen, presidents or other senior authorities. While such cases appeared in the press from time to time, journalists frequently failed to follow up cases or publish their conclusions. In part that was related to expansive libel laws that required journalists to provide extraordinary levels of proof before publishing an investigative story accusing a public figure of corruption or any other kind of misbehaviour. Publishing stories without reliable evidence could mean jail for the journalist. For example, when a journalist wrote a story accusing President José Maria Figueres Olsen (PLN 1994–98), while he was in office, of financial irregularities in his dealings with state banks, no state agency investigated the veracity of the newspaper reports, and neither charges nor prosecution followed; rather, it was the journalist who was reprimanded and lost his job (Gudmundson 1996, p. 80). The restrictions on press freedoms arising from the 1902 press law kept a close gag on journalists; as a result many stories that should have been published were not.

Secondly, taken together the shackled media and understaffed accountability agencies that operated under the two-party system resulted in reciprocal control but little public exposure of wrong-doing. That meant that the highest appointments to those institutions were distributed between the two parties, and ordinary citizens rarely became aware of corruption by public officials. Even when stories did make it into the media, high-ranking politicians or public officials were seldom prosecuted. Finally, it is true that citizen participation was rare, in particular relating to subjects such as transparency or accountability. Citizens had no direct access to control institutions nor tools such as social media; the only channels available to denounce acts of corruption were the traditional media or the judiciary.

8.7   TIPPING POINT #4: CONTEMPORARY COSTA RICA: APPROXIMATING ETHICAL UNIVERSALISM

At first glance Costa Rica's contemporary period appears to be a huge backward step in its journey towards ethical universalism. In 2004 for example, two former presidents were charged, tried, convicted and

sentenced for their part in a major corruption scandal.[27] Scandals reported
in the newspapers surrounding political party election financing, and the
daily abuse of office, produced a general popular sense that corruption
is a pervasive and unresolved problem in Costa Rica. However, we will
argue that although such recent high-profile scandals are indeed serious,
and highlight some of the significant weaknesses in Costa Rican anti-
corruption agencies and practices, they also mark the last tipping point
and the final transition to ethical universalism in Costa Rica.[28]

The 2006 Costa Rican elections proved the 'selective affinity' between
accountability and elections when the main party involved in the 2004
corruption scandals, the PUSC, saw its electoral support collapse from its
traditional levels of 35–40 per cent to approximately 3 per cent. That election also saw the rise of the Citizens' Action Party (PAC), a new party with
a high anti-corruption profile that almost won the presidency in only its
second national election.[29] In the 2014 election, while it won control of the
presidency, it failed to secure even plurality in Congress.

The scandals also illustrate the importance of new actors in the anti-
corruption arena – the traditional media and the new social media. It was
the newly assertive press,[30] particularly *La Nación* (the country's leading
daily newspaper) and its well-funded investigative unit, that scrutinized the
conspicuous consumption of some Costa Rican Social Security Agency
(CCSS) board members that led to the uncovering of a much larger corruption scandal which involved a former president. Once the conspiracy
had been revealed in newspaper reports, state agencies then initiated their
own investigation. The official investigation then culminated in the trials of
the former president and his collaborators, with their subsequent conviction, hefty fines and jail sentences – although they are under appeal at the
time of writing (Wilson 2014). It is worth noting that in these cases, Costa
Rica became the first country to charge perpetrators of corrupt acts with
'social damage',[31] an extra penalty in addition to any asset recovery that
might occur.

Although civil society related to political questions tends to be weak
in Costa Rica, citizen participation in anti-corruption action has become
increasingly common. Because the new institutions actively encourage
individuals to bring cases without having to pay fees, the need for well-
organized, well-funded, civil society anti-corruption organizations is less
pressing, and many of the cases taken up by the anti-corruption agencies
were brought to their attention by individual citizens. During this last
period the Comptroller's Office, the judiciary and the Ombudsman have
opened a wide range of new channels such as online forms, email, telephone and paper through which citizens can denounce perceived acts of
corruption and give anonymous reports. Coupled with that has come the

unleashing of traditional media and the rise of social media, both of which have increased the capacity of state anti-corruption agencies to identify, reveal and investigate acts of public corruption in a manner not previously possible.[32]

Accountability agencies explicitly follow stories of interest in traditional and social media, and can use what they find to initiate investigations and prosecute acts of illicit enrichment. The Electoral Court (TSE) has been another addition to the control system, because since the 2010 elections it has been responsible for the supervision of campaign finances. Tighter legislation and closer supervision have led to a number of trials for mis-management of campaign funds and corruption. The control agencies also practise preventive approaches to anti-corruption by developing indicators such as indexes of transparency and an index of effectiveness, for example; and they have held regular events to educate public servants about trans-parency, anti-corruption legislation and good practice.

Newspapers and social media, emboldened by changes in the laws that previously criminalized errors in reporting, now use sophisticated com-puter software to investigate and shine a light on corrupt acts by public officials. In addition, new laws and institutions allow the state to respond to newspaper stories and claims made by citizens with thorough investiga-tions and prosecutions. For example, the CGR uses the system of 'asset declaration' to cross-check these public claims. In 2012 a change in the law allowed the wider application of this new preventive tool to a larger number of public servants, including approximately 3000 judges, which has probably had the effect of forestalling possible corrupt schemes by politicians or public officials. However, the very real weaknesses in the funding and training of personnel within these anti-corruption agencies have left potential gaps in the state's anti-corruption vigilance.

Much of the awareness of and discussion about corruption stems not from individual politicians dedicated to eradicating corruption, but instead originates in an active press aided by the advent of the internet and social media. While on the surface therefore it might appear that Costa Rica has regressed and become more corrupt, as polling data appear to suggest, the opposite story can be told in compelling terms. Both traditional and social media have overcome some of the weakness of social movements in Costa Rica, and have invigorated the state's anti-corruption agencies and facilitated their capacity to identify, investigate and prosecute acts of illicit enrichment and misuse of public office. The unshackled media and strengthened laws and institutions allow state agencies to respond to news-paper, internet and other social media stories, or to citizens' claims brought to the attention of those agencies.[33]

The key difference distinguishing the current period from the earlier ones is the fact that the tackling of corruption was designed as the main purpose of the new adjustments to the legal and institutional framework, and was not therefore a secondary effect. For example, in 2000 an accountability principle was included explicitly in the 1949 Constitution, and the *Ley Orgánica de la CRG* established a true system of accountability, coordinated by the CGR.[34] In 2000 a constitutional reform included for the first time the principle of accountability (*rendición de cuentas*) for all public servants.

This third generation was when accountability mechanisms were developed in an evolving political context. Under the traditional two-party system control of the executive and legislature alternated between a social democratic-leaning party (PLN) and a Christian social party (PUSC); but that system collapsed and was replaced by a multi-party system littered with small parties and with no party winning a working majority in Congress after 1994. During this transition period one of the leading questions in election campaigns has been corruption perpetrated by political elites. It is not surprising therefore that the current president (since 2014), Luis Solís, represents a party (the PAC) that was created specifically in response to the corruption scandals of the 1990s. Nor is it any wonder that once in office, from 2014 to 2018, it included 'open government, transparency and anti-corruption' among the three priorities of its National Development Plan, along with poverty reduction and economic growth. Wilson (2014) develops in more detail the extent, scope and popular perception of corruption that allowed a party focusing on an anti-corruption agenda to win the 2014 presidential election.[35] Despite such flux among their political parties and Costa Ricans' general belief that corruption is endemic, more than 68 per cent have 'pride in their political system', a higher percentage than in any other country in the Americas. However, that figure is still relatively low when compared to its own historical record after 1978 (Alfaro and Seligson 2014).

While a revitalized media has been fundamental to bringing cases of corruption to the attention of both the public and the anti-corruption agencies, it was a series of institutional reforms that enhanced the role of those agencies. Together with ten years of Constitutional Court jurisprudence, four important pieces of accountability legislation have been approved since the start of the 21st century. First came the Law of Financial Management and Public Budget (LAFPP, 2002), then the Law of Internal Controls (2002), the law of citizen protection against excessive administrative procedures (2002) and the Law against Corruption and Illicit Enrichment in the Public Sector (2004). Even though it is always possible to improve legislation, most interviewees concur that for now the legal framework is sufficient to combat corruption. As one former deputy minister asserted:

Legally and institutionally speaking the chances of taking public resources almost disappeared with the new legislation. If I, as a minister, needed one cheque, it had to pass through a long chain of approvals; it would not be easy at all because you'd have to co-opt the whole chain. Basically that means that the nature of corruption has changed; now it is more likely to have irregularities in appointments of personnel, trading in influences, government procurement, etc.[36]

The anti-corruption landscape since the start of the new millennium amplified the remit and funding of existing institutions, and added new ones. In 2002, for example, the Office of the Public Prosecutor (MP) was expanded to include a section to deal specifically with corruption and fraud – the *Fiscalía Penal de Hacienda y Función Pública*, later known by various names and currently called the *Fiscalía Anticorrupción y Probidad*. Similarly, the PGR's remit was expanded with the addition of a *Procuraduría de la Ética Pública* (Public Ethics Office). In recent years, most of the institutions of control have experienced an increase in their functions, their budgets in real terms and in their personnel. Congressional appointments of the heads of the institutions now follow more transparent and technical procedures that have removed even more political influence. Supreme Court magistrates appointed in the last decade, for example, have had few political connections, but instead have tended to have had almost exclusively judicial careers or backgrounds in higher education – an important change from the previous political appointments (PEN 2015).

8.8   CONCLUSIONS

Costa Rica is currently regarded among the least corrupt countries in its hemisphere, having robust control institutions, independent media able to act as a watchdog and significant up-to-date anti-corruption legislation. Even though efforts can be further improved, the current situation is considered a success story when compared with Costa Rica's historical levels of corruption or the patterns of corruption among its regional neighbours. At the time of its independence from Spain, Costa Rica already had a long tradition of authoritarian leaders and an acceptance of the melding of public and private interests. The country gradually moved from particularism to ethical universalism in four stages beginning at the start of the 20th century, although it never had a well-mapped anti-corruption strategy. The country's democratization went hand in hand with the strengthening of the rule of law, both of which generally happened prior to significant economic development. However, in spite of that, for most of the 20th century the systematic abuse of power coexisted with progressive efforts to promote a modern, corruption-free state based on the rule of law.

Contemporary levels of corruption are significantly lower in Costa Rica than in any other Central American country, and the creation and funding of new agencies suggests that Costa Rica has taken its anti-corruption remit more seriously than have its neighbours. That two former presidents and their associates were exposed by newspaper reporters and then prosecuted for corrupt acts by the state illustrates the willingness of state anti-corruption agencies to prosecute anyone, no matter how powerful or important. Thus, the potential for public officials to profit from corrupt schemes has been greatly reduced. Citizens and the media have new avenues to uncover, and are prepared to publicize political corruption while raising public awareness of it. They hold elected and appointed officials of the state to account, and thereby put pressure on them to respond to corruption cases through investigation and prosecution as well as institutional reforms that set boundaries and limits on corruption. As has been noted by Alejandro Urbina, the former Editor-in-Chief of *La Nación*, such investigations by journalists make it 'much harder to keep a corrupt act secret; therefore, it's much harder to be a corrupt public servant today than it was 15 years ago' (quoted in Caryl 2015, p. 7).

Tracking these improvements to their origins shows that from early in the first half of the 20th century Costa Rica promoted a slow process of building a strong and independent judiciary and fostered respect for basic freedoms, such as of the press. The country did so in parallel with burgeoning electoral democracy, and even before major economic development came. The rules of the political game delineated by the 1949 Constitution distributed power among different branches of government and created one of the least powerful executives in Latin America. Recently, those tools have been complemented by more sophisticated control legislation and institutions in a context of a multi-party system, and that has helped motivate improved political controls. The result has been increasing awareness among ordinary citizens of corruption and their greater involvement in its suppression.

However, reaching the highest standards of ethical universalism remains a goal which has not quite been reached. Costa Ricans are now highly sensitive to corruption, and corruption scandals are more frequently reported in the media. There is also growing criticism of the capacity of the state to control corruption. What is clear, though, is that the country has the tools and the political context to fight corruption more effectively than any of its regional neighbours; cases are much more likely to be officially reported or brought to public awareness on social media, where they will be met with emphatic disapproval and even condemnation, which in time helps make corruption less acceptable. Changes to the institutions governing Costa Rican politics have made it easier to identify, label and condemn political corruption in its many forms. Recent convictions of senior politicians for electoral financial fraud suggest on the one hand that the new anti-corruption agencies have not been able to eradicate political corruption; but, on the other hand, they show that those agencies have the technical capacity to identify, investigate and prosecute even sophisticated electoral fraud. They show too that the state is committed to the principle that the rule of law must be respected and that all forms of corruption, no matter the perpetrator, are wholly unacceptable.

NOTES

1. The 'grey list' is compiled by the anti-money laundering NGO Financial Action Task Force (FATF), to identify the countries with major money laundering problems (Lohmuller 2015).
2. Research for this chapter spans more than two decades of academic fieldwork for Wilson, and many years of academic research focused on corruption and anti-corruption by Villarreal. Villarreal also brings to bear on the scholarship her years of experience as vice-president of Costa Rica Integra, the local Transparency International affiliate. Our research relies on reviews of primary and secondary sources in Spanish and English, and interviews with leading actors including politicians, judges, journalists, civil servants and academics.
3. The TSE is widely regarded as one of the most effective electoral agencies in the Americas. It acts as an electoral court and administers all aspects of elections – from voter registration, births and deaths registration, to ballot design, training for poll workers, and so on. It maintains a level playing field for political parties, and supervises elections that are ranked among the cleanest and freest in the Americas (Freedom House 2014; Wilson and Rodríguez 2011).
4. A third former president, José María Figueres, was also implicated, but refused to return to Costa Rica to face corruption charges.
5. Partido Acción Cuidadana (PAC) was created in 2000 largely in response to a series of major corruption scandals (Rodríguez 2013, p. 76; Wilson 2003). Although other parties now routinely campaign on anti-corruption platforms, it remains a fundamental part of PAC's identity and is still the central in the party's campaigns (Araya 2013).
6. It should also be noted that the contract with British builders for the railway collapsed partly because of corruption but from lack of funds too (Peraldo and Rojas 1998).
7. The 1871 Constitution survived, with amendments, until the civil war of 1948. It was replaced in 1949 by what is the current constitution.
8. However, even with the broadening of the franchise, there was still no secret ballot during these early elections; patrons were able to watch and record how their workers voted.
9. The highly corrupt Tinoco brothers' dictatorship (1917–19) failed to destroy the nascent social movements that had gown during the previous decades.
10. The 1871 Political Constitution and the 1887 *Ley Orgánica del Poder Judicial*.
11. The *Ley de Nulidades* (Annulments Act) cancelled government decisions taken during the dictatorship.
12. The Judicial Employees National Association (ANEJ) was formally created in 1934 and helped push for the 1937 judicial reforms that strengthened the position of judicial workers above all other public servants and included a generous retirement fund targeted at and controlled by judicial workers (Cascante 2014).

13. A large part of this force was made up of the Caribbean Legion, a multi-national force with the goal of removing dictatorships from across the Caribbean region.
14. He went on to become one of the founders of the *Partido Liberación Nacional*, the single most important post-civil war party.
15. Certain autonomous institutions existed prior to 1949, for example the Central Bank, the University of Costa Rica and the Social Security Agency. However, Facio believed this type of institution could facilitate a larger economic and social role for the state without increasing presidential power and the potential for abuse.
16. This was remarkable on many levels: Figueres had abolished the national army, but remained in control of his National Liberation Army; he was politically opposed to Ulate's ideology and his proposed policies; Figueres' Social Democratic party did poorly in a national election for a constituent assembly, which suggested his party might remain small and never win an election.
17. Constitutional Article 102 states that the role of the TSE is 'to interpret, with exclusive and compulsory effect, all constitutional and legal provisions on electoral matters'.
18. Only a two-thirds majority vote of the full Supreme Court can remove a TSE magistrate. Articles 99–104; TSE Organic Law (Ley No. 3504); Electoral Act (Ley No. 1536) regulate the work of the TSE.
19. Interview with Wilson, 2014.
20. This practice remains common in much of the rest of Central America.
21. The civil service was included in the 1949 Constitution (Title XV), and its statute approved in 1953. However, a draft of this law already existed in 1945, which also demonstrates that the 1949 Constitution was a catalyst for many of the reforms that had been promoted earlier. The Civil Service Law was complemented by other normative achievements, including the 1957 Public Administration Salaries Law (*Ley de Salarios para la adminsitración pública*), the 1970 *Ley de Carrera Docente* and the 1978 General Law for Public Administration.
22. The police force was one of the last bastions of political appointments. Until 1994 most police officers changed with each new government. The 1994 General Police Forces Law mandated that in each of the next four administrations, 25 per cent of the police force would become permanent civil servants. The goal of 100 per cent permanent staff was reached in 2010 (*Ley General de Policía* 7410, 1994; *Ley de Fortalecimiento de la Policía Civilista* 8096, 2001; Ministerio de Seguridad Pública, 2012).
23. Since the 1990 election no party has ever won a straight majority in the Legislative Assembly.
24. The court's decisions are not binding on the court itself, so that it may revisit cases at a later date.
25. Indeed, the transcripts of the parliamentary debates on the creation of the constitutional chamber and interviews with many of the architects and advocates show that the goal was not at all to create an institution that would limit the powers of the popular branches and animate anti-corruption mechanisms.
26. Parts of this law were declared unconstitutional by Sala IV in 1995, further diminishing its effectiveness.
27. A third former president was implicated, but declined to return to Costa Rica from Switzerland to face the charges.
28. For a detailed – and damning – rendition of the Calderón case, see an article by Giannina Segnini, Costa Rica's leading investigative journalist (Global Integrity 2007, pp. 1–20). For an overview of the scandals, see Wilson (2014).
29. For the first time in Costa Rican history, the margin between the main two presidential candidates was so tight that the Electoral Court (TSE) conducted a manual re-count before declaring an official result. Finally, although the new party (the PAC) lost the election by less than 2 per cent of the valid votes, it replaced the PUSC and became the second major political force in the country, and won the presidency outright in 2014.
30. In 2004 an Inter-American Court of Human Rights decision ruled Costa Rica's 1902 Printing Press Law incompatible with Article 13, paragraph 1 of the American

Convention of Human Rights [*Convención Americana de Derechos Humanos*], (*Sentencia de la Corte Interamericana de Derechos Humanos de 2 de julio de 2004. HU vs. C. R.*). Subsequently, in 2010 a Sala IV decision declared significant parts of the press law unconstitutional, effectively ending any significant sanction against journalists or publishers found guilty of 'criminal defamation and insults'.

31. The Ethics Office calculated $52 million of 'social damage' against the seven accused. Alcatel, the French company involved in one of the cases, had to pay $10 million for 'social damage' as part of a conciliatory process. See www.nacion.com/ln_ee/2010/enero/21/pais2233793.html [accessed January 18, 2017].

32. There are many examples of social media sites that publicize presumed wrongdoing by public officials in Costa Rica, including the popular Ticoblogger website 'el Cobrador de la CCSS', which publishes details of individuals (particularly public officials) who are delinquent in the payment of their debts to the state-run social security fund. Another, more general accountability social media site is 'El Infierno en Costa Rica', whose Facebook page has been 'liked' by almost 276,000 individual users.

33. The role of *La Nación*'s investigative journalism unit in revealing major corruption scandals involving three former presidents is well told in Caryl (2015).

34. Although it has broad legal and institutional support and enjoys public confidence, the agency's inefficacy remains a problem.

35. It should be noted that the PAC failed to surmount the 40 per cent required to win the presidency in the first round of elections, but won by a landslide in the second round. While the PAC won control of the presidency, it failed to win a majority or even a plurality of the seats in Congress.

36. Elaine White, political consultant, former vice-minister of foreign affairs, and former congressional advisor. Interview by Villarreal, 2005.

REFERENCES

Acuña, V. (1993). *Conflicto y reforma en Costa Rica (1940–1949)*. San José: Editorial Universidad Estatal a Distancia.

Alfaro, R. and Seligson, M. (2014). "Cultura política de la democracia en Costa Rica y en las Américas, 2014: Gobernabilidad democrática a través de 10 años del Barómetro de las Américas." Available at: www.estadonacion.or.cr/images/stories/biblioteca_virtual/otras_publicaciones/Lapop-2014.pdf [accessed April 18, 2014].

Ahmed, A. and Malkinsept, E. (2015). "Otto Pérez Molina of Guatemala is Jailed Hours after Resigning Presidency." *New York Times*. September 3. Available at: www.nytimes.com/2015/09/04/world/americas/otto-perez-molina-guatemalan-president-resigns-amid-scandal.html?_r=0 [accessed July 21st, 2017].

Ameringer, C. (1982). *Democracy in Costa Rica*. New York: Praeger.

Araya, A. (2013). "Precandidatos del PAC buscarán minimizar malestar de los ticos por corrupción." *La Nación*. July 18. Available at: www.nacion.com/nacional/Precandidatos-PAC-minimizar-malestar-corrupcion_0_1354464767.html [accessed April 18, 2014].

Bertelsmann Foundation. 2014. "Transformation Index." Available at: www.bti-project.org/index/ [accessed September 17, 2014].

Cambronero, N. (2015). "Movimiento Libertario condenado por ejecutar estafa contra el TSE." *La Nación*, October 24. Available at: www.nacion.com/nacional/politica/Movimiento-Libertario-condenado-ejecutar-TSE_0_1520048023.html [accessed October 27, 2015].

Cañas, A. (2010). *Chisporroteos.* Available at: www.larepublica.net/app/cms/cms_periodico_showpdf.php?id_menu=50&pk_articulo=33904&codigo_locale=es-CR [accessed March 12, 2011].

Caryl, C. (2015). "The Data Sleuths of San José: How Three Scrappy Costa Rican Reporters Used the Power of Data to Bring Down a System of Sleaze." Legatum Institute, Democracy Lab. Available at: https://lif.blob.core.windows.net/lif/docs/default-source/publications/the-data-sleuths-of-san-jose---curbing-corruption-may-2015.pdf?sfvrsn=8 [accessed January 20, 2017].

Cascante, C. (2014). "Estudio histórico del Poder Judicial en el marco del proceso de democratización de Costa Rica (1900–1990)." Serie Aportes para el análisis del desarrollo humano sostenible #13. Programa Estado de la Nación. Available at: www.estadonacion.or.cr/images/stories/biblioteca_virtual/otras_publicacion es/APORTES13.pdf [accessed February 27, 2015].

Castro, O. (2003). *El papel de Rodrigo Facio en la Asamblea Constituyente de 1949.* San José: Editorial Universidad Estatal a Distancia.

Cerdas, J. M. and Contreras, G. (1988). *Los años 40. Historia de una política de alianzas.* San José: Editorial Porvenir-ICES.

Cerdas, R. (1998). *La otra cara del 48.* San José: Editorial Universidad Estatal a Distancia. Constitution of the Republic of Costa Rica, Available at: www.wipo.int/wipolex/en/details.jsp?id=9161 [accessed January 19, 2017].

Creedman T. S. (1991). *Historical Dictionary of Costa Rica.* Second edition. Metuchen, NJ: Scarecrow.

Fernández, J. (2010). *Las Presidencias del Castillo Azul.* San José: Litografía e Imprenta LIL.

Freedom House. (2014). "Freedom in the World." [online] Available at: www.freedomhouse.org/report-types/freedom-world [accessed June 17, 2015].

Global Integrity. (2007). "Global Integrity Scorecard: Costa Rica." Available at: http://report.globalintegrity.org/reportPDFS/2007/Costa%20Rica.pdf [accessed June 18, 2015].

Gloppen, S., et al. (2010). *Courts and Power in Latin America and Africa.* New York: Palgrave Macmillan.

Gudmundson, L. (1996). "Costa Rica: New Issues and Alignments." In: Domínguez, J. and Lowenthal, A. (eds). *Constructing Democratic Governance: Mexico, Central America, and the Caribbean in the 1990s, Vol. 3.* Baltimore: Johns Hopkins University Press.

Hernández, A. (1977). "El control posterior ejercido por la Contraloría General de la República en las municipalidades." Thesis. San José, Universidad de Costa Rica.

Lakhani, N. (2015). "Guatemalan President's Downfall Marks Success for Corruption Investigators." *The Guardian.* September 9. Available at: www.theguardian.com/world/2015/sep/09/guatemala-president-otto-perez-molina-cicig-corruption-investigation [accessed September 26, 2015].

Lohmuller. M. (2015). "Did Panama's Former President Run a Criminal Regime?" *Insight Crime.* June 9. Available at: www.insightcrime.org/news-briefs/did-panama-former-president-run-criminal-regime [accessed June 20, 2015].

Luxner, L. (2014). "Costa Rica is Central America's most honest country, says TI corruption Index." *Tico Times.* December 25. Available at: www.ticotimes.net/2014/12/25 [accessed June 18, 2015].

MESICIC. (2012). "Reporte independiente para el Mecanismo de Seguimiento de la Convención Interamericana contra la Corrupción (2012), para Costa Rica."

Asociación Costa Rica Íntegra y Programa Estado de la Nación. Available at: www.oas.org/juridico/pdfs/mesicic4_cri_sc_inf.pdf [accessed June 18, 2015].

Ministerio de Seguridad Pública. (2012). *Memoria Institucional 2011–2012.* San José: Ministerio de Seguridad Pública.

Molina, I. and Lehoucq, F. (2002). *Stuffing the Ballot Box: Fraud, Election Reforms and Democratization in Costa Rica.* Cambridge: Cambridge University Press.

Navia, P. and Ríos-Figueroa, J. (2005). "The Constitutional Adjudication Mosaic of Latin America," *Comparative Political Studies*, **38**(2), 189–217.

OAS (Organization of American States). (1996). *Inter-American Convention Against Corruption.* Available at: www.oas.org/juridico/english/treaties/b-58. html [accessed January 4, 2017].

Programa Estado de la Nación. (2012). *XVII Informe Estado de la Nación.* San José: PEN, CONARE.

Programa Estado de la Nación. (2014). *XX Informe Estado de la Nación en desarrollo humano sostenible.* San José: PEN.

Programa Estado de la Nación (PEN). (2015). *Informe Estado de la Justicia.* San José: PEN.

Peraldo, G. and Rojas, E. (1998). "La deslizable historia del ferrocarril al Caribe de Costa Rica." *Anuario de Estudios Centroamericanos* (Universidad de Costa Rica), **24**(1–2), 97–128.

Pérez, H. 1997. *Breve historia comteporánea de Costa Rica.* México: Fondo de Cultura Económica.

Raventós, C. (2004). "Más allá del escandalo: bases políticas e institucionales de la corrupción." Mimeo, Universidad de Costa Rica.

Reuters. (1992). "Recibí dinero de narcos, admite Oscar Arias." *El Tiempo.* February 2.

Rinehart, R. (1984). "Historical Settings." In: Nelson, H. D. (ed.). *Costa Rica: A Country Study.* Washington, DC: American University.

Rodríguez, A. (2013). "Plan de acción para la implementación de las recomendaciones del MESICIC en Costa Rica." OAS/MESICIC.

Rojas, C. (2005). "El Poder Judicial y la lucha contra la corrupción." Mimeo, San José.

Salazar, O. (1990). *El apogeo de la República Liberal en Costa Rica 1870–1914.* San José: Editorial Universidad de Costa Rica.

Salazar, O. and Salazar, J. (1992). *Los partidos políticos en Costa Rica.* San José: Editorial Universidad Estatal a Distancia.

Shugart, M. and Carey, J. (1992). *Presidents and Assemblies.* Cambridge: Cambridge University Press.

Transparency International. (2014). "The 2014 Corruption Perception Index." [online]. Available at: www.transparency.org/cpi2014 [accessed January 4, 2015].

Tribunal Supremo de Elecciones. (2014). "Elecciones Generales en Cifras 1953–2014." Available at: www.tse.go.cr/pdf/elecciones/eleccionescifras.pdf [accessed May 6, 2015].

Uggla, F. (2003). "The Ombudsman in Latin America (The Uses of a Toothless Watchdog)." Paper presented at the conference Diagnosing Democracy: Methods of Analysis, Findings and Remedies. Santiago de Chile, Uppsala Universitet, April.

Vargas Cullell, J., Villarreal, E., Gutiérrez Saxe, M. and Proyecto Estado de la Nación. (2001). "Auditoría ciudadana sobre la calidad de la democracia." San José.

Vicenti, C. A. 1977. *El control económico en el Gobierno Central por parte de la Contraloría General.* San José: Universidad de Costa Rica.

Villarreal Fernández, E. (2004). "Evolución de los mecanismos de control y rendición de cuentas en la década de los noventa en Costa Rica." Ponencia preparada para el Décimo Informe Estado de la Nación. Programa Estado de la Nación, Consejo Nacional de Rectores. San José. Available at: www.estadona cion.or.cr [accessed April 20, 2014].

Villarreal Fernández, E. (2006). "Accountability System's Performance and Political Corruption: Beyond the 2004 Political Scandals in Costa Rica." MA thesis. University of Oxford.

Wilson, B. M. (1998). *Costa Rica: Politics, Economics, and Democracy*, Boulder, CO: Lynne Rienner.

Wilson, B. M. (2003). "The Elections in Costa Rica, February and April 2002," *Electoral Studies*, **22**(3), 509–16.

Wilson, B. M. (2014). "Costa Rica's Anti-Corruption Trajectory: Strengths and Limitations." Berlin: ANTICORRP. Available at: http://anticorrp.eu/publica tions/background-paper-on-costa-rica/ [accessed January 13, 2017].

Wilson, B. M. and Rodríguez, J. C. (2011). "Costa Rica's General Election, February 2010," *Electoral Studies*, **30**(1), 231–34.

World Bank. (2013). "World Bank Governance Indicators." [online]. Available at: http://data.worldbank.org/data-catalog/worldwide-governance-indicators [acce ssed January 18, 2017].

9. Chile: human agency against the odds

Patricio Navia, Alina Mungiu-Pippidi and Maira Martini

Chile stands today as Latin America's most developed economy and one of the three least corrupt countries in the region. In the mid-1960s, Chile was an economic underperformer in Latin America, but was already regarded as one of the least corrupt countries in the hemisphere. Ever since the first comparative perception indicators it was the only Latin American country close to or even outperforming some European countries. While the seeds of good governance were planted in different regimes, and reached an optimal equilibrium after democratization, some recent instability shows that Chile is not exempt from risks posed by competitive particularism. In the Index of Public Integrity (IPI) Chile scores very well on judicial independence, low red tape and e-citizenship, trailing only on budget transparency (Table 9.1). This chapter traces the historical roots of Chile's low tolerance for corruption, and analyses how the country has successfully remained free from significant corruption problems.

Chile has experienced the three types of regime: patrimonialism, competitive particularism and universalism (Mungiu-Pippidi 2006). During the colonial period, "ownership" of the state was concentrated in the

Table 9.1   Chile's public integrity framework

Components of Index of Public Integrity	Component Score	World Rank	Regional Rank	Income Group Rank
Judicial Independence	7.33	21/105	2/16	18/36
Administrative Burden	8.66	34/105	2/16	24/36
Trade Openness	8.24	27/105	3/16	23/36
Budget Transparency	6.14	83/105	13/16	31/36
E-Citizenship	7.32	25/105	1/16	24/36
Freedom of the Press	7.55	28/105	3/16	26/36

Source: Index of Public Integrity (IPI), www.integrity-index.org, 1–10 with 10 best.

hands of the few; power distribution was unequal and difficult to access; and informal institutions and rules were in place, making the distinction between private and public practically impossible to determine. After independence and the development of pluralism, elite groups began disputing important positions in the government, as well as disputing state rents. Access was only possible for those enjoying certain status or position in society, so that distribution of public goods was known to be unfair and unpredictable. The use of clientelistic practices was widespread and the distinction between private and public was poor, especially by the end of the 1960s and the beginning of the 1970s. In 1973, after the military coup, political parties and civil society organizations were outlawed, and Augusto Pinochet installed an authoritarian regime based on a power monopoly, whereby he closed access and acted as "owner of the state".

However, as opposed to other authoritarian regimes in the region, an economic reform based on decentralization and privatization took place, reducing the opportunities for rent-seeking behavior. After redemocratization in 1990, circumstances divided political parties into two large coalitions (for or against the authoritarian regime); and, although pluralism was quickly installed, politics have not returned to a competitive particularism model, where parties compete for the spoils (Altman 2008; Mungiu-Pippidi 2006). On the contrary, a political consensus emerged on ethical universalism and accountability as important principles of public administration and norms such as state autonomy from private interest, equal access to public goods distribution and a sharp distinction between private and public have come to enjoy wide acceptance. This does not mean that corruption, favoritism or, occasionally, "state capture" do not exist in the country, but those are exceptions rather than the norm. Here we will trace the development of good governance features successively across these regimes.

9.1   FOUNDATIONS OF CONSTITUTIONAL GOVERNMENT

Chile has come to be considered an exemption from Latin America's widespread corruption already in the early 19th century, although little evidence exists either way. Historians who studied Chile and those who specialized in regional comparisons agreed that Chile—for different reasons—was unique in that its governments enjoyed low levels of corruption and government officials were held to high standards of probity. The perception survived well into the 20th century, when Chile was regarded as one of the few countries in Latin America where police officers—the

Carabineros—were not normally bribed and where government officials were not prone to demand payments for special treatment. Corruption was widely believed to be much less common in Chile than in neighboring countries.

These stylized facts were associated with several untestable causes. Two stand out. One is associated with the colonial legacy and a second is linked to the creation of a strong, depersonalized and centralized state after independence.

First, Chile had little importance during the colonial period, as the country was located far from the Caribbean, the economic center of colonial Latin America. Second, because of its geographic distance and the absence of abundant gold deposits, Chile never evolved into an economic power house in South America. Thus, the country never attracted the kind of gold-diggers that flooded other Spanish colonies in the region. As a result, the landed oligarchy of Chile never developed the kind of taste for excessive wealth that became common in colonies blessed with gold and silver deposits, or in those whose agricultural exports made their landed oligarchies extremely wealthy. Scarcity and sobriety became the norm among government officials under colonial rule and, thus, established a precedent that survived after independence was achieved.

The Chilean elite composition was also more particular. The first generation (the Patricians) had studied in Europe, and they shared enlightened beliefs quite advanced for their time and place. By the end of the 19th century the Chilean elite, in comparison to other Latin American countries, had far more traders inspired by Anglo-Saxon liberalism than just landowners, with ideas on constitutionalism inspired by Anglo-Saxon British and American ideas rather than from continental, Catholic Europe. Unlike Argentina, where big landowners acting as principals used politicians (who were a separate class) as agents, in Chile the elite ruled directly, mostly through patronage.[1] But this was an enlightened elite, with no stake in personal enrichment: they saw themselves as stakeholders rather than office holders.[2]

An alternative but related explanation concerns the prominent figure of Diego Portales, an entrepreneur turned statesman who emerged as Chile's most prominent politician after independence and who is credited with the establishment of a strong non-personalist and centralized state in the 1830s. After independence was secured in 1818, Chile underwent—as other South American countries—a period of instability and political chaos. Several constitutions were enacted and quickly replaced by other documents. Independence leaders fought over political control and a number of civil wars ensued with liberal and conservative factions vying for power. The period of instability came to an end with the emergence of

Diego Portales, a minister in the cabinet of several presidents who became
Chile's most important politician after the 1829 civil war that gave power
to the conservatives. Portales served in different cabinet positions until his
assassination in 1837. As he consolidated his position, he was an influential force behind the 1833 constitution, which ruled the country for almost
a century until it was replaced in 1925. The 1833 constitution reflected
Portales's views in favor of a strong central government that could prevent
chaos and secure order in the emerging nation. Because Portales distrusted
politicians—he always rejected the possibility of becoming president
himself, even though he was more politically influential than the presidents he served under—the 1833 constitution sought to establish strong
institutions that would prevent the concentration of power in the hands of
a single individual. As a result, Chile avoided the emergence of *caudillos*
("strongmen") who were so prevalent elsewhere in Latin America.

These two explanations are commonly used by intellectuals and politicians when asked about the reasons why Chile acquired its reputation as a
non-corrupt country in the 19th century. Some historians have cast doubt
on the validity of these explanations, but they continue to be the dominant
reasons behind the alleged culture of probity that has characterized the
Chilean state since shortly after independence in 1818. But, even if Chile
experienced little graft, particularism was rife and the use of influence
through the manipulation of kinship, friendship, and educational and professional perspectives was common (Valenzuela 1978).

Throughout most of the 19th century, the Chilean economy experienced
periods of rapid economic growth and sharp decline, always associated
with export booms and fluctuating demand for agricultural and mineral
exports. Still, the country managed to emerge as one of the most stable
in Latin America, with a strong and highly centralized state. Despite its
smaller economy, Chile was successful in a war against Peru and Bolivia
(1879–1883) that resulted in a territorial loss for Peru and a larger and
more significant loss for Bolivia that left it landlocked. The territories
incorporated by Chile were rich in nitrates (saltpeter) and triggered a
period of rapid economic growth in the late 19th and early 20th centuries.

A civil war in 1891 resulted in the weakening of the presidency, but not
the central state. A period known as the parliamentary republic—given
the weak formal powers of the presidents—lasted from 1891 until 1925.
In the 1920 election, when the growth of the working class in mining areas
and a growing middle class in the capital city of Santiago and other urban
areas was putting pressure on the existing political party system, a populist
candidate, Arturo Alessandri, won the presidency on a platform aimed at
representing the emerging working class. Alessandri, who was a member of
the reformist Radical Party, attempted to undertake a number of reforms,

but was blocked by a powerful Congress that was dominated by the landed oligarchy and resistant to change. Eventually, a constitutional crisis ensued and Alessandri was forced to resign in 1924.

9.2   THE ORIGINS OF PUBLIC ACCOUNTABILITY

Alessandri's resignation represented the end of the parliamentary republic and the foundation of the new order that would result from the adoption of the 1925 constitution. A series of events led to the restoration of Alessandri to power and the adoption of a more presidentialist constitution in 1925. Drafted by Alessandri supporters, the constitution attempted to restore power to the executive and undermine the power of the landed oligarchy represented in Congress. The 1925 constitution guaranteed life tenure for all judges at all levels, irreducible salaries and an explicit non-partisan appointment process that removed virtually any role for political parties in the selection of judges (Valenzuela 1978). This was a first important step in the building of a state based on accountability, and elites need to be credited for it. However, after the adoption of the constitution, the country fell into a period of political instability. The 1929 depression negatively affected Chile and further deepened the political crisis. However, by 1932, stability had been regained and Alessandri was once again in power after being elected president. Since then, Chile experienced a long democratic period that lasted until the military coup of 1973.

Interestingly, one of the Chilean institutions most commonly mentioned when explaining the country's low tolerance for corruption and the high levels of probity present in government officials dates back to the period of instability that ensued after the adoption of the 1925 constitution. The Contraloría General de la República (Comptroller General) was created in 1927, at a time when Chile was undergoing a political crisis. Between 1925 and 1932, Chile had seven different governments, the highest turnover in the nation's history. It was in that period the Contraloría was created.

Interviewees cite the existence of the Contraloría as a leading cause of Chile's low levels of corruption, but the history behind its creation calls into question why the Contraloría came to be such a strong force to combat corruption. The Contraloría was created as a result of a suggestion made by Edwin Walter Kemmerer, an American economics professor at Princeton University. Kemmerer travelled to several Latin American countries between 1917 and 1931—including Mexico, Colombia, Chile, Ecuador, Bolivia and Peru (Drake 1989). In all those countries, he recommended the creation of a Central Bank and the consolidation of different government offices into what is known in the United States as the General

Accounting Office—a National Comptroller. Though Colombia, Bolivia and Chile created such offices, the Chilean Contraloría is the only one that evolved into a strong force in preventing government corruption. Thus, there must have been some prior conditions in Chile—or some developments prior to 1927—that explain why the Chilean Contraloría evolved into such a powerful and influential government agency. The only explanation we find was the commitment of the political elites of the time to have a state autonomous from private interest. This moment is the first critical juncture that empowered the state as an autonomous and impersonal apparatus towards private interests, which, however, continued their influence through party politics and Congress. The Contraloría could not prevent legal particularistic allocations of Congress, which followed pork-barrel logic but exercised considerable power over spending: for instance, by charging a mayor and a whole local council on grounds of changing the destination of a public expenditure category (Valenzuela 1978, p. 14, n. 27).

Why did politicians not fight back against this institution that got in their way? The simple answer is that its founding documents made it very difficult, due to the very competitive nature of Chile's party system (Valenzuela 1978, pp. 15–20); and since no party ever had an absolute majority in Congress (governments relied on coalitions and bargaining), replacing the head of the Contraloría proved virtually impossible. Since its creation, the Contraloría has had 16 different heads—or *Contralores*. Five of them served between 1927 and 1932, when the country was undergoing a period of political instability. Since 1932, 11 *Contralores* have served on average 7.5 years. The longest tenure belongs to Osvaldo Iturriaga (1978–1997), who was appointed under military rule and who retired in 1997 when he reached the maximum age of 75 allowed by the 1980 constitution. The shortest term belongs to Sergio Fernández, a civilian minister of the Pinochet administration who was appointed in December 1977 and resigned in April 1978. Fernández's appointment reflects the complicated relationship that the Pinochet dictatorship had with the Contraloría. When it took power, the military junta closed Congress, the Electoral Institute (Servicio Electoral) and many other government agencies. Yet, the military dictatorship did not intervene in the Supreme Court or the Contraloría. Contralor Hector Humeres, appointed in 1967, was confirmed in his position. For the most part, the Contraloría was not seen as an obstacle by the military dictatorship. In fact, it was perceived as an independent, non-political institution whose administrative duties would facilitate the proper, honest and efficient functioning of the government under military rule.

However, in late 1977, when the Pinochet dictatorship decided to convene a national referendum on January 4, 1978 to gain endorsement for the government—as a response to a United Nations decision to condemn human rights violations in Chile—Contralor Humeres decided not to validate the decision that would allow the referendum (as the Contraloría also has judicial review powers). As a result, Pinochet pressured the Contralor to resign and named his Interior Minister, Sergio Fernández, as a replacement to make sure that the Contraloría would go along with the referendum. That act by Pinochet would call into question the independence of the Contraloría under military rule. After all, the one time that the Contralor stood against Pinochet, the military junta had him removed. Yet, the fact of the matter is that the Contraloría did exercise some limited accountability on the actions of the military government, particularly among cabinet ministries and other agencies that are required to report their budgetary operations and administrative decisions to the Contraloría.

Although there are no publicly available studies that report on the level of independence exercised by the Contraloría under military rule, most interviewees suggest that the Contraloría continued to exercise its administrative control over government spending and procedures during the military government. In fact, Fernández himself resigned from the Contraloría a few months after he was appointed. He was replaced by Osvaldo Iturriaga, a lawyer who had worked at the Contraloría for many years. Iturriaga served for the remainder of the Pinochet dictatorship and stayed in his position until 1997—given a constitutional provision that made it almost impossible for the democratically elected president to remove him. Since then, three men have been named as Contralor following the rules established in the 1980 constitution. Those rules include a non-renewable eight-year term with a complicated procedure for impeachment.

Once democracy was restored in 1990, the Contraloría acquired more power and independence, and has actively exercised its mandate to review administrative decisions made by different government agencies and to oversee that government spending complies with regulations and budget allocations. The Comptroller General is appointed for an eight-year term by the president with senate approval and cannot be removed until he or she is 75 years old, unless impeached by the senate. It is an autonomous body which oversees all branches of the public service. Its budget is assigned by the treasury and confirmed by the state—60 million dollars in 2008 (Global Integrity 2008). As the Supreme Court also needs joint approval from the president and two-thirds of the senate, accountability mechanisms are strong in Chile.

The other important institutions for accountability are the independent judiciary and the Constitutional Tribunal. Their roots were also firmly established in the 1925 constitution. The 1980 constitution confirmed their absolute independence from other powers; and, although the heads of all three bodies are nominated by other state powers, the correct combination of checks and balances assures their political independence. Those institutions are essential in assuring that corruption scandals remain as individualized cases once, in general, authorities involved in corruption and/or misappropriation of public funds have been subjected to an audit by the Comptroller General's Office and the judiciary and have been severely punished.

The Supreme Court is the highest tribunal in the country, and is composed of 21 judges who are nominated by the president from a five-person list proposed by the court upon approval by two-thirds of the senate. Judges cannot be removed until they are 75 years old, unless sanctioned for wrongdoing.

9.3   RATIONALIZATION AND THE QUEST FOR EQUALITY

A highly competitive party system emerged in Chile in the 1930s that was able to mobilize and channel increasing waves of participation (Valenzuela 1978, pp. 15–20). The system was institutionalized with a stable number of parties, low party fragmentation and low electoral volatility. Chile has thus experienced electoral participation since the 1930s, giving citizens the opportunity to punish, in theory, corrupt politicians in elections. However, evidence suggests that partisan elites were able to control the nomination and election of their own candidates in a closed proportional representation system. In addition, they exerted control of elections until 1958, as vote-buying was a generalized practice. In fact, voters were given marked ballots in closed envelopes by party bosses in advance. This system allowed partisan elites to manipulate a growing electorate from the top through patronage networks. This scheme represented a form of particularistic manipulation restricting the exercise of free and secret universal voting and diminishing the chances to control corrupt politicians.

Over the years, several electoral reforms would be necessary to make elections more inclusive, the most important being in 1958 (Rehren 2002). Still, local brokers connected the voters with their congressional representatives for personal favors, which, of course, frequently resulted in particularistic transactions of the authorities (Valenzuela 1977). Accounts find little evidence, however, of undue profit sought through running public affairs, other, of course, than election or reelection of the patron. Despite the reforms of Presidents Frei Montalva and Allende, and a simultaneous trend towards rationalization and universalization in the sixties, it was only the dictatorship that killed political patronage. Officers in charge of villages or towns simply could not go to their hierarchical superior with demands for favors that they had received from locals, and could not bypass hierarchy going directly to technocratic ministers (who were not keen on expenses of any kind), so the military dictatorship by its very nature dried up personalistic allocations (Valenzuela 1977).

The demand for good governance rose gradually after the Second World War due to the ups and downs in Chile's economy, which resulted in high levels of poverty and inequality and insufficient government services. During most of the 20th century, Chile's development was below the Latin American average, and poverty and inequality rates were high. Chile's underperformance triggered a number of intellectual inquiries into the reasons behind its inability to achieve development (Ahumada 1990), but it is clear that development did not precede good governance in Chile. More importantly, the high levels of poverty and inequality also resulted in efforts by reformist and revolutionary political parties to bring about change that could help promote economic growth and reduce the high levels of poverty that were so prevalent in the nation. An important factor from the 1950s on was the popular demand for ethical universalism, which came in the form of egalitarian and anti-privilege demands rather than anti-graft, as there was no graft, just a patronage-organized rents system.

Among the most important subsequent political developments were the rise of the reformist Christian Democratic Party (PDC) in the late 1950s and the coalition formed by the Socialist and Communist parties behind the presidential aspirations of Salvador Allende starting in 1952. The PDC eventually won the presidential election in 1964 with its leader and popular candidate Eduardo Frei Montalva, who governed for the 1964–1970 term and attempted a number of reforms to reduce inequality of income and wealth and to restore economic growth. Frei Montalva's and Allende's presidencies also started the rationalization of clientelistic expenses driven by pork barrel Congress allocations. Though President Frei Montalva made some significant progress in reducing poverty and expanding opportunities by implementing an agrarian reform, pushing for educational reform to expand coverage and partially nationalizing copper production—Chile's most important export commodity—by the end of his administration rapid population growth and growing urbanization proved to be challenges too complex to solve. Frei Montalva's PDC was unable to retain power in 1970. In that presidential election, socialist candidate Salvador Allende, leading a broad front of leftwing parties, including the Communist Party, won a plurality vote and became president, promising to implement a Chilean road to socialism.

A 1968 report by the Contraloría after conducting investigations during 1965, 1966 and 1967 concluded innumerable cases of fraud and misuse of public resources. Many were related to the use of "slush funds" from state companies and the general secretariat of the government for pre-campaign advertisement, as well as irregular loans from the state bank for deputies disputing the 1969 parliamentarian elections (Rehren 2000). This highlights the fact that democratic politics have played their usual role in channeling state resources in a clientelistic manner to ensure election or reelection of offices. The Congress, considered the symbol of Chilean pluralistic traditions, has always been the decisive arena for partisan compromise of political elites (Valenzuela 1978, ch. 1). Due to the highly polarized political system, governments before Pinochet did not have a majority in Congress, and had very limited powers to rein in political pressures and to approve corrective legislation:

> While the proportional system encouraged competition among parties, it *also increased the transactions costs* required to govern and amplified the number of negotiating agents, at the same time that it reduced retaliatory powers by the Executive. Moreover, Congress had almost unlimited powers to legislate benefits for key constituencies, pension benefits being a prominent instrument. (Chumacero et al. 2007, p. 16)

However, the situation changed with the constitutional reform approved at the end of Eduardo Frei Montalva's administration, when the budgetary authority of the executive branch was expanded, meaning that congress no longer had the prerogative of legislating in the areas of social security, taxation, wages and fiscal budget. Laws that targeted spending aimed at specific constituencies were also forbidden (Montecinos 2003).

The deliberate attempts to curtail political clientelism as a system from 1958 on can therefore be assessed as moment zero in the transition, when particularism was still the rule of the game, with the constitutional amendment during Frei Montalva's administration to limit particularistic allocations as the next decisive step. The transition thus spanned several democratically elected presidents, in particular Jorge Alessandri (1958–1964), Eduardo Frei Montalva (1964–1970), Salvador Allende (1970–1973) and through General Pinochet's time; it ended with the first governments after the restoration of democracy, as the reinstating of elections did not bring back the old institutions. Figure 9.1 shows that after democratization the control of corruption increased in 1994, to arrive in 1996 at a value that afterwards remained as the higher point compared to the Pinochet regime, despite several ups and downs. In other words, the most important contributions to Chile's good performance came from before 1986, the first year of this measurement, and the maximum improvement by democrats (under the tenure of the second Frei Montalva president, the son of the first) was reached by 1996. Although many institutions have been introduced since then (for instance a Commissioner for Transparency), control

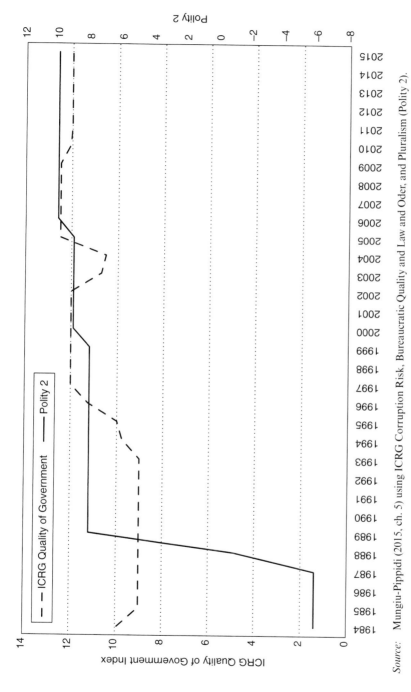

Source: Mungiu-Pippidi (2015, ch. 5) using ICRG Corruption Risk, Bureaucratic Quality and Law and Oder, and Pluralism (Polity 2).

Figure 9.1   The Chilean path: governance more stable than politics

of corruption pre-dates them and it was achieved with little transparency, rather based on strong audit and effective rule of law.

It is important to understand that none of the civilian presidents of Chile after the war and until the Pinochet regime—as different as they were in terms of background, ideology and commitment to democracy—was corrupt. Jorge Alessandri was the son of the constitutionalist reformer Arturo Alessandri. He was educated in Europe, an intellectual and a banker who walked to his office in La Moneda in downtown Santiago without a guard. His predecessor had already set the norm that a president lived at home and only went to the office at the presidency, which lasted until President Michelle Bachelet.[3] Eduardo Montalva Frei was an intellectual himself, a leading Christian Democrat thinker in whose library Jacques Maritain (a French anti-fascist theologian and thinker, member of the group who drafted the UN Human Rights Convention) and other Catholic authors promoting ethical universalism featured prominently. Montalva Frei's tiny house is today a museum where his library of 4 square meters with the two armchairs that he used for his top meetings can still be seen, together with all his books.[4] His son, Eduardo Frei was president after democratization, from 1994 to 2000. He created the National Commission on Public Ethics (1994) and reformed Law No. 19.653 on Administrative Probity (1999) and the Penal Code sanctioning influence trafficking, undue use of privileged information, conflict of interest, bribery and illicit enrichment (1999).

These "bourgeois" presidents were opposed to Allende, whose nationalizations and centralization they deemed to hurt the Chilean economy; but they were not in favor of a military regime either, beyond having the military intervention to protect property and the constitution. In other words, a highly educated political elite has existed in Chile promoting ethical universalism and public integrity across several generations and a few families whose work preceded and survived radicalization as a guiding thread.

Allende's Popular Unity government attempted a radical transformation of economic policies by nationalizing several economic sectors and establishing price controls. The agrarian reform process was accelerated and other reforms aimed at reducing inequality were implemented. The attacks on property in the countryside—some legal, others illegal and spontaneous— led to an alliance between conservative landowners and conservative officers. Corruption increased due to excessive state intervention and the shortages created as a result. The high levels of political polarization that already existed in Chile worsened as the government pushed for the transformation of the economy into a socialist state-led model, and the rightwing opposition—with support from the United States—resisted efforts to lead Chile away from the capitalist camp. The Allende socialist experiment came to a drastic end when the military stepped in and took power on September

11, 1973. President Allende committed suicide and a military junta, led by General Augusto Pinochet, took power. After 41 years of non-interrupted democratic governments, Chile joined other Latin American countries under military rule. Backed by the U.S. government, those authoritarian rulers aimed to prevent the spread of communism in Latin America.

9.4 THE DRYING OF RESOURCES UNDER THE DICTATORSHIP

The military dictatorship lasted for 17 years in Chile. In addition to human rights violations, the regime implemented sweeping economic reforms aimed at restoring a market-friendly economy. In fact, the economic reforms implemented under military rule went far beyond previous democratic governments in adopting reforms that minimized the size of the state, reduced regulations and offered market solutions to many problems that were historically addressed by government policies. As Figure 9.2 shows, Chile's economic rise began under military rule. After a recession triggered by the military government's decision to adopt a shock treatment

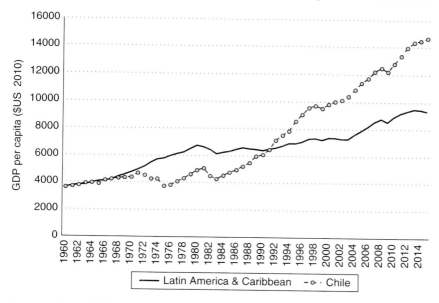

Source: Navia (2015) with data from the World Bank database.

Figure 9.2   *Chile's economic performance compared with the Latin America average*

to put the fiscal house in order when it took power—drastically reducing government spending, eliminating price controls and freezing wages to control runaway inflation—the economy experienced robust growth in the late 1970s. A new economic crisis, resulting from deregulation and excessive private borrowing, triggered a new crisis in 1982 when the economy shrank by more than 13 percent. But, starting in 1985, the economy began to grow again. By 1990, the year democracy was restored, Chile's economy reached the average per capita level of all the Latin American countries. Since then, its economy has continued to expand rapidly, making Chile the most developed country in Latin America today.

Thus, inconvenient as the fact may be for advocates of market-friendly policies, the Chilean economic model dates back to the brutal Augusto Pinochet dictatorship (1973–1990). The original sin of the so-called Chilean miracle results from this origin and the authoritarian conditions under which the reforms were first implemented. While on the one hand the economic model has lifted millions out of poverty, the legacy of human rights violations perpetrated by the dictatorship still haunt Chileans, and will always be an indelible mark on the nation's history.

As Figure 9.2 shows, compared to Latin America (and the rest of the world), the Chilean economy was an underperformer in the 1960s. In the 1970s and early 1980s, the country experienced two severe economic crises. After 1983—ten years into the authoritarian period—the Chilean economy entered a stable growth pattern that has lasted for more than three decades. Because the growth trajectory of the economy began under military rule, the origins of the 30-year period of economic expansion cannot be disassociated from the controversial legacy of the Pinochet dictatorship. However, since Chile only surpassed the Latin American average after democracy was restored—and because the period of economic growth has survived the authoritarian regime by more than two decades— credit for the successful performance of the Chilean economy must also go to the democratic governments that implemented reforms to (in their own words) transform the neoliberal economic model into a socially oriented neoliberal model, or as neoliberalism with a human face (Navia 2010).

The main implemented reforms that might have played a role in control of corruption under Pinochet were:

1. Property rights security, which had been severely undermined during the Allende regime, when many companies were nationalized or put under state management, with little or no compensation.
2. A subsidiary role of the state, which limited state interventions to cases of clear market failures, with the exception of the preservation of state-owned firms in the mining sector.

3. Freedom of choice: reflected in the elimination of trade permits and prohibitions, as well as of the rationing procedures and price controls which pervaded every activity by the end of Allende's government.

4. Fiscal consolidation and orthodox management of monetary and foreign exchange policies, which were a necessary condition for a well-functioning market economy and an area in which Chilean governments had failed in the past.

5. Systematic reduction of the spaces for public discretion and potential arbitrariness, introducing impersonal rules whenever possible. Rent seeking was seen as a major source of inefficiency and corruption, with a significant impact on overall factor productivity and growth.

6. Trade and financial openness, which would provide the impulse for growth that the limited size of the domestic economy could not provide, as well as creating competition in the local economy.

7. Institutionalization of the "rules of the game" in such a way that it would not be easy to change them, with the purpose of granting stability to those rules under different governments (Edwards and Lederman 1998).

As a general principle, the technocrats behind the reforms designed policies to address rent-seeking behavior and activities—for instance the price of all public utilities was established at marginal cost of production, and uniform import tariffs were set for all goods (Martini 2010).

The main tenet of the neoliberal reforms implemented under Pinochet was that the state was an obstacle to economic development. Thus, by reducing the size of the state and limiting its functions, the *creative destruction* power of capitalism would be unleashed and economic growth would bring about development. After increasing in the 1960s, central government consumption expenditure substantially decreased under the authoritarian regime and remained low until democracy was restored (Navia 2015). Though the democratic governments that have ruled the country since 1990 have introduced reforms to reduce poverty, increase social spending and strengthen the regulatory role of the state, the Chilean model can be properly characterized as a neoliberal model; and clearly the major contribution of the dictatorship to a successful control of corruption was a reduction in resources available for rent-seeking, for which the American-educated economists in the Pinochet government ("the Chicago boys") can be credited (Valdés 1995). The exception was the copper industry, which remained a source of rents until very late in time.

9.5   THE UNBEARABLE LIGHTNESS OF DEMOCRACY, AGAIN

Though failing to avert a change in regime, incumbent elites may well have exerted more control over the Chilean transition than in any other recent case of regime change (Munck and Leff 1997). The transition started on the basis of a constitutionally mandated plebiscite in 1988 won by the opposition. However, in order to remove the incumbent elite from power, the opposition had to form a broad coalition, opening the political process to a broad array of social forces. As part of the accommodation of powers, the constitution established the right of the president to appoint nine out of the 47 members of the state (and the first nine appointments were made by the national Security Council controlled by General Pinochet and the Supreme Court filled with Pinochet appointees, making it really hard for the democratic regime to approve constitutional amendments). General Pinochet could remain as chief of the army until 1998, and thereafter as senator for life. Last but not least, 10 percent of the annual export earning of the state copper company would go directly to the military forces. This "pacted transition" left many "enclaves of authoritarianism" in the Chilean constitution; nevertheless, it was an essential step to allow the transition to a democratic regime.

As a result of the conditions prevailing at the time, two large coalitions were formed, one center-right and the other center-left (in favor of or against the old regime). Under the new electoral system, negotiation within the coalitions for the definition of the ballots is the key factor to get elected, so that the power of the party leaders over members of congress has been greatly enhanced, which significantly reduces the number of players and gives strong retaliatory powers to party leaders. Stability was (and still is) a central goal in the democratic governments. The main difference between Chile before 1973 and after 1990 is that political parties were conscious of the need to advance to democracy using consensual mechanisms of conflict resolution (Fuentes 2000); that is to say, parties had to abandon ideological differences and build a common platform.

Since democracy was restored, the consolidation of democracy, economic development and the growth of the middle class have generated new challenges to the way government functions. In recent years, technological development has facilitated access to information, and an increasingly freer and more heterogeneous press has stepped up its investigative role. As the quality of democracy has improved—according to independent organizations such as Freedom House—demands for more transparency have resulted in institutional reforms that have limited the discretionary power of the executive and opened access to government information for citizen organizations, think tanks and NGOs.

The 1980 constitution continues to play a positive role due to the same budgetary rules that were already present in the legislation before the authoritarian regime; that is to say, the president has an exclusive mandate to propose legislation related to wages, public employment, social security and other entitlement programs. In this sense:

> [Congress] has limited opportunities and mechanisms to bargain with and extract concessions from the executive branch and it no longer serves as a major arena for resolving political conflicts. The type of particularistic legislation that in the past served as a system lubricant is widely discredited and unlikely to re-emerge, but no clear institutional alternatives have emerged in its place. (Montecinos 2003, p. 14)

Furthermore, Chile remained largely a neoliberal country, with a limited role for the state and fully fledged private alternatives in education and health, which keeps corruption opportunities limited.

However, political funding scandals show that funding of politics after democratization found new avenues. A campaign scandal that broke in 2002, associated with the use of government funds to overpay high government officials (including cabinet ministers) triggered a political crisis that resulted in comprehensive legislation on campaign finance. Before the so-called MOP Gate scandal (named after a company that was used to disguise government salary supplements as private consulting made on the side by government officials), there was simply no campaign finance legislation in Chile. Campaign spending was a black box that everyone knew existed but no one knew the extent to which campaign donations influenced the political process. As a result of the scandal, a broad political agreement was reached between the center-left Concertación government of Ricardo Lagos and the rightwing Alianza opposition to implement campaign finance reform.

The new legislation adopted before the 2004 municipal elections provides for some public campaign finance to political parties and candidates based on their electoral results from the previous election—thus marginally favoring incumbents over challengers; and it regulates private donations, creating three types of such donations. First, some donations can be anonymous. They are intended for small donations made by individuals to candidates. Those donations cannot account for more than 20 percent of all campaign contributions to any one candidate. Then, other donations are reserved. That is, the donor privately deposits the money to the Electoral Service and informs it of the name of the candidate who should receive the donation. The Electoral Service gives the donation to candidates in different amounts over different days so as to hide the identity of the donor and prevent a quid pro quo relationship between the donor and the candidate that wins an office. Finally, bigger donations are public and are intended to discourage large donations by private companies to individual candidates. In addition, the law established campaign spending limits associated with the number of voters in each district.

The campaign finance legislation has been in place since 2004 and has been used for three consecutive presidential and legislative elections (a new reform that bans private companies from making public or anonymous contributions was introduced in 2015 and was due be first tested in presidential and legislative elections in 2017). Since 2004, Chileans have more information than before on how money goes from donors to candidates. Moreover, precisely because there is regulation now, the legal cases and criminal investigations of illegal campaign finance are a sign of positive developments in terms of curbing corruption rather than evidence of increased corruption. Just like a patient who already had a life-threatening condition before going to the doctor but is only made aware of it after their visit, the cases of corruption associated with campaign finance in Chile have been uncovered only since new campaign finance legislation was promulgated in 2004 (Navia 2015). For instance, a fertilizer company belonging to Pinochet's former son-in-law allowed both rightwing and leftwing politicians to submit invoices for work that was never done, in what *Bloomberg* described as an "equal opportunity briber without concern for ideology" (Thomson and Quiroga 2016). Several post-Pinochet presidents are involved in this scandal, through their campaign managers or relatives, in an investigation which had indicted 17 political figures by the end of 2016.

Although this looks terrible, it has the potential to clean up politics. The same goes for the forced resignation of President Michelle Bachelet's son over an alleged preferential loan to his wife, or the charging of the same wife for tax evasion. By and large, the current generation of politicians, despite enjoying a larger and more educated middle class than their predecessors did, does not seem to rise to the integrity standards that are generally attributed to the generation of Frei Montalva, Alessandri or Allende. In the Chilean context, the middle class holds as little explanatory power as economic development.

Similarly, a judicial reform that began in the late 1990s and was fully implemented by 2005 has also had positive consequences in combating government corruption. The reform created an independent prosecutor's office to replace the old system where the judicial power was in charge of both investigating criminal wrongdoing and delivering justice. The creation of a Fiscalía Nacional—prosecutor's office—was met with some resistance by the political elite that feared the emergence of an unchecked power that could target elected authorities for investigations of wrong-doing. Anecdotal evidence exists that some prosecutors have gone after individual politicians overzealously to advance their careers (Navia 2015).

Two other institutional reforms implemented in recent years have helped uncover additional corruption scandals, though in most cases those scandals are associated with private companies. However, since many of the services normally provided by the state in other countries are provided by the private sector in Chile (with government subsidies), those cases can also be associated with some form of government corruption. The Fiscalía Nacional Económica (the special prosecutors' office charged with safeguarding fair competition) and the Tribunal de Defensa de la Libre Competencia (the tribunal in charge of ruling on antitrust cases) are two organizations whose powers and attributions were widely expanded in recent years, and whose investigations and rulings on oligopolistic practices have rocked the country. The fact that these two institutions have taken on a much bigger role in securing free competition and fighting price-fixing and market cartels has also fed on the perception of growing corruption and traffic of influence among politicians who have protected those unfair competition practices. However, there is no reason to believe that those types of collusion are new. If anything, the fact that two independent and powerful agencies are empowered to go after unfair competition and to protect consumers' rights is an indication of progress, especially in a country where the limited reach and attributions of the state in the provision of some public goods—such as education, health, housing, transportation and utilities—makes the private sector the leading provider of many public goods.

Finally, the increasing power of the press—and the more pluralistic nature of media outlets aided by the lower entry barriers for new media—and the growing influence of social media has also had positive effects in consolidating a culture of intolerance to corruption among the middle class. The growth of NGOs that serve as watchdogs to combat corruption has also resulted in the uncovering of more corruption scandals and in the greater diffusion in mass media and social media of corruption scandals involving government officials.

9.6   CONCLUSIONS

Although in recent years Chile has been shaken by a number of corruption scandals involving high government officials and legislators and the perception of corruption increased in the 2016 CPI, there is no evidence that the number of corruption cases has actually increased. Prior corruption is now more likely to be uncovered by the many instances created to combat corruption—beyond the office of the Contraloría General de la República—and by a more vocal and demanding middle class empowered with new technology that gives it more access to information and more power to disseminate the information and publicize the corruption cases. However, it is also clear that the virtuous circle of Chile, which made it the most developed country in Latin America, is not the work of the generation that was swept to government by democratization, but a hard-built equilibrium over the preceding 50 years. To this equilibrium, patrician politicians, radical challengers, libertarian economists and bureaucratic auditors all brought contributions, sometimes in defiance of one another. The virtuous circle came from their extraordinary agency, not the copper, not the GDP and not the middle class. The role of the latter ranged from negative to less positive than the theory would have predicted, but remains marginal on all counts.

NOTES

1. Interviews with Marta Lagos and Alfredo Joignant in Santiago de Chile, May 2014.
2. Interview with Marta Lagos, Latinobarometer, Santiago, May 2014, by Alina Mungiu-Pippidi.
3. Interview with Alfredo Joignant. See also Joignant (2009); Collier and Sater (1996, p. 151).
4. On the intellectual legacy of Eduardo Frei Montalva see also Mungiu-Pippidi (2015, ch. 5).

REFERENCES

Ahumada, J. (1990). *En vez de la miseria. 10a edición*. Santiago: BAT ediciones.
Altman D. (2008). Régimen de Gobierno y Sistema de Partidos en Chile. In: Fontaine, A., et al (eds.) *Reforma de los partidos políticos en Chile*. Santiago: Libertad y Desarrollo, Proyectamérica y cieplan.
Chumacero, R., Fuentes, R., Lüders, R. and Vial, J. (2007). Understanding Chilean Reforms. In Fanelli, J. M. (ed.) *Understanding Market Reforms in Latin America: Similar Reforms, Diverse Constituencies, Varied Results*. New York: Palgrave Macmillan.
Collier, S. and Sater, W. (1996). *A History of Chile: 1808–1994*. Cambridge: Cambridge University Press.
Drake, P. (1989). *The Money Doctor in the Andes: The Kemmerer Missions, 1923–1933*. Durham, NC: Duke University Press.
Edwards, S. and Lederman, D. (1998). The Political Economy of Unilateral Trade Liberalization: The Case of Chile. NBER working paper 6510.
Fuentes, C. A. (2000). After Pinochet: Civilian Policies toward the Military in

the 1990s Chilean Democracy. *Latin American Politics and Society*, **42**(3), pp. 111–42.

Global Integrity. (2008). Global Integrity Scorecard: Chile. [online] Washington, DC: Global Integrity. Available at: http://report.globalintegrity.org/Chile/2008/scorecard [accessed June 18, 2015].

Joignant A. (2009). El Estudio de las Élites: Un Estado del Arte. Série de Políticas Públicas Universidad Diego Portales (UDP).

Martini, M. (2010). Political Economy Analysis of Control of Corruption in Chile. European Research Center for Anti-Corruption and State Building Berlin: ERCAS working paper. Available at: www.againstcorruption.eu/reports/politi cal-economy-of-corruption-chile/ [accessed June 3, 2015].

Montecinos, V. (2003). Economic Policy Making and Parliamentary Accountability in Chile. United Nations Research Institute for Social Development. Democracy, Governance and Human Rights Programme, Paper Number 11, December.

Munck, G. and Leff, C. (1997). Modes of Transition and Democratisation: South America and Eastern Europe in Comparative Perspective. *Comparative Politics*, **29**(3), special issue, pp. 343–62.

Mungiu-Pippidi A. (2006). Corruption: Diagnosis and Treatment. *Journal of Democracy*, **17**(3), pp. 86–99.

Mungiu-Pippidi, A. (2015). *The Quest for Good Governance: How Societies Develop Control of Corruption*. Cambridge: Cambridge University Press.

Navia, P. (2010). Chile: Democracy to the Extent Possible. *Latin American Research Review*, **45**, (special issue), pp. 298–328.

Navia, P. (2015). The Chilean Transition from No Corrupt Economic Underperformer to Most Developed and Least Corrupt Country in Latin America. ANTICORRP Project: Anti-Corruption Policies Revisited. Available at: http://anticorrp.eu/wp-content/uploads/2015/07/D3.3.1-Chile_Process-traci ng-report-Navia.pdf [accessed June 14, 2015].

Rehren A. (2000). *Clientelismo Político, Corrupción y Reforma del Estado en Chile*. Santiago, Chile: Centro de Estudios Públicos.

Rehren, A. (2002). Clientelismo político, corrupción y reforma del estado en Chile. *Reforma de Estado*, **2**, pp. 127–64.

Rehren, A. (2014). Background Paper on Chile. ANTICORRP Project: Anti-Corruption Policies Revisited. Available at: http://anticorrp.eu/wp-content/uplo ads/2014/03/Chile-Background-Report_Final.pdf [accessed January 4, 2017].

Thomson, E. and Quiroga, J. (2016). Another Latin American State, Chile, Hit by Brazil-like Scandal. *Bloomberg*. [online] Available at: www.bloomberg.com/news/articles/2016-03-22/another-latin-american-state-chile-hit-by-brazil-like-scandal [accessed March 28, 2016].

Valdés, J. (1995). *Pinochet's Economists: The Chicago School of Economics in Chile*. New York: Cambridge University Press.

Valenzuela, A. (1977). *Political Brokers in Chile: Local Government in a Centralized Polity*. Durham, NC: Duke University Press.

Valenzuela, A. (1978). *The Breakdown of Democratic Regimes. Chile*. Baltimore: Johns Hopkins University Press.

10. Conclusions and lessons learned

Alina Mungiu-Pippidi and Michael Johnston

10.1   A DEVELOPMENTAL MODEL OF CHANGE

Statistical evidence cannot add much on top of our cases and our previous equilibrium model. Econometric literature has tested both structural and policy factors of corruption, with poor separation between them and major reverse causality and endogeneity problems, despite advances in econometric techniques over the years (Treisman 2007).

However, a review of some basic hypotheses of the long-term development of control of corruption, even with the imperfect, 30-year data that we possess, may complement the findings from the process-tracing. The dependent variables are the aggregated Control of Corruption (CoC) expert score from the World Bank (see Kaufmann et al. 2011), which is however only a 15-year time-series (by 2015), and the ICRG corruption risk by PRS, the longest-running corruption expert score, since 1986, for most countries (PRS 2016).

The first countries to achieve good control of corruption—such as Britain, the Netherlands, Switzerland and Prussia—were also the first countries to modernize and, in Max Weber's terms, to rationalize. This implied an evolution from the brutal material interests as espoused, for instance, by Spanish conquistadors who despoiled the gold and silver of the New World, to the more rationalistic, capitalistic channeling of the economic surplus, with an adjacent ideology highlighting personal austerity and achievement (Weber 2002). The market and capitalism, despite their obvious limitations, have gradually emerged in these cases as the main means of allocating resources, replacing the previous discretionary allocation by means of more or less organized violence (Weber 1981). The past 150 years have seen a multitude of attempts around the world to replicate these few advanced historical cases of Western modernization. But a similar reduction in the arbitrariness and power discretion of rulers like in the West and some Western Anglo-Saxon colonies has not occurred, regardless of whether the said rulers were monopolists or won power after contested elections.

Despite adopting—in the form of constitutions, constitutional courts, political parties, elections, bureaucracies, free markets and courts—most of the formal institutions that are associated with Western modernity, many countries never managed to achieve a similar rationalization of both the state and the broader society (North et al. 2009). This unfinished rationalization syndrome is frequently labeled under the loose name of "corruption" (Wallace and Haerpfer 2000). Perhaps elections are the best example of formal institutions which can become entirely useless in delivering the goods if the vote is rigged or bought, or simply if a society does not yet have the modern social structure that would allow the interests to aggregate in representative parties and clans, cliques or cartels result instead.

Some disclaimers are needed. There is no universally agreed-upon scale of modernity, and we find only a very imperfect consistency between progress in economic development, good governance, freedom and human happiness. Authoritarian China seems to have better mass educational attainment than pluralistic India, and some of the most equal and developed countries in the world have the highest suicide rates. Social sciences do not have an equivalent of the hierarchical classification system of species devised by Swedish scientist Carl Linnaeus in the eighteenth century, which guided Charles Darwin and is still in use today (Mungiu-Pippidi 2015). Social scientists also fail to keep a good count of extinct species in the way that biologists do. Norman Davies's 2011 book *Vanished Kingdoms* offers only a small selection. Even for Europe alone, one could add dozens of vanished city-states and a few empires, including some that were highly successful for a time, with good quality of governance (for example Siena in the twelfth century and at least the last two decades of Emperor Franz Joseph's Austrian Empire) but could not endure. In other words, the kind of evidence that we can summon in social science might be insufficient to answer such grand questions.

With this disclaimer, we need to look at what benchmarks social scientists use to assess degrees of modernity. The traditional literature, for instance Samuel Huntington's *Political Order in Changing Societies* (1968), used the urban–rural dichotomy to explain why developing societies change or resist change. Seymour Martin Lipset (1956) used the degree of economic autonomy of individuals in a society to explain why political inclusiveness grew. A frequently used option in practice is to equate modernity with economic and social development, using the Human Development Index, HDI (Anand 1994). But, as this is a composite index formed by education, income and life expectancy, questions can be raised on the causal mechanisms linking the three elements. Another option is to use administrative capacity as a proxy for modernity. Using a scale of meritocracy in public service for a sample of 35 developing countries for the period 1970–90, Evans and Rauch (1999) found that these "Weberian" characteristics enhanced prospects for economic growth, even when controlling for initial levels of GDP per capita and human capital.

North et al. (2009) describe certain "doorstep" conditions which are close to the classic Lipset political modernization theory, followed by a tipping point in favor of an open access order, when elites choose competition versus rent extraction. For the nineteenth-century US, for instance, the tipping point came when openings on the political side reached high enough to push through effective open access rules for the top of the economy (Wallis 2006). Acemoglu and Robinson (2012) argue for a development explanation built on the primacy of politics—political institutions being forged and changing as a result of conflict, and in turn shaping economic institutions and then innovation and investment. The passage from extractive to inclusive institution thus precedes economic development, and a sustainable take-off does not take place in its absence.

We combine the data from cases and the statistical trends from the mid-1980s onwards to discuss these mechanisms, before turning to the more specific policy lessons from the cases themselves.

10.1.1 Economic Development

Except for Georgia, our achievers are quite developed. However, they did not start out that way. Chile was less developed than the Latin American average; Estonia was not more developed than Latvia; and Botswana was certainly not better than either South Africa or Zimbabwe. Only the Asian cases have started out comparatively better than some of their neighbors, as they had previously been run by dictators as "development states". However, for different periods, since the mid-1980s for the Latin American cases, for two decades for Eastern European cases and starting after the Asian economic crisis for the Asian cases, a clear argument can be made that political reforms with the aim of controlling corruption and empowering ethical universalism drove growth in all the cases, and not the other way around.

The global evidence complements these findings. The number of low-income countries only declined since the mid-1990s, with more countries moving to high incomes or high middle incomes than ever before (see Figure 10.1). But this only led to a decrease in the average of control of corruption for both the top income groups (see Figure 10.2). Countries can grow without political reforms, and growth seems neither necessary nor sufficient for control of corruption. Control of corruption improvement, however, drives economic development (Tanzi and Davoodi 2000;

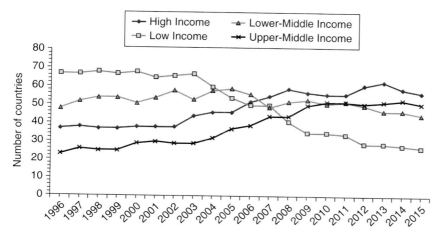

Note: The sample of countries for 1996 includes 190 countries, whereas the sample for 2015 includes 209 countries.

Sources: GNI per capita (US$ 2010) and income classification by the World Bank.

Figure 10.1 *Distribution of countries by income group, 1996–2015*

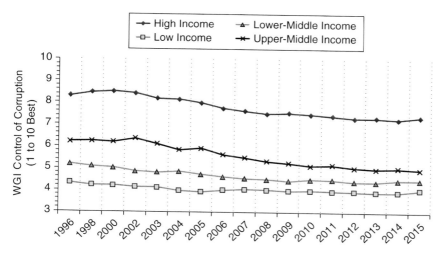

Note: The sample of countries for 1996 includes 190 countries, whereas the sample for 2015 includes 209 countries.

Sources: WGI Control of Corruption (recoded 1–10 Best), GNI per capita (US$ 2010) World Bank.

Figure 10.2 *Evolution of the WGI Control of Corruption average by income group, 1996–2015*

Keefer 2004; Méon and Sekkat 2005). We do not find significant advances in control of corruption that are not followed by sustainable growth in the area of middle income. In the area of very low income it is possible that anti-corruption reforms existed, but they had no impact on corruption, and therefore no impact on growth either. This does not mean that at very low incomes good governance policies do not matter, but precisely that the just selection of effective policies is more important there than elsewhere.

10.1.2 Modernization of Society

While growth remains of major policy interest, development has grown to be perceived in a more holistic way over the past decades. The question is then to check what other specific developments within society are more conducive to control of corruption, so we checked again over cases and statistical trends, the most tested factors in the literature.

At first sight, despite the fact that there is a strong correlation between corruption and life expectancy in comparative, cross-sectional analysis, and that corrupt countries invest less in health (Mauro 1995; Mungiu-Pippidi et al. 2014), the successful upward trend in life expectancy across the world in the past decades is not due to better control of corruption—and it is definitely not driving control of corruption upwards as well. The increase is global, due to progress in medicine, hygiene and better nutrition; but it is disproportionately spread, with EU-28 driving the changes, with a ten-year increase in life expectancy for both men and women at birth since the mid-1960s (Eurostat 2016). Estonia has had a far better transition for life expectancy compared to Russia since 1990—its life expectancy expanded by the full average ten European years, the highest across all former Soviet Republics, while that of Russia, which has the worst control of corruption, expanded the least (Figure 10.3). But the relation between health outcomes, economic development and control of corruption remains loose. Botswana is a good example of this. Despite its good control of corruption, and a rate of 5 percent growth since the mid-1990s (the highest in the world), its HIV/AIDS pandemic remains a danger to the sustainability of development, and its health indicators are well below those of countries in the same income group.

The evolution of education and control of corruption tells the next story in the complicated relation between corruption and modernization (Uslaner and Rothstein 2012). We know from the case studies that education played a role in at least the Asian cases. Jong-sung You argues in his chapter that land reforms after the Second World War in Taiwan and South Korea created a new category of farmers who were sufficiently well off to send their children to school. This is the generation that asked for

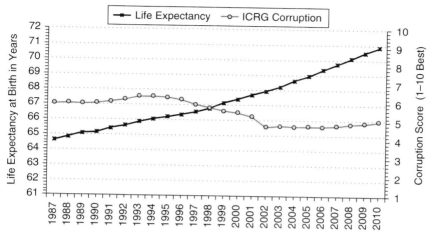

Note: N = 123 countries.

Sources: International Country Risk Guide (PRS 2016) (recoded 1–10 best) and Life Expectancy World Bank Database.

Figure 10.3 Evolution of life expectancy and control of corruption

reforms in 1968, who pushed the doors of state bureaucracy employment and eventually had to be accommodated, which meant more meritocracy. So education is part of the virtuous circle. But it seems to be just a part, or we would not have such an expansion of education as we have seen in the last two to three decades, with so little progress in control of corruption. It is true that normative constraints increased in many countries where governance has not yet changed—Brazil and Mexico are obvious examples.

There are other examples related to education which creep into the process-tracing:

- the elites educated abroad in Georgia, Chile, South Korea and Botswana;
- the island of resistance to communism of Estonia's oldest university, where most of Mart Laar's people were educated or teaching;
- the alternative university that Georgians founded with George Soros's money, as well as their deep-cutting reforms in university governance right after the Rose Revolution; and
- the fact that Uruguay was always the most educated Latin American country, investing even more in education after control of corruption was reached.

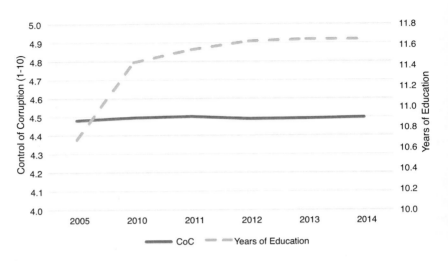

Note: N = 122.

Sources: WGI Control of Corruption and Human Development Index (Years of Education).

Figure 10.4   Evolution of education and control of corruption

But then again, education has to be seen as an indispensable feature of an autonomous, critical and rational citizenry exercising constraints on rulers' behavior for many years, if a high integrity minded ruling elite (or an enlightened leader, like Botswana's founder) do not exist from the onset. Education by itself is not a determining factor of control of corruption; Greece and Italy are highly educated countries (the cradles of European civilization) and also high-income countries, but also high on particularism.

Summing up the three major development components—education, income and life expectancy—we use their aggregated measure by the UNDP Human Development Index (HDI). This time we are just mapping the change between the largest interval for which data is available on both variables (HDI and CoC)—ten years. The result shows that the change in HDI has not significantly driven the change in control of corruption. (The influence is certainly reciprocal, but as HDI changed far more than corruption we will stick to the modernization narrative, that HDI is supposed to trigger the change.) We can definitely find a number of countries (the anonymous spots on the line) which improved on both dimensions. But the greatest changes in HDI (Zimbabwe or Burkina Faso) did not improve significantly on corruption, and the top achievers in control of corruption

(Rwanda, Georgia, Tonga, and Côte d'Ivoire at the very top) have clearly not improved on corruption on account of any big progress in HDI. By and large, even with great improvement in HDI recently (2.5 percent per annum for Zimbabwe between 2010 and 2014), the level reached matters, and Zimbabwe is still at 0.5 after a sluggish 0.08 percent growth since 2000, while Rwanda is nearly catching up at 0.49 with a rapid growth of 2.89 percent per annum over the same period. Botswana, however, approaches 0.7, so the control of corruption regional leader is also a leader in HDI, although Botswana's achievement on governance is superior to what its HDI would predict.

From the other modernity components we can track urbanization and the development of a middle class. On both, data is incomplete, but still we find in a panel regression that the more countries reduced their rural population, the more they progressed between 1996 and 2011. In the same panel regression, education is plainly not significant. As to the middle class, there is simply not enough time-series country data to run a panel regression, but we can rely on recently released sources that the middle class has increased insufficiently. The Pew Center found that in the decade 2001–2011 nearly 700 million people escaped poverty, but did not travel so far up as to the middle class (Kochhar 2015). In any event, clear evidence does not exist that the middle class delivers control of corruption. It may be due to the looseness of the concept, but many cases exist which would invalidate this hypothesis: for example, Greece and Italy in Europe have large middle classes, but so does Argentina. Estonia had no middle class by the mid-1990s, when its essentials of corruption control were already built; what it had was staunch anti-communism and nationalism in all strata. Georgia does not have a middle class today any more than Denmark did in 1824, when the meritocratic principle was introduced for public office employment. Chile's and Uruguay transitions also were not middle-class driven.

10.1.3 Political Agency

Everything indicates that political agency matters. Let us now check the political modernization and political agency hypotheses, in all their forms. Starting with the basic Freedom House measures, political and civil rights, we notice that political rights registered some progress globally, of about one point since the mid-1980s (on a scale of 1–10), no doubt on account of the third democratization wave and post-1989 liberalization, although later on the progress slowed down. Clearly, this is not tied to the evolution of corruption in this interval, as it was already obvious from Chapter 1: more than half of the new democracies present symptoms of

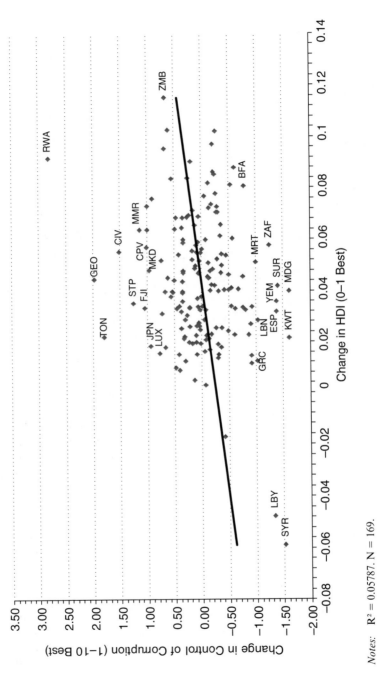

Notes: R² = 0.05787. N = 169.

Sources: UNDP HDI; WGI CoC (recoded 1–10 best).

Figure 10.5 Correlation between change in HDI and change in corruption control, 2005–2014

institutionalized corruption, so elections by themselves do not deliver less corruption. Civil rights progressed less, so could have driven control of corruption change even less. Of all Freedom House indicators, freedom of the press, which has the closest correlation with control of corruption (Brunetti and Weder 2003), being a crucial component of normative constraints, has actually regressed, especially since 2000. By 2014, global press freedom had declined to its lowest point in more than ten years, with more than twice as many countries regressing as progressing. According to Freedom House, the share of the world's population living in countries where the press was free stood at 14 percent by that time, "meaning only one in seven people lived in countries where coverage of political news was robust, the safety of journalists was guaranteed, state intrusion in media affairs is minimal, and the press was not subject to onerous legal or economic pressure" (Dunham et al. 2015).

Political agency can be good as well as bad, and we find that a measurement which captures institutionalized political violence, such as the Physical Integrity Index, captures a lot of the variance in control of corruption (Mungiu-Pippidi et al. 2014). However, on average, this index declined for the past ten years, so it cannot trigger an improvement in corruption (Figure 10.6). Corruption and violence are complementary forms of coercion limiting access, as North et al. (2009) argued; but their relation is neither linear nor simple. The tale the case studies tell is not one of simple democratization. While Costa Rica, Uruguay and Chile have the longest democratic history on their continent, they also experienced dictatorships and civil wars which had decisive influence—without which their post-conflict or post-dictatorship regimes would have been different. The threat posed by these circumstances shaped the behavior of democrats. South Korea and Taiwan reached control of corruption only after democratization; but some foundations, like a strong meritocratic civil service, preceded it and were laid down by previous regimes. Asking therefore if democracy is conducive to control of corruption is quite a simplistic question. Some factors which are essential for control of corruption are more present in a democracy, but electoral democracy by itself has not yet produced control of corruption anywhere.

While the bulk of econometric research focuses on formal political institutions ("constitutions"), political agency is thus best captured by the Physical Integrity Index, which includes de facto violence and abuse. Control of corruption is also very well explained (over 40 percent variance) by *political mentality*, as captured in the social psychologist Geert Hofstede's (2010) "power distance" concept.[1] Power distance is a measure of Weber's "status" concept, illustrating engrained particularism in a society, as it also captures acceptance of asymmetric power relations

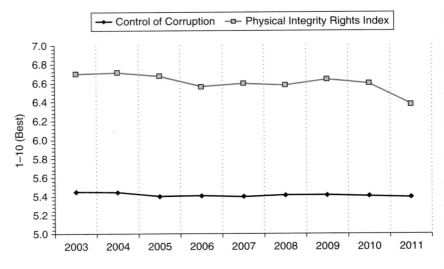

Note: N = 179.

Sources: WGI CoC and Cingranelli-Richards (CIRI) Human Rights Dataset (both recoded 1–10 best).

Figure 10.6   *Evolution of physical integrity rights and control of corruption, 2003–2011*

(Figure 10.7). Unfortunately, as Hofstede famously claims even on his website, such cultural elements do not change except over many generations, so we do not have enough change in power distance in the past 20–30 years to compare it with the change in control of corruption.[2] If in Figure 10.7 we replace corruption with change in corruption we no longer have any significant correlation. Rather, what we have is everybody's favorite explanation of why institutionalized corruption is so resilient—the persistence of hard-to-change cultural factors.

External agency has played an uneven role. The international anti-corruption movement from the mid-1990s onwards cannot claim credit for any of the success stories discussed in this book. South Korea and Taiwan, both on the front lines of the Cold War, received foreign assistance at critical moments, part of it conditional upon reforms. Emulation of foreign models, in particular the Anglo-Saxon liberal model, played a role in Chile, Estonia and Georgia, where local elites in charge of the economy had often spent time studying in the United States. Uruguay had a Swiss constitutional model and its population is descended from

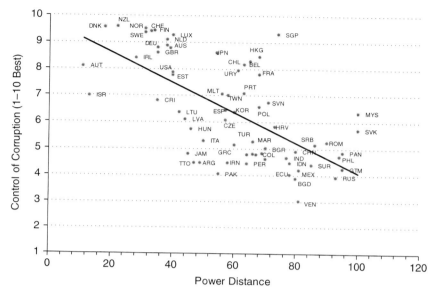

Notes: R² = 0.42435. N = 69.

Sources: Hofstede 2015* (0–100); WGI CoC (1–10 best).

Figure 10.7 The strong link between power distance and corruption

immigrants from various European countries, giving it a far more diverse mix than other Latin American countries. A similar dynamic is at play in South Korea, where a considerable number of local elites were educated in Japan. Estonia has benefited from its emulation of the Finnish corruption-control model as well as the help received from the Scandinavian countries (whose investments in Estonian local media outlets kept post-Soviet oligarchs from buying them up). By and large, external agency helped shape a political context that empowered local actors. But these countries worked because local actors committed to change existed in the first place to emulate these models, and had local support (Mungiu-Pippidi 2016).

10.1.4 Modernization of the State

What about the direct instruments of the state, an autonomous bureaucracy and an independent judiciary? We have no fact-based measure to

---

* https://geert-hofstede.com/countries.html

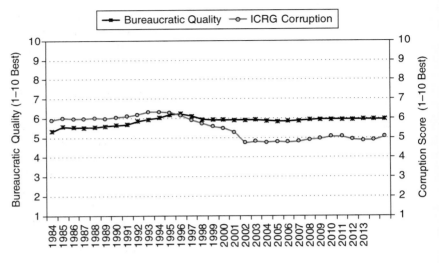

Note: N = 120.

Source: PRS *International Country Risk Guide* (recoded 1–10 best).

Figure 10.8   Evolution of bureaucracy and control of corruption

assess quality of bureaucracy, so we have to resort again to another PRS score. Figure 10.8 shows that bureaucratic quality registered a slight evolution (under one point in the global average), which was not, however, followed by control of corruption. Case studies clearly show that improvement of bureaucracy depends on top-down political will. Unlike with e-government or trade openness, the bureaucracy does not become autonomous as a side effect; it needs a clear political decision to stop politicization and introduce merit-based reforms, or at least to be scrupulous on merit even if the nature of appointment remains political (as in Uruguay). And this is why a corrupt principal cannot be pushed away by bureaucratic reforms—we are dealing with a primacy of politics and not with one of administration. A reform-minded politician can always introduce merit if, as Mart Laar says, he is willing to let the bureaucracy be autonomous.[3] But how can it work the other way around, if a patrimonial political actor controls civil service appointments and dismissals? Then no bureaucratic intervention can help, and this is a frequent waste area of anti-corruption: ethical codes and training for civil servants are introduced when the bureaucracy is not at all autonomous from the rule of corrupt principals.

Independence of the judiciary is similar only in part to bureaucracy. It also depends very much on the decision of politicians to let the magistrates be free, but in a democracy the formal appointment and the dismissal of judges by politicians is far more remote than for bureaucrats; so, although imperfect, we do find some correlation between the organization of a judiciary and its de facto independence (Hayo and Voigt 2007). Independence of the judiciary is a strong predictor of control of corruption, even in complex time-series (Ades and Tella 1996; Mungiu-Pippidi 2015). However, using our only valid time-series for judiciary independence, the Global Competitiveness Report expert survey, we discover that independence of the judiciary could not have driven much control of corruption in the last ten years since it was monitored because there was just too little of it (CESifo 2014). Many countries doing reasonably well on corruption regressed (countries as different as Austria and Turkey), while many with a corruption problem have further declined over ten years (India, Bulgaria, Mexico, Greece, Slovakia, Spain) and only a few have progressed, but not sufficiently (Latvia, Brazil, China, Romania).[4]

In the absence of rule of law (RoL) and judiciary independence, the tools that the anti-corruption industry advocates do not work. Control of corruption on average declined in the group of countries which do not enjoy rule of law or freedom. Slight progress was registered only in the groups of rule of law, free and partly free countries (Figure 10.9). As we have a very close correlation between rule of law and control of corruption (at over 90 percent in World Governance Indicators), it follows that wherever corruption is high, rule of law is also poor, so legal approaches to anti-corruption can hardly be expected to work. For instance, change in control of corruption in countries with an anti-corruption agency (ACA) but without rule of law is on average (marginally) lower than in those which introduced an ACA and reached a certain level of rule of law. But even among the countries with rule of law, those without ACA seem, on average, to progress more (Table 10.1).[5]

The same happens with the floods of anti-corruption regulation meant to modernize states. Alongside anti-corruption agencies, the Council of Europe's Group of States against Corruption (GRECO) and the EU insist on *restrictive rules on party finance* as a key to solving political corruption. Using updated data from the Political Finance Database provided by the International Institute for Democracy and Electoral Assistance (IDEA) we compiled a score that captures political finance (PF) regulations. The IDEA database lists specific indicators which cover legal practices on private and public funding to political parties and candidates, including restrictions on their spending, requirements for reporting and oversight as well as sanctions. Our score is an average of the dichotomous variables (1/0) that capture the (non)-existence of these regulations. That is, the higher the score, the stricter the legal framework for political financing.

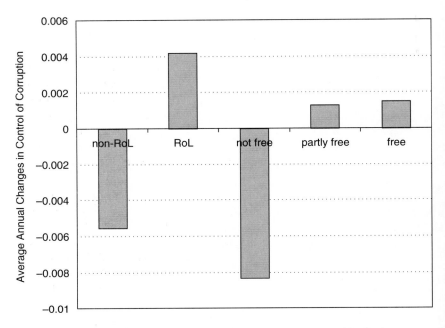

Note: N = 105 (non-RoL), 91 (RoL), 46 (not free), 58 (partly free), and 83 (free).

Sources: Worldwide Governance Indicators. Freedom House for non-RoL/RoL: countries with WGI "rule of law" scores below/above the sample median; not/partly/free— corresponding freedom status by Freedom House.

Figure 10.9   *Average values of the changes in control of corruption, 2002–2014*

Table 10.1   *Progress on corruption by anti-corruption agency in different rule of law contexts*

	ACA	No ACA
RoL	−0.003	0.086
	N = 46	N = 34
Non-RoL	−0.062	−0.052
	N = 52	N = 38

Note: Non-RoL/RoL: countries with "rule of law" scores below/above the sample median; no ACA—(non) presence of an anti-corruption agency.

Sources: Worldwide Governance Indicators; ANTICORRP; own calculation.

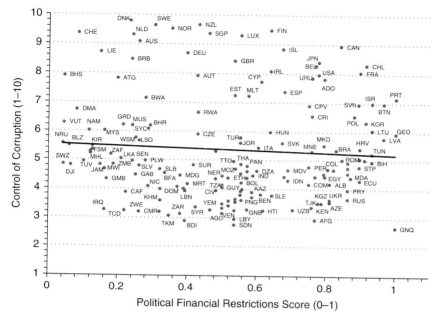

Note: N = 173.

Sources: WGI CoC (recoded 1–10 best) and IDEA Political Finance Database (0–1); own calculation (2012).

Figure 10.10 *Control of corruption and political finance restrictions*

However, as Figure 10.10 shows, the relationship between PF score and control of corruption is negative, indicating that the more restrictions a country has on political financing, the more corrupt it is (or vice versa).[6]

Though this might be because the country tries to fix the problem, even on cross-country panel regression and difference-in-difference models, introducing additional political financing restrictions does not have a measurable negative impact on public procurement corruption risks measured by fact-based objective indicators, such as non-competitive bids on almost 3 million public contracts awarded across 29 European countries in the interval 2009–14 (Fazekas and Cingolani 2016). In fact, the observed effect is positive in most models, and remains the same for most constitutive components of political financing regulations (Fazekas and Cingolani 2016). As the results are reproduced for the whole IDEA database, *legal restrictions on party finance do not reduce corrupt practices—they might even prompt more illegal behavior.* The countries with cleanest politics

(Switzerland, Denmark and Sweden) are on the top left of the graph, with few restrictions but good control of corruption. It may be that making campaign finance fully transparent is all that a country needs to do to reap some benefit while avoiding unintended consequences.

10.1.5 Structure and Agency

The lessons derived from such indicators are completed by the analytic narratives in this book. They do, however, give us the crucial intimation: control of corruption could not have taken off globally in recent years as some of its essential components, such as freedom of the press and the independence of the judiciary, kept regressing. The little progress and in fact even the stagnation (versus a backslide) are due to overall progress of other elements of the equilibrium model—global expansion of broadband Internet, Facebook, reduction of red tape prompted by the need for foreign investment, and even some modest advances in fiscal transparency due to the Open Government Partnership (OGP). And we still lack a test of progress as a by-product or side effect of other policies.

Further constrained by the existence of time-series data, we propose a parsimonious model which reunites both the findings from the case studies and the equilibrium cross-sectional model (see also Mungiu-Pippidi et al. 2014). To test policies that may reduce corruption as a side effect we introduce two new indicators which have not been used in the previous analysis and are part of the so-called KOF Index of Globalization: one is a measure of the degree of economic globalization that captures trade as well as financial openness; and the second measures the degree of social openness that is mostly based on the data on information flows and usage of telecommunication services.

The data covers the years 1996–2011 and a sample of 148 countries (Table 10.2). We use three-year averages to take the persistence of institutional indicators into account, and apply two standard estimation methods for panel data analysis: a random effects model and fixed effects model. The latter is used to additionally account for potential effects of country-specific unobserved time invariant factors such as political culture, tradition and so on. We include indicators for rural population and education to control for the effect of development because the data on HDI is not available annually. Furthermore, since the results might be driven by the inclusion of developed countries, columns (5)–(8) in Table 10.2 repeat the estimations from the previous four models considering only middle- and low-income countries.

Overall the models explain more than 70 percent of the differences in the level of control of corruption in our total data sample, most of which,

Table 10.2 *Panel regressions*

Variables	All countries				Middle- and low-income countries			
	RE	RE	FE	FE	RE	RE	FE	FE
Physical integrity index (0–8 best)	0.056***	0.056***	0.053***	0.049***	0.048***	0.046***	0.050***	0.046***
	(−5.03)	(−4.8)	(−4.46)	(−3.85)	(−4.24)	(−3.7)	(−3.88)	(−3.17)
Freedom of the press (1–100 most free)	0.006***	0.008***	0.002	0.004	0.005***	0.007***	0.002	0.005**
	(−3.69)	(−4.03)	(−1.22)	(−1.47)	(−2.95)	(−3.33)	(−1.27)	(−1.98)
Social openness (1–100 most open)	0.019***	0.015***	0.009**	0.006	0.012***	0.011***	0.013***	0.012**
	(−8.17)	(−5.11)	(−2.18)	(−1.56)	(−5.81)	(−3.56)	(−3.14)	(−2.5)
Economic openness (1–100 most open)	0.006***	0.007***	0.006**	0.007**	0.005**	0.006**	0.005**	0.007**
	(−3.29)	(−3.23)	(−2.61)	(−2.67)	(−2.58)	(−2.54)	(−2.15)	(−2.09)
Natural resource rents (% GDP)	−0.073**	−0.068*	−0.083**	−0.089	−0.073**	−0.064*	−0.068	−0.058
	(−2.37)	(−1.79)	(−2.03)	(−1.59)	(−2.41)	(−1.81)	(−1.62)	(−1.04)
Rural population (% total pop.)		−0.005*		−0.002		0.001		0
		(−1.84)		(−0.28)		(−0.44)		−0.02
Tertiary school enrollment (% total pop.)		0		−0.001		0		0.002
		(−0.13)		(−0.51)		(−0.09)		−0.65
Constant	−1.667***	−1.373***	−0.964***	−0.779	−1.377***	−1.541***	−1.331***	−1.525**
	(−12.19)	(−4.73)	(−4.37)	(−1.43)	(−10.25)	(−5.68)	(−6.53)	(−2.36)
Observations	724	525	724	525	559	384	559	384
Countries	148	137	148	137	121	111	121	111
R-squared (overall)	0.72	0.71	0.69	0.69	0.49	0.47	0.47	0.45
R-squared (within)	0.12	0.12	0.13	0.13	0.15	0.17	0.15	0.17

Notes: Dependent variable WGI Control of Corruption. Data for 1996–2011. Sample of 148 countries; three-year averages. Random effects model and fixed effects models. * p<0.05, ** p<0.01, *** p<0.001.

however, resulting from the cross-country rather than time variation (which endorses the hypothesis that causes leading to evolution or change in control of corruption are different than causes explaining why in a given moment in time certain countries enjoy it and others not).

Our general findings are consistent with those obtained from the cross-sectional analysis and time-series presented in Mungiu-Pippidi (2015) and Mungiu-Pippidi and Dadašov (2016). In particular, the results show that structural factors associated with incomplete modernization, such as power discretion, rural residence and dependency on natural resource revenues, tend to undermine control of corruption. By contrast, agency-driven factors such as economic openness, resulting in a higher degree of competitiveness, and normative constraints, captured by the degree of social openness as well as press freedom, positively influence control of corruption. We removed the independence of judiciary and the quality of bureaucracy, considering them endogenous, but we left press freedom, as in the time of digital media and social networks there is far more to media freedom than the will of governments alone. As mentioned earlier, we controlled for education, which did not however turn out to be significant.

10.2 WHAT VIRTUOUS CIRCLES DO, AND DO NOT, TEACH US

10.2.1 "Just Tell Us What Works"

Anyone reading our process-tracing chapters in hope of finding a succinct to-do list for reformers will no doubt have been disappointed by now. If our case studies tell us anything it is something we should have known already: that there is no single recipe for corruption control or, if you wish, no single well-marked road to Denmark. Indeed, the notion that our virtuous cases—identified by the most inclusive and rigorous assessment process yet devised—have conclusively checked corruption is open to dispute in a few cases. The historical and political processes, innovations, institutional changes and other choices that have helped them resist corruption are far from identical; the causal chains involved are long and indirect; and the attributes they share may strike many as far removed from the immediate challenges of fighting corruption. Indeed, one reading of our cases might be that each story is unique, contingent upon a variety of factors both local and fortuitous, and that the most general lesson they have to teach us is that there are no general lessons.

But that view would be wrong. While we do not derive any neat anti-corruption "toolkit" from these reform histories—and, in truth, had no expectation of finding one—process-tracing can teach us a great deal about the sources, nature and pace of changes that have helped check corruption, and about how to understand causality and the enabling conditions for effective reform. As we will discuss below, they also cast considerable doubt on some favorite reform ideas—for example, that countries struggling with corruption should compile "best practices" from elsewhere and implement them post-haste, "get civil society involved", or that what we really need is high-level "political will". In fact the struggles of reform and reformers in our ten featured countries, if we will look closely, can tell us a great deal about what does not "work", and about some of the reasons why successful strategies have had the effects they did. Those lessons, however, may well not be the ones we expect to hear.

10.2.2   The Complexities of Change

There is an understandable desire, reinforced by growing understanding of the social, economic and political costs of corruption, to attempt to "tackle" the problem directly and quickly. None of our virtuous countries has done so, however, and many others that have publicly proclaimed such an effort have failed. In many of our cases progress has been long term, indirect and often independent of deliberate reforms. Within the context of longer-term social and economic change and global or regional political trends, human agency has played a critical role in corruption control. But the most important such action has at times been debate, contention or outright conflict over issues more fundamental than specific corrupt practices:

- Who is to govern whom, and with what justification?
- By what means, and within what limits?
- Whose voices will be heard, and whose interests taken into account, as policy is made and decisions are taken?

There are no guarantees that disputes revolving around those fundamental issues will come out well, or even that they will be definitely resolved. But without the kinds of energy, expectations and grievances that drive such contention, and without the lasting interests that sustain them, even the best corruption controls will accomplish little.

Therein lies the real value of the process-tracing approach. "Tell us what works" is in effect to detach apparently successful corruption controls from the processes that brought them into being, and from the enabling conditions, events and trends that engendered *those* processes. Further, it is to ignore the possible reasons why many other reform efforts, sometimes involving much the same set of controls, have failed. A conscientious process-tracing methodology gives us a much more complete and realistic view of the challenges and opportunities reformers confront in practice, and of the range of influences and events any reform-oriented analysis or effort must take into account.

10.2.3 Understanding What We See

Process-tracing presents us with at least two conundrums. The first has to do with causation and opportunities for human agency to have a positive impact. The chances of success for any reform we propose today are profoundly shaped by deeper conditions with more distant origins: geography, economic development, demographic changes, the outcomes of domestic and international struggles, and the rise (or absence) of key personalities are just a few of those conditioning or enabling factors. But those often date to long ago or are under no one's control, and in either event lie well beyond our reach. In light of those contingencies, what does human agency in the service of corruption control seem likely to accomplish?

The answer depends upon what we expect this approach to teach us. Process-tracing, in the full depth and complexity of causal analysis it should provide, will almost by definition never give us direct and short-term remedies—"Do X and Y will happen"—or produce certainty about causation. It can, however, tell us much about the complexity and embedded nature of corruption, making it clear that just attacking specific practices is to treat symptoms while ignoring deeper, and more serious, problems. It can attune us to the range of evidence and events that must be taken into account in any reform scenario. Above all it reminds us that building social and political support for reform, based on interests and issues that are sufficiently important to sustain opposition to corruption in the face of major challenges, is of the essence:

- Who, in a given social, political and institutional setting, will likely back a given reform?
- Who will be opposed, and why?
- What longer-term developments give us reason to think there will be such social support, and to choose a given tactic over others?
- How can we measure or assess the state of those deeper influences as well as the effects—if any—of the controls we implement?

That sort of thinking, difficult and speculative as it must be, can help us anticipate and address collective-action problems and begin to sort out questions of sequencing: what do we do immediately, later or not at all?

How can one reform, or some other form of change we can bring to pass, help later ones succeed? All too often such issues have not been given sufficient thought, and thus anti-corruption groups have ended up bombarding the problem with one bright idea after another in no particular sequence.

The second conundrum has to do with a seemingly obvious issue: what does success look like? The tempting answers—"less corruption" or even "eradicating corruption"—do not tell us much, particularly if we aim for integrity in its broadest and most fundamental sense of wholeness. Total eradication is not even a real possibility, as the lingering problems in even our most successful case-study countries should make clear. Indeed, any leader who proclaims a "zero tolerance" approach to corruption has probably not thought things through very clearly. As for "less corruption," it is a fine idea; but, as we lack even a clear and authoritative definition of "corruption", much less valid and reliable ways of measuring it, what does that really mean? Having fewer police officers soliciting bribes, fewer politicians buying (and citizens selling) votes, and fewer tax collectors and inspectors abusing their authority are eminently worthy objectives.

But even if we apparently move toward those goals, have we addressed the deeper reasons for corruption—such as excessive discretion, value conflicts, insufficient accountability, a poor citizenry with low expectations, poorly institutionalized markets and government processes or weak property rights, to name but a few? And (despite my references to "the problem" of corruption, for reasons of convenience) is corruption a singularity—a national attribute distributed evenly across society, having a consistent set of causes and effects everywhere? Or does it come in qualitatively different varieties, varying not only among whole societies but also from one sector, or city, or agency, or administrative function to the next? Is the problem really that police demand money from citizens, or is it that government itself is poorly structured, lacks legitimacy and credibility and, in some respects, cannot govern?

10.2.4 Deeply Rooted Dilemmas

Process-tracing as exemplified in our case studies puts all such questions in a new light, emphasizing the importance of looking at historical and international variations, considering both deep-rooted causes and contingent or contextualized effects and, above all, highlighting those questions of who shall govern whom, by what justification, using what means and within what limits. With respect to those sorts of change, history does indeed matter, and can powerfully constrain or enable human agency. Process-tracing often recasts that process of fighting corruption in terms of the development of open and accountable government within a climate of resources and conditions, and of realizing and protecting justice—not just preventing bribery. It does so because lasting progress against corruption requires no less.

Those sorts of reform scenarios are long term in nature, open to many reversals and may well not take shape smoothly: after all, basic questions of power and justice are at stake. Clearly that sets up corruption control as far more than just rebalancing positive and negative incentives and building social support for reform as much more than appealing to people to "be good" or to uphold civic values. At stake is the fundamental political issue of where power comes from, who should have it, what the real and acceptable relationships between power and wealth are, and how both should and should not be used. Those questions, as our cases make clear, are rarely if ever settled easily. What our virtuous cases have done, by contrast, is build resistance to corruption in society at large—not just in administrative or legal frameworks—and convince citizens that they have a stake in a government that can perform basic tasks effectively, credibly and, above all, in ways that are demonstrably fair. That last point is another common denominator among our cases, even if it has not been achieved from the same starting points or in the same ways and at similar paces.

As noted, the paths to such outcomes will often be rough and uneven. Neither long processes of evolution nor rapid, qualitative changes are likely to be sufficient by themselves. Our cases suggest that much more of the time the gradual development of enabling conditions (economic development, the widening social consequences of land reform, a strengthening and increasingly self-conscious intelligentsia and/or civil society) will be punctuated by disruptive events (civil war, the fall of communism, a military coup and the regime to which it gives way) or by legal or institutional changes whose full impact may not be understood until well after the fact. But those discontinuous changes often depend, for their full effects or even for occurring at all, upon the longer-term developments. Trying somehow to plan for that mixed scenario in its entirety will likely be fruitless: the deeper causes will have started long ago, and causal relationships among them, precipitating events, and positive outcomes are exceedingly complex. It will remain important, however, to be conscious of historical and other fundamental influences as any corruption control choice is made.

10.2.5 Doing Things Indirectly

Some of the more important changes contributing to virtuous circles were not envisioned as anti-corruption measures as such. Land reform in the Republic of Korea, the limitation of citizenship in Estonia and simplified taxation schemes there and in Georgia, and the establishment of Costa

Rica's Constitutional Chamber all contributed to better government and reduced corruption, but reflected wider agendas and expectations. Their anti-corruption effects were indirect: empowering new constituencies with property and an interest in protecting it; excluding from Estonian citizenship and politics those more likely to cling to the old Soviet ways of doing things; providing greater tax revenue for government and underlining the system's credibility and fairness; and reinforcing the rule of law in Costa Rica made key contributions to better government. Other causal factors were not the doing of anyone at all: histories of democratic politics in Chile and Uruguay; Estonia's proximity to Western news media and linguistic similarity to Finland; the rise of a middle class in several of our cases; the post-2003 economic and political crisis that left Georgia no choice but to make government work better (reminiscent, in a way, of the dilemmas faced by Lee Kuan Yew when Singapore was expelled from the Federation of Malaysia).

Most, though not all, of our virtuous-circle cases are small-scale societies marked by relatively high levels of social homogeneity, a characteristic that (while it by no means prevents opposition to reforms) we might expect to aid the process of building support for corruption controls and ease the administrative and logistical challenges of implementation. And several of the precipitating events—civil wars in Uruguay and Costa Rica, Chile's 1973 coup and aftermath—would not be recommended by reformers anywhere (similarly, Estonia's radical limitations on citizenship required a highly unusual set of circumstances and, in most societies, would be neither feasible nor desired).

Two additional, somewhat different lessons are that in fighting corruption it can be hard to tell the good news from the bad, and that in reform (as in politics generally) no good deed ever goes unpunished. In Costa Rica, for example, it has not been immediately clear whether there has been a resurgence of corruption in recent years or whether more cases are being reported and brought to the public's attention. For that reason perceptions make a poor metric for the effects of reform, and better measures are needed. Some years ago, at a panel presentation, one of us (Johnston) was asked to name a country where some anti-corruption progress was being made; my nominee was South Korea. The panelist next to me snorted dismissively and said, "They just arrested the president of the stock exchange last week." My response was that at least he had been arrested, whereas in years past he might well have pursued his schemes with impunity.

It was unclear which of us the audience found more, or less, persuasive, and in truth the significance of the arrest was open to legitimate debate. But as a country gets more serious about checking corruption, scandals and new evidence of wrongdoing are likely to surface, controversy and political disruptions can ensue and, for a time, the country's image may well suffer as a result of having done the right things. Indeed, a number of countries whose officials have invested major resources, political and otherwise, in corruption control have complained that, as judged by the popular global indices, their efforts have hardly moved the needle. Effective detection and controls may initially seem to move things backward as more cases of corruption come to light.

For that reason, reformers must assemble indicators of progress (or lack of it) that are credible and engage citizens' own interests. Evidence in Georgia that formerly black-market economic activities are returning to the legitimate realm is one such indicator; so too might be evidence that capital flight has slowed, or been reversed, in countries that are strengthening their security and economic institutions. Government performance data of many sorts, dealing with functions such as utility services, schools, law enforcement, housing and procurement, can be gathered, benchmarked across agencies and jurisdictions and published on a regular basis. Such indicators and benchmarks do not directly measure corruption: no such measure exists; and while numerous interesting proxy measures are routinely proposed, they are often complex, require unusual data or are not easy for the public to understand. But they can provide clear evidence (assuming matters go well) that government is doing a better job of governing, and of serving its citizens.

Expectations of those sorts are of critical importance when we ask citizens to undertake the risks, uncertainties and all-too-real sacrifices of challenging corruption; those who have reason to expect better services and treatment and more responsive government are more likely to stay the course. Moreover, they can point to highly specific vulnerabilities such as long delays, large numbers of bureaucratic hurdles and excessive official discretion and negotiability of decisions that create incentives making for more corrupt dealings. Those "hot spots" in turn give reformers clear signals as to where to attack and what to do: if a permit process in one city takes twice as long and involves many more steps than it does elsewhere, enabling officials to press clients for "speed money" and creating incentives for the clients to pay up, then it is a prime candidate for rationalization. By contrast, national corruption-index scores, even if they do reliably track underlying changes, give little guidance as to what to do or whether our controls are having any effect.

To be sure, some varieties of corruption will go untouched by an indicators and benchmarks scheme; the public will need to be informed and reminded as to what the data mean; and reformers must be prepared for cases or time periods in which the indicators move in the wrong directions. Autocratic governments and bureaucratic resistance can also be clear problems for such monitoring processes, but where they are feasible and can be sustained they can help reduce collective-action problems by showing people and businesses that they have a real stake in continuing reform. Similarly, indications of improving performance—consider, for example, an agency that had been paying 50 percent more than a sensible benchmark price for fuel, but which has brought its prices much closer to that norm—can send shady operators important signals that the scope for illicit profits is being squeezed out of that agency's procurement processes.

10.2.6   Taking It on the Road

If history matters as much as process-tracing suggests, if important events enabling reform are unique or beyond anyone's deliberate choice and if the effects of some of the most important reform measures in these case studies have entailed long and indirect causal chains, how transferable are these scenarios? Do Korea, Chile and Georgia, for example, have anything to teach the Philippines, Venezuela or Tajikistan?

The answer to that question depends upon what we expect those lessons to be. As already noted, our cases yield no reform toolkits or recipes. They do not generate a list of specific anti-corruption "best practices"; nor do they reflect any process of importing such practices from elsewhere. While human agency has played a critical role in all of our cases in various ways, we do not find heroic tales of "political will". Much more often human agency has involved people coping with difficult circumstances as best they could: the aftermath of the collapse of the USSR, recovering from civil war or military rule, coping with a dangerous geopolitical situation in South Korea, or reforming government in Georgia post-2003 because those in charge looked at the nation's dilemma and realized that, as an old saying has it, "there was no way out of it but through it."

As they coped and improvised, however, these countries and their citizens seem to have taken a broad, historically aware view of their challenges, and to have been guided (in quite different ways and through evolving processes) by important principles of openness, effective government and accountability. Therein lie the lessons of our virtuous-circle countries: not a do this, do that plan, but rather a sound assessment of the role of government within a society, an appreciation of what corruption represents within those relationships, and a comprehension of the full scope of changes needed.

Some common denominators do emerge. In all of our countries key figures, interest groups and significant numbers of citizens realized, at various points and on contrasting timetables, that they had a stake in effective, credible, accountable government. Decisions needed to be made and implemented, services had to be provided, threats to the society's survival had to be addressed and political legitimacy had to be won and preserved—not just proclaimed. That legitimacy needed to be invested in institutions and political processes, not just in a particular leader or party, and it had to reflect the history, current situation and aspirations of a nation. Corruption was not just a set of undesirable actions and exchanges, or a bundle of crimes to be detected, prevented and punished. Instead, it was both cause and effect of basic weaknesses in the ability to govern, and to govern in ways that citizens and potential bad actors would see as credible. Both government and the process of reform had to deliver benefits for the nation and address very real problems, not just pursue nebulous public goods such as "better government for everyone". In no way did those lessons dawn upon those involved in identical form or sequence, or in some flash of good-government insight; more often they emerged in evolving ways or were realized after the fact. For those reasons among others, the reflections on history and recent events that are reported in our case studies are of great interest and value.

Our most important lessons, therefore, involve ways to think about: what government is and must be able to do; the importance and fragility of the rule of law; the nature of corruption; the sources and pace of political change and continuity; the complexities of causality; the sorts of effects we might, and might well not, observe; and, above all, the full scale of challenges involved in building a society that operates effectively and fairly. Attacking specific corrupt practices will normally be a necessary aspect of reform, but expecting it to be sufficient is like trying to control illegal racecourse gambling by arresting the horses. "Best practices" may usefully guide some specific aspects of those attacks, if carefully chosen; but, given the vagaries and importance of history and circumstance, importing them wholesale in the expectation that what seems to have "worked" in other societies (with their own histories and challenges, resources and constraints) is an exercise in self-delusion. Indeed, what worked well in another country might be irrelevant, impossible or downright harmful in one's own.

Our cases also suggest a useful, if negative, perspective on two of the more common blanket recommendations within the anti-corruption debate. One is the frequently asserted need for "political will". As a positive concept, political will is an empty cliché: will is a matter of intentions and dispositions, both of which are fundamentally unknowable. In practice, therefore, there is no way to validate the existence of political will apart from the outcomes that we presume it will produce. But (perhaps) apart from a case such as Singapore, how confident should we be that even when we see those outcomes they have been produced by "will" alone? Countries such as Pinochet's Chile, the old Estonian SSR or Georgia during those same days, and pre-democratic Korea and Taiwan had no shortage of "political will", but it was a will that had to be checked, dismantled or otherwise balanced by countervailing political forces.

Even if a reform champion were to emerge—an unlikely development in most settings—will corruption control so closely tied to one person, or to a small ruling circle, survive the passing of those figures? If political will accounts for the positive developments in our case studies, it seems much more likely to have been will, expectations and demand flowing from major segments of society itself, in a setting in which its development and expression have been facilitated by many long-term and broader developments, and aided by elites with strong incentives to heed those social messages. It is much better, clearly, to think in terms of human agency, taking place at several levels within a complex and shifting environment, than to reduce reform to a matter of political will. No doubt most who resort to the political will argument will acknowledge such complexities, particularly in the face of a rich process-tracing analysis; the real danger lies in the temptation—seen in my experience among some Peruvians and other observers in the wake of Alberto Fujimori's *autogolpe* (self-coup), and all too often in anti-corruption justifications for military coups elsewhere—to yield too readily to strongmen claiming their will alone can cure society's problems. (In that precise connection, see the comments below on contemporary democracies.)

The other common prescription, one that is better founded but still open to misapprehension, is to rely heavily on civil society itself to check corruption. That notion is not without merit: the growing strength of a middle class in Estonia, Chile and Uruguay, and the proliferation of civil society organizations (CSOs) in Costa Rica, for example, point not only to growing social resistance to corruption but also to an apparent convergence with successful affluent democracies whose civil societies are presumed to be strong (even though, in many cases, that view is open to serious question). But the argument typically encounters problems: "civil society" is often weak, vulnerable, divided or manipulated from above in extensively corrupt situations. The term, moreover, is too often assumed to refer to dedicated organizations with anti-corruption or other civic agendas. But those sorts of organization are vulnerable to collective-action problems, particularly if they conceive of corruption control in terms of public goods ("better government for all"). Even under favorable circumstances such groups embody only a part of what "civil society" really means, and of what it brings to the table in a well-governed society. True, civil society will include purposive groups with civic agendas, but it also includes social clubs, ethnic and neighborhood associations, recreational and hobby groups, and many others whose reasons for being have little immediate connection to the political world (indeed, in societies emerging from authoritarian regimes the latter may be virtually the only segments of civil society with a viable history). Far from being irrelevant to corruption control, however, they help build networks, teach and diffuse organizational skills, raise levels of social trust and solidarity (the latter, at times, in counterproductive ways) and produce legitimate grassroots leadership cadres.

Focusing only on dedicated reform organizations tends to miss all of that, and to overlook some of the enduring strengths of civil societies where they are strong. Indeed, observing struggling countries from the vantage point of more privileged places, and concluding that their civil societies have failed to play the reform roles we might hope for, can come perilously close to blaming the victims. A final problem with many civil society arguments becomes apparent from a process-tracing perspective: the relatively strong civil societies in affluent democracies were not created overnight; nor have they been permanent aspects of those countries. Many of the attributes shared by today's better-governed, more success-ful societies—a middle class, strong civil society, democratic values, sound institutions—are not necessarily the ones that launched them toward that status or got them there once changes were under way. To put the argu-ment another way: countries with relatively low corruption do tend to have comparatively strong civil societies, but it seems likely that both attributes are *outcomes* of the sorts of deeper, long-term trends and events that are so important in our case studies.

Finally, our virtuous-circle countries and process-tracing approach hold a pointed lesson for outwardly successful countries, many of which have taken the lead in advising struggling societies on improving government. Essentially, it is that those countries should take nothing for granted. Deeper changes and trends do not stop happening once affluence has been attained or democracy is seemingly consolidated. Similarly, the law of unintended consequences—often so helpful in the cases under consid-eration, but inherently unpredictable everywhere—remains very much in force. Sound institutions can weaken or become out of touch; anti-system parties and would-be strongmen can capitalize on economic and cultural stresses, and on global and regional population movements, to undermine consensus, legitimacy, tolerance and democratic values. Political cam-paigns geared ever more skillfully to raising expectations before elections may contribute to mass disillusionment after the votes are in and the routine difficulties of governing are found to remain very much in place. Widening inequalities in income and wealth can create the image—and, in some cases, the reality—of electoral politics and representative institutions as rich people's preserves.

In those fortunate countries corruption may appear to have receded in the midst of general affluence and stability, but two subtle yet worrisome variations (in addition to more familiar varieties that have by no means been eradicated) are growing. One is the way in which the liberalization of economies and pullback of the state's regulatory and supervisory presence in such economies, together with the ways in which wealthy interests can arrange to have special privileges and concessions written into law, may have in effect replaced a great deal of corruption with the legal, even constitutionally protected, political clout of wealth and of those who possess it. In such a setting, corruption has not been reduced by stronger institutions or some unprecedented outbreak of mass honesty; rather, friendly policies and policymakers have reduced the reasons to engage in it in the first place. Why break in through a basement window when you can just walk through the front door? The second worrisome trend, linked both to the monetization of political influence and to widening inequalities, is a mass sense of exclusion and estrangement from the governing processes in which citizens have been promised a voice. Majorities, or at least large minorities, in virtually every liberal democracy tend to agree with the notion that "politicians nowadays don't care about people like me", and to see their role as citizens as being crowded out by the influence of money.

Those processes may not directly fit formal definitions of corruption, although they might suggest a need for rethinking those definitions to include more subtle variations; but they should raise alarms with anyone who has contemplated our case studies of societies that have, against long odds, apparently made significant progress against corruption by opening up government, making it more accountable and making its functions more credibly beneficial. Even in the most outwardly successful democracies, if the answers to "Who governs whom, by what means, within what limits, and by what justification?" become the wealthy governing the rest, using money without limits, because the wealthy want it that way, we are likely to be tracing some very grim processes indeed before many years have passed.

NOTES

1. The Power Distance Index (PDI) expresses the degree to which the less powerful members of a society accept and expect that power is distributed unequally. The fundamental issue here is how a society handles inequalities among people. People in societies exhibiting a large degree of power distance accept a hierarchical order in which everybody has a place and which needs no further justification. In societies with low power distance, people strive to equalize the distribution of power and demand justification for inequalities of power. See Hofstede et al. (2010).

2. See the answer to the question "Do dimension scores get updated?" Available at: http://geerthofstede.com/research-and-vsm/, last accessed January 29, 2017.
3. See interview of Estonian Prime Minister Mart Laar by Alina Mungiu-Pippidi, available at: www.youtube.com/watch?v=LzwW37T-MUs.
4. The Executive Opinion Survey, administered each year in over 140 economies, captures valuable information on a broad range of factors that are critical for a country's competitiveness and sustainable development, and for which data sources are scarce or, frequently, nonexistent on a global scale. Among several examples of otherwise unavailable data are the quality of the educational system, indicators measuring business sophistication, and labor market variables such as flexibility in wage determination. The survey results are used in the calculation of the Global Competitiveness Index (GCI) and other indexes of the World Economic Forum.
5. However, the values between different groups are statistically not significant, as the results of simple t-tests have shown. Furthermore, Figure 10.9 and Table 10.1 show the changes in country scores of control of corruption. We would get similar results if we used the percentile ranks instead.
6. In a global sample, we also obtain a negative significant relationship between corruption control and the extent of political finance regulation once we control for the differences in the level of development among countries.

REFERENCES

Acemoglu, D., and Robinson. J. A. (2012). *Why Nations Fail: The Origins of Power, Prosperity, and Poverty.* New York: Crown Business.

Ades, A., and Tella, R. D. (1996). "The causes and consequences of corruption: a review of recent empirical contributions." *IDS Bulletin,* **27**(2), pp. 6–11.

Anand, S. (1994). "Human development index: methodology and measurement (No. HDOCPA-1994-02)." Human Development Report Office (HDRO), United Nations Development Programme (UNDP).

Brunetti, A., and Weder, B. (2003). "A free press is bad news for corruption." *Journal of Public Economics,* **87**, pp. 1801–24.

CESifo DICE (2014). "Judicial independence (according to the World Economic Forum)" [online]. Cesifo Group. Available at: www.cesifo-group.de/ifoHome/facts/DICE/Public-Sector/Public-Governance-and-Law/Judiciary-System/judicial-independence-WEF/fileBinary/judicial-independence-WEF.xls [accessed January 14, 2017].

Davies, N. (2011). *Vanished Kingdoms: The Rise and Fall of States and Nations.* New York: Penguin.

Dunham, J., et al. (2015). "Harsh laws and violence drive global decline." [online] Washington, DC: Freedom House. Available at: https://freedomhouse.org/report/freedom-press-2015/harsh-laws-and-violence-drive-global-decline [accessed December 3, 2016].

Eurostat. (2016). "Life expectancy at birth, 1980–2014." [online] Strasbourg: European Commission. Available at: http://ec.europa.eu/eurostat/statistics-explained/index.php/File:Life_expectancy_at_birth,_1980%E2%80%932014_(years)_YB16.png [accessed January 15, 2017].

Evans, P., and Rauch, J. E. (1999). "Bureaucracy and growth: a cross-national analysis of the effects of 'Weberian' state structures on economic growth." *American Sociological Review,* **64**(5), pp. 748–65.

Fazekas, M., and Cingolani, L. (2016). "Breaking the cycle? How (not) to use political finance regulations to counter public procurement corruption." Government Transparency Institute (GTI) working paper. Available at www. researchgate.net/profile/Mihaly_Fazekas/publication/303966472_Breaking_the_c ycle_How_not_to_use_political_finance_regulations_to_counter_public_procur ement_corruption/links/57608edc08aeeada5bc306ce.pdf [accessed July 20, 2016].

Gakidou, E., Cowling, K., Lozano, R., and Murray, C. J. L. (2010). "Increased educational attainment and its effect on child mortality in 175 countries between 1970 and 2009: a systematic analysis." *Lancet*, 376(9745), pp. 959–74.

Hayo, B., and Voigt, S. (2007). "Explaining de facto judicial independence." *International Review of Law and Economics*, 27(3), pp. 269–90.

Hofstede, G., Hofstede, G. J., and Minkov, M. (2010). *Cultures and Organizations: Software of the Mind.* Revised and expanded. New York: McGraw-Hill.

Huntington, S. P. (1968 [2006]). *Political Order in Changing Societies.* New Haven, CT: Yale University Press.

Kaufmann, D., Kraay, A., and Mastruzzi, M. (2011). "The worldwide governance indicators: methodology and analytical issues." *Hague Journal on the Rule of Law*, 3(2), pp. 220–46.

Keefer, P. (2004). "What does political economy tell us about economic development—and vice versa?" *Annual Review of Political Science*, 7, pp. 247–72.

Kochhar, R. (2015). "A global middle class is more promise than reality." [online] Washington, DC: Pew Research Center. Available at: www.pewglobal. org/2015/07/08/a-global-middle-class-is-more-promise-than-reality/ [accessed January 14, 2017].

Lipset, S. M. (1956 [1981]). *Political Man: The Social Bases of Politics.* Baltimore, MD: Johns Hopkins University Press.

Mauro, P. (1995). "Corruption and growth." *Quarterly Journal of Economics*, 110(3), pp. 681–712.

Méon, P. G., and Sekkat, K. (2005). "Does corruption grease or sand the wheels of growth?" *Public Choice*, 122(1–2), pp. 69–97.

Mungiu-Pippidi, A., et al. (2014) "Quantitative report on causes of performance and stagnation in the global fight against corruption." [online] Berlin: ANTICORRP. Available at: http://anticorrp.eu/publications/quantitative-report-on-causes/ [accessed May 25, 2015].

Mungiu-Pippidi, A. (2015). "The evolution of political order." *Journal of Democracy*, 26(4), pp. 169–75.

Mungiu-Pippidi, A. (2016). "Learning from virtuous circles." *Journal of Democracy*, 27(1), pp. 95–109.

Mungiu-Pippidi, A., and Dadašov, R. (2016). "Measuring control of corruption by a new index of public integrity." *European Journal on Criminal Policy and Research*, 22(3), pp. 415–38.

North, D. C., Wallis J. J., and Weingast B. R. (2009). *Violence and Social Orders: A Conceptual Framework for Interpreting Recorded Human History.* New York: Cambridge University Press.

PRS. (2016). *International Country Risk Guide.* [online] East Syracuse, NY: PRS Group. Available at: www.prsgroup.com/about-us/our-two-methodologies/icrg [accessed January 12, 2017].

Tanzi, V., and Davoodi, H. R. (2000). "Corruption, growth, and public finances." International Monetary Fund (IMF) working paper 00/182.

Treisman, D. (2007). "What have we learned about the causes of corruption from ten years of cross-national empirical research?" *Annual Review of Political Science*, **10**, pp. 211–44.

Uslaner, E., and Rothstein, B. (2012). "Mass education, state-building and equality," QoG working paper series 5.

Wallis, J. J. (2006). "The concept of systematic corruption in American history." In Glaeser, E. L. and Goldin, C. (eds.), *Corruption and Reform: Lessons from America's Economic History*. Chicago: University of Chicago Press, pp. 23–62.

Wallace, C., and Haerpfer, C. W. (2000). *Democratisation, Economic Development and Corruption in East-Central Europe: An 11-Nation Study*. Vienna: Institute for Advanced Studies.

Weber, M. (1981). *General Economic History*. New Brunswick, NJ: Transaction

Weber, M. (2002). *The Protestant Ethic and the "Spirit" of Capitalism and Other Writings*. New York: Penguin.

Appendices

APPENDIX I

Table A1.1   National average of control of corruption (2010-2015): Asia and the Pacific

Country	Average
Singapore	9.35
Hong Kong	8.66
Japan	8.43
Guam	7.25
Taiwan	6.89
Brunei Darussalam	6.82
Macao	6.53
South Korea	6.36
Vanuatu	6.10
Malaysia	5.98
Micronesia	5.76
Kiribati	5.71
Marshall Islands	5.19
Tuvalu	5.11
Tonga	4.93
Sri Lanka	4.92
Thailand	4.88
Fiji	4.85
Solomon Islands	4.81
China	4.73
Maldives	4.68
India	4.59
Vietnam	4.52
Philippines	4.50
Mongolia	4.49
Indonesia	4.38
Nepal	4.31
East Timor	3.95
Bangladesh	3.82

Table A1.1   (continued)

Country	Average
Pakistan	3.79
Laos	3.72
Papua New Guinea	3.62
Cambodia	3.51
Myanmar	3.29
North Korea	3.10
Afghanistan	2.90

Source: WGI CoC (Scale 1–10 Best).

Table A1.2   *National average of control of corruption (2010–2015): Eastern Europe and Baltics*

Country	Average
Estonia	7.42
Slovenia	6.91
Poland	6.46
Lithuania	6.17
Czech Republic	6.01
Latvia	5.95
Hungary	5.91
Slovakia	5.76
Croatia	5.63
Macedonia, the former Yugoslav Republic of	5.47
Montenegro	5.23
Romania	5.19
Serbia	5.04
Bulgaria	5.03
Bosnia and Herzegovina	4.96
Kosovo	4.45
Albania	4.44

Source: WGI CoC (Scale 1–10 Best).

Table A1.3   National average of control of corruption (2010–2015):
former Soviet Union (except Baltics)

Country	Average
Georgia	6.06
Armenia	4.56
Belarus	4.55
Moldova, Republic of	4.19
Kazakhstan	3.92
Russian Federation	3.75
Azerbaijan	3.69
Ukraine	3.68
Kyrgyzstan	3.50
Tajikistan	3.49
Uzbekistan	3.32
Turkmenistan	3.08

Source: WGI CoC (Scale 1–10 Best).

Table A1.4   National average of control of corruption (2010-2015): Latin
America

Country	Average
Chile	8.16
Uruguay	7.84
Costa Rica	6.66
Brazil	5.25
Belize	5.23
El Salvador	4.90
Panama	4.86
Colombia	4.82
Peru	4.74
Suriname	4.66
Argentina	4.62
Mexico	4.56
Guatemala	4.43
Bolivia	4.42
Guyana	4.29
Ecuador	4.18
Nicaragua	4.06
Honduras	4.02
Paraguay	3.92
Venezuela	3.22

Source: WGI CoC (Scale 1–10 Best).

Table A1.5   National average of control of corruption (2010–2015): Middle East and Northern Africa

Country	Average
Qatar	7.65
United Arab Emirates	7.55
Bhutan	7.15
Israel	6.94
Bahrain	6.04
Oman	5.77
Jordan	5.72
Turkey	5.54
Saudi Arabia	5.43
Kuwait	5.42
Tunisia	5.26
Morocco	4.94
Algeria	4.53
Egypt	4.44
Iran	4.12
Lebanon	3.85
Syria	3.22
Iraq	3.18
Yemen	3.16
Libya	2.87

Source: WGI CoC (Scale 1–10 Best).

Table A1.6   National average of control of corruption (2010–2015): sub-Saharan Africa

Country	Average
Botswana	7.13
Cape Verde	7.02
Rwanda	6.62
Mauritius	6.37
Seychelles	6.30
Namibia	6.00
Lesotho	5.78
South Africa	5.41
Ghana	5.36
Senegal	4.99

Table A1.6 (continued)

Country	Average
Swaziland	4.95
Sao Tome and Principe	4.93
Djibouti	4.76
Zambia	4.72
Burkina Faso	4.68
Ethiopia	4.50
Madagascar	4.48
Malawi	4.48
Mozambique	4.42
Niger	4.40
Liberia	4.36
Gambia	4.35
Comoros	4.30
Gabon	4.27
Mali	4.27
Tanzania	4.21
Benin	4.14
Mauritania	4.13
Côte d'Ivoire	4.12
Eritrea	4.07
Sierra Leone	3.94
Togo	3.80
Uganda	3.71
Kenya	3.70
Central African Republic	3.69
Guinea	3.57
Cameroon	3.49
Nigeria	3.44
Congo	3.40
Burundi	3.28
Guinea-Bissau	3.23
Chad	3.20
Congo, DR	3.11
Zimbabwe	3.07
Angola	3.06
Sudan	2.97
Equatorial Guinea	2.57
Somalia	2.52

Source: WGI CoC (Scale 1–10 Best).

Table A1.7   National average of control of corruption (2010–2015):
Western Europe and North America

Country	Average
Denmark	9.76
New Zealand	9.70
Sweden	9.56
Norway	9.50
Finland	9.49
Switzerland	9.35
Luxembourg	9.31
Netherlands	9.23
Australia	9.01
Canada	8.98
Liechtenstein	8.95
Iceland	8.93
Germany	8.70
United Kingdom	8.53
Ireland	8.35
Belgium	8.32
Austria	8.16
France	7.98
United States	7.87
Andorra	7.82
Cyprus	7.43
Portugal	7.23
Malta	7.13
Spain	6.99
Italy	5.46
Greece	5.19

Note: This classification includes Australia and New Zealand.

Source: WGI CoC (Scale 1–10 Best).

APPENDIX II

Table A2.1 Estimates of corruption by Human Development Index (HDI)

Region	Bottom 5 Under-Achievers	CoC Score	Predicted Score	Residual	Top 5 Achievers	CoC Score	Predicted Score	Residual
Asia and the Pacific	Sri Lanka	4.89	5.95	-1.06	Bhutan	7.79	4.36	3.43
	South Korea	6.38	7.38	-0.99	Micronesia	7.02	4.65	2.37
	Mongolia	4.65	5.54	-0.89	Vanuatu	6.62	4.31	2.31
	Thailand	4.77	5.54	-0.77	Singapore	9.31	7.51	1.80
	China	4.91	5.55	-0.65	Kiribati	6.05	4.30	1.76
Eastern Europe and Former USSR	Russia	3.93	6.40	-2.46	Georgia	6.84	5.91	0.93
	Kazakhstan	4.13	6.34	-2.21	Estonia	7.78	6.94	0.85
	Ukraine	3.71	5.81	-2.10				
	Azerbaijan	3.84	5.88	-2.04				
	Turkmenistan	3.31	5.04	-1.73				
Latin America	Venezuela	3.01	6.01	-3.00	Uruguay	7.93	6.39	1.54
	Argentina	4.45	6.77	-2.32	Chile	8.16	6.73	1.43
	Mexico	4.18	5.93	-1.75	Costa Rica	6.81	6.08	0.74
	Ecuador	4.03	5.62	-1.59				
	Panama	4.86	6.25	-1.38				

Table A2.1 (continued)

Region	Bottom 5 Under-Achievers	CoC Score	Predicted Score	Residual	Top 5 Achievers	CoC Score	Predicted Score	Residual
Middle East and North Africa	Libya	2.60	5.51	-2.90	UAE	7.72	6.76	0.96
	Lebanon	3.59	6.10	-2.51	Qatar	7.47	6.86	0.61
	Iraq	3.09	4.75	-1.66	Cyprus	7.42	6.86	0.56
	Iran	4.47	6.08	-1.60	Morocco	5.03	4.56	0.48
	Syria	2.71	4.31	-1.60				
Sub-Saharan Africa	Equatorial Guinea	2.19	4.29	-2.09	Rwanda	6.99	3.66	3.33
	Angola	2.89	4.02	-1.13	Cape Verde	7.12	4.68	2.44
	Congo, Rep.	3.31	4.30	-0.99	Senegal	5.53	3.49	2.04
	Zimbabwe	3.00	3.90	-0.90	Lesotho	5.77	3.80	1.96
	Sudan	2.90	3.63	-0.73	Botswana	6.94	5.13	1.81
Western Europe and North America (includes Australia and New Zealand)	Greece	5.14	6.96	-1.82	Finland	9.42	7.17	2.26
	Italy	5.30	7.03	-1.72	New Zealand	9.59	7.53	2.06
	Spain	6.45	7.05	-0.61	Denmark	9.57	7.57	2.00
					Luxembourg	9.26	7.31	1.95
					Norway	9.51	7.62	1.89

Note: The difference between expected values and real values is shown as residuals, with countries overperforming their HDI labelled 'achievers' and those underperforming labelled 'under-achievers'.

Sources: World Bank WGI; United Nations Development Programme.

APPENDIX III

Table A3.1 Variables and sources

Variable	Description/measurement	Scale	Time period	Country coverage	Source
Average years of schooling in 1900	Average years of schooling among the population older than 15	Numerical $(0-\infty)$	1900	74	Morrisson, C. and Murtin, F. (2009), "The Century of Education", *Journal of Human Capital*, **3**(1), 1–42
Civil liberties	This score is made taking into account information about freedom of expression and belief, associational and organizational rights, rule of law, and personal autonomy and individual rights	1–7, where 7 is the least free; recoded to 1–10, where 10 is the most free	1986–2015	194	Freedom House, Freedom in the World Report
Corruption Perception Index (TI)	The CPI focuses on corruption in the public sector and defines corruption as the abuse of public office for private gain. The surveys used in compiling the CPI tend to ask questions in line with the misuse of public power for private benefit, with a focus, for example, on	0 (highly corrupt)–10 (very clean)	2014	172	Transparency International

Variable	Description/measurement	Scale	Time period	Country coverage	Source
	bribe-taking by public officials in public procurement. The sources do not distinguish between administrative and political corruption. The CPI score relates to perceptions of the degree of corruption as seen by business people, risk analysts and the general public				
Costa Rica's socio-economic indicators	Costa Rica's major socio-economic indicators for the time frame 1940–2010, including: population, urban population, poverty, life expectancy, child mortality, fecundity rate, malnutrition, social security coverage, illiteracy, years of education, access to drinking water, forest coverage, GDP per capita, women's participation in the labor force, the agriculture sector and the number of women in Congress	Different values	2014	1	Programa Estado de la Nación (PEN)

Variable	Description	Scale	Year	N	Source
Democracy	Scale ranges from 0–10, where 0 is least democratic and 10 most democratic. Average of Freedom House (political rights and civil liberties, transformed to a scale of 0–10) and Polity (Polity II, transformed to a scale of 0–10). These variables were averaged as a new variable	0–10 (least to most democratic)	2010	158	Freedom House, Freedom in the World Report and Center for Systemic Peace, Polity IV Project
Ease of doing business	Ease of doing business ranks economies from 1–183, with first place being the best. A high rank (a low numerical rank) means that the regulatory environment is conducive to business operation. The index averages the country's percentile rankings on 10 topics covered in the World Bank's Doing Business. The ranking on each topic is the simple average of the percentile rankings on its component indicators	1 (best)–183 (worst)	2010	183	World Bank Database
Economic Globalization Index	Economic globalization is characterized as long-distance flows of goods and services as well as information and perceptions that accompany market exchanges	0 (least globalized)–100 (most globalized)	1970–2010	207	KOF Globalization Index: Dreher, A. (2006), "Does Globalization affect Growth? Evidence from a New Index on Globalization", *Applied Economics*, **38**(10), 1091–1100

Table A3.1 (continued)

Variable	Description/measurement	Scale	Time period	Country coverage	Source
Freedom in the world	Average of a country's or territory's scores on political rights and civil liberties; it determines the status of free (1.0–2.5), partly free (3.0–5.0) or not free (5.5–7.0)	1–7, where 7 is the least free; recoded to 1–10, where 10 is the most free	1986–2015	194	Freedom House, Freedom in the World Report
Freedom of the press	The press freedom index is computed by adding three component ratings: laws and regulations; political pressure and controls; economic influences and repressive actions	0 (most free)–100 (least free)	2010	189	Freedom House, Freedom of the Press Report
GDP per capita	Constant 2010 US$	Numerical (0–∞)	1990–2015	176	World Bank Database
GNI per capita	PPP (current international $)	Numerical (0–∞)	1990–2015	168	World Bank Database

Government favoritism	The extent of government officials showing favoritism to well-connected firms and individuals when deciding on policies and contracts (1 = always show favoritism; 7 = never show favoritism), weighted average	01-07-17	2006–2015	151	World Economic Forum
Human Development Index (HDI)	Summary composite index that measures a country's average achievements in three basic aspects of human development: longevity, knowledge, and a decent standard of living. Longevity is measured by life expectancy at birth; knowledge is measured by a combination of the adult literacy rate and the combined primary, secondary, and tertiary gross enrollment ratio; standard of living is measured by GDP per capita. The HDI, reported in the UN's Human Development Report, is an indication of how developed a country is. The index can take a value between 0 and 1. Countries with an index over 0.800 are part of the High Human Development	0 (lowest human development)–1 (highest human development)	2000–2014	185	UNDP database

Table A3.1 (continued)

Variable	Description/measurement	Scale	Time period	Country coverage	Source
	group; between 0.500 and 0.800 countries are part of the Medium Human Development group; and below 0.500 they are part of the Low Human Development group				
HDI education index	The education component of the HDI is now measured by mean of years of schooling for adults aged 25 years and expected years of schooling for children of school entry age. The indicators are normalized using a minimum value of zero, and maximum values are set to the actual observed maximum value of mean years of schooling from the countries in the time series, 1980–2010, that is 13.1 years estimated for the Czech Republic in 2005. Expected years of schooling is maximized by its cap at 18 years. The education index is the geometric mean of the two	Numerical $(0-\infty)$	2000–2014	186	UNDP Database

Variable	Description	Scale	Year	N	Source
Index of Public Integrity	A society's capacity to control corruption and ensure that public resources are spent without corrupt practices	1–10	2014	105	European Research Centre for Anti-Corruption and State-Building
International Country Risk Guide: Bureaucratic quality, law and order and pluralism	The *International Country Risk Guide* (ICRG) rating comprises 22 variables in three subcategories of risk: political, financial, and economic. The Bureaucratic Quality estimation awards more points to countries where the bureaucracy has the strength and expertise to govern without drastic changes in policy or interruptions to government services	0–4	1984–2015	140	The PRS Group
International Country Risk Guide: Corruption	The *International Country Risk Guide* (ICRG) rating comprises 22 variables in three subcategories of risk: political, financial, and economic. In Political Risk, corruption is an assessment of corruption within the political system where the higher score indicates better control of corruption	0–6	1984–2015	140	The PRS Group
Internet users (per 100 people)	Internet users (per 100 people)	%	2010	192	World Bank Database

Table A3.1 (continued)

Variable	Description/measurement	Scale	Time period	Country coverage	Source
Judicial independence	Part of the Global Competitiveness Report, this index records answers to the question "To what extent is the judiciary in your country independent from influences of members of government, citizens, or firms?" asked of key business leaders	1 (heavily influenced)–7 (entirely independent)	2010	135	World Economic Forum, Global Competitiveness Report
Life expectancy at birth, total (years)	Life expectancy at birth, total (years)	Numerical (0–∞)	1987–2010	194	World Bank Database
Literacy rate	Total adult literacy rate (% of people aged 15 and above)	%	2000–2010	148	World Bank Database
Open Budget Index (OBI)	The OBI rates countries on how open their budget books are to their citizens. It is intended to provide citizens, legislators, and civil society advocates with the comprehensive and practical information needed to gauge a government's commitment to budget transparency and accountability	0 (scant or no information available)–100 (extensive information available)	2010	100	International Budget Partnership, Open Budget Survey 2010

Indicator	Description	Scale	Year	N	Source
Perception of corruption of public officials/civil servants	% of respondents who consider public officials/civil servants as "not at all corrupt" or "a little corrupt" (1 + 2)	%	2013	107	Global Corruption Barometer 2012
Perception of corruption of public officials/civil servants	% of respondents who answered the question: "To what extent do you see public officials/civil servants to be affected by corruption in this country?" with 4 (corrupt) or 5 (extremely corrupt)	%	2013	110	Global Corruption Barometer 2012
Physical integrity rights index	This is an additive index constructed from the Torture (ciri_tort), Extrajudicial Killing (ciri_kill), Political Imprisonment (ciri_polpris), and Disappearance indicators (ciri_disap). It ranges from 0 (no government respect for these four rights)–8 (full government respect for these rights)	0 (no government respect for physical integrity)–8 (full government respect for physical integrity)	2002–2010	187	Cingranelli, D. and Richards, D.L. (2010). _The Cingranelli-Richards (CIRI) Human Rights Dataset_
Political finance restrictions	Data on: (a) bans and limits on private income; (b) public funding; (c) regulations; and (d) spending and reporting, oversight and sanctions	Numerical (0–∞)	2012	180	International IDEA Database
Political rights	This score is made taking into account information about the electoral process, political pluralism and participation, and functioning of government	1–7, where 7 is the least free; recoded to 1–10, where 10 is the most free	1986–2015	194	Freedom House, Freedom in the World Report

Table A3.1 (continued)

Variable	Description/measurement	Scale	Time period	Country coverage	Source
Poverty rate	The poverty rate at $1.25 a day is the proportion of the population living on less than $1.25 a day, measured at 2005 international prices, adjusted for purchasing power parity (PPP)	%	1979–2007	115	World Bank Development Research Group
Power distance	The extent to which the less powerful members of organizations and institutions (like the family) accept and expect that power is distributed unequally	0–100 (more acceptant to unequal distribution of power)	2010	69	Hofstede, G., Hofstede, G.J. and Minkov, M. (2010), *Cultures and Organizations: Software of the Mind.* New York: McGraw-Hill
Region	This is a politico-geographic classification of world regions adapted from the World Bank classification, which is based on a mixture of two considerations: geographical proximity (with the partial exception of category 5 below) and demarcation by area specialists. The categories are as follows: (1) Eastern Europe and the Baltics	Numerical $(0-\infty)$	2010	189	Quality of Government Dataset

	(2) Latin America (including Cuba, Haiti and the Dominican Republic)				
	(3) North Africa and the Middle East (including Israel, Turkey and Cyprus)				
	(4) Sub-Saharan Africa				
	(5) Western Europe and North America (including Australia and New Zealand)				
	(6) Asia and the Pacific				
	(7) Former Soviet Union (and Central Asia)				
Rural population	% of total population living in rural areas	%	2010	210	World Bank Database
Social Globalization Index	Social globalization is expressed as the spread of ideas, information, images and people	1 (least globalized)–100 (most globalized)	1970–2010	207	KOF Globalization Index; Dreher, A. (2006), "Does Globalization affect Growth? Evidence from a New Index on Globalization", *Applied Economics*, **38**(10), 1091–1100
Tax collection	Gross tax collection in Uruguay	Numerical $(0–\infty)$	1998–2012		Dirección General Impositiva – Aseosría Estadística

Table A3.1 (continued)

Variable	Description/measurement	Scale	Time period	Country coverage	Source
Tertiary school enrollment	Total enrollment in tertiary education (ISCED 5–8), regardless of age, expressed as a percentage of the total population of the five-year age group following on from secondary school leaving	%	1990–2010	180	World Bank Database
Total pensions/ population over 60 and government employees	Total pensions/population over 60 and government employees for Uruguay. Base de Datos – Series Históricas	%	1911–2010	1	Instituto de Economia, Facultad de Ciencias Economicas y de Administracion, Universidad de la Republica
WGI Control of Corruption estimate	"Control of Corruption" measures perceptions of corruption, conventionally defined as the exercise of public power for private gain. The particular aspect of corruption measured by the various sources differs somewhat, ranging from the frequency of "additional payments to get things done", to the effects of corruption on	−2.5 (weak control of corruption)–2.5 (strong control of corruption). Alternatively recoded to a C50 scale from 1 (lowest control of corruption)–10	1996–2015	200	Worldwide Governance Indicators

286

	the business environment, to measuring "grand corruption" in the political arena or in the tendency of elite forms to engage in "state capture". Estimate of governance ranges from approximately -2.5 (weak) to 2.5 (strong). The recoded version of this variable ranges to a scale of 1 (lowest control)-10 (highest control) was also used throughout this report	(highest control of corruption)			
Years of education	Number of years of education at the national level	Numerical (0-∞)	1970–2009	175	Gakidou, E., Cowling, K., Lozano, R. and Murray, C.J.L (2010), "Increased Educational Attainment and its Effect on Child Mortality in 175 Countries between 1970 and 2009: A Systematic Analysis", *The Lancet*, 376(9745), 959–74

Index